NATIONAL IDEALS AND PROBLEMS

NATIONAL IDEALS AND PROBLEMS

ESSAYS FOR COLLEGE ENGLISH

BY

MAURICE GARLAND FULTON

PROFESSOR OF ENGLISH, DAVIDSON COLLEGE

Essay Index Reprint Series

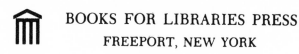

BOOKS FOR LIBRARIES PRESS
FREEPORT, NEW YORK

First Published 1918
Reprinted 1968

LIBRARY OF CONGRESS CATALOG CARD NUMBER:
68-54346

PRINTED IN THE UNITED STATES OF AMERICA

In Honor of
Davidson College Students

WHO IN CHEERFUL WILLINGNESS TO
GIVE SUPREME DEVOTION JOINED THE
NATIONAL FORCES BANDED TO UPHOLD
LIBERTY, PEACE, AND JUSTICE
THROUGHOUT THE WORLD

PREFACE

In this book my purpose has been to bring together a number of significant essays, addresses, and state papers which should be helpful in showing students what others, chiefly their fellow-Americans, have thought or now think about their country—its people, its ideals, and its significance both at home and abroad.

The time is opportune for seeking a more intelligent acquaintance with our national ideals and problems. The war thrusts upon the nation the need of burnishing ideals as well as weapons. We should use this war to clarify our vision and intensify our national purposes, and we must, in our schools and colleges, make it a means for developing catholicity of spirit, human sympathy, sacrificial devotion to convictions, and passion for truth and justice.

Realizing the danger of doing violence in the stress of conflict to the very ideals we seek to defend and exalt, President Wilson early addressed a plea to the teachers in all grades of schools urging the conservation of our ideals. Said he, "The war is bringing to the minds of our people a new appreciation of the problems of national life and a deeper understanding of the meaning and aims of democracy. Matters which we have heretofore deemed commonplace and trivial are seen in a truer light. . . . When the war is over we must apply the wisdom we have acquired in purging and ennobling the life of the world."

An intelligent understanding of American democracy is not merely a matter of interest; it is a patriotic duty for making both better Americans and better citizens of the world. Democracy is a body of ideals. Armies and navies alone cannot make the world safe for democracy. The world must be wrought to sympathy with democratic ideals, and, in accomplishing this, the schools—institutions devoted to the conserving of ideals and agencies able to reach the next generation—must undertake to inculcate these principles for which we are fighting. For what shall it profit us if we gain the whole world for democracy and thereby lose the soul of democracy?

In this work the teacher of English has a large part. Those who teach history or political science may give the facts, but those who handle the nation's literature impart the spirit of the nation. Since American literature affords the best possible interpretation of American ideals, the English teacher should have his students give attention more largely than heretofore to the history and progress of American thought as recorded in American literature.

The selections in this volume do not, of course, belong under the classification "literature" in the narrower sense of the term. Nevertheless they are discussions of value in reaching conclusions regarding the American spirit and ideals, and as such may be appropriately brought into the literary vista of the student. Such study of American life and institutions as this book contemplates may be made in connection with the course in American literature.

But this book would seem to have its most useful place in the so-called "thought-courses" in composition. This type of course has become so widely popular in recent years that it needs no defense or explanation. Its fundamental principle of accompanying the reading of thought-provoking selections with discussion, oral or written, upon questions and topics suggested by the reading is a most stimulating way to come to an understanding of national ideals. Furthermore, this method is a replica of the way in which definite national ideals must be reached. Each person must reach his own independent conclusions and then compound them by intelligent discussion in public and in private. Under this natural method, the student is brought to his own conclusions and to correcting or modifying them in the light of those formed by his classmates.

The selections have been arranged into a rough sequence and grouped under certain headings. Despite the fact that in some cases positions may seem arbitrarily assigned, the arrangement will be found of practical value in emphasizing the larger aspects of the study. A convenient starting-point is had in a group of selections discussing the predominant characteristics of the American people. Next, to make this study of American characteristics more concrete, come selections dealing with a few great Americans who seem to exemplify the special make-up of mind and faculties that is the specific product of American democracy. The third group is composed of epoch-making addresses and state papers which every young American should know at first hand. These are followed by a group of selections discussing in a general way the aims and tendencies of American democracy. The next two groups present the closely related topics of the citizen's part in government and the especial responsibilities that rest upon the college-trained. After these comes a section devoted to a discussion of the principles that must be adhered to in making such changes and adjustments as the future may require. The last division contains selections discussing how and why America became a participant in the world war, and what she desires the outcome of the struggle to be.

In order to keep the book of moderate size, much important material had to be omitted. At no point was it harder to make rejections than in the second division, Patterns of Americanism. Jefferson, Jackson, Grant, Lee, Lowell, and many others, representative of Americanism in one way or another, seemed to demand inclusion, but finally the list was left with but four upon whom there would be almost universal agreement.

A word of explanation seems needed regarding the absence of selections from Bryce's *The American Commonwealth.* My first intention was to include several chapters from this source. But when it became possible for me to prepare for the moderate-priced English and American classics series of the Macmillan Company a volume including some twelve or fifteen of the most significant chapters of Bryce's book, under the title *American Democracy,* I thought it advisable to use all the space in this book for material from other quarters, and to suggest to those who may desire material from *The American Commonwealth* that they may find it in the collection referred to.

I take this opportunity of recording in a general way grateful thanks to those writers who have generously permitted me to use their work and to those publishers who have courteously dismissed copyright restrictions in my favor. Specific acknowledgements have been made at appropriate places throughout the book.

M. G. F.

CONTENTS

American Traits

Patterns of Americanism

Landmark Addresses and State Papers

American Democracy

Citizenship and Patriotism

Educated Leadership

Changes and Adjustments

In Arms for Democracy

After the Conflict

NATIONAL IDEALS AND PROBLEMS

AMERICAN TRAITS

AMERICAN QUALITY[1]

Nathaniel Southgate Shaler

[Nathaniel Southgate Shaler (1841–1906) was a distinguished American geologist, born in Newport, Kentucky. He graduated in 1862 at the Lawrence Scientific School of Harvard University. A few years later he became connected with the instructional staff in that institution, and held, from time to time, different professorships in his field of work. In 1891 be became dean of the Lawrence Scientific School. His interesting analysis of American character which is here reprinted shows the scientific attitude which is not content with the actual facts, but must seek probable explanations of its origin. It also shows traces of a favorite thesis of the writer—that human characteristics are the result largely of environment. This view is developed at length in respect to the United States in his book, *Nature and Man in America*.]

The most important, because the most fundamental, of problems concerning the quality of the American man, concerns his physical condition, as compared with that of his kindred beyond the seas. As to this point the evidence is so clear that it needs little discussion. It is evident that the American Indians, a race evidently on the ground for many thousand years before the coming of the Europeans, had found the land hospitable. For savages they were remarkably well developed, and though unfitted for steady labor, their bodies were well made and enduring. Taking their place, the North Europeans, representing a wide range of local varieties, English, Irish, Highland Scotch, Germans, Scandinavians, Normans, French, and many other groups of Old World peoples, have, since their implantation a hundred years or more ago, shown that the area of the continent from the Rio Grande to the far north is as suited to our kind as is any part of the earth. This is sufficiently proved by the statistics of American soldiers gathered during the Civil War; the American

[1]From *International Monthly*, vol. iv, p. 48 (July, 1901). Reprinted by permission.

white man of families longest in this country, is, on the average, larger than his European kinsman; the increase being mainly in the size of head and chest. It is further indicated by the endurance of these men in the trials of the soldier's life and by the remarkable percentage of recoveries from wounds. This endurance of wounds was regarded by the late Dr. Brown-Sequard as a feature common to all the mammals of this continent, being, as he claimed on the basis of an extensive experience, as characteristic of American rabbits as of American men. Moreover, the statistics of life insurance companies doing business in this country appear to indicate that the expectation of life is greater here than in the Old World. . . .

Accepting the conclusion that the bodily condition of our race is, in this country at least, as good as in the continent whence they came, we will now turn to the questions as to their moral and intellectual development in the new land. First of these to be considered is that which relates to the attitude of the individual man toward his fellows of the commonwealth. However we may state this question, it is likely to appear to be of a shadowy nature; seen clearly, however, it will be recognized as of fundamental importance. It were best approached by a comparison of the usual state of mind of communities in Europe as regards other groups of the same race and country, from which they are separated, as are people dwelling in neighboring villages. Having journeyed much afoot in England and continental Europe, I have often had occasion to remark the very general lack of confidence which the common men of any place have in those who, though dwelling nearby, are personally unknown to them. Traces of this humor may be found in England and northern Germany, where it may commonly be noted in a good natured contempt for the unknown compatriot. Further southward this limitation of sympathy becomes more definite. Ancient hatreds between the citizens of neighboring communes find expression in legends and songs that continue the bitterness to this day. In Italy this partition of the people in spirit goes so far that the pedestrian who has become friendly with those who dwell in any little rural society will often be warned that he will be in danger as soon as he comes among the dreadful folk who dwell on the other side of the divide.

To an observant American who journeys in Europe in a way that brings him in contact with its people, this *morcellement* of states into little bits which are united not by any common direct sympathy, but only by the bond of a common rule, is not only very evident, but in singular contrast to what he has been accustomed to in his own country. Though from its familiarity it escapes the attention of most people, it is one of the most noteworthy social phenomena of the New World, that the citizen of Maine accepts, as by a kind of instinct, his fellowman of Texas or California as a real compatriot, as a person who feels and acts as he does himself. It is evident that this is no recently acquired state of mind; its existence clearly antedates the formation of our government; it, indeed, made the Federal union possible. For a half century slavery limited the extension of the motive, though it did not altogether part the people of the North and South. This habit of confidence in the neighbor, however remote, which is at the foundation of the quality of our people, goes beyond the national limits. It has effectively made an end of the rancors which once existed toward the mother country. Watch as one may the talk of our people, we now hear nothing indicating more than a good-humored quirk concerning John Bull and his ways.

At first sight it may seem as if this confidence in the fellowman, which is the foundation of American quality, is but a manifestation of their prevailing good nature. That it is other and more than this is fairly well shown by many incidents occurring in and after the Civil War. Those who remember that mighty clutch will recall how in its worst days the soldiers of the contending armies trusted one another much as they would their own comrades. It is said that in the Fredericksburg campaign a number of Federal soldiers spent Christmas with a Confederate regiment with whom they had made acquaintance in the campaign. All the hard usage of war could not sweep away the neighborly trust between men who were yet ready for the bitterest fighting to accomplish their objects.

This feature of confidence in the essential likeness of the fellowman which holds among our people is, perhaps, best shown in the closing incidents of the Civil War. There was at the time much talk about guerrilla warfare, such as the Dutch have waged in South Africa; but when it became evident that effective national resistance was no longer possible, the subjugated people turned to their conquerors as to their fellow-citizens, with a measure of trust in their quality such as under like conditions the world had not before known. Owing to an unhappy series of political accidents and much actual knavery, the trust of the southerners in the quality of their northern brethren seemed for a time ill-founded. During the so-called reconstruction period, the states which had revolted were subjected to a very oppressive rule. Yet, through it all, the people trusted, happily not in vain, to the American quality of their sometime enemies to set them right. So, too, in the last step in the work of reconstruction, when the northern people found the southern undoing, in an indirect way, that provision of the Constitution which gives the negro the ballot on the same terms with the white man; the acquiescence of the Republican party in this course finds its explanation in the general conviction that the southern people are doing about as well as can be expected with a problem of exceeding difficulty. The history of secession and reconstruction discloses a consensus among the citizens of this country such as may be sought in vain in any other.

It is easy to see that the American's belief in the unseen neighbor as like unto himself is not only the foundation of his true democracy, but the basis on which rest certain other important elements of his quality. To it is due the exceptional range and activity of the sympathetic motives, such as led to the war with Spain, and to the almost preposterous welcome of the captured officers of the Spanish fleet; and such now moves so many of our folk to protest against the doings of this nation in the Philippines. It is also marked in the constant sympathy with suffering, whenceever comes the cry. Not that this accord with the fellowman is peculiar to Americans; it is, indeed, a part of modern life, but the effect of it is evidently felt by a larger part of our people, is more national with us than else-where. This quality of sympathy is, indeed, near to being, if it be not in fact, a national weakness. Too little limited by reason, it led to the war with Spain for the rescue of Cuba, with the common consequence of war, a series of difficulties of which no man can see the end.

A most important result of this belief in the essential likeness of men is the eminently kindly quality of the American. The proof of this on a large scale is again to be had in the history of the Rebellion. Though this contest, like all war whatsoever, was replete with brutality and horror, it was singularly distin-guished from all like contentions by the mercy shown to non-combatants, by the care for women and children, and by the leniency with which the subjugated leaders were treated. The evidence to support these statements cannot be here given in any detail. To exhibit it fitly would require an extended study of the matter; I cannot, however, forbear to set forth a few in-cidents which came to my knowledge at the time, and which served to illustrate the temper of our people in conditions which bring out the worst qualities of men.

Shortly after the close of the Rebellion, I questioned many persons who had been in the most sanguinary contests, to find whether they had observed any instances where prisoners, taken in the heat of battle, had been harmed. As the result of this inquiry, which was made of over one hundred ex-soldiers, I learned of one or two cases where prisoners had been shot by members of a rabble home guard, men generally of a much lower grade than the embodied troops and without adequate control by officers. Among disciplined troops, there was but one ex-ample of cruelty, if such it may be called, where a Federal soldier, as he clutched the musket of a surrendering Confederate, slapped him on the face; and he was at once put under arrest for his brutal conduct.

In the campaign of 1862, between the armies of Buell and Bragg for the possession of Kentucky, movements which led to the fiercest action of the war, the conditions were such as have elsewhere always brought vast suffering to non-combatants. It was a more truly internecine struggle than occurred in any other part of the great field. The state was divided against itself, communities and families were rent. In instances, probably numbering thousands, brothers, or fathers and sons, were in opposing armies. It is doubtful if in any other time have people of our race been so moved by fury to the foundations of their souls. Yet at the end of it, I recall that none of the many I questioned knew of harm having come to woman or child; that whenever a flag of truce gave the chance of meeting, there was expression of a mutual anxiety to "keep the fighting clean," and a determination to insure this end by slaying all offenders against decency.

The evidence of good nature afforded by the treatment of the leaders of the Rebellion is so general and well known that it needs no setting forth. One such came under my eyes when, just after the war, Alexander Stephens, the ex-Vice-President of the ex-Confederacy, because he was a cripple, was, by general consent, allowed to select his seat in the hall of the House at Washington, before the other members drew lots for their places. There were some marring deeds, as, for instance, the execution of Wertz, and the chaining of Jefferson Davis, an unoffending prisoner; but the conduct of our people at the end of the Rebellion, indeed we may say the whole conduct of that vast struggle, displays their eminently merciful quality.

In the interchange of wit and humor, wherein men show their quality in an unpremeditated way, we have a chance to discern another evidence of the singular confidence of the American as to the likeness of the fellowman to himself. Among other peoples this instinctive criticism of life is commonly turned upon the personal differences between men, those of individuals, classes, or races. It usually exhibits an essentially narrow, hedonistic motive. In this country, on the other hand, the criticism most often assumes the similarity of men, and finds the amusement in larger features of identity and contrast of situations. Thus, the humor of the Mississippi Valley, especially that of the frontiersman, has a sympathetic motive which is not found elsewhere. It is apt to relate to the insufficiencies of mankind rather than to the defects of particular men; not rarely it takes the fine allegorical form, wherein much apparent profanity does not hide the really high moral tone. Thus it comes about that the American is by no means witty as compared with the Frenchman; from that point of view, he may fairly be termed dull; but in him there is characteristically an inextinguishable spirit of humor. Like his prototype, Mercutio, even the wound that ends him is a fair subject for a quirk. Like the other accidents of life, "'tis not so deep as a well, nor so wide as a churchdoor; but 'tis enough, 'twill serve." If this view be true, our much-discussed American humor is a very natural product of our assumption as to the intimate kinship of men.

Turning from the simpler emotions which lie at the foundations of human nature, let us consider what evidence is to be had that shows us something concerning the permanent ideals that have been developed among our people. So far as ideals relate to the home, they appear to be, with slight exceptions, essentially those that were transmitted to us from the mother country; the difference being that the head of the house is far less its master than in the Old World. Here, again, we have the primary concept of democracy, that of the essential likeness of human beings, working to break down the ancient idea as to the rightful power of the father over the family, with the result that the normal American household is a type of the democracy of which it forms a part. It is not likely that this change of view has, in any measure, weakened the hold of parents on their children; but to it is probably due, in some degree, the rapid increase of the divorce rate, which, as is well known, is higher in this than in any other country.

The ideal of the commonwealth came to us, with that of the family, by inheritance; the name itself is an importation, but there is an evident change in the contents of the conception. Until our government was founded, there was no instance in which men had developed patriotic instincts relating to such a complex as the United States presents. In the Old World, except in some measure in Switzerland, for all the experiments in governing that have there been essayed, men have not proved themselves able to maintain a divided allegiance, such as is required of American citizens, and by them effectively rendered, in the love and duty they give to the state and the Union in which they are included. In all experiments previously made, it was evident that the sense of obligation had to relate to one center; with rare exceptions—in fact only in small oligarchies where the motives due to personal association of all the leaders existed— the reference of allegiance had to be to a sovereign, whether king or Cromwell, an evident leader beheld upon a throne. It is true that the American complex was the result of an accident of government which united several centers of growth, but it is none the less a remarkable fact that the system of allegiance within allegiance, with no reference to any devotion to individuals or dynasties and with no association with religious faiths, should have been accepted by our people without debate except as to the mere details, and with no sense of the novelty of the conditions they were establishing. This course of action, apparently so spontaneous and immediate, indicates that the political sense of the American people had undergone an unrecognized development in the century and a half of colonial life before the Revolution. It is impossible here to essay an analysis of this growth. It may, however, be noted that, more than any other feature, it indicates the subtle effect of the conditions of the New World on the spirit of men.

The essence of the political allegiance of the American people is evidently not to a definite bit of the earth, nor to the memories of the past, which are to a great extent the basis of that motive in the Old World, but to ideals of government. The people of France, for instance, and the same is true of most other countries, love their land and its traditions equally well, whatever kind of government manages to set itself over them. Here, however, as is well shown by the history of the Civil War, the affection is for the system of the commonwealth as a system, even more than for the results attained by it. Love of the land of a romantic kind, such as has been the basis of so much that is noble as well as unhappy in other realms, is evidently not a leading motive with us. It is true that slavery, in an immediate

way, brought about the War of Secession, but the question
which was debated, which moved the people as men have rarely
if ever before been moved, concerned the relative weight of
the allegiance the citizen owed to his state and to the Nation.
It is conceivable that the American might be transplanted
to some other land, and that the deportation would bring
with it little if any sense of exile, provided his political order
went with him. But for this order he is prepared to do battle
to the end.

It appears like a contradiction to say that the love of our
people for their government does not include a devotion to the
instruments which set it forth. We are much given to patching
our constitutions and, at times, to juggling with them, but the
essence of the motive appears to be love of a definite political
order, an intense need of a distinctly stated body of negative
law which will permit the largest possible measure of liberty.
The clinging to the system of states in a nation apparently rests
on the conviction that under that system the maximum of freedom may be attained. . . .

The most indicative feature in American quality is that
which is expressed in the religious freedom which has been
attained in this country. In a rude, imperfect form this ideal
existed in the Elizabethan time. Evidently it was not brought
from the Old World, for the colonies began with the ancient
intolerance. This motive was variously expressed, sometimes in
a brutal manner, again with a milder accent, but it was essentially universal. At the time the Federal union was formed,
religious freedom or at least the understanding that the law
had no right to dictate religious beliefs, was well established.
Since then the development of this quality has been continued
until it has so far penetrated the minds of men that the barriers
of faith have little effect in limiting social relations. Even the
ancient dislike of Roman Catholics and Jews has nearly passed
away; what is left of it relates rather to race hatreds than to
religious prejudices. It may fairly be claimed that the efface-
ment of sectarian rancors is the greatest and most unique accomplishment of our people. It is evident that this gain has also

been due to the fundamental belief of our people as to the likeness of men to one another.

The ideal of public education, like the many other elements of American quality, came to us from the mother country. Except, however, in the fancies of idealists the projects of instruction which were developed in the Old World were not intended to apply to all sorts and conditions of men, but to a chosen few. Although in the several colonies the motive which led to the development of educational systems differed much in intensity, it appears in some degree to have existed in all, and to have been active in the minds of the hardest pressed of their frontiersmen. Thus, with the first settlers of Kentucky, who were facing the trials and perils of an unknown wilderness, we find among the brief proceedings of their first parliament, held in 1775 under a tree, a provision for the establishment of a school. Another of these memorable enactments provided for the suppression of profane swearing; yet another for the improvement of the breed of horses—all of which goes to show how the ideal and the practical went together in the minds of our pioneers, whether they were of Massachusetts Bay or of the Virginia plantations.

Beginning doubtfully in the colonial period, the ideal of public education has grown with the growth of the fundamental concept of democracy, that of the essential likeness of men, and with the sympathetic bond which this view of life creates, until it is one of the most characteristic elements of the quality of our people. It has commanded a share of devotion such as has been given to no other feature of our public life. It has so far entered into our hearts that the greediest of fortune seekers may be said to dream of founding schools. It is to be noted that this desire that the youth be adequately trained, has little relation to the economic results of such training. So far from desiring that the end to be attained shall be instruction in crafts or professions, the intent of our people has ever been that their schools shall lead toward culture; to enlargement rather than to more immediate profit; to the quality of the citizen rather than to that of the artisan. It has, indeed, been difficult to obtain from public money or from private gifts the means imperatively demanded for instruction in applied science. It is in the character of the educational system which has been developed in this country that we find the most indisputable evidence as to the essential quality of the American man. Seen in his money-hunting form, he seems to the ordinary observer as devoid of all ideals as was the Indian he has replaced. Considered in the light of his lofty devotion to the interests of the unborn, we gain another and better view of his complicated nature. It may be granted that these schools are in many ways most imperfect, but the concept on which they are founded and the devotion with which they have been supported tell much of American quality.

Looking at the social organization of this country in a broad way, we may note another feature, exhibited in very legible facts, which deserves our attention. This is the ease with which this society has taken in, and, as we may say, assimilated a vast body of very foreign people, very generally converting them or their immediate descendants into characteristic Englishmen of the American variety. To see the nature of this accomplishment, we should first note that in the fifteen decades or so of colonial life our people had a chance to shape their society with relatively little disturbing invasions from other than English countries. The Dutch colonists, then, were near kinsmen to the Palatinate Germans of Pennsylvania, and those of North Carolina, though more remote, were akin in race and religion and bound to the English people by the memory of the help lent them in their extremity; as were, also, the Huguenot French. Perhaps nine-tenths of the folk at the beginning of the Revolutionary War were of English stock, and the remainder no hindrance to the prevailing race. It is evident that these colonies had attained to a social organization which was singularly efficient in making a common serviceable product out of the odds and ends of humanity that immigration began to bring to the new nation in the early part of the nineteenth century. For near a hundred years the tide of foreigners has poured into the United States with increasing volume. To many good observers it has appeared impossible that grave changes in the quality of the country should not be brought about by this invasion. Yet this material, so far as it is of European origin, has been effectively, if not completely, Americanized.

It is true there has been no considerable adoption of the aborigines into the commonwealth, but this failure is due to the nature of the Indian. It is also true that the adjustment of the African is yet to be brought about, but there is some reason to believe that it may be accomplished. But, so far as the progress of our own race is concerned, the entrance of foreigners into our life, while here and there highly disadvantageous, has not been disastrous. In one or two generations, even where they retain, as in the case of the Pennsylvania Germans, their native speech and customs, they are, in all important regards, completely naturalized. This swift digestion of the millions from countries of a spirit very alien to its own, indicates what we may term the organic intensity of American society; in other words, the eminently political quality of the association. Into this invisible, intangible, yet most real, social whole the ardent quality of its citizens so enters that it can quickly efface the imprint of the ages upon those who come to it from foreign lands, and stamp them as its own.

It has been the purpose of this writing to consider only those elements of American quality of which we have evidence in recorded or evident facts. Only by such limitation can we avoid those highly romantic speculations as to the character of our folk which so fill the pages of would-be observers from abroad. In summing up the story, it seems not unreasonable to consider what is to be the future of the evidently novel type of Englishman; we might, indeed, term him this spiritually new variety of man. It is clear that his most eminent quality consists in his detachment from the control of the past, his self-sufficiency in the better sense of the term. He has learned to feel, beyond others of his kind, the value of his individuality. It is, perhaps, as a reflection of this sense that he places a like high rating on his neighbor. He feels the bond of human brotherhood in a curiously intense degree. As all the coöperative work of man depends upon this sense of human kinship, his large measure of it should carry the American far—in just what direction it is not easy to foretell.

It requires no analysis to see that the fundamental judgment of democracy, that of the essential likeness of men, though a truth of vast import, is but a half truth. True for the primary qualities which should determine the rights of all, it is profoundly untrue as regards those secondary features of the intelligence which give to human minds a range and variety of capacity really greater than the differences in the frames of men. An apparent consequence of this excessive idea of common likeness in his kind, is the comparative absence of critical ability in the American people. In a large sense of the term, criticism rests upon a conception of the very great difference of one individual from another. As applied to life, it leads to an understanding of its vast complication, of its far-reaching interdependencies, of its splendors and its shames. In the field of morals, it teaches that there are herds and leaders; that men have won the heights because they knew their prophets, or have gone to the deep because they knew them not.

It is evident that the path on which this America-shaping and America-shaped man has journeyed separates him from the critical state of mind. Yet he has so prospered in his journey on it, has gained such a measure of will and discernment, that the critic would not really know his cautious trade if he ventured to forecast his limits. The most reasonable judgment concerning this essentially new form of strong man is, that on this deep and broad foundation of his sympathies and understandings he will, in time, build all that his friendly critics could wish him of enlargement.

AMERICAN CHARACTER[1]

Brander Matthews

[Brander Matthews (1852——) was born in New Orleans, Louisiana, but early in life went to New York to live. After a brief experience with law, he turned to literature in which he distinguished himself as a writer of fiction and criticism. Since 1892 he has been a professor in the English department of Columbia University. The discussion of American character, which is here given, supplements the selection from Shaler in approaching the matter from a somewhat different angle. It was originally an address delivered on several academic occasions.]

I

In a volume recording a series of talks with Tolstoi, published by a French writer in the final months of 1904, we are told that the Russian novelist thought the Dukhobors had attained to a perfected life, in that they were simple, free from envy, wrath, and ambition, detesting violence, refraining from theft and murder, and seeking ever to do good. Then the Parisian interviewer asked which of the peoples of the world seemed most remote from the perfection to which the Dukhobors had elevated themselves; and when Tolstoi returned that he had given no thought to this question, the French correspondent suggested that we Americans deserved to be held up to scorn as the least worthy of nations.

The tolerant Tolstoi asked his visitor why he thought so ill of us; and the journalist of Paris then put forth the opinion that we Americans are " a people terribly practical, avid of pleasure, systematically hostile to all idealism. The ambition of the American's heart, the passion of his life, is money; and it is rather a delight in the conquest and possession of money than in the use of it. The Americans ignore the arts; they despise disinterested beauty. And, now, moreover, they are imperialists. They could have remained peaceful without danger to their national existence; but they had to have a fleet and an army.

[1]From *The American of the Future and Other Essays.* (Copyright, 1909, Charles Scribner's Sons.) Reprinted by permission.

They set out after Spain and attacked her; and now they begin
to defy Europe. Is there not something scandalous in this
revelation of the conquering appetite in a new people with no
hereditary predisposition toward war?"

It is to the credit of the French correspondent that, after
setting down this fervid arraignment, he was honest enough to
record Tolstoi's dissent. But although he dissented, the great
Russian expressed little surprise at the virulence of this diatribe.
No doubt it voiced an opinion familiarized to him of late by many
a newspaper of France and of Germany. Fortunately for us,
the assertion that foreign nations are a contemporaneous
posterity is not quite true. Yet the opinion of foreigners, even
when most at fault, must have its value for us as a useful cor-
rective of conceit. We ought to be proud of our country; but we
need not be vain about it. Indeed, it would be difficult for the
most patriotic of us to find any satisfaction in the figure of the
typical American which apparently exists in the mind of most
Europeans, and which seems to be a composite photograph of
the backwoodsman of Cooper, the negro of Mrs. Stowe, and
the Mississippi river-folk of Mark Twain, modified, perhaps, by
more vivid memories of Buffalo Bill's Wild West. Surely this is
a strange monster; and we need not wonder that foreigners
feel toward it as Voltaire felt toward the prophet Habakkuk,
whom he declared to be "capable of anything."

It has seemed advisable to quote here what the Parisian
journalist said of us, not because he himself is a person of consequence, indeed, he is so obscure that there is no need even to
mention his name, but because he has had the courage to
attempt what Burke declared to be impossible—to draw an
indictment against a whole nation. It would be easy to retort
on him in kind, for, unfortunately,—and to the grief of all her
friends,—France has laid herself open to accusations as sweeping and as violent. It would be easy to dismiss the man himself
as one whose outlook on the world is so narrow that it seems to
be little more than what he can get through a chance slit in the
wall of his own self-sufficiency. It would be easy to answer him
in either of these fashions, but what is easy is rarely worth while;

and it is wiser to weigh what he said and to see if we cannot find our profit in it.

Sifting the essential charges from out the mass of his malevolent accusation, we find this Frenchman alleging, first, that we Americans care chiefly for making money; second, that we are hostile to art and to all forms of beauty; and thirdly, that we are devoid of ideals. These three allegations may well be considered, one by one, beginning with the assertion that we are mere money-makers.

II

Now, in so far as this Frenchman's belief is but an exaggeration of the saying of Napoleon's, that the English were a nation of shopkeepers, we need not wince, for the Emperor of the French found to his cost that those same English shopkeepers had a stout stomach for fighting. Nor need we regret that we can keep shop profitably, in these days when the doors of the bankers' vaults are the real gates of the Temple of Janus, war being impossible until they open. There is no reason for alarm or for apology so long as our shopkeeping does not cramp our muscle or curb our spirit, for, as Bacon declared three centuries ago, "walled towns, stored arsenals and armories, goodly races of horse, chariots of war, elephants, ordnance, artillery and the like, all this is but a sheep in a lion's skin, except the breed and disposition of the people be stout and warlike."

Even the hostile French traveler did not accuse us of any flabbiness of fiber; indeed, he declaimed especially against our "conquering appetite," which seemed to him scandalous "in a new people with no hereditary predisposition toward war." But here he fell into a common blunder; the United States may be a new nation—although, as a fact, the stars-and-stripes is now older than the tricolor of France, the union-jack of Great Britain, and the standards of those newcomers among the nations, Italy and Germany—the United States may be a new nation, but the people here have had as many ancestors as the population of any other country. The people here, moreover, have "a hereditary predisposition toward war," or at least toward adventure, since they are, every man of them, descended from some European more venturesome than his fellows, readier to risk the perils of the western ocean and bolder to front the unknown dangers of an unknown land. The warlike temper, the aggressiveness, the imperialistic sentiment—these are in us no new development of unexpected ambition; and they ought not to surprise anyone familiar with the way in which our forefathers grasped this Atlantic coast first, then thrust themselves across the Alleghanies, spread abroad to the Mississippi, and reached out at last to the Rockies and to the Pacific. The lust of adventure may be dangerous, but it is no new thing; it is in our blood, and we must reckon with it.

Perhaps it is because "the breed and disposition of the people" is "stout and warlike" that our shopkeeping has been successful enough to awaken envious admiration among other races whose energy may have been relaxed of late. After all, the arts of war and the arts of peace are not so unlike; and in either a triumph can be won only by an imagination strong enough to foresee and to divine what is hidden from the weakling. We are a trading community, after all and above all, even if we come of fighting stock. We are a trading community, just as Athens was, and Venice and Florence. And like the men of these earlier commonwealths, the men of the United States are trying to make money. They are striving to make money, not solely to amass riches, but partly because having money is the outward and visible sign of success—because it is the most obvious measure of accomplishment.

In his talk with Tolstoi, our French critic revealed an unexpected insight when he asserted that the passion of American life was not so much the use of money as a delight in the conquest of it. Many an American man of affairs would admit without hesitation that he would rather make half a million dollars than inherit a million. It is the process he enjoys, rather than the result; it is the tough tussle in the open market which gives him the keenest pleasure, and not the idle contemplation of wealth safely stored away. He girds himself for battle and fights for his own hand; he is the son and the grandson of the stalwart adven-

B

turers who came from the Old World to face the chances of the new. This is why he is unwilling to retire as men are wont to do in Europe when their fortunes are made. Merely to have money does not greatly delight him—although he would regret not having it; but what does delight him unceasingly is the fun of making it.

The money itself often he does not know what to do with; and he can find no more selfish use for it than to give it away. He seems to recognize that his making it was in some measure due to the unconscious assistance of the community as a whole; and he feels it his duty to do something for the people among whom he lives. It must be noted that the people themselves also expect this from him; they expect him sooner or later to pay his footing. As a result of this pressure of public opinion and of his own lack of interest in money itself, he gives freely. In time he comes to find pleasure in this as well; and he applies his business sagacity to his benefactions. Nothing is more characteristic of modern American life than this pouring out of private wealth for public service. Nothing remotely resembling it is to be seen now in any country of the Old World; and not even in Athens in its noblest days was there a larger-handed lavishness of the individual for the benefit of the community.

Again, in no country of the Old World is the prestige of wealth less powerful than it is here. This, of course, the foreigner fails to perceive; he does not discover that it is not the man who happens to possess money that we regard with admiration but the man who is making money, and thereby proving his efficiency and indirectly benefiting the community. To many it may sound like an insufferable paradox to assert that nowhere in the civilized world today is money itself of less weight than here in the United States; but the broader his opportunity the more likely is an honest observer to come to this unexpected conclusion. Fortunes are made in a day almost, and they may fade away in a night; as the Yankee proverb put it pithily, "It's only three generations from shirt-sleeves to shirt-sleeves." Wealth is likely to lack something of its glamor in a land where well-being is widely diffused and where a large proportion of the population have either had a fortune and lost it or else expect to gain one in the immediate future.

Probably also there is no country which now contains more men who do not greatly care for large gains and who have gladly given up money-making for some other occupation they found more profitable for themselves. These are the men like Thoreau —in whose *Walden*, now half a century old, we can find an emphatic declaration of all the latest doctrines of the simple life. We have all heard of Agassiz,—best of Americans, even though he was born in another republic,—how he repelled the proffer of large terms for a series of lectures, with the answer that he had no time to make money. Closely akin was the reply of a famous machinist in response to an inquiry as to what he had been doing, —to the effect that he had accomplished nothing of late,—"we have just been building engines and making money, and I'm about tired of it." There are not a few men today in these toiling United States who hold with Ben Jonson that "money never made any man rich,—but his mind."

But while this is true, while there are some men among us who care little for money, and while there are many who care chiefly for the making of it, ready to share it when made with their fellow-citizens, candor compels the admission that there are also not a few who are greedy and grasping, selfish and shameless, and who stand forward, conspicuous and unscrupulous, as if to justify to the full the aspersions which foreigners cast upon us. Although these men manage for the most part to keep within the letter of the law, their morality is that of the wrecker and of the pirate. It is a symptom of health in the body politic that the proposal has been made to inflict social ostracism upon the criminal rich. We need to stiffen our conscience and to set up a loftier standard of social intercourse, refusing to fellowship with the men who make their money by overriding the law or by undermining it—just as we should have declined the friendship of Captain Kidd laden down with stolen treasure.

In the immediate future these men will be made to feel that they are under the ban of public opinion. One sign of an acuter sensitiveness is the recent outcry against the acceptance of "tainted money" for the support of good works. Although it is wise always to give a good deed the credit of a good motive, yet it is impossible sometimes not to suspect that certain large gifts have an aspect of "conscience money." Some of them seem to be the result of a desire to divert public attention from the evil way in which the money was made to the nobler manner in which it is spent. They appear to be the attempt of a social outlaw to buy his peace with the community. Apparently there are rich men among us, who, having sold their honor for a price, would now gladly give up the half of their fortunes to get it back.

Candor compels the admission also that by the side of the criminal rich there exists the less noxious but more offensive class of the idle rich, who lead lives of wasteful luxury and of empty excitement. When the French reporter who talked with Tolstoi called us Americans "avid of pleasure" it was this little group he had in mind, as he may have seen the members of it splurging about in Paris, squandering and self-advertising. Although these idle rich now exhibit themselves most openly and to least advantage in Paris and in London, their foolish doings are recorded superabundantly in our own newspapers; and their demoralizing influence is spread abroad. The snobbish report of their misguided attempts at amusement may even be a source of danger in that it seems to recognize a false standard of social success or in that it may excite a miserable ambition to emulate these pitiful frivolities. But there is no need of delaying longer over the idle rich; they are only a few, and they have doomed themselves to destruction, since it is an inexorable fact that those who break the laws of nature can have no hope of executive clemency.

> "Patience a little; learn to wait,
> Years are long on the clock of fate."

III

The second charge which the wandering Parisian journalist brought against us was that we ignore the arts and that we despise disinterested beauty. Here again the answer that is easiest is not altogether satisfactory. There is no difficulty in declaring that there are American artists, both painters and sculptors, who have gained the most cordial appreciation in Paris itself, or in drawing attention to the fact that certain of the minor arts—that of the silversmith, for one, and for another, that of the glass-blower and the glass-cutter—flourish in the United States at least as freely as they do anywhere else, while the art of designing in stained glass has had a new birth here, which has given it a vigorous vitality lacking in Europe since the Middle Ages. It would not be hard to show that our American architects are now undertaking to solve new problems wholly unknown to the builders of Europe, and that they are often succeeding in this grapple with unprecedented difficulty. Nor would it take long to draw up a list of the concerted efforts of certain of our cities to make themselves more worthy and more sightly with parks well planned and with public buildings well proportioned and appropriately decorated. We might even invoke the memory of the evanescent loveliness of the White City that graced the shores of Lake Michigan a few years ago; and we might draw attention again to the Library of Congress, a later effort of the allied arts of the architect, the sculptor, and the painter.

But however full of high hope for the future we may esteem these several instances of our reaching out for beauty, we must admit—if we are honest with ourselves—that they are all more or less exceptional, and that to offset this list of artistic achievements the Devil's Advocate could bring forward a damning catalogue of crimes against good taste which would go far to prove that the feeling for beauty is dead here in America and also the desire for it. The Devil's Advocate would bid us consider the flaring and often vulgar advertisements that disfigure our highways, the barbaric ineptness of many of our public buildings, the squalor of the outskirts of our towns and villages, the hideousness and horror of the slums in most of our cities, the negligent toleration of dirt and disorder in our public conveyances, and many another pitiable deficiency of our civilization present in the minds of all of us.

The sole retort possible is a plea of confession and avoidance, coupled with a promise of reformation. These evils are evident and they cannot be denied. But they are less evident today than they were yesterday; and we may honestly hope that they will be less evident tomorrow. The bare fact that they have been observed warrants the belief that unceasing effort will be made to do away with them. Once aroused, public opinion will work its will in due season. And here occasion serves to deny boldly the justice of a part of the accusation which the French reporter brought against us. It may be true that we "ignore the arts"— although this is an obvious overstatement of the case; but it is not true that we "despise beauty." However ignorant the American people may be as a whole, they are in no sense hostile toward art—as certain other peoples seem to be. On the contrary, they welcome it; with all their ignorance, they are anxious to understand it; they are pathetically eager for it. They are so desirous of it that they want it in a hurry, only too often to find themselves put off with an empty imitation. But the desire itself is indisputable; and its accomplishment is likely to be helped along by the constant commingling here of peoples from various other stocks than the Anglo-Saxon, since the mixture of races tends always to a swifter artistic development.

It is well to probe deeper into the question and to face the fact that not only in the arts but also in the sciences we are not doing all that may fairly be expected of us. Athens was a trading city as New York is, but New York has had no Sophocles and no Phidias. Florence and Venice were towns whose merchants were princes, but no American city has yet brought forth a Giotto, a Dante, a Titian. It is now nearly threescore years and ten since Emerson delivered his address on the "American Scholar," which has well been styled our intellectual Declaration of Independence, and in which he expressed the hope that "perhaps the time is already come . . . when the sluggard intellect of this continent will look from under its iron lids and fulfil the postponed expectation of the world with something better than the exertions of a mechanical skill." Nearly seventy years ago was this prophecy uttered which still echoes unaccomplished.

In the nineteenth century, in which we came to maturity as a nation, no one of the chief leaders of art, even including literature in its broadest aspects, and no one of the chief leaders in science, was native to our country. Perhaps we might claim that Webster was one of the world's greatest orators and that Parkman was one of the world's greatest historians; but probably the experts outside of the United States would be found unprepared and unwilling to admit either claim, however likely it may be to win acceptance in the future. Lincoln is indisputably one of the world's greatest statesmen; and his fame is now firmly established throughout the whole of civilization. But this is all we can assert; and we cannot deny that we have given birth to very few indeed of the foremost poets, dramatists, novelists, painters, sculptors, architects or scientific discoverers of the last hundred years.

Alfred Russell Wallace, whose renown is linked with Darwin's and whose competence as a critic of scientific advance is beyond dispute, has declared that the nineteenth century was the most wonderful of all since the world began. He asserts that the scientific achievements of the last hundred years, both in the discovery of general principles and in their practical application, exceed in number the sum total of the scientific achievements to be credited to all the centuries that went before. He considers, first of all, the practical applications, which made the aspect of civilization in 1900 differ in a thousand ways from what it had been in 1801. He names a dozen of these practical applications: railways, steam navigation, the electric telegraph, the telephone, friction-matches, gas-lighting, electric-lighting, the phonograph, the Roentgen rays, spectrum analysis, anesthetics, and antiseptics. It is with pride that an American can check off not a few of these utilities as being due wholly or in large part to the ingenuity of one or another of his countrymen.

But his pride has a fall when Wallace draws up a second list, not of mere inventions but of those fundamental discoveries, of those fecundating theories underlying all practical applications and making them possible, of those principles "which have extended our knowledge or widened our conceptions of the uni-

verse." Of these he catalogues twelve; and we are pained to find
that no American has had an important share in the establishment of any of these broad generalizations. He may have added
a little here and there, but no single one of all the twelve discoveries is mainly to be credited to any American. It seems as
if our French critic was not so far out when he asserted that we
were "terribly practical." In the application of principles, in
the devising of new methods, our share was larger than that of
any other nation. In the working out of the stimulating principles themselves, our share was less than "a younger brother's
portion."

It is only fair to say, however, that even though we may not
have brought forth a chief leader of art or of science to adorn
the wonderful century, there are other evidences of our practical sagacity than those set down by Wallace, evidences
more favorable and of better augury for our future. We
derived our language and our laws, our public justice and our
representative government from our English ancestors, as we
derived from the Dutch our religious toleration and perhaps
also our large freedom of educational opportunity. In our time
we have set an example to others and helped along the progress
of the world. President Eliot holds that we have made five
important contributions to the advancement of civilization.
First of all, we have done more than any other people to further
peace-keeping and to substitute legal arbitration for the brute
conflict of war. Second, we have set a splendid example of the
broadest religious toleration—even though Holland had first
shown us how. Thirdly, we have made evident the wisdom of
universal manhood suffrage. Fourthly, by our welcoming of
newcomers from all parts of the earth, we have proved that men
belonging to a great variety of races are fit for political freedom.
Finally, we have succeeded in diffusing material well-being
among the whole population to an extent without parallel in
any other country in the world.

These five American contributions to civilization are all of
them the result of the practical side of the American character.
They may even seem commonplace as compared with the con-

quering exploits of some other races. But they are more than merely practical; they are all essentially moral. As President Eliot insists, they are "triumphs of reason, enterprise, courage, faith and justice over passion, selfishness, inertness, timidity, and distrust. Beneath each of these developments there lies a strong ethical sentiment, a strenuous moral and social purpose. It is for such work that multitudinous democracies are fit."

IV

A "strong ethical sentiment," and a "strenuous moral purpose" cannot flourish unless they are deeply rooted to idealism. And here we find an adequate answer to the third assertion of Tolstoi's visitor, who maintained that we are "hostile to all idealism." Our idealism may be of a practical sort, but it is idealism none the less. Emerson was an idealist, although he was also a thrifty Yankee. Lincoln was an idealist, even if he was also a practical politician, an opportunist, knowing where he wanted to go, but never crossing a bridge before he came to it. Emerson and Lincoln had ever a firm grip on the facts of life; each of them kept his gaze fixed on the stars—and he also kept his feet firm on the soil.

There is a sham idealism, boastful and shabby, which stares at the moon and stumbles in the mud, as Shelley and Poe stumbled. But the basis of the highest genius is always a broad common sense. Shakspere and Molière were held in esteem by their comrades for their understanding of affairs; and they each of them had money out at interest. Sophocles was entrusted with command in battle; and Goethe was the shrewdest of the Grand Duke's counselors. The idealism of Shakspere and of Molière, of Sophocles and of Goethe, is like that of Emerson and of Lincoln; it is unfailingly practical. And thereby it is sharply set apart from the aristocratic idealism of Plato and of Renan, of Ruskin and of Nietzsche, which is founded on obvious self-esteem and which is sustained by arrogant and inexhaustible egotism. True idealism is not only practical, it is also liberal and tolerant.

Perhaps it might seem to be claiming too much to insist on certain points of similarity between us and the Greeks of old. The points of dissimilarity are only too evident to most of us; and yet there is a likeness as well as an unlikeness. Professor Butcher has recently asserted that "no people was ever less detached from the practical affairs of life" than the Greeks, "less insensible to outward utility; yet they regarded prosperity as a means, never as an end. The unquiet spirit of gain did not take possession of their souls. Shrewd traders and merchants, they were yet idealists. They did not lose sight of the higher and distinctively human aims which give life its significance." It will be well for us if this can be said of our civilization two thousand years after its day is done; and it is for us to make sure that "the unquiet spirit of gain" shall not take possession of our souls. It is for us also to rise to the attitude of the Greeks, among whom, as Professor Butcher points out, "money lavished on personal enjoyment was counted vulgar, oriental, inhuman."

There is comfort in the memory of Lincoln and of those whose death on the field of Gettysburg he commemorated. The men who there gave up their lives that the country might live, had answered to the call of patriotism, which is one of the sublimest images of idealism. There is comfort also in the recollection of Emerson, and in the fact that for many of the middle years of the nineteenth century he was the most popular of lecturers, with an unfading attractiveness to the plain people, perhaps, because, in Lowell's fine phrase, he "kept constantly burning the beacon of an ideal life above the lower region of turmoil." There is comfort again in the knowledge that idealism is one manifestation of imagination, and that imagination itself is but an intenser form of energy. That we have energy and to spare, no one denies; and we may reckon him a nearsighted observer who does not see also that we have our full share of imagination even though it has not yet expressed itself in the loftiest regions of art and of science. The outlook is hopeful, and it is not true that

> "We, like sentries are obliged to stand
> In starless nights and wait the appointed hour."

The foundations of our commonwealth were laid by the sturdy Elizabethans who bore across the ocean with them their portion of that imagination which in England flamed up in rugged prose and in superb and soaring verse. In two centuries and a half the sons of these stalwart Englishmen have lost nothing of their ability to see visions and to dream dreams, and to put solid foundations under their castles in the air. The flame may seem to die down for a season, but it springs again from the embers most unexpectedly, as it broke forth furiously in 1861. There was imagination at the core of the little war for the freeing of Cuba—the very attack on Spain, which the Parisian journalist cited to Tolstoi as the proof of our predatory aggressiveness. We said that we were going to war for the sake of the ill-used people in the suffering island close to our shores; we said that we would not annex Cuba; we did the fighting that was needful—and we kept our word. It is hard to see how even the most bitter of critics can discover in this anything selfish.

There was imagination also in the sudden stopping of all the steam-craft, of all the railroads, of all the street-cars, of all the incessant traffic of the whole nation, at the moment when the body of a murdered chief magistrate was lowered into the grave. This pause in the work of the world was not only touching, it had a large significance to anyone seeking to understand the people of these United States. It was a testimony that the Greeks would have appreciated; it had the bold simplicity of an Attic inscription. And we would thrill again in sympathetic response if it was in the pages of Plutarch that we read the record of another instance: When the time arrived for Admiral Sampson to surrender the command of the fleet he had brought back to Hampton Roads, he came on deck to meet there only those officers whose prescribed duty required them to take part in the farewell ceremonies as set forth in the regulations. But when he went over the side of the flagship he found that the boat which was to bear him ashore was manned by the rest of the officers, ready to row him themselves and eager to render this last personal service; and then from every other ship of the fleet there put out a boat, also manned by officers,

to escort for the last time the commander whom they loved
and honored.

V

As another illustration of our regard for the finer and loftier
aspects of life, consider our parks, set apart for the use of the
people by the city, the state, and the nation. In the cities of this
new country the public playgrounds have had to be made, the
most of them, and at high cost—whereas the towns of the Old
World have come into possession of theirs for nothing, more often
than not inheriting the private recreation-grounds of their
rulers. And Europe has little or nothing to show similar either
to the reservations of certain states, like the steadily enlarging
preserves in the Catskills and the Adirondacks, or to the ampler
national parks, the Yellowstone, the Yosemite and the Grand
Canyon of the Colorado, some of them far larger in area than one
at least of the original thirteen states. Overcoming the pressure
of private greed, the people have ordained the preservation of
this natural beauty and its protection for all time under the
safe guardianship of the nation and with free access to all who
may claim admission to enjoy it.

In like manner many of the battlefields, whereon the nation
spent its blood that it might be what it is and what it hopes to
be—these have been taken over by the nation itself and set apart
and kept as holy places of pilgrimage. They are free from the
despoiling hand of any individual owner. They are adorned with
monuments recording the brave deeds of the men who fought
there. They serve as constant reminders of the duty we owe
to our country and of the debt we owe to those who made
it and who saved it for us. And the loyal veneration with
which these fields of blood have been cherished here in the
United States finds no counterpart in any country in Europe,
no matter how glorious may be its annals of military prowess.
Even Waterloo is in private hands; and its broad acres,
enriched by the bones of thousands, are tilled every year by
the industrious Belgian farmers. Yet it was a Frenchman,
Renan, who told us that what welds men into a nation, is

"the memory of great deeds done in common and the will to accomplish yet more."

According to the theory of the conservation of energy, there ought to be about as much virtue in the world at one time as at another. According to the theory of the survival of the fittest, there ought to be a little more now than there was a century ago. We Americans today have our faults, and they are abundant enough and blatant enough, and foreigners take care that we shall not overlook them; but our ethical standard—however imperfectly we may attain to it—is higher than that of the Greeks under Pericles, of the Romans under Cæsar, of the English under Elizabeth. It is higher even than that of our forefathers who established our freedom, as those know best who have most carefully inquired into the inner history of the American Revolution. In nothing was our advance more striking than in the different treatment meted out to the vanquished after the Revolution and after the Civil War. When we made our peace with the British the native Tories were proscribed, and thousands of loyalists left the United States to carry into Canada the indurated hatred of the exiled. But after Lee's surrender at Appomattox, no body of men, no single man indeed, was driven forth to live an alien for the rest of his days; even though a few might choose to go, none were compelled.

This change of conduct on the part of those who were victors in the struggle was evidence of an increasing sympathy. Not only is sectionalism disappearing, but with it is departing the feeling that really underlies it—the distrust of those who dwell elsewhere than where we do. This distrust is common all over Europe today. Here in America it has yielded to a friendly neighborliness which makes the family from Portland, Maine, soon find itself at home in Portland, Oregon. It is getting hard for us to hate anybody—especially since we have disestablished the devil. We are good-natured and easy-going. Herbert Spencer even denounced this as our immediate danger, maintaining that we were too good-natured, too easy-going, too tolerant of evil; and he insisted that we needed to strengthen our wills to protest against wrong, to wrestle with it resolutely, and to overcome it before it is firmly rooted.

VI

We are kindly and we are helpful; and we are fixed in the belief that somehow everything will work out all right in the long run. But nothing will work out all right unless we so make it work; and excessive optimism may be as corrupting to the fiber of the people as "the Sabbathless pursuit of fortune," as Bacon termed it. When Mr. John Morley was last in this country he seized swiftly upon a chance allusion of mine to this ingrained hopefulness of ours. "Ah, what you call optimism," he cried, "I call fatalism." But an optimism which is solidly based on a survey of the facts cannot fairly be termed fatalism; and another British student of political science, Mr. James Bryce, has recently pointed out that the intelligent native American has—and by experience is justified in having—a firm conviction that the majority of qualified voters are pretty sure to be right.

Then he suggested a reason for the faith that is in us, when he declared that no such feeling exists in Europe, since in Germany the governing class dreads the spread of socialism, in France the republicans know that it is not impossible that Monarchism and Clericalism may succeed in upsetting the republic, while in Great Britain each party believes that the other party, when it succeeds, succeeds by misleading the people, and neither party supposes that the majority are any more likely to be right than to be wrong.

Mr. Morley and Mr. Bryce were both here in the United States in the fall of 1904, when we were in the midst of a presidential election, one of those prolonged national debates, creating incessant commotion, but invaluable agents of our political education, in so far as they force us all to take thought about the underlying principles of policy by which we wish to see the government guided. It was while this political campaign was at its height that the French visitor to the Russian novelist was setting his notes in order and copying out his assertion that we Americans were mere money-grubbers, "systematically hostile to all idealism." If this unthinking Parisian journalist had only taken the trouble to consider the addresses which the chief speakers of the two parties here in the United States were then making to their fellow-citizens in the hope of winning votes, he would have discovered that these practical politicians, trained to perceive the subtler shades of popular feeling, were founding all their arguments on the assumption that the American people as a whole wanted to do right. He would have seen that the appeal of these stalwart partisans was rarely to prejudice or to race-hatred—evil spirits that various orators have sought to arouse and to intensify in the more recent political discussions of the French themselves.

An examination of the platforms, of the letters of the candidates, and of the speeches of the more important leaders on both sides revealed to an American observer the significant fact that "each party tried to demonstrate that it was more peaceable, more equitable, more sincerely devoted to lawful and righteous behavior than the other;" and "the voter was instinctively credited with loving peace and righteousness, and with being stirred by sentiments of good-will toward men." This seems to show that the heart of the people is sound, and that it does not throb in response to ignoble appeals. It seems to show that there is here the desire ever to do right and to see right done, even if the will is weakened a little by easy-going good-nature, and even if the will fails at times to stiffen itself resolutely to make sure that the right shall prevail.

"Liberty hath a sharp and double edge fit only to be handled by just and virtuous men," so Milton asserted long ago, adding that "to the bad and dissolute, it becomes a mischief unwieldy in their own hands." Even if we Americans can clear ourselves of being "bad and dissolute," we have much to do before we may claim to be "just and virtuous," Justice and virtue are not to be had for the asking; they are the rewards of a manful contest with selfishness and with sloth. They are the results of an honest effort to think straight, and to apply eternal principles to present needs. Merely to feel is only the beginning; what remains is to think and to act.

A British historian, Mr. Frederic Harrison, who came here to spy out the land three or four years before Mr. Morley and Mr. Bryce last visited us, was struck by the fact—and by the many consequences of the fact—that "America is the only land on earth where caste has never had a footing, nor has left a trace." It seemed to him that "vast numbers and the passion of equality tend to low averages in thought, in manners, and in public opinion, which the zeal of the devoted minority tends gradually to raise to higher planes of thought and conduct." He believed that we should solve our problems one by one because "the zeal for learning, justice and humanity" lies deep in the American heart. Mr. Harrison did not say it in so many words, but it is implied in what he did say, that the absence of caste and the presence of low averages in thought, in manners, and in public opinion, impose a heavier task on the devoted minority, whose duty it is to keep alive the zeal for learning, justice and humanity.

Which of us, if haply the spirit moves him, may not elect himself to this devoted minority? Why should not we also, each in our own way, without pretence, without boastfulness, without bullying, do whatsoever in us lies for the attainment of justice and of virtue? It is well to be a gentleman and a scholar; but after all it is best to be a man, ready to do a man's work in the world. And indeed there is no reason why a gentleman and a scholar should not also be a man. He will need to cherish what Huxley called "that enthusiasm for truth, that fanaticism for veracity, which is a greater possession than much learning, a nobler gift than the power of increasing knowledge." He will need also to remember that

> "Kings have their dynasties—but not the mind;
> Cæsar leaves other Cæsars to succeed,
> But Wisdom, dying, leaves no heir behind."

EFFECTS OF THE FRONTIER UPON AMERICAN CHARACTER[1]

Frederick Jackson Turner

[Frederick Jackson Turner (1861———) was born at Portage, Wisconsin. After his graduation from the University of Wisconsin in 1884, he pursued historical studies at Johns Hopkins University. Afterward he was appointed professor of American history in the University of Wisconsin, and since 1910 he has held a professorship of history at Harvard. He is regarded as one of the foremost authorities on phases of western history. This article on the effects of the habits of pioneer days on American life and character is an excellent example of the interesting and thorough way in which the writer discusses matters connected with western America.]

Behind institutions, behind constitutional forms and modifications, lie the vital forces that call these organs into life and shape them to meet changing conditions. The peculiarity of American institutions is the fact that they have been compelled to adapt themselves to the changes of an expanding people— to the changes involved in crossing a continent, in winning a wilderness, and in developing at each area of this progress out of the primitive economic and political conditions of the frontier into the complexity of city life. Said Calhoun in 1817, "We are great, and rapidly—I was about to say fearfully—growing!" So saying, he touched the distinguishing feature of American life. All people show development; the germ theory of politics has been sufficiently emphasized. In the case of most nations, however, the development has occurred in a limited area; and if the nation has expanded, it has met other growing peoples whom it has conquered. But in the case of the United States we have a different phenomenon. Limiting our attention to the Atlantic coast, we have the familiar phenomenon of the evolution of institutions in a limited area, such as the rise of representative government; the differentiation of simple colonial governments into complex organs; the progress from primitive industrial society, without division of labor, up to manufacturing civili-

[1] From "The Significance of the Frontier in American History" in the *Fifth Yearbook of the National Herbart Society*. Reprinted by permission.

C

zation. But we have in addition to this a recurrence of the process of evolution in each western area reached in the process of expansion. Thus, American development has exhibited not merely advance along a single line, but a return to primitive conditions on a continually advancing frontier line, and a new development for that area. American social development has been continually beginning over again on the frontier. This perennial rebirth, this fluidity of American life, this expansion westward with its new opportunities, its continuous touch with the simplicity of primitive society, furnish the forces dominating American character. The true point of view in the history of this nation is not the Atlantic coast: it is the great West. Even the slavery struggle, which is made so exclusive an object of attention by some historians, occupies its important place in American history because of its relation to westward expansion.

In this advance, the frontier is the outer edge of the wave— the meeting-point between savagery and civilization. Much has been written about the frontier from the point of view of border warfare and the chase, but as a field for the serious study of the economist and the historian it has been neglected.

The American frontier is sharply distinguished from the European frontier—a fortified boundary-line running through dense populations. The most significant thing about the American frontier is that it lies at the hither edge of free land. In the census reports it is treated as the margin of that settlement which has a density of two or more to the square mile. The term is an elastic one, and for our purposes does not need sharp definition. We shall consider the whole frontier belt, including the Indian country and the outer margin of the "settled area" of the census reports. This paper will make no attempt to treat the subject exhaustively; its aim is simply to call attention to the frontier as a fertile field for investigation, and to suggest some of the problems which arise in connection with it.

In the settlement of America we have to observe how European life entered the continent, and how America modified and developed that life and reacted on Europe. Our early history is the history of European germs developing in an American environment. Too exclusive attention has been paid by institutional students to the Germanic origins, too little to the American factors. The frontier is the line of most rapid and effective Americanization. The wilderness masters the colonist. It finds him a European in dress, industries, tools, modes of travel, and thought. It takes him from the railroad car and puts him in the birch canoe. It strips off the garments of civilization and arrays him in the hunting-shirt and moccasin. It puts him in the log-cabin of the Cherokee and Iroquois and runs an Indian palisade around him. Before long he has gone to planting Indian corn and plowing with a sharp stick; he shouts the war-cry and takes the scalp in orthodox Indian fashion. In short, at the frontier the environment is at first too strong for the man. He must accept the conditions which it furnishes, or perish, and so he fits himself into the Indian clearings and follows the Indian trails. Little by little he transforms the wilderness, but the outcome is not the old Europe, not simply the development of Germanic germs, any more than the first phenomenon was a case of reversion to the Germanic mark. The fact is, that here is a new product that is American. At first, the frontier was the Atlantic coast. It was the frontier of Europe in a very real sense. Moving westward, the frontier became more and more American. As successive terminal moraines result from successive glaciations, so each frontier leaves its traces behind it, and when it becomes a settled area the region still partakes of the frontier characteristics. Thus the advance of the frontier has meant a steady movement away from the influence of Europe, a steady growth of independence on American lines. And to study this advance, the men who grew up under these conditions, and the political, economic, and social results of it, is to study the peculiarly American part of our history.

Let us then grasp the conception of American society steadily expanding into new areas. How important it becomes to watch the stages, the processes, and the results of this advance! The conception will be found to revolutionize our study of American history. . . .

We next inquire what were the influences on the East and on the Old World. A rapid enumeration of some of the more noteworthy effects is all that I have space for.

Composite Nationality

First, we note that the frontier promoted the formation of a composite nationality for the American people. The coast was preponderantly English, but the later tides of continental immigration flowed across to the free lands. This was the case from the early colonial days. The Scotch-Irish and the Palatine-Germans, or "Pennsylvania Dutch," furnished the dominant element in the stock of the colonial frontier. With these peoples were also the freed indented servants, or redemptioners, who, at the expiration of their time of service, passed to the frontier. Governor Spotswood, of Virginia, writes, in 1717, "The inhabitants of our frontiers are composed generally of such as have been transported hither as servants, and, being out of their time, settle themselves where land is to be taken up and that will produce the necessarys of life with little labour." Very generally these redemptioners were of non-English stock. In the crucible of the frontier the immigrants were Americanized, liberated, and fused into a mixed race, English in neither nationality nor characteristics. The process has gone on from the early days to our own. Burke and other writers in the middle of the eighteenth century believed that Pennsylvania was "threatened with the danger of being wholly foreign in language, manners, and perhaps even inclinations." The German and Scotch-Irish elements in the frontier of the South were only less great. In the middle of the present century the German element in Wisconsin was already so considerable that leading publicists looked to the creation of a German state out of the commonwealth by concentrating their colonization. By the census of 1890 South Dakota had a percentage of persons of foreign parentage to total population of sixty; Wisconsin, seventy-three; Minnesota, seventy-five; and North Dakota, seventy-nine. Such examples teach us to beware of misinterpreting the fact that there is a common English speech in America into a belief that the stock is also English.

Industrial Independence

In another way the advance of the frontier decreased our dependence on England. The coast, particularly of the South, lacked diversified industries, and was dependent on England for the bulk of its supplies. In the South there was even a dependence on the northern colonies for articles of food. Governor Glenn, of South Carolina, writes in the middle of the eighteenth century: "Our trade with New York and Philadelphia was of this sort, draining us of all the little money and bills we could gather from other places for their bread, flour, beer, hams, bacon, and other things of their produce, all which, except beer, our new townships began to supply us with, which are settled with very industrious and thriving Germans. This no doubt diminishes the number of shipping and the appearance of our trade, but it is far from being a detriment to us." Before long the frontier created a demand for merchants. As it retreated from the coast it became less and less possible for England to bring her supplies directly to the consumers' wharves and carry away staple crops, and staple crops began to give way to diversified agriculture for a time. The effect of this phase of the frontier action upon the northern section is perceived when we realize how the advance of the frontier aroused seaboard cities like Boston, New York, and Baltimore to engage in rivalry for what Washington called "the extensive and valuable trade of a rising empire."

Effects on National Legislation

The legislation which most developed the powers of the national government, and played the largest part in its activity, was conditioned on the frontier. Writers have discussed the subjects of tariff, land, and internal improvement as subsidiary to the slavery question. But when American history comes to be rightly viewed it will be seen that the slavery question is an incident. In the period from the end of the first half of the present century to the close of the Civil War slavery rose to primary, but far from exclusive, importance. But this does not justify Dr. von Holst (to take an example) in treating our constitutional history in its formative period down to 1828 in a single volume, giving six volumes chiefly to the history of slavery from 1828 to 1861, under the title *Constitutional History of the United States*. The growth of nationalism and the evolution of American political institutions were dependent on the advance of the frontier. Even so recent a writer as Rhodes, in his history of the United States since the Compromise of 1850, has treated the legislation called out by the western advance as incidental to the slavery struggle.

This is a wrong perspective. The pioneer needed the goods of the coast, and so the grand series of internal improvement and railroad legislation began, with potent nationalizing effects. Over internal improvements occurred great debates, in which grave constitutional questions were discussed. Sectional groupings appear in the votes, profoundly significant for the historian. Loose construction increased as the nation marched westward. But the West was not content with bringing the farm to the factory. Under the lead of Clay—"Harry of the West"—protective tariffs were passed, with the cry of bringing the factory to the farm. The disposition of the public lands was a third important subject of national legislation influenced by the frontier.

Effects on Institutions

It is hardly necessary to do more than mention the fact that the West was a field in which new political institutions were to be created. It offered a wide opportunity for speculative creation and for adjustment of old institutions to new conditions. The study of the evolution of western institutions shows how slight was the proportion of actual theoretic invention of institutions; but there is abundance of opportunity for study of the sources of the institutions actually chosen, the causes of the selection, the degree of transformation by the new conditions, and the new institutions actually produced by the new environment.

The Public Domain

The public domain has been a force of profound importance in the nationalization and development of the government. The effects of the struggle of the landed and the landless states, and of the ordinance of 1787, need no discussion. Administratively the frontier called out some of the highest and most vitalizing activities of the general government. The purchase of Louisiana was perhaps the constitutional turning point in the history of the republic, inasmuch as it afforded both a new area for national legislation and the occasion of the downfall of the policy of strict construction. But the purchase of Louisiana was called out by frontier needs and demands. As frontier states accrued to the Union the national power grew. In a speech on the dedication of the Calhoun monument, Mr. Lamar explained, "In 1789 the states were the creators of the federal government; in 1861 the federal government was the creator of a large majority of the states."

When we consider the public domain from the point of view of the sale and disposal of the public lands, we are again brought face to face with the frontier. The policy of the United States in dealing with its lands is in sharp contrast with the European system of scientific administration. Efforts to make this domain a source of revenue, and to withhold it from emigrants in order that settlement might be compact, were in vain. The jealousy and the fears of the East were powerless in the face of the demands of the frontiersmen. John Quincy Adams was obliged to confess: "My own system of administration, which was to make the national domain the inexhaustible fund for progressive and unceasing internal improvement, has failed." The reason is obvious: a system of administration was not what the West demanded; it wanted land. Adams states the situation as follows: "The slave-holders of the South have bought the co-operation of the western country by the bribe of the western lands, abandoning to the new western states their own proportion of the public property and aiding them in the design of grasping all the lands into their own hands. Thomas H. Benton was the author of this system, which he brought forward as a substitute for the American system of Mr. Clay, and to supplant him as the leading statesman of the West. Mr. Clay, by his tariff compromise with Mr. Calhoun, abandoned his own American system. At the same time he brought forward a plan for distributing among all the states of the Union the proceeds of the sales of the public lands. His bill for that purpose passed both houses of Congress, but was vetoed by President Jackson, who, in his annual message of December, 1832, formally recommended that all public lands should be gratuitously given away to individual adventurers and to the states in which the lands are situated.

"No subject," said Henry Clay, "which has presented itself to the present, or perhaps any preceding, Congress, is of greater magnitude than that of the public lands." When we consider the far-reaching effects of the government's land policy upon political, economic, and social aspects of American life, we are disposed to agree with him. But this legislation was framed under frontier influences, and under the lead of western statesmen like Benton and Jackson. Said Senator Scott, of Indiana, in 1841: "I consider the preëmption law merely declaratory of the custom or common law of the settlers."

National Tendencies of the Frontier

It is safe to say that the legislation with regard to land, tariff, and internal improvements—the American system of the nationalizing Whig party—was conditioned on frontier ideas and needs. But it was not merely in legislative action that the frontier worked against the sectionalism of the coast. The economic and social characteristics of the frontier worked against sectionalism. The men of the frontier had closer resemblances to the middle region than to either of the other sections. Pennsylvania had been the seed plot of southern frontier emigration, and although she passed on her settlers along the Great Valley into the west of Virginia and the Carolinas, yet the industrial society of these southern frontiersmen was always more like that of the middle region than like that of the tidewater portion of the South, which later came to spread its industrial type throughout the South.

The middle region, entered by New York harbor, was an open door to all Europe. The tidewater part of the South represented typical Englishmen, modified by a warm climate and servile labor, and living in baronial fashion on great plantations; New England stood for a special English movement—Puritanism. The middle region was less English than the other sections. It had a wide mixture of nationalities, a varied society, the mixed town and county system of local government, a varied economic life, many religious sects. In short, it was a region mediating between New England and the South, and the East and the West. It represented the composite nationality which the contemporary United States exhibits, that juxtaposition of non-English groups, occupying a valley or a little settlement, and presenting reflections of the map of Europe in their variety. It was democratic and non-sectional, if not national; "easy, tolerant, and contented;" rooted strongly in material prosperity. It was typical of the modern United States. It was least sectional, not only because it lay between North and South, but also because with no barriers to shut out its frontiers from its settled region, and with a system of connecting waterways, the middle region mediated between East and West as well as between North and South. Thus it became the typically American region. Even the New Englander, who was shut out from the frontier by the middle region, tarrying in New York or Pennsylvania on his westward march, lost the acuteness of his sectionalism on the way.

Moreover, it must be recalled that the western and central New England settler who furnished the western movement was not the typical tidewater New Englander: he was less conservative and contented, more democratic and restless.

The spread of cotton culture into the interior of the South finally broke down the contrast between the tidewater region and the rest of the South, and based southern interests on slavery. Before this process revealed its results, the western portion of the South, which was akin to Pennsylvania in stock, society, and industry, showed tendencies to fall away from the faith of the fathers into internal improvement legislation and nationalism. In the Virginia convention of 1829–30, called to revise the constitution, Mr. Leigh, of Chesterfield, one of the tidewater counties, declared:

"One of the main causes of discontent which led to this convention, that which had the strongest influence in overcoming our veneration for the work of our fathers, which taught us to contemn the sentiments of Henry and Mason and Pendleton, which weaned us from our reverence for the constituted authorities of the state, was an overweening passion for internal improvement. I say this with perfect knowledge, for it has been avowed to me by gentlemen from the West over and over again. And let me tell the gentleman from Albemarle (Mr. Gordon) that it has been another principal object of those who set this ball of revolution in motion, to overturn the doctrine of state rights, of which Virginia has been the very pillar, and to remove the barrier she has interposed to the interference of the federal government in that same work of internal improvement, by so reorganizing the legislature that Virginia, too, may be hitched to the federal car."

It was this nationalizing tendency of the West that transformed the democracy of Jefferson into the national republicanism of Monroe and the democracy of Andrew Jackson. The West of the War of 1812, the West of Clay and Benton and Harrison and Andrew Jackson, shut off by the Middle States and the mountains from the coast sections, had a solidarity of its own with national tendencies. On the tide of the Father of Waters, North and South met and mingled into a nation. Interstate migration went steadily on—a process of cross-fertilization of ideas and institutions. The fierce struggle of the sections over slavery on the western frontier does not diminish the truth of this statement; it proves the truth of it. Slavery was a sectional trait that would not down, but in the West it could not remain sectional. It was the greatest of frontiersmen who declared: "I believe this government cannot endure permanently half slave and half free. It will become all of one thing or all of the other." Nothing works for nationalism like intercourse within the nation. Mobility of population is death to localism, and the western frontier worked irresistibly in unsettling population. The effects reached back from the frontier, and affected profoundly the Atlantic coast and even the Old World.

Growth of Democracy

But the most important effect of the frontier has been in the promotion of democracy here and in Europe. As has been indicated, the frontier is productive of individualism. Complex society is precipitated by the wilderness into a kind of primitive organization based on the family. The tendency is antisocial. It produces antipathy to control, and particularly to any direct control. The taxgatherer is viewed as a representative of oppression. Professor Osgood, in an able article,[1] has pointed out that the frontier conditions prevalent in the colonies are important factors in the explanation of the American Revolution, where individual liberty was sometimes confused with absence of all effective government. The same conditions aid in explaining the difficulty of instituting a strong government in the period of the Confederacy. The frontier individualism has from the beginning promoted democracy.

The frontier states that came into the Union in the first quarter of a century of its existence came in with democratic suffrage provisions, and had reactive effects of the highest importance upon the older states whose peoples were being attracted there. An extension of the franchise became essential. It was *western* New York that forced an extension of suffrage in the constitutional convention of that state in 1821; and it was *western* Virginia that compelled the tidewater region to put a more liberal suffrage provision in the constitution framed in 1830, and to give to the frontier region a more nearly proportionate representation with the tidewater aristocracy. The rise of democracy as an effective force in the nation came in with western preponderance under Jackson and William Henry Harrison, and it meant the triumph of the frontier—with all of its good and with all of its evil element. An interesting illustration of

[1] *Political Science Quarterly*, vol. ii, p. 457; Sumner, *Alexander Hamilton*, chaps. ii–vii; Turner, in *Atlantic Monthly*, January, 1903. [Turner's note.]

the tone of frontier democracy in 1830 comes from the same debates in the Virginia convention already referred to. A representative from western Virginia declared:

"But, sir, it is not the increase of population in the West which this gentleman ought to fear. It is the energy which the mountain breeze and western habits impart to those emigrants. They are regenerated, politically I mean, sir. They soon become *working politicians;* and the difference, sir, between a *talking* and a *working* politician is immense. The Old Dominion has long been celebrated for producing great orators; the ablest metaphysicians in policy; men that can split hairs in all abstruse questions of political economy. But at home, or when they return from Congress, they have negroes to fan them asleep. But a Pennsylvania, a New York, an Ohio, or a western Virginia statesman, though far inferior in logic, metaphysics, and rhetoric to an old Virginia statesman, has this advantage, that when he returns home he takes off his coat and takes hold of the plow. This gives him bone and muscle, sir, and preserves his republican principles pure and uncontaminated."

So long as free land exists, the opportunity for a competency exists, and economic power secures political power. But the democracy born of free land, strong in selfishness and individualism, intolerant of administrative experience and education, and pressing individual liberty beyond its proper bounds, has its dangers as well as its benefits. Individualism in America has allowed a laxity in regard to governmental affairs which has rendered possible the spoils system and all the manifest evils that follow from the lack of a highly developed civic spirit. In this connection may be noted also the influence of frontier conditions in permitting inflated paper currency and wild-cat banking. The colonial and revolutionary frontier was the region whence emanated many of the worst forms of paper currency.[1] The West in the War of 1812 repeated the phenomenon on the frontier of that day, while the speculation and wild-cat banking of the period of the crisis of 1837 occurred on the new frontier belt of the next tier of states. Thus each one of the periods of paper-money projects coincides with periods when a new set of frontier communities had arisen, and coincides in area with

[1]On the relation of frontier conditions to Revolutionary taxation, see Sumner, *Alexander Hamilton*, chap. iii. [Turner's note.]

these successive frontiers, for the most part. The recent radical Populist agitation is a case in point. Many a state that now declines any connection with the tenets of the Populists itself adhered to such ideas in an earlier stage of the development of the state. A primitive society can hardly be expected to show the appreciation of the complexity of business interests in a developed society. The continual recurrence of these areas of paper-money agitation is another evidence that the frontier can be isolated and studied as a factor in American history of the highest importance. . . .

Intellectual Traits

From the conditions of frontier life came intellectual traits of profound importance. The works of travelers along each frontier from colonial days onward describe certain common traits, and these traits have, while softening down, still persisted as survivals in the place of their origin, even when a higher social organization succeeded. The result is that to the frontier the American intellect owes its striking characteristics. That coarseness and strength combined with acuteness and inquisitiveness; that practical, inventive turn of mind, quick to find expedients; that masterful grasp of material things, lacking in the artistic, but powerful to effect great ends; that restless, nervous energy;[1] that dominant individualism, working for good and for evil, and, withal, that buoyancy and exuberance which come with freedom—these are traits of the frontier, or traits called out elsewhere because of the existence of the frontier. We are not easily aware of the deep influence of this individualistic way of thinking upon our present conditions. It persists in the midst of a society that has passed away from the conditions that occasioned it. It makes it difficult to secure social regulation of business enterprises that are essentially

[1]Colonial travelers agree in remarking on the phlegmatic characteristics of the colonists. It has frequently been asked how such a people could have developed that strained nervous energy now characteristic of them. Cf. Sumner, *Alexander Hamilton*, p. 98, and Adams, *History of the United States*, vol. i, p. 60; vol. ix, pp. 240, 241. The transition appears to become marked at the close of the War of 1812, a period when interest centered upon the development of the West, and the West was noted for restless energy.—Grund, *Americans*, vol. ii, p. 1. [Turner's note.]

public; it is a stumbling-block in the way of civil-service reform; it permeates our doctrines of education;[1] but with the passing of the free lands a vast extension of the social tendency may be expected in America.

Ratzel, the well-known geographer, has pointed out the fact that for centuries the great unoccupied area of America furnished to the American spirit something of its own largeness. It has given a largeness of design and an optimism to American thought.[2] Since the days when the fleet of Columbus sailed into the waters of the New World, America has been another name for opportunity, and the people of the United States have taken their tone from the incessant expansion which has not only been open, but has even been forced upon them. He would be a rash prophet who should assert that the expansive character of American life has now entirely ceased. Movement has been its dominant fact, and, unless this training has no effect upon a people, the American energy will continually demand a wider field for its exercise.[3] But never again will such gifts of free land offer themselves. For a moment, at the frontier, the bonds of custom are broken and unrestraint is triumphant. There is not *tabula rasa*. The stubborn American environment is there with its imperious summons to accept its conditions; the inherited ways of doing things are also there; and yet, in spite of environment, and in spite of custom, each frontier did indeed furnish a new field of opportunity, a gate of escape from the bondage of the past; and freshness, and confidence, and scorn of older society, impatience of its restraints and its ideas, and indifference to its lessons have accompanied the frontier. What the Mediterranean Sea was to the Greeks, breaking the bond of custom, offering new experiences, calling out new institutions and activities, that, and more, the ever-retreating frontier has been to the United States directly, and to the nations of Europe more remotely. And now, four centuries from the discovery of America, at the end

[1] See the able paper by Professor de Garno on "Social Aspects of Moral Education," in the *Third Yearbook of the National Herbart Society*, 1897, p. 37. [Turner's note.]

[2] See paper on "The West as a Field for Historical Study," in *Report of American Historical Association for* 1896, pp. 279–319. [Turner's note.]

[3] The commentary upon this sentence—written in 1893—lies in the recent history of Hawaii, Cuba, Porto Rico, the Philippines, and the Isthmian Canal. [Turner's note.]

of a hundred years of life under the Constitution, the frontier has gone, and with its going has closed the first period of American history.

THE INFLUENCE OF THE IMMIGRANT ON AMERICA[1]

WALTER EDWARD WEYL

[Walter Edward Weyl (1873———) was born in Philadelphia, Pennsylvania. After graduating from the University of Pennsylvania in 1892, he made a special study of political economy at Halle, Berlin, and Paris. He has written much on economic subjects and is a statistical expert on commerce and labor.]

We must not forget that these men and women who file through the narrow gates at Ellis Island, hopeful, confused, with bundles of misconceptions as heavy as the great sacks upon their backs—we must not forget that these simple, rough-handed people are the ancestors of our descendants, the fathers and mothers of our children.

So it has been from the beginning. For a century a swelling human stream has poured across the ocean, fleeing from poverty in Europe to a chance in America. Englishman, Welshman, Scotchman, Irishman; German, Swede, Norwegian, Dane; Jew, Italian, Bohemian, Serb; Syrian, Hungarian, Pole, Greek— one race after another has knocked at our doors, been given admittance, has married us and begot our children. We could not have told by looking at them whether they were to be good or bad progenitors, for racially the cabin is not above the steerage, and dirt, like poverty and ignorance, is 'but skin-deep. A few hours, and the stain of travel has left the immigrant's cheek; a few years, and he loses the odor of alien soils; a generation or two, and these outlanders are irrevocably our race, our nation, our stock.

That stock, a little over a century ago, was almost pure British. True, Albany was Dutch, and many of the signs in the Philadelphia streets were in the German language. Neverthe-

[1]From "New Americans," *Harper's Monthly Magazine*, vol. cxxix, p. 615 (1914).

less, five-sixths of all the family names collected in 1790 by the
census authorities were pure English, and over nine-tenths
(90.2 per cent.) were British. Despite the presence of Germans,
Dutch, French, and Negroes, the American was essentially an
Englishman once removed, an Englishman stuffed with English
traditions, prejudices, and stubbornnesses, reading English
books, speaking English dialects, practising English law and
English evasions of the law, and hating England with a truly
English hatred. In all but a political sense America was still
one of "His Majesty's dominions beyond the sea." Even after
immigration poured in upon us, the English stock was strong
enough to impress upon the immigrating races its language,
laws, and customs. Nevertheless, the incoming millions profoundly altered our racial structure. Today over thirty-two
million Americans are either foreign-born or of foreign parentage.
No longer an Anglo-Saxon cousin, America has become the
most composite of nations.

We cannot help seeing that such a vast transfusion of blood
must powerfully affect the character of the American. What that
influence is to be, however, whether for better or for worse, is a
question more baffling. Our optimists conceive the future American, the child of this infinite intermarrying, as a glorified, syn-
thetical person, replete with the best qualities of all component
races. He is to combine the sturdiness of the Bulgarian peasant,
the poetry of the Pole, the vivid artistic perceptions of the Italian, the Jew's intensity, the German's thoroughness, the Irishman's *verve*, the tenacity of the Englishman, with the initiative
and versatility of the American. The pessimist, on the other hand,
fears the worst. America, he believes, is committing the un-
pardonable sin, is contracting a *mésalliance*, grotesque and
gigantic. We are diluting our blood with the blood of lesser
breeds. We are suffering adulteration. The stamp upon the
coin—the flag, the language, the national sense—remains, but
the silver is replaced by lead.

All of which is singularly unconvincing. In our own families,
the children do not always inherit the best qualities of father
and mother, and we have no assurance that the children of

mixed races have this selective gift and rise superior to their parent stocks. Nor do we know that they fall below. We hear much concerning "pure" races and "mongrel" races. But is there in all the world a pure race? The Jew, once supposed to be of Levitical pureness, is now known to be racially unorthodox. The Englishman is not pure Anglo-Saxon; the German is not Teutonic; the Russian is not Slav. To be mongrel may be a virtue or a vice—we do not know. The problem is too subtle, too elusive, and we have no approved receipts in this vast eugenic kitchen. Intermarrying will go on, whether we like it or loathe it, for love laughs at racial barriers, and the maidens of one nation look fair to the youth of another. Let the kettle boil and let us hope for the best.

But the newcomer brings with him more than his potential parenthood, and he influences America and the American in other ways than by marriage and procreation. He creates new problems of adjustment. He enters into a new environment. He creates a new environment for us. Unconsciously but irresistibly he transforms an America which he does not know. He forces the native American to change, to change that he may feel at home in his own home.

When we seek to discover what is the exact influence of the immigrant upon his new environment, we are met with difficulties almost as insurmountable as those which enter into the problem of the immigrant's influence upon our common heredity. Social phenomena are difficult to isolate. The immigrant is not merely an immigrant; he is also a wage-earner, a city-dweller, perhaps an illiterate. Wage-earning, city-dwelling, and illiteracy are all contributing influences. Your immigrant is a citizen of the new factory, of the great industrial state, within, yet almost overshadowing, the political state. Into each of our problems—wages and labor, illiteracy, crime, vice, insanity, pauperism, democracy—the immigrant enters.

There is in all the world no more difficult, no more utterly bewildering problem than this of the intermingling of races. Already thirty million immigrants have arrived, of whom considerably over twenty millions have remained. To interpret

D

this pouring of new, strange millions into the old, to trace its result upon the manners, the morals, the emotional and intellectual reactions of the Americans, is like searching out the yellow waters of the Missouri in the vast flood of the lower Mississippi. Our immigrating races are many, and they meet diverse kinds of native Americans on varying planes and at innumerable contact points. So complex is the resulting pattern, so multitudinous are the threads interwoven into so many perplexing combinations, that we struggle in vain to unweave this weaving. At best we can merely follow a single color, noting its appearance here and its reappearance there, in this vast and many-hued tapestry which we call American life.

Fortunately we are not compelled to embark upon so ambitious a study. We are here concerned, not with the all-inclusive question, "Is immigration good or bad?" but with the problem of how immigration has contributed to certain broad developments in the character and habits of the American, and even to this question we must be content with a half-answer.

When we compare the America of today with the America of half a century ago, certain differences stand out sharply. America today is far richer. It is also more stratified. Our social gamut has been widened. There are more vivid contrasts, more startling differences, in education and in the general chances of life. We are less rural and more urban, losing the virtues and the vices, the excellences and the stupidities, of country life and gaining those of the city. We are massing in our cities armies of the poor to take the place of country ne'er-do-wells and village hangers-on. We are more sophisticated. We are more lax and less narrow. We have lost our earlier frugal simplicity, and have become extravagant and competitively lavish. We have, in short, created a new type of American, who lives in the city, reads newspapers and even books, bathes frequently, travels occasionally; a man, fluent intellectually and physically restless, ready but not profound, intent upon success, not without idealism, but somewhat disillusioned, pleasure-loving, hard-working, humorous. At the same time there grows a sense of a social mal-adjustment, a sense of a failure of America to live up to expectations, and an intensifying desire to right a not clearly perceived wrong. There develops a vigorous, if somewhat vague and untrained, moral impulse, an impulse based on social rather than individual ethics, unesthetic, democratic, headlong.

Although this development might have come about, in part at least, without immigration, the process has been enormously accelerated by the arrival on our shores of millions of Europeans. These men came to make a living, and they made not only their own but other men's fortunes. They hastened the dissolution of old conditions; they undermined old standards by introducing new; their very traditions facilitated the growth of that traditionless quality of the American mind which hastened our material transformation. . . .

The attraction of America penetrates ever deeper into Europe, from the maritime peoples living on the fringe of the ocean, to the inland plains, and then into somnolent, winter-locked mountain villages. Simultaneously Europe changes America. You can alter any country if you pour in enough millions. These immigrants, moreover, are of a character to effect changes. America's attraction is not to the good or to the bad, to the saint or to the sinner, but to the young, the aggressive, the restless, the ambitious. The Europeans in America are chosen men, for there is a rigorous selection at home and a rigorous selection here, the discouraged and defeated returning by the shipload. These immigrating races are virile, tenacious, prolific. Each shipload of newcomers carries to American life an impulse like the rapidly succeeding explosions of a gasolene engine.

Moreover, these immigrants, peasants at home, become city-dwellers here. The city is the heart of our body social. It is the home of education, amusement, culture, crime, discontent, social contacts—and power. The immigrant, even in the gutter of the city, is often nearer to the main currents of our national life than is the average resident of the country. His children are more literate, more restless, more wide-awake.

With such numbers, such qualities, and such a position within the social network, one might imagine that the immigrant would gradually transform us in his own likeness. But no such direct influence is visible. As a nation we have not learned politeness, although we have drawn millions of immigrants from the politest peoples in the world. Our national irreverence is not decreased, but, on the contrary, is actually increased, by the mass of idols, of good old customs, memories, religions, which come to us in the steerage. Nor is the immigrant's influence in any way intentional. Though he hopes that America will make him, the immigrant has no presumptuous thought of making America. To him, America is a fixed, unchanging environmental thing, a land to browse on.

This very passivity of the newly arrived immigrant is the most tremendous of influences. The workman who does not join a union, the citizen who sends his immature children to the factory, the man who does not become naturalized, or who maintains a standard of living below an inadequate wage, such a one by contagion and pressure changes conditions and lowers standards all about him, undermining to the extent of his lethargy our entire social edifice. The aim of Americanization is to combat this passive influence. Two forces, like good and evil, are opposed on that long frontier line where the immigrant comes into contact with the older resident. The American, through self-protection, not love, seeks to raise the immigrant to his economic level; the immigrant, through self-protection, not through knowledge, involuntarily accepts conditions which tend to drag the American down to his. In this contest much that we ordinarily account virtue is evil; much that is ugly is good. The immigrant girl puts on a corset, exchanges her picturesque headdress for a flowering monstrosity of an American hat, squeezes her honest peasant's foot into a narrow, thin-soled American shoe—and behold, it is good. It is a step toward assimilation, toward a more expensive if not a more lovely standard of living. It gives hostages to America. It makes the frenzied saving of the early days impossible. Docility, abnegation, and pecuniary abasement are not economic virtues, however highly they may be rated in another category.

In still other ways this assimilation alters and limits the

alien's influence. Much is lost in the process. The immigrant comes to us laden with gifts, but we have not the leisure to take nor he the opportunity to tender. The brilliant native costumes, the strange, vibrant dialects, the curious mental molds are soon faded or gone. The old religions, the old customs, the traditional manners, the ancient lace do not survive the melting-pot. Assimilation, however necessary, ends the charm and rareness of our quaint human importations.

For this esthetic degeneration the immigrant must not be blamed. To gain himself he must lose himself. He must adopt "our ways." The Italian day laborer finds that macaroni and lettuce are not a suitable diet for ten hours' work on the subway or the Catskill dam. The politeness of sunny southern Europe is at a discount in our skurrying, elbowing crowds. The docility of the peasant damns a man irretrievably in the struggle to rise, and conservatism in gentle, outlandish manners is impossible in kaleidoscopic America. The immigrant, therefore, accepts our standards wholesale and indiscriminately. He "goes the limit" of assimilation—slang, clothes, and chewing-gum. He accommodates himself quickly to that narrow fringe of America which affects him most immediately. The Talmudist in Russia is, for better or worse, no Talmudist here: he is a cloak-presser or a real-estate broker. The Greek shepherd becomes an elevator-boy or a hazardous speculator in resuscitated violets. The Sicilian bootblack learns to charge ten cents for a five-cent shine; the candy-vender from Macedonia haggles long before he knows a hundred English words; the Pole who never has seen a coal-mine becomes adept at the use of the steam-shovel.

Another limit to the immigrant's influence is due to the fact that the America to which he adapts himself is the America that he first meets, the America at the bottom. That bottom changes as America changes from an agricultural to an industrial nation. For the average immigrant there is no longer a free farm on a western frontier: there is only a job as an unskilled or semi-skilled workman. For that job a knowledge of his letters is not absolutely necessary. Nor is a knowledge of English. There are in America today a few millions of aliens who cannot speak English or read or write their native tongue, and who, from an industrial point of view, are almost mere muscle. The road from bottom to top becomes steeper and more inaccessible. Stratification begins.

Because of his position at the bottom of a stratified society, the immigrant—especially the recent immigrant—does not exert any large direct influence. Taken in the mass, he does not run our businesses, make our laws, write our books, paint our pictures, preach to us, teach us or prescribe for us. His indirect influence, on the other hand, is increased rather than diminished by his position at the bottom of the structure. When he moves, all superincumbent groups must of necessity shift their positions. This indirect influence is manifold. The immigration of enormous numbers of unskilled "interchangeable" laborers, who can be moved about like pawns, standardizes our industries, facilitates the growth of stupendous business units, and generally promotes plasticity. The immigrant, by his mere presence, by his mere readiness to be used, speeds us up; he accelerates the whole *tempo* of our industrial life. He changes completely "the balance of power" in industry, politics, and social life generally. The feverish speed of our labor, which is so largely pathological, is an index of this. The arrival of ever-fresh multitudes adds to the difficulties of securing a democratic control of either industry or politics. The presence of the unskilled, unlettered immigrant excites the cupidity of men who wish to make money quickly and do not care how. It makes an essentially kind-hearted people callous. Why save the lives of "wops"? What does it matter if our industry kills a few thousands more or less, when, if we wish, we can get millions a year from inexhaustible Europe? Immigration acts to destroy our brakes. It keeps us, as a nation, transitional.

Of course this transitional quality of America was due partly to our virgin continent. There was always room in the West; a man did not settle, but merely lighted on a spot, like a migratory bird on its southern journey. Immigration, however, intensified and protracted this development. Each race had to fight for its place. Natives were displaced by Irish, who were displaced in turn by Germans, Russians, Italians, Portuguese, Greeks, Syrians. Whole trades were deserted by one nation and conquered by another. The peoples of eastern Europe inundated the Pennsylvania mining districts, displacing Irish, English, and Welsh miners. The Irish street laborer disappeared; the Italian quietly took his shovel. Russian Jews revolutionized the clothing trade, driving out Germans as these had driven out native Americans. The old homes of displaced nations were inhabited by new peoples; the old peoples were shoved up or down, but, in any case, out. Cities, factories, neighborhoods changed with startling rapidity. Connecticut schools, once attended by descendants of the Pilgrims, became overfilled with dark-eyed Italian lads and tow-headed Slavs. Protestant churches were stranded in Catholic or Jewish neighborhoods. America changed rapidly, feverishly. That peculiar quiet restlessness of America, the calm fear with which we search with the tail of our eye to avoid swirling automobiles, the rush and recklessness of our life, were increased by the mild, law-abiding people who came to us from abroad.

There was a time when all these qualities were good, or at least had their good features. So long as we had elbow-room in the West, so long as we were young and growing, with a big continent to make our mistakes in, even recklessness was a virtue. But today America is no longer elastic, the road from bottom to top is not so short and not so unimpeded as it once was. We cannot any longer be sure that the immigrant will find his proper place in our eastern mills or on our western farms without injury to others—or to himself.

The time has passed when we exulted in the number of grown-up men, bred at another country's expense, who came to work for us and fertilize our soils with their dead bones. The time has passed when we believed that mere numbers were all. Today, despite night schools, settlements, and a whole network of Americanizing agencies, we have teeming, polyglot slums and the clash of race with race in sweatshop and factory, mine and lumber-camp. We have a mixture of ideals, a confusion of standards, a conglomeration of clashing views of life. We, the many-nationed nation of America, bring the Puritan tradition, a trifle anemic and thin, a little the worse for disuse. The immigrant brings a Babel of traditions, an all too plastic mind, a willingness to copy our virtues and vices, to imitate us for better or for worse. All of which hampers and delays the formation of a national consciousness.

From whatever point we view the new America, we cannot help seeing how intimately the changes have been bound up with our immigration, especially with that of recent years. The widening of the social gamut becomes more significant when we recall that with unrestricted immigration our poorest citizens are periodically recruited from the poor of the poorest countries of Europe. Our differences in education, while they have other causes, are sharply accentuated by our enormous development of university and high schools at the one end, and by the increasing illiteracy of our immigrants at the other. In cities where there are large immigrant populations we note the beginning of a change in our attitude toward the public schools, toward universal suffrage, toward many of the pious, if unrealized, national ideals of an earlier period.

Fundamentally, however, the essential fact about our present-day immigration is not that the immigrant has changed (though that fact is of great importance), but that the America to which the immigrant comes has changed fundamentally and permanently. And the essential fact about the immigrant's effect on American character is this, that the gift of the immigrant to the nation is not the qualities which he himself had at home, but the very qualities which Americans have always had. In other words, at a time when American industrial, political, and social conditions are changing, partly as a result of immigration itself, the immigrant hampers our psychological adjustment to such changes by giving scope and exercise to old national characteristics which should be obsolescent.

America today is in transition. We have moved rapidly from one industrial world to another, and this progress has been aided and stimulated by immigration. The psychological change, however, which should have kept pace with this industrial transition, has been slower and less complete. It has been retarded by the very rapidity of our immigration and by the tremendous educational tasks which that influx placed upon us. The immigrant is a challenge to our highest idealism, but the task of Americanizing the extra millions of newcomers has hindered progress in the task of democratizing America.

PATTERNS OF AMERICANISM

FRANKLIN: THE CITIZEN[1]

GEORGE WILLIAM ALGER

[George William Alger (1872———) is a lawyer in New York City. In
his own activities as a citizen he has taken great interest in labor and child
labor matters. In this article, he has in an interesting way discussed Benjamin Franklin as a concrete example of Americanism.]

It is unfortunate for the fame of Franklin that most of us
form our ideas of our great historical characters from school
histories. We were introduced to him in our youth and under
the worst of auspices. For in that part of the story of the Revolution where each daily lesson is full of exciting events, when
the great embattled farmers are chasing Redcoats and killing
Hessians, fighting thrilling battles and doing those interesting
things which make the story of the Revolution a schoolboy's
romance, the music seems to stop suddenly and the rapidly
moving figures of our fighting fathers are swept ruthlessly from
the stage and out shuffles an old man, with a broad, shrewd,
and homely face, queer glasses, and a head surmounted by an
atrocious fur hat—Benjamin Franklin.

How can a boy see anything heroic in an old man, no fighter,
whose biography is in a footnote, which does not count in
examination? An old man, moreover, whose footnote biography
generally contains nothing exciting, or even interesting, except
the story of his kite or the ridiculous figure he made with his
three loaves of bread, one under each arm and one in his mouth
on his first entry into Philadelphia.

Every American schoolboy, as he reads the history of his
country, has born in him an essentially dramatic ambition—

[1]From the *American Magazine*, vol. vii, p. 318 (January, 1906).

the ambition that at some far-off day, in some far-off crisis of his country's existence, he, too, may add a thrilling page to some schoolboy's history, may do some deed of daring—like mad Anthony Wayne may carry some post by storm, die generously like Hale or De Kalb, may scourge the seas like Paul Jones. But what boy's ambition does the old man in the fur hat inspire? What schoolboy knows that it was really a great thing to finance the American Revolution?

It is precisely because he is the great American whom most of us failed to appreciate in our youth—not entirely through our fault—that in this month, which contains the second centennial of Franklin's birth, we should in our maturer years return to a study of one who was perhaps the first great American citizen and pay to his memory a belated tribute.

It is fortunate for Franklin that the second centenary of his birth falls as it does, for we are realizing, year by year, the supreme importance of the things he stood for, the supreme importance to a country whose future is to be won through the arts of peace and not of war, of his type of citizenship. We have suffered from the military ideal of citizenship, for it made and makes the citizenship of peace seem dull, tame, and not worth while. The country has never lacked men who would die for it. Such danger as it is in today lies in its lack of men willing to do something for it while they are alive with their skins not in danger.

The newspapers and magazines are full of the crooked doings of men who are today undermining the foundations of a government for which, in times of war, they would carry a gun. Our supreme problem in these days, when so much is being said of corruption in office and the corrupting influences of businessmen on public life, the supreme problem is, how shall we make the ideal of citizenship, plain everyday citizenship—seem something highly important and worth striving for? The lesson which we can learn from the career of Franklin is the tremendous, permanent value of this type of citizenship.

In point of time he was the first great American citizen. He was widely and favorably known and nearing the middle of his career before Washington was in his teens. He was nearly seventy when the crisis of the Revolution came, and when as an old man, full of honors and years, feeble and afflicted with gout and rheumatism, he brought France to our aid at the critical day of our struggle for independence, and secured the funds which made the success of the Revolution possible.

Though he was born two hundred years ago, on the 17th of January, and the social conditions of his time were so unlike our own, there is a marked similarity between Franklin and the type of big businessmen of whom we complain so bitterly to-day. For up to a certain point his career and his interests in life were curiously like not a few of our own great magnates.

He was born poor, had little school education, and began life with an insatiable desire to improve himself and his condition. Economy and frugality were his in a marked degree. No man ever lived who had a greater notion of the value of time. Sparks tells an anecdote illustrating this, which we have no reason to consider as merely a jest. Franklin's father, like every good old-time New Englander, said grace before meals three times a day. One day when a barrel of pork was received at the house, young Benjamin earnestly entreated his parent to bless the meat in the barrel and thereby save the time spent on blessing at each meal the portion put on the table. He worked with enormous industry. When he set up his printing shop in Philadelphia in partnership with Meredith, it was this industry which gave the young firm credit. "For the industry of that Franklin," said Dr. Baird at the Merchants' Every Night Club, "is superior to anything I have ever seen of the kind. I see him still at work when I go from the club and he is at work again before his neighbors are out of bed."

He lived simply—almost parsimoniously—and spent nothing on display. Generous though he was to his immediate relatives, to his friends, and to those in distress, he was close in his ordinary business dealings. He allowed himself few luxuries and saved money rigorously from his youth up. No reader of his autobiography can help feeling sympathy with his poor London landlady, the widow in Duke Street, "who was so lame in her knees with the gout and therefore seldom stirred out of her room," and who found young Franklin so interesting. He found her equally good company, but when after patient searching he discovered a boarding place which was thirty-six cents a week cheaper, he threatened to leave and she had to "abate him" forty-eight cents a week to keep her congenial boarder.

He certainly cared a great deal about money. He was shrewd and long-headed in getting it. He believed in it and was forever writing about it, and advising young tradesmen on "The Way to Wealth" and how to find it. *Poor Richard's Almanack* is a materialist's catechism, full of wise saws on the saving of money and the tangible advantages of industry. The qualities which Franklin possessed, the business shrewdness and foresight, the executive ability and the combination in him of industry, economy and endless patience would make him a multi-millionaire today. It made him very well-to-do in his own time. He left a fortune of over $150,000.

At the height of his business career he was, in his chosen calling, the best as well as the most successful printer in the Colonies, earning annually four times as much as his most fortunate rival. He was editor, composer, publisher, bookbinder, stationer; he made lamp-black and ink, dealt in rags, sold soap and live geese feathers and "very good sack at six shillings a gallon." He had the best jobs of printing of New Jersey, Maryland, Pennsylvania, and by partnership in Virginia, New York, the Carolinas and Georgia. He published schoolbooks and handbooks in medicine and farriery. *Poor Richard's Almanack* had to go to press in October, so as to be ready for the New Year, so great was the demand for it. He was postmaster-general and clerk of the Pennsylvania General Assembly and earned by all these separate irons in these different fires $10,000 per year. At forty-two he was a free man, for he had an estate of $3,500 per year. He had earned leisure, that leisure which Poor Richard describes as "the time for doing something useful. This leisure the diligent man will obtain, the lazy man never."

Thus much has been said of Franklin in his character as a businessman, because it is the substructure of his character as a public man. He was the original American businessman in public life. It should be borne in mind that it was while he was actively and laboriously engaged in a pursuit which he loved, that of making money, he found time to perform those many acts of wise citizenship which form the substantial foundation of his later career as a statesman. He could do successful business and still find time for public service.

He was particular about the way of doing that business, moreover. He was particular about the way in which he made his money. He was not of that too familiar type of big businessmen who square extortion and oppression by philanthropy. He took no rebates. When he first started his newspaper in Philadelphia, his rival was Bradford, who, in addition to publishing a paper, was postmaster-general of the Colonies. Bradford used his authority as postmaster-general to practically exclude Franklin's papers from the mail by forbidding the postriders to carry them. Franklin shortly after succeeded Bradford as postmaster-general. Here was the opportunity to build a monopoly and crush his old rival. But the thought never seems to have entered his head that the newspaper business of the Colonies belonged to him. He says of Bradford in his attempt to crush Franklin's newspaper: "I thought so meanly of him for it that when I afterward came into his situation, I took care never to imitate him."

He believed in fair competition, in freedom for others as well as himself, and cared more for his personal independence in the conduct of his business than for the business itself. The story of the sawdust pudding should be known in every newspaper office in the country. When he first started his *Gazette*, he made some free comments on certain public officials, and some of the influential patrons of the paper resented it and tried to stop it. He invited them to dinner. When they came they found nothing on the table but a pudding made of coarse meal and a jug of water. They sat down. Franklin filled their plates and then his own and proceeded to eat heartily, but his guests could not swallow the stuff. After a few moments Franklin rose, and, looking at them, said quietly: "My friends, any man who can subsist on sawdust pudding as I can, needs no man's patronage."

This is what the liberty of the press meant to the first great American printer.

There is something humorous to us in these days about the simple-mindedness of Franklin's honesty. His autobiography affords us one unconscious example. When Braddock came over in the French and Indian War with his British regulars, and before he met the historic disaster which cost him his life, he had great difficulty in getting horses and wagons to pull ordnance and carry camp supplies, and Franklin set about helping him to get the necessary transportation. The Pennsylvania farmers were suspicious. They did not know Braddock, they did not know Franklin, and insisted on his bond for the performance of Braddock's promises. There was absolutely no reason why Franklin should give it, for he was in no sense an army contractor, but was simply trying to be of practical help in an emergency in the war. But he gave his personal bond and advanced considerable sums from his own funds to procure the wagons. As everybody knows, Braddock was defeated and the wagons and horses were lost. The farmers came back to Franklin, and he nearly had to pay twenty thousand pounds, which would have ruined him, but a commission was finally created to adjust and pay the claims. As for the cash advances he had made, Braddock's successor intimated that Franklin had probably made enough "rake off," on the transportation contracts so that he could stand the loss of his advances, and laughed incredulously at him when the honest printer declared indignantly that he had not pocketed a farthing. "I have since learned," says Franklin in his autobiography, "that immense fortunes are often made in such employments." What homespun simplicity! How curiously, in an age of directors, do these words sound! How remote and foreign seems the honest, wise old man's innocence of "graft"!

Franklin never was a rich man. The things which he accomplished, the permanent monuments which he left, were created, not by gifts of his money, but by gifts of himself. He had an extremely practical mind. He was always looking around for opportunities to do something useful, for improvements which could be made which should be of benefit to the public, and he found time to accomplish them.

He founded the first high school of the state, which before his death developed into the present Universtiy of Pennsylvania. It was through his great influence in supporting Dr. Bond that the Philadelphia Hospital was established. Through the "Junto," the debating society which he had established, was founded by his active management the Philadelphia Library, the first circulating library in America from which books could be taken to the homes of the readers—the parent of thousands of circulating libraries all over the land. These are a portion of the local interests with which Franklin's name is associated. The association of his name with these public enterprises should not be understood, however, as meaning that they were built on his money, either wholly or mainly. He never had enough money for that. They were founded on his wise plans, on his generous expenditure of time, trouble and thought.

These things were done amidst the engrossing demands of a growing business by a man who made the public business a part of his business, and refused to allow his own personal interests to command all his time. When the University of Pennsylvania proudly describes itself today as "founded by Benjamin Franklin," the word founded means not cash but character.

He invented a long list of useful things and sought no personal gain from them. The Franklin stove which he devised, and upon which he refused to accept a patent, became the standard stove among our forefathers. He devised what the oculists today call Franklinic lenses—bifocal glasses—combining in one pair of spectacles long-distance and reading lenses. He studied the causes of smoky chimneys and how to avoid them, and published a pamphlet on his discoveries. His electrical experiments are familiar to students of electricity. His discoveries in this branch of knowledge made his name known, long before the Revolution, in European as well as in American scientific societies, and long before the war cloud grew black on the horizon, the farmer and laborer in England as well as in America read the wise maxims of *Poor Richard's Almanack*, and knew and respected its author.

He was the first American diplomat. Practically thirty years of his life were devoted to American interests abroad, first as agent of Pennsylvania carrying on a patient and successful attack on the vested selfishness of the Penn Proprietaries who refused to permit their Pennsylvania land to be taxed for the common benefits which they received from the Colony.

At last the Revolution came, and at an age when few men perform any work of great importance, he rendered his services in the cause of American liberty, second only to those of Washington himself. To those who still insist on considering history as a form of romantic drama, no contrast to the thrilling war story of the Revolution can be apparently more ridiculous than the story of the financiering by which that war was for the most part carried on. Congress had no money. Its requisitions on the several states were discounted or ignored. Individual patriots of means contributed heavily. Franklin loaned all his own ready money. Rich Robert Morris gave all he had and died in a poorhouse, but the funds thus obtained were utterly inadequate for the war. The Colonies were miserably poor. Where, indeed, was the money to come from to buy uniforms, guns, provisions, ships, and all the various supplies of an army and navy? The answer which Congress finally hit upon was very simple. They drew drafts on Franklin. Without any previous notice to him, without any inquiry as to whether he had funds or could raise them, they drew on him for anything and everything which the conduct of the war required. His simple duty was to find in France somehow the funds to meet these drafts. He did it.

He was perhaps the only American who at the time was known and respected for his personal worth in continental Europe. He was famous as scientist and philosopher. He was as engaging as he was wise. With a keen knowledge of human nature he knew how to deal with the French character. He was

E

a splendid borrower. Saddled as he was with two perfectly useless associates, who hampered him in France and slandered him at home, and with practically no other assistance than a sixteen-year-old grandson as his secretary, himself afflicted with the infirmities of old age, he persuaded a nation, deep in financial straits, to loan the struggling colonies the funds necessary for the war. In the critical year of the war his diplomacy obtained at last from France the recognition of American independence, and the active and open aid of French arms, obtained sixteen men-of-war, 4,000 men, and last but not least, $5,000,000, nearly $2,000,000 of which was a free gift.

Well might Paul Jones name his flagship the *Bonnehomme Richard*, for it was the pseudonym of the man who made his career possible, who fitted out his ships and found the pay for his sailors.

But this is no place to trace in detail the long story of Franklin's career of public service. The record of that service should, however, not stand alone as his claim on the memory of posterity. We must not overlook the vast, almost tangible influence of his plain, simple, hard-working life, its struggles, high purposes, its practical accomplishments upon the great artisan class in which he was born, on the vast army of young men whose lives depend upon their intelligence applied through their hands, working at his own trade of printing, or in the other practical arts.

That he had faults must be admitted. His enemies said that he had an inordinate desire for public office. He certainly filled many, and a desire for power is wrong only when the purposes are wrong for which it is coveted.

If he had so chosen, the immense powers of the mind which he had devoted to public service could have been devoted successfully to accumulating a fortune. He had great executive capacity. He devoted it to public rather than to private ends. When great businessmen of today prefer to be remembered by the form in which they leave their fortunes, by the endowments or funds they create, Franklin chose that succeeding generations should remember not the endowments of his fortune but the stamp of his mind and character that he should leave for us, his descendants, the memory of a good citizen.

THE AMERICANISM OF WASHINGTON[1]

HENRY VAN DYKE

[Henry Van Dyke (1852———) was born at Germantown, Pennsylvania. He· was graduated from Princeton and later studied at Berlin. For some years he was pastor of the Brick Presbyterian Church in New York City. In 1899 he was appointed to the Murray professorship of English literature at Princeton, his writings both in prose and in poetry having won for him acknowledged literary position. In 1913 he was appointed Minister of the United States to the Netherlands, a position which he filled with great ability until his resignation in 1917. The portions of his brochure, *The Americanism of Washington*, here reprinted, give the essential points of the discussion.]

What shall we say, then, of the Americanism of Washington? It was denied, during his lifetime for a little while, by those who envied his greatness, resented his leadership, and sought to shake him from his lofty place. But he stood serene and imperturbable, while that denial, like many another blast of evil-scented wind, passed into nothingness, even before the disappearance of the party strife out of whose fermentation it had arisen. By the unanimous judgment of his countrymen for two generations after his death he was hailed as *Pater Patriæ;* and the age which conferred that title was too ingenuous to suppose that the father could be of a different race from his own offspring.

But the modern doubt is more subtle, more curious, more refined in its methods. It does not spring, as the old denial did, from a partisan hatred, which would seek to discredit Washington by an accusation of undue partiality for England, and thus to break his hold upon the love of the people. It arises, rather, like a creeping exhalation, from a modern theory of what true Americanism really is: a theory which goes back,

[1]From *The Americanism of Washington*. (Copyright, 1906, Harper Brothers.) Reprinted by permission.

indeed, for its inspiration to Dr. Johnson's somewhat crudely expressed opinion that "the Americans were a race whom no other mortals could wish to resemble;" but which, in its later form, takes counsel with those British connoisseurs who demand of their typical American not depravity of morals but depravation of manners, not vice of heart but vulgarity of speech, not badness but bumptiousness, and at least enough of eccentricity to make him amusing to cultivated people. I find that not a few of our native professors and critics are inclined to accept some features of this view, perhaps in mere reaction from the unamusing character of their own existence. They are not quite ready to subscribe to Mr. Kipling's statement that the real American is "unkempt, disreputable, vast," but they are willing to admit that it will not do for him to be prudent, orderly, dignified. He must have a touch of picturesque rudeness, a red shirt in his mental as well as in his sartorial outfit. The poetry that expresses him must recognize no metrical rules. The art that depicts him must use the primitive colors, and lay them on thick. I remember reading somewhere that Tennyson had an idea that Longfellow, when he met him, would put his feet upon the table. And it is precisely because Longfellow kept his feet in their proper place, in society as well as in verse, that some critics, nowadays, would have us believe that he was not a truly American poet.

Traces of this curious theory of Americanism in its application to Washington may now be found in many places. You shall hear historians describe him as a transplanted English commoner, a second edition of John Hampden. You shall read, in a famous poem, of Lincoln as

"New birth of our new soil, the *first* American."

That Lincoln was one of the greatest Americans, glorious in the largeness of his heart, the vigor of his manhood, the heroism of his soul, none can doubt. But to affirm that he was the first American is to disown and disinherit Washington and Franklin and Adams and Jefferson. Lincoln himself would have been the man to extinguish such an impoverishing claim with huge and hearty laughter. He knew that Grant and Sherman and Seward and Farragut and the men who stood with him were Americans, just as Washington knew that the Boston maltster, and the Pennsylvania printer, and the Rhode Island anchor-smith, and the New Jersey preacher, and the New York lawyer, and the men who stood with him were Americans.

He knew it, I say: and by what divination? By a test more searching than any mere peculiarity of manners, dress, or speech: by a touchstone able to divide the gold of essential character from the alloy of superficial characteristics; by a standard which disregarded alike Franklin's fur cap and Putnam's old felt hat, Morgan's leather leggings and Witherspoon's black silk gown and John Adam's lace ruffles, to recognize and approve, beneath these various garbs, the vital sign of America woven into the very souls of the men who belonged to her by a spiritual birthright.

For what is true Americanism, and where does it reside? Not on the tongue, nor in the clothes, nor among the transient social forms, refined or rude, which mottle the surface of human life. The log-cabin has no monopoly of it, nor is it an immovable fixture of the stately pillared mansion. Its home is not on the frontier nor in the populous city, not among the trees of the wild forest nor the cultured groves of Academe. Its dwelling is in the heart. It speaks a score of dialects but one language, follows a hundred paths to the same goal, performs a thousand kinds of service in loyalty to the same ideal which is its life. . . .

To believe that the inalienable rights of man to life, liberty, and the pursuit of happiness are given by God.

To believe that any form of power that tramples on these rights is unjust.

To believe that taxation without representation is tyranny, that government must rest upon the consent of the governed, and that the people should choose their own rulers.

To believe that freedom must be safeguarded by law and order, and that the end of freedom is fair play for all.

To believe not in a forced equality of conditions and estates, but in a true equalization of burdens, privileges, and opportunities.

To believe that the selfish interests of persons, classes, and sections must be subordinated to the welfare of the commonwealth.

To believe that union is as much a human necessity as liberty is a divine gift.

To believe, not that all people are good, but that the way to make them better is to trust the whole people.

To believe that a free state should offer an asylum to the oppressed, and an example of virtue, sobriety, and fair dealing to all nations.

To believe that for the existence and perpetuity of such a state a man should be willing to give his whole service, in property, in labor, and in life.

That is Americanism; an ideal embodying itself in a people; a creed heated white hot in the furnace of conviction and hammered into shape on the anvil of life; a vision commanding men to follow it whithersoever it may lead them. And it was the subordination of the personal self to that ideal, that creed, that vision, which gave eminence and glory to Washington and the men who stood with him. . . .

Washington, no doubt, was preëminent among his contemporaries in natural endowments. Less brilliant in his mental gifts than some, less eloquent and accomplished than others, he had a rare balance of large powers which justified Lowell's phrase of "an imperial man." His athletic vigor and skill, his steadiness of nerve restraining an intensity of passion, his undaunted courage which refused no necessary risks and his prudence which took no unnecessary ones, the quiet sureness with which he grasped large ideas and the pressing energy with which he executed small details, the breadth of his intelligence, the depth of his convictions, his power to apply great thoughts and principles to everyday affairs, and his singular superiority to current prejudices and illusions,—these were gifts in combination which would have made him distinguished in any company, in any age. But what was it that won and kept a free field for the exercise of these gifts? What was it that secured for them a long, unbroken opportunity of development in the activities of leadership, until they reached the summit of their perfection? It was a moral quality. It was the evident magnanimity of the man which assured the people that he was no self-seeker who would betray their interests for his own glory or rob them for his own gain. It was the supreme magnanimity of the man, which made the best spirits of the time trust him implicitly, in war and peace, as one who would never forget his duty or his integrity in the sense of his own greatness.

From the first, Washington appears not as a man aiming at prominence or power, but rather as one under obligation to serve a cause. Necessity was laid upon him and he met it willingly. After his marvelous escape from death in his first campaign for the defence of the Colonies, the Rev. Samuel Davies, fourth president of Princeton College, spoke of him in a sermon as "that heroic youth, Colonel Washington, whom I can but hope Providence has hitherto preserved in so signal a manner for some important service to his country." It was a prophetic voice, and Washington was not disobedient to the message. Chosen to command the Army of the Revolution in 1775, he confessed to his wife his deep reluctance to surrender the joys of home, acknowledged publicly his feeling that he was not equal to the great trust committed to him, and then, accepting it as thrown upon him "by a kind of destiny," he gave himself body and soul to its fulfilment, refusing all pay beyond the mere discharge of his expenses, of which he kept a strict account, and asking no other reward than the success of the cause which he served. . . .

There are a hundred other points in Washington's career in which the same supremacy of character, magnanimity focused on service to an ideal, is revealed in conduct. I see it in the wisdom with which he, a son of the South, chose most of his generals from the North, that he might secure immediate efficiency and unity in the army. I see it in the generosity with which he praised the achievements of his associates, disregarding jealous rivalries, and ever willing to share the credit of victory as he was to bear the burden of defeat. I see it in the patience with which he suffered his fame to be imperiled for the moment by reverses and retreats, if only he might the more surely guard the frail hope of ultimate victory for his country. I see it in the quiet dignity with which he faced the Conway Cabal, not anxious to defend his own reputation and secure his own power, but nobly resolute to save the army from being crippled and the cause of liberty from being wrecked. I see it in the splendid self-forgetfulness which cleansed his mind of all temptation to take personal revenge upon those who had sought to injure him in that base intrigue. I read it in his letter of consolation and encouragement to the wretched Gates after the defeat at Camden. I hear the prolonged reëchoing music of it in his letter to General Knox in 1798, in regard to military appointments, declaring his wish to "avoid feuds with those who are embarked in the same general enterprise with myself."

Listen to the same spirit as it speaks in his circular address to the governors of the different states, urging them to "forget their local prejudices and policies; to make those mutual concessions which are requisite to the general prosperity, and in some instances to sacrifice their individual advantages to the interest of the community." Watch how it guides him unerringly through the critical period of American history which lies between the success of the Revolution and the establishment of the nation, enabling him to avoid the pitfalls of sectional and partisan strife, and to use his great influence with the people in leading them out of the confusion of a weak Confederacy into the strength of an indissoluble Union of sovereign states. See how he once more sets aside his personal preferences for a quiet country life, and risks his already secure popularity, together with his reputation for consistency, by obeying the voice which calls him to be a candidate for the Presidency. See how he chooses for the cabinet and for the Supreme Court, not an exclusive group of personal friends, but men who can be trusted to serve the great cause of Union with fidelity and power— Jefferson, Randolph, Hamilton, Knox, John Jay, Wilson, Cushing, Rutledge. See how patiently and indomitably he gives himself to the toil of office, deriving from his exalted station no gain "beyond the lustre which may be reflected from its connection with a power of promoting human felicity." See how he retires, at last, to the longed-for joys of private life, confessing that his career has not been without errors of judgment, beseeching the Almighty that they may bring no harm to his country, and asking no other reward for his labors than to partake, "in the midst of my fellow-citizens, the benign influence of good laws under a free government, the ever favorite object of my heart."

Oh, sweet and stately words, revealing through their calm reserve, the inmost secret of a life that did not flare with transient enthusiasm but glowed with unquenchable devotion to a cause! "The ever favorite object of my heart"—how quietly, how simply he discloses the source and origin of a sublime consecration, a lifelong heroism. Thus speaks the victor looking back upon the long battle. But if you would know the depth and the intensity of the divine fire that burned within his breast you must go back to the dark and icy days of Valley Forge, and hear him cry in passion unrestrained: "If I know my own mind, I could offer myself a living sacrifice to the butchering enemy, provided that would contribute to the people's ease. I would be a living offering to the savage fury and die by inches to save the people."

The ever favorite object of my heart! It is the capacity to find such an object in the success of the people's cause, to follow it unselfishly, to serve it loyally, that distinguishes the men who stood with Washington and who deserve to share his fame. I read the annals of the Revolution, and I find everywhere this secret and searching test dividing the strong from the weak, the noble from the base, the heirs of glory from the captives of oblivion and the inheritors of shame. It was the unwillingness to sink and forget self in the service of something greater that made the failures and wrecks of those tempestuous times, through which the single-hearted and the devoted pressed on to victory and honor. . . .

Is not this, after all, the root of the whole matter? Is not this the thing that is vitally and essentially true of all those great men, clustering about Washington, whose fame we honor and revere with his? They all left the community, the commonwealth, the race, in debt to them. This was their purpose and the ever favorite object of their hearts. They were deliberate and joyful creditors. Renouncing the maxim of worldly wisdom which bids men "get all you can and keep all you get," they resolved rather to give all they had to advance the common cause, to use every benefit conferred upon them in the service of the general welfare, to bestow upon the world more than they received from it, and to leave a fair and unblotted account of business done with life which should show a clear balance in their favor.

LINCOLN AS AN AMERICAN[1]

HERBERT CROLY

[Herbert Croly (1869————) was born in New York City. After attending the College of the City of New York and Harvard University, he has devoted himself to literary work. He has held editorial positions on several magazines and is the author of several books. The selection here given is from his *The Promise of American Life* and is an attempt to show Lincoln as an example of the kind of human excellence that is possible under a democracy like that of the United States.]

Lincoln's services to his country have been rewarded with such abundant appreciation that it may seem superfluous to insist upon them once again; but I believe that from the point of view of this book an even higher value may be placed, if not upon his patriotic service, at least upon his personal worth. The Union might well have been saved and slavery extinguished without his assistance; but the life of no other American has revealed with anything like the same completeness the peculiar moral promise of genuine democracy. He shows us by the full but unconscious integrity of his example the kind of human excellence which a political and social democracy may and should fashion; and its most grateful and hopeful aspect is, not merely that there is something partially American about the manner of his excellence, but that it can be fairly compared with the classic types of consummate personal distinction.

To all appearance nobody could have been more than Abraham Lincoln a man of his own time and place. Until 1858 his outer life ran much in the same groove as that of hundreds of other western politicians and lawyers. Beginning as a poor and ignorant boy, even less provided with props and stepping-stones than were his associates, he had worked his way to a position of ordinary professional and political distinction. He was not,

[1]From *The Promise of American Life.* (Copyright, 1909, The Macmillan Company.)
Reprinted by permission.

like Douglas, a brilliant success. He was not, like Grant, an apparently hopeless failure. He had achieved as much and as little as hundreds of others had achieved. He was respected by his neighbors as an honest man and as a competent lawyer. They credited him with ability, but not to any extraordinary extent. No one would have pointed him out as a remarkable and distinguished man. He had shown himself to be desirous of recognition and influence; but ambition had not been the compelling motive in his life. In most respects his ideas, interests, and standards were precisely the same as those of his associates. He accepted with them the fabric of traditional American political thought and the ordinary standards of contemporary political morality. He had none of the moral strenuousness of the reformer, none of the exclusiveness of a man whose purposes and ideas were consciously perched higher than those of his neighbors. Probably the majority of his more successful associates classed him as a good and able man who was somewhat lacking in ambition and had too much of a disposition to loaf. He was most at home, not in his own house, but in the corner grocery store, where he could sit with his feet on the stove swapping stories with his friends; and if an English traveler of 1850 had happened in on the group, he would most assuredly have discovered another instance of the distressing vulgarity to which the absence of an hereditary aristocracy and an established church condemned the American democracy. Thus no man could apparently have been more the average product of his day and generation. Nevertheless, at bottom, Abraham Lincoln differed as essentially from the ordinary western American of the middle period as St. Francis af Assisi differed from the ordinary Benedictine monk of the thirteenth century.

The average western American of Lincoln's generation was fundamentally a man who subordinated his intelligence to certain dominant practical interests and purposes. He was far from being a stupid or slow-witted man. On the contrary, his wits had been sharpened by the traffic of American politics and business, and his mind was shrewd, flexible, and alert.

But he was wholly incapable either of disinterested or of concentrated intellectual exertion. His energies were bent in the conquest of certain stubborn external forces, and he used his intelligence almost exclusively to this end. The struggles, the hardships, and the necessary self-denial of pioneer life constituted an admirable training of the will. It developed a body of men with great resolution of purpose and with great ingenuity and fertility in adapting their insufficient means to the realization of their important business affairs. But their almost exclusive preoccupation with practical tasks and their failure to grant their intelligence any room for independent exercise bent them into exceedingly warped and one-sided human beings.

Lincoln, on the contrary, much as he was a man of his own time and people, was precisely an example of high and disinterested intellectual culture. During all the formative years in which his life did not superficially differ from that of his associates, he was in point of fact using every chance which the material of western life afforded to discipline and inform his mind. These materials were not very abundant; and in the use which he proceeded to make of them Lincoln had no assistance, either from a sound tradition or from a better educated master. On the contrary, as the history of the times shows, there was every temptation for a man with a strong intellectual bent to be betrayed into mere extravagance and aberration. But with the sound instinct of a well-balanced intelligence Lincoln seized upon the three available books, the earnest study of which might best help to develop harmoniously a strong and many-sided intelligence. He seized, that is, upon the Bible, Shakspere, and Euclid. To his contemporaries the Bible was for the most part a fountain of fanatic revivalism, and Shakspere, if anything, a mine of quotations. But in the case of Lincoln, Shakspere and the Bible served, not merely to awaken his taste and fashion his style, but also to liberate his literary and moral imagination. At the same time he was training his powers of thought by an assiduous study of algebra and geometry. The absorbing hours he spent over his Euclid were apparently of no use to him in his profession; but Lincoln was in his way an intellectual gymnast and enjoyed the exertion for its own sake. Such a use of his leisure must have seemed a sheer waste of time to his more practical friends, and they might well have accounted for his comparative lack of success by his indulgence in such secret and useless pastimes. Neither would this criticism have been beside the mark, for if Lincoln's great energy and powers of work had been devoted exclusively to practical ends, he might well have become in the early days a more prominent lawyer and politician than he actually was. But he preferred the satisfaction of his own intellectual and social instincts, and so qualified himself for achievements beyond the power of a Douglas.

In addition, however, to these private gymnastics Lincoln shared with his neighbors a public and popular source of intellectual and human insight. The western pioneers, for all their exclusive devotion to practical purposes, wasted a good deal of time on apparently useless social intercourse. In the middle western towns of that day there was, as we have seen, an extraordinary amount of good-fellowship, which was quite the most wholesome and humanizing thing which entered into the lives of these hard-working and hard-featured men. The whole male countryside was in its way a club; and when the presence of women did not make them awkward and sentimental, the men let themselves loose in an amount of rough pleasantry and free conversation which added the one genial and liberating touch to their lives. This club life of his own people Lincoln enjoyed and shared much more than did his average neighbor. He passed the greater part of what he would have called his leisure time in swapping stories with his friends, in which the genial and humorous side of western life was embodied. Doubtless his domestic unhappiness had much to do with his vagrancy; but his native instinct for the wholesome and illuminating aspect of the life around him brought him more frequently than any other cause to the club of loafers in the general store. And whatever the promiscuous conversation and the racy yarns meant to his associates, they meant vastly more to Lincoln. His hours of social vagrancy really completed the process of his intellectual training. It relieved his culture from the taint of bookishness.

It gave substance to his humor. It humanized his wisdom and enabled him to express it in a familiar and dramatic form. It placed at his disposal, that is, the great classic vehicle of popular expression, which is the parable and the spoken word.

Of course, it was just because he shared so completely the amusements and the occupations of his neighbors that his private personal culture had no embarrassing effects. Neither he nor his neighbors were in the least aware that he had been placed thereby in a different intellectual class. No doubt the loneliness and sadness of his personal life may be partly explained by a dumb sense of difference from his fellows; and no doubt this very loneliness and sadness intensified the mental preoccupation which was both the sign and the result of his personal culture. But his unconsciousness of his own distinction, as well as his regular participation in political and professional practice, kept his will as firm and vigorous as if he were really no more than a man of action. His natural steadiness of purpose had been toughened in the beginning by the hardships and struggles which he shared with his neighbors; and his self-imposed intellectual discipline in no way impaired the stability of his character, because his personal culture never alienated him from his neighbors and threw him into a consciously critical frame of mind. The time which he spent in intellectual diversion may have diminished to some extent his practical efficiency previous to the gathering crisis. It certainly made him less inclined to the aggressive self-assertion which a successful political career demanded. But when the crisis came, when the minds of northern patriots were stirred by the ugly alternative offered to them by the South, and when Lincoln was by the course of events restored to active participation in politics, he soon showed that he had reached the highest of all objects of personal culture. While still remaining one of a body of men who, all unconsciously, impoverished their minds in order to increase the momentum of their practical energy, he none the less achieved for himself a mutually helpful relation between a firm will and a luminous intelligence. The training of his mind, the awakening of his imagination, the formation of his taste and style, the humorous dramatizing of his experience—all this discipline had failed to pervert his character, narrow his sympathies, or undermine his purposes. His intelligence served to enlighten his will, and his will to establish the mature decisions of his intelligence. Late in life the two faculties became in their exercise almost indistinguishable. His judgments, in so far as they were decisive, were charged with momentum, and his actions were instinct with sympathy and understanding.

Just because his actions were instinct with sympathy and understanding, Lincoln was certainly the most humane statesman who ever guided a nation through a great crisis. He always regarded other men and acted toward them, not merely as the embodiment of an erroneous or harmful idea, but as human beings, capable of better things; and consequently all of his thoughts and actions looked in the direction of a higher level of human association. It is this characteristic which makes him a better and, be it hoped, a more prophetic democrat than any other national American leader. His peculiar distinction does not consist in the fact that he was a "man of the people" who passed from the condition of splitting rails to the condition of being President. No doubt he was in this respect as good a democrat as you please, and no doubt it was desirable that he should be this kind of a democrat. But many other Americans could be named who were also men of the people, and who passed from the most insignificant to the most honored positions in American life. Lincoln's peculiar and permanent distinction as a democrat will depend rather upon the fact that his thoughts and his actions looked toward the realization of the highest and most edifying democratic ideal. Whatever his theories were, he showed by his general outlook and behavior that democracy meant to him more than anything else the spirit and principle of brotherhood. He was the foremost to deny liberty to the South, and he had his sensible doubts about the equality between the negro and the white man; but he actually treated everybody—the southern rebel, the negro slave, the northern deserter, the personal enemy—in a just and kindly spirit. Neither was this kindliness merely an instance of ordinary

American amiability and good nature. It was the result, not of superficial feeling which could be easily ruffled, but of his personal, moral, and intellectual discipline. He had made for himself a second nature, compact of insight and loving-kindness.

It must be remembered, also, that this higher humanity resided in a man who was the human instrument partly responsible for an awful amount of slaughter and human anguish. He was not only the commander-in-chief of a great army which fought a long and bloody war, but he was the statesman who had insisted that, if necessary, the war should be fought. His mental attitude was dictated by a mixture of practical common sense with genuine human insight, and it is just this mixture which makes him so rare a man and, be it hoped, so prophetic a democrat. He could at one and the same moment order his countrymen to be killed for seeking to destroy the American nation and forgive them for their error. His kindliness and his brotherly feeling did not lead him, after the manner of Jefferson, to shirk the necessity and duty of national defence. Neither did it lead him, after the manner of William Lloyd Garrison, to advocate non-resistance, while at the same time arousing in his fellow-countrymen a spirit of fratricidal warfare. In the midst of that hideous civil contest which was provoked, perhaps unnecessarily, by hatred, irresponsibility, passion, and disloyalty, and which has been the fruitful cause of national disloyalty down to the present day, Lincoln did not for a moment cherish a bitter or unjust feeling against the national enemies. The southerners, filled as they were with a passionate democratic devotion to their own interests and liberties, abused Lincoln until they really came to believe that he was a military tyrant, yet he never failed to treat them in a fair and forgiving spirit. When he was assassinated, it was the South, as well as the American nation, which had lost its best friend, because he alone among the Republican leaders had the wisdom to see that the divided House could only be restored by justice and kindness; and if there are any defects in its restoration today, they are chiefly due to the baleful spirit of injustice and hatred which the Republicans took over from the Abolitionists.

His superiority to his political associates in constructive states-manship is measured by his superiority in personal character. There are many men who are able to forgive the enemies of their country, but there are few who can forgive their personal ene-mies. I need not rehearse the well-known instances of Lincoln's magnanimity. He not only cherished no resentment against men who had intentionally and even maliciously injured him, but he seems at times to have gone out of his way to do them a service. This is, perhaps, his greatest distinction. Lincoln's magnanimity is the final proof of the completeness of his self-discipline. The quality of being magnanimous is both the con-summate virtue and the one which is least natural. It was cer-tainly far from being natural among Lincoln's own people. Americans of his time were generally of the opinion that it was dishonorable to overlook a personal injury. They considered it weak and unmanly not to quarrel with another man a little harder than he quarreled with you. The pioneer was good-natured and kindly; but he was aggressive, quick-tempered, un-reasonable, and utterly devoid of personal discipline. A slight or an insult to his personality became in his eyes a moral wrong which must be cherished and avenged, and which relieved him of any obligation to be just or kind to his enemy. Many con-spicuous illustrations of this quarrelsome spirit are to be found in the political life of the middle period, which, indeed, cannot be understood without constantly falling back upon the influ-ence of lively personal resentments. Every prominent politician cordially disliked or hated a certain number of his political ad-versaries and associates; and his public actions were often dic-tated by a purpose either to injure these men or to get ahead of them. After the retirement of Jackson these enmities and resent-ments came to have a smaller influence; but a man's right and duty to quarrel with anybody who, in his opinion, had done him an injury was unchallenged, and was generally considered to be the necessary accompaniment of American democratic virility.

As I have intimated above, Andrew Jackson was the most conspicuous example of this quarrelsome spirit, and for this reason he is wholly inferior to Lincoln as a type of democratic

F

manhood. Jackson had many admirable qualities and on the whole he served his country well. He also was a "man of the people" who understood and represented the mass of his fellow-countrymen, and who played the part, according to his lights, of a courageous and independent political leader. He also loved and defended the Union. But with all his excellence he should never be held up as a model to American youth. The world was divided into his personal friends and followers and his personal enemies, and he was as eager to do the latter an injury as he was to do the former a service. His quarrels were not petty, because Jackson was, on the whole, a big rather than a little man, but they were fierce and they were for the most part irreconcilable. They bulk so large in his life that they cannot be overlooked. They stamp him a type of the vindictive man without personal discipline, just as Lincoln's behavior towards Stanton, Chase, and others stamps him a type of the man who has achieved magnanimity. He is the kind of national hero the admiring imitation of whom can do nothing but good.

Lincoln had abandoned the illusion of his own peculiar personal importance. He had become profoundly and sincerely humble, and his humility was as far as possible from being either a conventional pose or a matter of nervous self-distrust. It did not impair the firmness of his will. It did not betray him into shirking responsibilities. Although only a country lawyer without executive experience, he did not flinch from assuming the leadership of a great nation in one of the gravest crises of its national history, from becoming commander-in-chief of an army of a million men, and from spending $3,000,000,000 in the prosecution of a war. His humility, that is, was precisely an example of moral vitality and insight rather than of moral awkwardness and enfeeblement. It was the fruit of reflection on his own personal experience—the supreme instance of his ability to attain moral truth both in discipline and in idea; and in its aspect of a moral truth it obtained a more explicit expression than did some other of his finer personal attributes. His practice of cherishing and repeating the plaintive little verses which inquire monotonously whether the spirit of mortal has any right to be proud indicates the depth and the highly conscious character of this fundamental moral conviction. He is not only humble himself, but he feels and declares that men have no right to be anything but humble; and he thereby enters into possession of the most fruitful and the most universal of all religious ideas.

Lincoln's humility, no less than his liberal intelligence and his magnanimous disposition, is more democratic than it is American; but in this, as in so many other cases, his personal moral dignity and his peculiar moral insight did not separate him from his associates. Like them, he wanted professional success, public office, and the ordinary rewards of American life; and like them, he bears no trace of political or moral purism. But unlike them, he was not the intellectual and moral victim of his own purposes and ambitions; and unlike them, his life is a tribute to the sincerity and depth of his moral insight. He could never have become a national leader by the ordinary road of insistent and clamorous self-assertion. Had he not been restored to public life by the crisis, he would have remained in all probability a comparatively obscure and a wholly undervalued man. But the political ferment of 1856 and the threat of ruin overhanging the American Union pushed him again on to the political highway; and once there, his years of intellectual discipline enabled him to play a leading and a decisive part. His personality obtained momentum, direction, and increasing dignity from its identification with great issues and events. He became the individual instrument whereby an essential and salutary national purpose was fulfilled; and the instrument was admirably effective, precisely because it had been silently and unconsciously tempered and formed for high achievement. Issue as he was of a society in which the cheap tool, whether mechanical or personal, was the immediately successful tool, he had none the less labored long in the making of a consummate individual instrument.

Some of my readers may protest that I have over-emphasized the difference between Lincoln and his contemporary fellow-countrymen. In order to exalt the leader have I not too much disparaged the followers? Well, a comparison of this kind always involves the risk of unfairness; but if there is much truth in the foregoing estimate of Lincoln, the lessons of the comparison are worth its inevitable risks. The ordinary interpretation of Lincoln as a consummate democrat and a "man of the people" has implied that he was, like Jackson, simply a bigger and a better version of the plain American citizen; and it is just this interpretation which I have sought to deny and to expose. In many respects he was, of course, very much like his neighbors and associates. He accepted everything wholesome and useful in their life and behavior. He shared their good-fellowship, their strength of will, their excellent faith, and above all their innocence; and he could never have served his country so well, or reached as high a level of personal dignity, in case he had not been good-natured and strong and innocent. But, as all commentators have noted, he was not only good-natured, strong, and innocent; he had made himself intellectually candid, concentrated, and disinterested, and morally humane, magnanimous, and humble. All these qualities, which were the very flower of his personal life, were not possessed either by the average or the exceptional American of his day; and not only were they not possessed, but they were either wholly ignored or consciously undervalued. Yet these very qualities of high intelligence, humanity, magnanimity, and humility are precisely the qualities which Americans, in order to become better democrats, should add to their strength, their homogeneity, and their innocence; while at the same time they are just the qualities which Americans are prevented by their individualistic practice and tradition from attaining or properly valuing. Their deepest convictions make the average unintelligent man the representative democrat, and the aggressive successful individual the admirable national type; and in conformity with these convictions their uppermost ideas in respect to Lincoln are that he was a "man of the people" and an example of strong will. He was both of these things, but his great distinction is that he was also something vastly more and better. He cannot be fully understood and properly valued as a national hero without an implicit criticism of these traditional convictions. Such a criticism he himself did not and could not make. In case he had made it, he could never have achieved his great political task and his great personal triumph. But other times bring other needs. It is as desirable today that the criticism should be made explicit as it was that Lincoln himself in his day should preserve the innocence and integrity of a unique unconscious example.

EMERSON[1]

Matthew Arnold

[Matthew Arnold (1822–1888) is well known in nineteenth century English literature as a poet, but more particularly as a critic of literature and of society. He twice visited America on lecture tours—once in 1883–1884 and again in 1886—and it was during the first of these visits that he delivered his notable address on Emerson, which was subsequently published, together with others of his lectures, in the volume entitled, *Discourses in America.* The high opinion which Arnold in this essay expresses for Emerson is all the more convincing because it is entirely unprejudiced. Arnold's discussion brings out the fact that Emerson's great achievement lay in impressing upon Americans, apart from all theological speculations, the supreme importance of the higher nature, the moral life, the intellectual being. As an American critic, George Edward Woodberry, puts it, "He was closer to the soil in his democracy, nearer to the plain people of the country, than any other man of letters; and in his works he embodied more vitally the practical ideal of the American—industrious, successful, self-reliant, not embarrassed by the past, not disturbed by the future, confident, not afraid. . . . The fortune of the republic was for him not accumulated wealth but widespread welfare. He was by birth a patriot, by tradition a Puritan democrat, and these views were natural to him. His Americanism undoubtedly endears him to his countrymen. But it is not within narrow limits of political or worldly wisdom that his influence and teachings have their effect; but in the invigoration of the personal life with which his pages are electric."]

Forty years ago, when I was an undergraduate at Oxford, voices were in the air there which haunt my memory still. Happy the man who in that susceptible season of youth hears such voices! they are a possession to him forever. No such

[1]Matthew Arnold's *Discourses in America.*

voices as those which we heard in our youth at Oxford are sounding there now. Oxford has more criticism now, more knowledge, more light; but such voices as those of our youth it has no longer. The name of Cardinal Newman is a great name to the imagination still; his genius and his style are still things of power. But he is over eighty years old; he is in the Oratory at Birmingham; he has adopted, for the doubts and difficulties which beset men's minds today, a solution which, to speak frankly, is impossible. Forty years ago he was in the very prime of life; he was close at hand to us at Oxford; he was preaching in St. Mary's pulpit every Sunday; he seemed about to transform and to renew what was for us the most national and natural institution in the world, the Church of England. Who could resist the charm of that spiritual apparition, gliding in the dim afternoon light through the aisles of St. Mary's, rising into the pulpit, and then, in the most entrancing of voices, breaking the silence with words and thoughts which were a religious music—subtle, sweet, mournful? I seem to hear him still, saying: "After the fever of life, after wearinesses and sicknesses, fightings and despondings, langour and fretfulness, struggling and succeeding; after all the changes and chances of this troubled, unhealthy state—at length comes death, at length the white throne of God, at length the beatific vision." Or, if we followed him back to his seclusion at Littlemore, that dreary village by the London road, and to the house of retreat and the church which he built there—a mean house such as Paul might have lived in when he was tent-making at Ephesus, a church plain and thinly sown with worshipers—who could resist him there either, welcoming back to the severe joys of church fellowship, and of daily worship and prayer, the firstlings of a generation which had well-nigh forgotten them? Again I seem to hear him: "The season is chill and dark, and the breath of the morning is damp, and worshipers are few; but all this befits those who are by their profession pentitents and mourners, watchers and pilgrims. More dear to them that loneliness, more cheerful that severity, and more bright that gloom, than all those aids and appliances of luxury by which men nowadays attempt to make prayer less disagreeable to them. True faith does not covet comforts; they who realize that awful day, when they shall see Him face to face whose eyes are as a flame of fire, will as little bargain to pray pleasantly now as they will think of doing so then."

Somewhere or other I have spoken of those "last enchantments" of the Middle Age which Oxford sheds around us, and here they were! But there were other voices sounding in our ear besides Newman's. There was the puissant voice of Carlyle; so sorely strained, over-used, and misused since, but then fresh, comparatively sound, and reaching our hearts with true, pathetic eloquence. Who can forget the emotion of receiving in its first freshness such a sentence as that sentence of Carlyle upon Edward Irving, then just dead: "Scotland sent him forth a herculean man; our mad Babylon wore and wasted him with all her engines—and it took her twelve years!" A greater voice still—the greatest voice of the century—came to us in those youthful years through Carlyle: the voice of Goethe. To this day—such is the force of youthful associations—I read the *Wilhelm Meister* with more pleasure in Carlyle's translation than in the original. The large, liberal view of human life in *Wilhelm Meister*, how novel it was to the Englishman in those days! and it was salutary, too, and educative for him, doubtless, as well as novel. But what moved us most in *Wilhelm Meister* was that which, after all, will always move the young most—the poetry, the eloquence. Never, surely, was Carlyle's prose so beautiful and pure as in his rendering of the Youths' dirge over Mignon!— "Well is our treasure now laid up, the fair image of the past. Here sleeps it in the marble, undecaying; in your hearts, also, it lives, it works. Travel, travel, back into life! Take along with you this holy earnestness, for earnestness alone makes life eternity." Here we had the voice of the great Goethe;—not the stiff, and hindered, and frigid, and factitious Goethe who speaks to us too often from those sixty volumes of his, but of the great Goethe, and the true one.

And besides those voices, there came to us in that old Oxford time a voice also from this side of the Atlantic—a clear and pure voice, which for my ear, at any rate, brought a strain as new, and moving, and unforgettable, as the strain of Newman, or Carlyle, or Goethe. Mr. Lowell has well described the apparition of Emerson to your young generation here, in that distant time of which I am speaking, and of his workings upon them. He was your Newman, your man of soul and genius visible to you in the flesh, speaking to your bodily ears, a present object for your heart and imagination. That is surely the most potent of all influences! nothing can come up to it. To us at Oxford Emerson was but a voice speaking from three thousand miles away. But so well he spoke that from that time forth Boston Bay and Concord were names invested to my ear with a sentiment akin to that which invests for me the names of Oxford and of Weimar; and snatches of Emerson's strain fixed themselves in my mind as imperishably as any of the eloquent words which I have been just now quoting. "Then dies the man in you; then once more perish the buds of art, poetry, and science, as they have died already in a thousand thousand men." "What Plato has thought, he may think; what a saint has felt, he may feel; what at any time has befallen any man, he can understand." "Trust thyself! every heart vibrates to that iron string. Accept the place the Divine Providence has found for you, the society of your contemporaries, the connection of events. Great men have always done so, and confided themselves childlike to the genius of their age; betraying their perception that the Eternal was stirring at their heart, working through their hands, predominating in all their being. And we are now men, and must accept in the highest spirit the same transcendent destiny; and not pinched in a corner, not cowards fleeing before a revolution, but redeemers and benefactors, pious aspirants to be noble clay plastic under the Almighty effort, let us advance and advance on chaos and the dark!" These lofty sentences of Emerson, and a hundred others of like strain, I never have lost out of my memory; I never *can* lose them.

At last I find myself in Emerson's own country, and looking upon Boston Bay. Naturally I revert to the friend of my youth. It is not always pleasant to ask oneself questions about the friends of one's youth; they cannot always well support it.

Carlyle, for instance, in my judgment, cannot well support such a return upon him. Yet we should make the return; we should part with our illusions; we should know the truth. When I come to this country, where Emerson now counts for so much, and where such high claims are made for him, I pull myself together, and ask myself what the truth about this object of my youthful admiration really is. Improper elements often come into our estimate of men. We have lately seen a German critic make Goethe the greatest of all poets, because Germany is now the greatest of military powers, and wants a poet to match. Then, too, America is a young country; and young countries, like young persons, are apt sometimes to evince in their literary judgments a want of scale and measure. I set myself, therefore, resolutely to come at a real estimate of Emerson, and with a leaning even to strictness rather than to indulgence. That is the safer course. Time has no indulgence; any veils of illusion which we may have left around an object because we loved it, Time is sure to strip away.

I was reading the other day a notice of Emerson by a serious and interesting American critic. Fifty or sixty passages in Emerson's poems, says this critic—who had doubtless himself been nourished on Emerson's writings, and held them justly dear—fifty or sixty passages from Emerson's poems have already entered into English speech as matter of familiar and universally current quotation. Here is a specimen of that personal sort of estimate which, for my part, even in speaking of authors dear to me, I would try to avoid. What is the kind of phrase of which we may fairly say that it has entered into English speech as matter of familiar quotation? Such a phrase, surely, as the "Patience on a monument" of Shakspere; as the "Darkness visible" of Milton; as the "Where ignorance is bliss" of Gray. Of not one single passage in Emerson's poetry can it be truly said that it has become a familiar quotation like phrases of this kind. It is not enough that it should be familiar to his admirers, familiar in New England, familiar even throughout the United States; it must be familiar to all readers and lovers of English poetry. Of not more than one or two passages in

Emerson's poetry can it, I think, be truly said, that they stand ever-present in the memory of even many lovers of English poetry. A great number of passages from his poetry are no doubt perfectly familiar to the mind and lips of the critic whom I have mentioned, and perhaps a wide circle of American readers. But this is a very different thing from being matter of universal quotation, like the phrases of the legitimate poets.

And, in truth, one of the legitimate poets, Emerson, in my opinion, is not. His poetry is interesting, it makes one think; but it is not the poetry of one of the born poets. I say it of him with reluctance, although I am sure that he would have said it of himself; but I say it with reluctance, because I dislike giving pain to his admirers, and because all my own wish, too, is to say of him what is favorable. But I regard myself, not as speaking to please Emerson's admirers, not as speaking to please myself; but rather, I repeat, as communing with Time and Nature concerning the productions of this beautiful and rare spirit, and as resigning what of him is by their unalterable decree touched with caducity, in order the better to mark and secure that in him which is immortal.

Milton says that poetry ought to be simple, sensuous, impassioned. Well, Emerson's poetry is seldom either simple, or sensuous, or impassioned. In general it lacks directness; it lacks concreteness; it lacks energy. His grammar is often embarrassed; in particular, the want of clearly-marked distinction between the subject and the object of his sentence is a frequent cause of obscurity in him. A poem which shall be a plain, forcible, inevitable whole he hardly ever produces. Such good work as the noble lines graven on the Concord Monument is the exception with him; such ineffective work as the *Fourth of July Ode* or the *Boston Hymn* is the rule. Even passages and single lines of thorough plainness and commanding force are rare in his poetry. They exist, of course; but when we meet with them they give us a slight shock of surprise, so little has Emerson accustomed us to them. Let me have the pleasure of quoting one or two of these exceptional passages:

"So nigh is grandeur to our dust,
    So near is God to man,
When Duty whispers low, *Thou must,*
    The youth replies, *I can.*"

Or again this:

"Though love repine and reason chafe,
    There came a voice without reply:
'Tis man's perdition to be safe,
    When for the truth he ought to die.' "

Excellent! but how seldom do we get from him a strain blown so clearly and firmly! Take another passage where his strain has not only clearness, it has also grace and beauty:

"And ever, when the happy child
    In May beholds the blooming wild,
    And hears in heaven the bluebird sing,
'Onward,' he cries, 'your baskets bring!
    In the next field is air more mild,
    And in yon hazy west is Eden's balmier spring.' "

In the style and cadence here there is a reminiscence, I think, of Gray; at any rate the pureness, grace, and beauty of these lines are worthy even of Gray. But Gray holds his high rank as a poet, not merely by the beauty and grace of passages in his poems; not merely by a diction generally pure in an age of impure diction: he holds it, above all, by the power and skill with which the evolution of his poems is conducted. Here is his grand superiority to Collins, whose diction in his best poem, the *Ode to Evening,* is purer than Gray's; but then the *Ode to Evening* is like a river which loses itself in the sand, whereas Gray's best poems have an evolution sure and satisfying. Emerson's *May-Day,* from which I just now quoted, has no real evolution at all; it is a series of observations. And, in general, his poems have no evolution. Take, for example, his *Titmouse.* Here he has an excellent subject; and his observation of Nature, moreover, is always marvelously close and fine. But compare what he makes of his meeting with his titmouse with what Cowper or Burns makes of the like kind of incident! One never quite arrives at learning what the titmouse actually did for him at all, though one feels a strong interest and desire to learn it; but one is reduced to guessing, and cannot be quite sure that after all one has guessed right. He is not plain and concrete enough—in other words, not poet enough—to be able to tell us. And a failure of this kind goes through almost all his verse, keeps him amid symbolism and allusion and the fringes of things, and, in spite of his spiritual power, deeply impairs his poetic value. Through the inestimable virtue of concreteness, a simple poem like *The Bridge* of Longfellow, or the *School Days* of Mr. Whittier, is of more poetic worth, perhaps, than all the verse of Emerson.

I do not, then, place Emerson among the great poets. But I go further, and say that I do not place him among the great writers, the great men of letters. Who are the great men of letters? They are men like Cicero, Plato, Bacon, Pascal, Swift, Voltaire—writers with, in the first place, a genius and instinct for style; writers whose prose is by a kind of native necessity true and sound. Now the style of Emerson, like the style of his transcendentalist friends and of the *Dial* so continually—the style of Emerson is capable of falling into a strain like this, which I take from the beginning of his *Essay on Love:* "Every soul is a celestial being to every other soul. The heart has its sabbaths and jubilees, in which the world appears as a hymeneal feast, and all natural sounds and the circle of the seasons are erotic odes and dances." Emerson altered this sentence in the later editions. Like Wordsworth, he was in later life fond of altering; and in general his later alterations, like those of Wordsworth, are not improvements. He softened the passage in question, however, though without really mending it. I quote it in its original and strongly marked form. Arthur Stanley used to relate that about the year 1840, being in conversation with some Americans in quarantine at Malta, and thinking to please them, he declared his warm admiration for Emerson's *Essays*, then recently published. However, the Americans shook their heads, and told him that for home taste Emerson was decidedly too *greeny*. We will hope, for their sakes, that the sort of thing they had in their heads was such writing as I have just quoted. Unsound it is, indeed, and in a style almost impossible to a born man of letters.

It is a curious thing, that quality of style which marks the great writer, the born man of letters. It resides in the whole tissue of one's work, and of his work regarded as a composition for literary purposes. Brilliant and powerful passages in a man's writings do not prove his possession of it; it lies in their whole tissue. Emerson has passages of noble and pathetic eloquence, such as those which I quoted at the beginning; he has passages of shrewd and felicitous wit; he has crisp epigram; he has passages of exquisitely touched observation of nature. Yet he is not a great writer; his style has not the requisite wholeness of good tissue. Even Carlyle is not, in my judgment, a great writer. He has surpassingly powerful qualities of expression, far more powerful than Emerson's, and reminding one of the gifts of expression of the great poets—of even Shakspere himself. What Emerson so admirably says of Carlyle's "devouring eyes and portraying hand," "those thirsty eyes, those portrait-eating, portrait-painting eyes of thine, those fatal perceptions," is thoroughly true. What a description is Carlyle's of the first publisher of *Sartor Resartus*, "to whom the idea of a new edition of *Sartor* is frightful, or rather ludicrous, unimaginable;" of this poor Fraser, in whose "wonderful world of Tory pamphleteers, conservative Younger-brothers, Regent Street loungers, Crockford gamblers, Irish Jesuits, drunken reporters, and miscellaneous unclean persons (whom niter and much soap will not wash clean), not a soul has expressed the smallest wish that way!" What a portrait, again, of the well-beloved John Sterling! "One, and the best, of a small class extant here, who, nigh drowning in a black wreck of Infidelity (lighted up by some glare of Radicalism only, now growing *dim* too), and about to perish, saved themselves into a Coleridgian Shovel-Hattedness." What touches in the invitation of Emerson to London! "You shall see blockheads by the million; Pickwick himself shall be visible—innocent young Dickens, reserved for a questionable fate. The great Wordsworth shall talk till you yourself pronounce him to be a bore. Southey's complexion is still healthy mahogany brown, with a fleece of white hair, and eyes that seem running at full gallop. Leigh Hunt, man of genius in the shape of a cockney, is my near neighbor, with good humor and no common sense; old Rogers with his pale head, white, bare, and cold as snow, with those large blue eyes, cruel, sorrowful, and that sardonic shelf chin." How inimitable it all is! And, finally for one must not go on forever, this version of a London Sunday, with the public houses closed during the hours of divine service! "It is silent Sunday; the populace not yet admitted to their beer-shops, till the respectabilities conclude their rubric mummeries—a much more audacious feat than beer." Yet even Carlyle is not, in my judgment, to be called a great writer; one cannot think of ranking him with men like Cicero and Plato and Swift and Voltaire. Emerson freely promises to Carlyle immortality for his histories. They will not have it. Why? Because the materials furnished to him by that devouring eye of his, and that portraying hand, were not wrought in and subdued by him to what his work, regarded as a composition for literary purposes, required. Occurring in conversation, breaking out in familiar correspondence, they are magnificent, inimitable; nothing more is required of them; thus thrown out anyhow, they serve their turn and fulfil their function. And, therefore, I should not wonder if really Carlyle lived, in the long run, by such an invaluable record as that correspondence between him and Emerson, of which we owe the publication to Mr. Charles Norton—by this and not by his works, as Johnson lives in Boswell, not by his works. For Carlyle's sallies, as the staple of a literary work, become wearisome; and as time more and more applies to Carlyle's works its stringent test, this will be felt more and more. Shakspere, Molière, Swift—they, too, had, like Carlyle, the devouring eye and the portraying hand. But they are great literary masters, they are supreme writers, because they knew how to work into a literary composition their materials, and to subdue them to the purposes of literary effect. Carlyle is too willful for this, too turbid, too vehement.

You will think I deal in nothing but negatives. I have been saying that Emerson is not one of the great poets, the great writers. He has not their quality of style. He is, however, the propounder of a philosophy. The Platonic dialogues afford us the example of exquisite literary form and treatment given to philosophical ideas. Plato is at once a great literary man and a great philosopher. If we speak carefully, we cannot call Aristotle or Spinoza or Kant great literary men, or their productions great literary works. But their work is arranged with such constructive power that they build a philosophy, and are justly called great philosophical writers. Emerson cannot, I think, be called with justice a great philosophical writer. He cannot build; his arrangement of philosophical ideas has no progress in it, no evolution; he does not construct a philosophy. Emerson himself knew the defects of his method, or rather want of method, very well; indeed, he and Carlyle criticise themselves and one another in a way which leaves little for anyone else to do in the way of formulating their defects. Carlyle formulates perfectly the defects of his friend's poetic and literary production when he says of the *Dial:* "For me it is too ethereal, speculative, theoretic; I will have all things condense themselves, take shape and body, if they are to have my sympathy." And, speaking of Emerson's *Orations*, he says: "I long to see some concrete Thing, some Event, Man's Life, American Forest, or piece of Creation, which this Emerson loves and wonders at, well *Emersonized*—depictured by Emerson, filled with the life of Emerson, and cast forth from him, then to live by itself. If these *Orations* balk me of this, how profitable soever they may be for others, I will not love them." Emerson himself formulates perfectly the defect of his own philosophical productions when he speaks of his "formidable tendency to the lapidary style. I build my house of bowlders." "Here I sit and read and write," he says again, "with very little system, and, as far as regards composition, with the most fragmentary result; paragraphs incomprehensible, each sentence an infinitely repellent particle." Nothing can be truer; and the work of a Spinoza or Kant, of the men who stand as great philosophical writers, does not proceed in this wise.

Some people will tell you that Emerson's poetry, indeed, is

too abstract, and his philosophy too vague, but that his best work is his *English Traits*. The *English Traits* are beyond question very pleasant reading. It is easy to praise them, easy to commend the author of them. But I insist on always trying Emerson's work by the highest standards. I esteem him too much to try his work by any other. Tried by the highest standards, and compared with the work of the excellent markers and recorders of the traits of human life—of writers like Montaigne, La Bruyère, Addison—the *English Traits* will not stand the comparison. Emerson's observation has not the disinterested quality of the observation of these masters. It is the observation of a man systematically benevolent, as Hawthorne's observation in *Our Old Home* is the work of a man chagrined. Hawthorne's literary talent is of the first order. His subjects are generally not to me subjects of the highest interest; but his literary talent is of the first order, the finest, I think, which America has yet produced—finer, by much, than Emerson's. Yet *Our Old Home* is not a masterpiece any more than *English Traits*. In neither of them is the observer disinterested enough. The author's attitude in each of these cases can easily be understood and defended. Hawthorne was a sensitive man, so situated in England that he was perpetually in contact with the British Philistine; and the British Philistine is a trying personage. Emerson's systematic benevolence comes from what he himself calls somewhere his "persistent optimism;" and his persistent optimism is the root of his greatness and the source of his charm. But still let us keep our literary conscience true, and judge every kind of literary work by the laws really proper to it. The kind of work attempted in the *English Traits* and in *Our Old Home* is work which cannot be done perfectly with a bias such as that given by Emerson's optimism or by Hawthorne's chagrin. Consequently, neither *English Traits* nor *Our Old Home* is a work of perfection in its kind.

Not with the Miltons and Grays, not with the Platos and Spinozas, not with the Swifts and Voltaires, not with the Montaignes and Addisons, can we rank Emerson. His work of various kinds, when one compares it with the work done in a corresponding kind by these masters, fails to stand the comparison. No man could see this clearer than Emerson himself. It is hard not to feel despondency when we contemplate our failures and shortcomings; and Emerson, the least self-flattering and the most modest of men, saw so plainly what was lacking to him that he had his moments of despondency. "Alas, my friend," he writes in reply to Carlyle, who had exhorted him to creative work—"Alas, my friend, I can do no such gay thing as you say. I do not belong to the poets, but only to a low department of literature—the reporters; suburban men." He deprecated his friend's praise; praise "generous to a fault," he calls it; praise "generous to the shaming of me—cold, fastidious, ebbing person that I am. Already in a former letter you had said too much good of my poor little arid book, which is as sand to my eyes. I can only say that I heartily wish the book were better; and I must try and deserve so much favor from the kind gods by a bolder and truer living in the months to come— such as may perchance one day release and invigorate this cramped hand of mine. When I see how much work is to be done; what room for a poet, for any spiritualist, in this great intelligent, sensual, and avaricious America—I lament my fumbling fingers and stammering tongue." Again, as late as 1870, he writes to Carlyle: "There is no example of constancy like yours, and it always stings my stupor into temporary recovery and wonderful resolution to accept the noble challenge. But 'the strong hours conquer us;' and I am the victim of miscellany— miscellany of designs, vast debility, and procrastination." The forlorn note belonging to the phrase, "vast debility," recalls that saddest and most discouraged of writers, the author of *Obermann*, Senancour, with whom Emerson has in truth a certain kinship. He has, in common with Senancour, his pureness, his passion for nature, his single eye; and here we find him confessing, like Senancour, a sense in himself of sterility and impotence.

And now I think I have cleared the ground. I have given up to envious Time as much of Emerson as Time can fairly expect ever to obtain. We have not in Emerson a great poet, a great writer, a great philosophy maker. His relation to us is not that of one of those personages; yet it is a relation of, I think, even superior importance. His relation to us is more like that of the Roman Emperor, Marcus Aurelius. Marcus Aurelius is not a great writer, a great philosophy maker; he is the friend and aider of those who would live in the spirit. Emerson is the same. He is the friend and aider of those who would live in the spirit. All the points in thinking which are necessary for this purpose he takes; but he does not combine them into a system, nor present them as a regular philosophy. Combined in a system by a man with the requisite talent for this kind of thing, they would be less useful than as Emerson gives them to us; and the man with the talent so to systematize them would be less impressive than Emerson. They do very well as they now stand—like "bowlders," as he says—in "paragraphs incompressible, each sentence an infinitely repellent particle." In such sentences his main points recur again and again, and become fixed in the memory.

We all know them. First and foremost, character. Character is everything. "That which all things tend to educe—which freedom, cultivation, intercourse, revolutions, go to form and deliver—is character." Character and self-reliance. "Trust thyself! every heart vibrates to that iron string." And yet we have our being in a *not ourselves*. "There is a power above and behind us, and we are the channels of its communications." But our lives must be pitched higher. "Life must be lived on a higher plane; we must go up to a higher platform, to which we are always invited to ascend; there the whole scene changes." The good we need is forever close to us, though we attain it not. "On the brink of the waters of life and truth, we are miserably dying." This good is close to us, moreover, in our daily life, and in the familiar, homely places. "The unremitting retention of simple and high sentiments in obscure duties—that is the maximum for us. Let us be poised and wise, and our own today. Let us treat the men and women well—treat them as if they were real; perhaps they are. Men live in their fancy, like drunkards

whose hands are too soft and tremulous for successful labor. I
settle myself ever firmer in the creed, that we should not post-
pone and refer and wish, but do broad justice where we are, by
whomsoever we deal with; accepting our actual companions and
circumstances, however humble or odious, as the mystic officials
to whom the universe has delegated its whole pleasure for us.
Massachusetts, Connecticut River, and Boston Bay, you think
paltry places, and the ear loves names of foreign and classic
topography. But here we are; and if we will tarry a little we
may come to learn that here is best. See to it only that thyself
is here." Furthermore, the good is close to us *all*. "I resist the
skepticism of our education and of our educated men. I do not
believe that the differences of opinion and character in men are
organic. I do not recognize, besides the class of the good and
the wise, a permanent class of skeptics, or a class of conservatives, or of malignants, or of materialists. I do not believe in
the classes. Every man has a call of the power to do something
unique." Exclusiveness is deadly. "The exclusive in social life
does not see that he excludes himself from enjoyment in the
attempt to appropriate it. The exclusionist in religion does not
see that he shuts the door of Heaven on himself in striving to
shut out others. Treat men as pawns and ninepins, and you
shall suffer as well as they. If you leave out their heart you
shall lose your own. The selfish man suffers more from his
selfishness than he from whom that selfishness withholds some
important benefit." A sound nature will be inclined to refuse
ease and self-indulgence. "To live with some rigor of temperance,
or some extreme of generosity, seems to be an asceticism which
common good-nature would appoint to those who are at ease
and in plenty, in sign that they feel a brotherhood with the
great multitude of suffering men." Compensation, finally, is the
great law of life; it is everywhere, it is sure, and there is no
escape from it. This is that "law alive and beautiful, which
works over our heads and under our feet. Pitiless, it avails
itself of our success when we obey it, and of our ruin when we
contravene it. We are all secret believers in it. It rewards actions
after their nature. The reward of a thing well done is to have

done it. The thief steals from himself, the swindler swindles himself. You must pay at last your own debt."

This is tonic indeed! And let no one object that it is too general; that more practical, positive direction is what we mean; that Emerson's optimism, self-reliance, and indifference to favorable conditions for our life and growth have in them something of danger. "Trust thyself;" "what attracts my attention shall have it;" "though thou shouldest walk the world over thou shalt not be able to find a condition inopportune or ignoble;" "what we call vulgar society is that society whose poetry is not yet written, but which you shall presently make as enviable and renowed as any." With maxims like these, we surely, it may be said, run some risk of being made too well satisfied with our own actual self and state, however crude and imperfect they may be. "Trust thyself?" It may be said that the common American or Englishman is more than enough disposed already to trust himself. I often reply, when our sectarians are praised for following conscience: Our people are very good in following their conscience; where they are not so good is in ascertaining whether their conscience tells them right. "What attracts my attention shall have it?" Well, that is our people's plea when they run after the Salvation Army, and desire Messrs. Moody and Sankey. "Thou shalt not be able to find a condition inopportune or ignoble?" But think of the turn of the good people of our race for producing a life of hideousness and immense ennui; think of that specimen of your own New England life which Mr. Howells gives us in one of his charming stories which I was reading lately; think of the life of that ragged New England farm in the *Lady of the Aroostook;* think of Deacon Blood, and Aunt Maria, and the straight-backed chairs with black horsehair seats, and Ezra Perkins with perfect self-reliance depositing his travelers in the snow! I can truly say that in the little which I have seen of the life of New England, I am more struck with what has been achieved than with the crudeness and failure. But no doubt there is still a great deal of crudeness also. Your own novelists say there is, and I suppose they say true. In the New England, as in the Old, our people have to learn, I suppose, not that their modes of life are beautiful and excellent already; they have rather to learn that they must transform them.

To adopt this line of objection to Emerson's deliverances would, however, be unjust. In the first place, Emerson's points are in themselves true, if understood in a certain high sense; they are true and fruitful. And the right work to be done, at the hour when he appeared, was to affirm them generally and absolutely. Only thus could he break through the hard and fast barrier of narrow, fixed ideas, which he found confronting him, and win an entrance for new ideas. Had he attempted developments which may now strike us as expedient, he would have excited fierce antagonism, and probably effected little or nothing. The time might come for doing other work later, but the work which Emerson did was the right work to be done then.

In the second place, strong as was Emerson's optimism, and unconquerable as was his belief in a good result to emerge from all which he saw going on around him, no misanthropical satirist ever saw shortcomings and absurdities more clearly than he did, or exposed them more courageously. When he sees "the meanness," as he calls it, "of American politics," he congratulates Washington on being "long already happily dead," on being "wrapt in his shroud and forever safe." With how firm a touch he delineates the faults of your two great political parties of forty years ago! The Democrats, he says, "have not at heart the ends which give to the name of democracy what hope and virtue are in it. The spirit of our American radicalism is destructive and aimless; it is not loving; it has no ulterior and divine ends, but is destructive only out of hatred and selfishness. On the other side, the conservative party, composed of the most moderate, able, and cultivated part of the population, is timid, and merely defensive of property. It vindicates no right, it aspires to no real good, it brands no crime, it proposes no generous policy. From neither party, when in power, has the world any benefit to expect in science, art, or humanity, at all commensurate with the resources of the nation." Then with what subtle though kindly irony he follows the gradual withdrawal in New England, in the last half century, of tender consciences from the

social organizations—the bent for experiments such as that of
Brook Farm and the like—follows it in all its "dissidence of
dissent and Protestantism of the Protestant religion!" He even
loves to rally the New Englander on his philanthropical activity,
and to find his beneficence and its institutions a bore! "Your
miscellaneous popular charities, the education at college of fools,
the building of meetinghouses to the vain end to which many of
these now stand, alms to sots, and the thousandfold relief
societies—though I confess with shame that I sometimes succumb and give the dollar, yet it is a wicked dollar, which by and
by I shall have the manhood to withhold." "Our Sunday
schools and churches and pauper societies are yokes to the neck.
We pain ourselves to please nobody. There are natural ways of
arriving at the same ends at which these aim, but do not arrive."
"Nature does not like our benevolence or our learning much
better than she likes our frauds and wars. When we come out
of the caucus, or the bank, or the Abolition convention, or the
Temperance meeting, or the Transcendental club, into the fields
and woods, she says to us: 'So hot, my little sir?'"

Yes, truly, his insight is admirable; his truth is precious. Yet
the secret of his effect is not even in these; it is in his temper.
It is in the hopeful, serene beautiful temper wherewith these, in
Emerson, are indissolubly joined; in which they work, and have
their being. He says himself: "We judge of a man's wisdom by
his hope, knowing that the perception of the inexhaustibleness of
nature is an immortal youth." If this be so, how wise is Emerson! for never had man such a sense of the inexhaustibleness of
nature, and such hope. It was the ground of his being; it never
failed him. Even when he is sadly avowing the imperfection of
his literary power and resources, lamenting his fumbling fingers
and stammering tongue, he adds: "Yet, as I tell you, I am very
easy in my mind and never dream of suicide. My whole philosophy which is very real teaches acquiescence and optimism.
Sure I am that the right word will be spoken, though I cut out
my tongue." In his old age, with friends dying and life failing,
his note of cheerful, forward-looking hope is still the same. "A
multitude of young men are growing up here of high promise,

and I compare gladly the social poverty of my youth with the power on which these draw." His abiding word for us, the word by which being dead he yet speaks to us, is this: "That which befits us, embosomed in beauty and wonder as we are, is cheerfulness and courage, and the endeavor to realize our aspirations. Shall not the heart, which has received so much, trust the Power by which it lives?"

One can scarcely overrate the importance of thus holding fast to happiness and hope. It gives to Emerson's work an invaluable virtue. As Wordsworth's poetry is, in my judgment, the most important work done in verse, in our language, during the present century, so Emerson's *Essays* are, I think, the most important work done in prose. His work is more important than Carlyle's. Let us be just to Carlyle, provoking though he often is. Not only has he that genius of his which makes Emerson say truly of his letters, that "they savor always of eternity." More than this may be said of him. The scope and upshot of his teaching are true; "his guiding genius," to quote Emerson again, is really "his moral sense, his perception of the sole importance of truth and justice." But consider Carlyle's temper, as we have been considering Emerson's! take his own account of it! "Perhaps London is the proper place for me after all, seeing all places are *im*proper: who knows? Meanwhile, I lead a most dyspeptic, solitary, self-shrouded life; consuming, if possible in silence, my considerable daily allotment of pain; glad when any strength is left in me for writing, which is the only use I can see in myself—too rare a case of late. The ground of my existence is black as death; too black, when all *void* too; but at times there paint themselves on it pictures of gold, and rainbow, and lightning; all the brighter for the black ground, I suppose. Withal, I am very much of a fool." No, not a fool, but turbid and morbid, willful and perverse. "We judge of a man's wisdom by his hope."

Carlyle's perverse attitude towards happiness cuts him off from hope. He fiercely attacks the desire for happiness; his grand point in *Sartor*, his secret in which the soul may find rest, is that one shall cease to desire happiness, that one should learn to say to oneself: "What if thou wert born and predestined not to be happy, but to be unhappy!" He is wrong; Saint Augustine is the better philosopher, who says: "Act we *must* in pursuance of what gives us most delight." Epictetus and Augustine can be severe moralists enough; but both of them know and frankly say that the desire for happiness is the root and ground of man's being. Tell him and show him that he places his happiness wrong, that he seeks for delight where delight will never be really found; then you illumine and further him. But you only confuse him by telling him to cease to desire happiness: and you will not tell him this unless you are already confused yourself.

Carlyle preached the dignity of labor, the necessity of righteousness, the love of veracity, the hatred of shams. He is said by many people to be a great teacher, a great helper for us, because he does so. But what is the due and eternal result of labor, righteousness, veracity?—Happiness. And how are we drawn to them by one who, instead of making us feel that with them is happiness, tells us that perhaps we were predestined not to be happy but to be unhappy?

You will find, in especial, many earnest preachers of our popular religion to be fervent in their praise and admiration of Carlyle. His insistence on labor, righteousness, and veracity, pleases them; his contempt for happiness pleases them too. I read the other day a tract against smoking, although I do not happen to be a smoker myself. "Smoking," said the tract, "is liked because it gives agreeable sensations. Now it is a positive objection to a thing that it gives agreeable sensations. An earnest man will expressly avoid what gives agreeable sensations." Shortly afterwards I was inspecting a school, and I found the children reading a piece of poetry on the common theme that were are here today and gone tomorrow. I shall soon be gone, the speaker in this poem was made to say—

> "And I shall be glad to go,
> For the world at best is a dreary place,
> And my life is getting low."

How usual a language of popular religion that is, on our side of the Atlantic at any rate! But then our popular religion, in disparaging happiness here below, knows very well what it is after. It has its eye on a happiness in a future life above the clouds, in the New Jerusalem, to be won by disliking and rejecting happiness here on earth. And so long as this ideal stands fast, it is very well. But for very many it now stands fast no longer; for Carlyle, at any rate, it had failed and vanished. Happiness in labor, righteousness, and veracity—in the life of the spirit— here was a gospel still for Carlyle to preach, and to help others by preaching. But he baffled them and himself by preferring the paradox that we are not born for happiness at all.

Happiness in labor, righteousness, and veracity; in all the life of the spirit; happiness and eternal hope;—that was Emerson's gospel. I hear it said that Emerson was too sanguine; that the actual generation in America is not turning out so well as he expected. Very likely he was too sanguine as to the near future; in this country it is difficult not to be too sanguine. Very possibly the present generation may prove unworthy of his high hopes; even several generations succeeding this may prove unworthy of them. But by his conviction that in the life of the spirit is happiness, and by his hope that this life of the spirit will come more and more to be sanely understood, and to prevail, and to work for happiness—by this conviction and hope Emerson was great, and he will surely prove in the end to have been right in them. In this country it is difficult, as I said, not to be sanguine. Very many of your writers are over-sanguine, and on the wrong grounds. But you have two men who in what they have written show their sanguineness in a line where courage and hope are just, where they are also infinitely important, but where they are not easy. The two men are Franklin and Emerson.[1] These two are, I think, the most distinctively and honorably American of your writers; they are the most original and the most valuable. Wise men everywhere know that

[1] I found with pleasure that this conjunction of Emerson's name with Franklin's had already occurred to an accomplished writer and a delightful man, a friend of Emerson, left almost the sole survivor, alas! of the famous

we must keep up our courage and hope; they know that hope is, as Wordsworth well says—

> "The paramount *duty* which heaven lays,
> For its own honor, on man's suffering heart."

But the very word *duty* points to an effort and a struggle to maintain our hope unbroken. Franklin and Emerson maintained theirs with a convincing ease, an inspiring joy. Franklin's confidence in the happiness with which industry, honesty, and economy will crown the life of this work-day world, is such that he runs over with felicity. With a like felicity does Emerson run over, when he contemplates the happiness eternally attached to the true life in the spirit. You cannot prize him too much, nor heed him too diligently. He has lessons for both the branches of our race. I figure him to my mind as visible upon earth still, as still standing here by Boston Bay, or at his own Concord, in his habit as he lived, but of heightened stature and shining feature, with one hand stretched out toward the East, to our laden and laboring England; the other toward the ever-growing West, to his own dearly-loved America,—"great, intelligent, sensual, avaricious America." To us he shows for guidance his lucid freedom, his cheerfulness and hope; to you his dignity, delicacy, serenity, elevation.

literary generation of Boston—Dr. Oliver Wendell Holmes. Dr. Holmes has kindly allowed me to print here the ingenious and interesting lines, hitherto unpublished, in which he speaks of Emerson thus:

> "Where in the realm of thought, whose air is song,
> Does he, the Buddha of the West, belong?
> He seems a wingéd Franklin, sweetly wise,
> 'Born to unlock the secret of the skies;
> And which the nobler calling—if 'tis fair
> Terrestrial with celestial to compare—
> To guide the storm-cloud's elemental flame,
> Or walk the chambers whence the lightning came
> Amidst the sources of its subtile fire,
> And steal their effluence for his lips and lyre?"
>
> [Arnold's Note.]

LANDMARK ADDRESSES AND STATE PAPERS

DECLARATION OF INDEPENDENCE

Thomas Jefferson

[Thomas Jefferson (1743–1826), the third President of the United States, was born in Albemarle County, Virginia. He was graduated from William and Mary College, admitted to the bar, and began his long public career as a member of the Virginia legislature. He was a delegate to the Continental Congress, and, because of his well-known skill in composing state papers, was appointed upon the drafting committee of the Congress. The Declaration of Independence, though it embodies emendations by John Adams and Benjamin Franklin, is mainly the work of Jefferson, and his name will always be indissolubly connected with it. Despite the fact that it has been common to sneer at certain features of the Declaration (see article by Moses Coit Tyler, "The Declaration of Independence in the Light of Modern Criticism," reprinted in this volume on page 158), it remains, as someone has said, "the most powerful, the most significant piece of literature that ever came from the pen of a statesman." It is not needful to enumerate the public positions held by Jefferson in his later career. After retiring from the Presidency in 1809, he spent the remainder of his life at Monticello, his country estate in Virginia.]

In Congress, July 4, 1776.

THE UNANIMOUS DECLARATION OF THE THIRTEEN UNITED STATES OF AMERICA

When, in the course of human events, it becomes necessary for one people to dissolve the political bands which have connected them with another, and to assume, among the powers of the earth, the separate and equal station to which the laws of nature and of nature's God entitle them, a decent respect to the opinions of mankind requires that they should declare the causes which impel them to the separation.

We hold these truths to be self-evident: that all men are created equal; that they are endowed by their Creator with certain unalienable rights; that among these are life, liberty, and the pursuit of happiness. That, to secure these rights, governments are instituted among men, deriving their just powers from the consent of the governed; that, whenever any form of government becomes destructive of these ends, it is the right of the people to alter or to abolish it, and to institute new government, laying its foundation on such principles, and organizing its powers in such form, as to them shall seem most likely to effect their safety and happiness. Prudence, indeed, will dictate that governments long established should not be changed for light and transient causes; and, accordingly, all experience hath shown that mankind are more disposed to suffer, while evils are sufferable, than to right themselves by abolishing the forms to which they are accustomed. But, when a long train of abuses and usurpations, pursuing invariably the same object, evinces a design to reduce them under absolute despotism, it is their right, it is their duty, to throw off such government, and to provide new guards for their future security. Such has been the patient sufference of these colonies; and such is now the necessity which constrains them to alter their former systems of government. The history of the present king of Great Britain is a history of repeated injuries and usurpations, all having in direct object the establishment of an absolute tyranny over these States. To prove this, let facts be submitted to a candid world:

He has refused his assent to laws the most wholesome and necessary for the public good.

He has forbidden his governors to pass laws of immediate and pressing importance, unless suspended in their operation till his assent should be obtained; and, when so suspended, he has utterly neglected to attend to them.

He has refused to pass other laws for the accommodation of large districts of people, unless those people would relinquish the right of representation in the legislature, a right inestimable to them and formidable to tyrants only.

He has called together legislative bodies at places unusual, uncomfortable, and distant from the depository of their public records, for the sole purpose of fatiguing them into compliance with his measures.

He has dissolved representative houses repeatedly, for opposing, with manly firmness, his invasions on the rights of the people.

He has refused, for a long time after such dissolutions, to cause others to be elected; whereby the legislative powers, incapable of annihilation, have returned to the people at large for their exercise; the State remaining, in the meantime, exposed to all the dangers of invasion from without, and convulsions within.

He has endeavored to prevent the population of these States; for that purpose obstructing the laws for naturalization of foreigners; refusing to pass others to encourage their migration hither, and raising the conditions of new appropriations of lands.

He has obstructed the administration of justice, by refusing his assent to laws for establishing judiciary powers.

He has made judges dependent on his will alone for the tenure of their offices, and the amount and payment of their salaries.

He has erected a multitude of new offices and sent hither swarms of officers to harass our people, and eat out their substance.

He has kept among us in times of peace, standing armies, without the consent of our legislature.

He has affected to render the military independent of, and superior to, the civil power.

He has combined, with others, to subject us to a jurisdiction foreign to our constitution, and unacknowledged by our laws; giving his assent to their acts of pretended legislation:

For quartering large bodies of armed troops among us:

For protecting them, by a mock trial, from punishment for any murders which they should commit on the inhabitants of these States:

For cutting off our trade with all parts of the world:

For imposing taxes on us without our consent:

For depriving us, in many cases, of the benefits of trial by jury:

For transporting us beyond seas to be tried for pretended offenses:

For abolishing the free system of English laws in a neighboring province, establishing therein an arbitrary government and enlarging its boundaries, so as to render it at once an example and fit instrument for introducing the same absolute rule into these colonies:

For taking away our charters, abolishing our most valuable laws, and altering, fundamentally, the forms of our governments:

For suspending our own legislatures, and declaring themselves invested with power to legislate for us in all cases whatsoever.

He has abdicated government here by declaring us out of his protection, and waging war against us.

He has plundered our seas, ravaged our coasts, burnt our towns, and destroyed the lives of our people.

He is, at this time, transporting large armies of foreign mercenaries to complete the works of death, desolation, and tyranny, already begun, with circumstances of cruelty and perfidy scarcely paralleled in the most barbarous ages, and totally unworthy the head of a civilized nation.

He has constrained our fellow-citizens, taken captive on the high seas, to bear arms against their country, to become the executioners of their friends and brethren, or to fall themselves by their hands.

He has excited domestic insurrections amongst us, and has endeavored to bring on the inhabitants of our frontiers, the merciless Indian savages, whose known rule of warfare is an undistinguished destruction of all ages, sexes, and conditions.

In every stage of these oppressions, we have petitioned for redress in the most humble terms: our repeated petitions have been answered only by repeated injury. A prince, whose character is thus marked by every act which may define a tyrant, is unfit to be the ruler of a free people.

Nor have we been wanting in attention to our British brethren. We have warned them, from time to time, of attempts by their legislature to extend an unwarrantable jurisdiction over us. We have reminded them of the circumstances of our emigration and settlement here. We have appealed to their native justice and magnanimity, and we have conjured them, by the ties of our common kindred, to disavow these usurpations, which would inevitably interrupt our connections and correspondence. They, too, have been deaf to the voice of justice and consanguinity. We must, therefore, acquiesce in the necessity which denounces our separation, and hold them, as we hold the rest of mankind, enemies in war—in peace, friends.

We, therefore, the representatives of the United States of America, in General Congress assembled, appealing to the Supreme Judge of the world for the rectitude of our intentions, do, in the name, and by authority of the good people of these colonies, solemnly publish and declare, That these United Colonies are, and of right ought to be, free and independent States; that they are absolved from all allegiance to the British crown, and that all political connection between them and the state of Great Britain is, and ought to be, totally dissolved; and that, as free and independent States, they have full power to levy war, conclude peace, contract alliances, establish commerce, and to do all other acts and things which independent States may of right do. And for the support of this declaration, with a firm reliance on the protection of Divine Providence, we mutually pledge to each other our lives, our fortunes, and our sacred honor.

JOHN HANCOCK.

New Hampshire
Josiah Bartlett,
Wm. Whipple,
Matthew Thornton.

Massachusetts Bay
Saml. Adams,
John Adams,
Robt. Treat Paine,
Elbridge Gerry.

Rhode Island
Step. Hopkins,
William Ellery.

Connecticut
Roger Sherman,
Sam'el Huntington,
Wm. Williams,
Oliver Wolcott.

New York
Wm. Floyd,
Phil. Livingston,
Frans. Lewis,
Lewis Morris.

New Jersey
Richd. Stockton,
Jno. Witherspoon,

Fras. Hopkinson,
John Hart,
Abra. Clark.

Pennsylvania
Robt. Morris,
Benjamin Rush,
Benja. Franklin,
John Morton,
Geo. Clymer,
Jas. Smith,
Geo. Taylor,
James Wilson,
Geo. Ross.

Delaware	*Virginia*	*South Carolina*
Cæsar Rodney,	George Wythe,	Edward Rutledge,
Geo. Read,	Richard Henry Lee,	Thos. Heyward, Junr.,
Tho. M'Kean.	Th Jefferson,	Thomas Lynch, Junr.,
	Benja. Harrison,	Arthur Middleton.
Maryland	Thos. Nelson, jr.,	
Samuel Chase,	Francis Lightfoot Lee,	*Georgia*
Wm. Paca,	Carter Braxton.	Button Gwinnett,
Thos. Stone,		Lyman Hall,
Charles Carroll of Car-	*North Carolina*	Geo. Walton.
rollton.	Wm. Hooper,	
	Joseph Hewes,	
	John Penn.	

FAREWELL ADDRESS

George Washington

[George Washington (1732–1799), the first President of the United States, was born in Westmoreland County, Virginia, and died at Mount Vernon, his famous estate, not many miles from his birthplace. The details of his life are so well known that no attempt is made in this note to recount them. Light on his character as an American citizen will be found in the selection, Van Dyke's *The Americanism of Washington*, page 67, this volume. After being twice elected President without opposition, Washington felt that he had done his work in founding the Republic and resolved to withdraw to private life. His Farewell Address was written upon this occasion and issued in 1796. It is a simple, touching letter of advice, caution, and bene-diction, in spite of the stiff and formal diction in which, according to the literary fashion of that time, it is couched. As has been long known, the Address is a composite production. The substance and spirit of it, the main idea and the trend, are wholly Washington's; the language, in great part, is undoubtedly Madison's and Hamilton's (see Horace Binney's *Inquiry into the Formation of Washington's Farewell Address;* also a briefer account in the *Forum*, vol. xxvii, p. 145). In reprinting the address here a few opening paragraphs are omitted.]

In looking forward to the moment, which is intended to ter-minate the career of my public life, my feelings do not permit me to suspend the deep acknowledgment of that debt of grati-tude, which I owe to my beloved country for the many honors it has conferred upon me; still more for the steadfast confidence with which it has supported me; and for the opportunities I have thence enjoyed of manifesting my inviolable attachment, by services faithful and persevering, though in usefulness unequal to my zeal. If benefits have resulted to our country from these services, let it always be remembered to your praise, and as an instructive example in our annals, that under circumstances in which the passions, agitated in every direction, were liable to mislead, amidst appearances sometimes dubious, vicissitudes of fortune often discouraging, in situations in which not unfrequently want of success has countenanced the spirit of criticism, the constancy of your support was the essential prop of the efforts, and a guarantee of the plans by which they were affected. Profoundly penetrated with this idea, I shall carry it with me to my grave, as a strong incitement to unceasing vows that Heaven may continue to you the choicest tokens of its beneficence; that your union and brotherly affection may be perpetual, that the free constitution, which is the work of your hands, may be sacredly maintained, that its administration in every department may be stamped with wisdom and virtue; that, in fine, the happiness of the people of these states, under the auspices of liberty, may be made complete, by so careful a preservation and so prudent a use of this blessing, as will acquire to them the glory of recommending it to the applause, the affection, and adoption of every nation, which is yet a stranger to it.

Here, perhaps, I ought to stop. But a solicitude for your welfare, which cannot end but with my life and the apprehension of danger, natural to that solicitude, urge me, on an occasion like the present, to offer to your solemn contemplation, and to recommend to your frequent review, some sentiments, which are the result of much reflection, of no inconsiderable observation, and which appear to me all-important to the permanency of your felicity as a people. These will be offered to you with the more freedom, as you can only see in them the disinterested warnings of a parting friend, who can possibly have no personal motive to bias his counsel. Nor can I forget, as an encouragement to it, your indulgent reception of my sentiments on a former and not dissimilar occasion.

H

Interwoven as is the love of liberty with every ligament of your hearts, no recommendation of mine is necessary to fortify or confirm the attachment.

The unity of government, which constitutes you one people, is also now dear to you. It is justly so, for it is a main pillar in the edifice of your real independence, the support of your tranquility at home, your peace abroad, of your safety; of your prosperity; of that very liberty, which you so highly prize. But as it is easy to foresee, that, from different causes and from different quarters, much pains will be taken, many artifices employed, to weaken in your minds the conviction of this truth; as this is the point in your political fortress against which the batteries of internal and external enemies will be most constantly and actively (though often covertly and insidiously) directed, it is of infinite moment that you should properly estimate the immense value of your national union to your collective and individual happiness; that you should cherish a cordial, habitual, and immovable attachment to it; accustoming yourselves to think and speak of it as of the palladium of your political safety and prosperity; watching for its preservation with jealous anxiety; discountenancing whatever may suggest even a suspicion, that it can in any event be abandoned; and indignantly frowning upon the first dawning of every attempt to alienate any portion of our country from the rest, or to enfeeble the sacred ties which now link together the various parts.

For this you have every inducement of sympathy and interest. Citizens, by birth or choice, of a common country, that country has a right to concentrate your affections. The name of American, which belongs to you, in your national capacity, must always exalt the just pride of patriotism, more than any appellation derived from local discriminations. With slight shades of difference, you have the same religion, manners, habits, and political principles. You have in a common cause fought and triumphed together; the independence and liberty you possess are the work of joint counsels, and joint efforts, of common dangers, sufferings, and successes.

But these considerations, however powerfully they address

themselves to your sensibility, are greatly outweighed by those which apply more immediately to your interest. Here every portion of our country finds the most commanding motives for carefully guarding and preserving the union of the whole.

The North, in an unrestrained intercourse with the South, protected by the equal laws of a common government, finds in the productions of the latter, great additional resources of maritime and commercial enterprise and precious materials of manufacturing industry. The South, in the same intercourse, benefiting by the agency of the North, sees its agriculture grow and its commerce expand. Turning partly into its own channels the seamen of the North, it finds its particular navigation invigorated; and, while it contributes, in different ways, to nourish and increase the general mass of the national navigation, it looks forward to the protection of a maritime strength, to which itself is unequally adapted. The East, in a like intercourse with the West, already finds, and in the progressive improvement of interior communications by land and water, will more and more find, a valuable vent for the commodities which it brings from abroad, or manufactures at home. The West derives from the East supplies requisite to its growth and comfort, and, what is perhaps of still greater consequence, it must of necessity owe the secure enjoyment of indispensable outlets for its own productions to the weight, influence, and the future maritime strength of the Atlantic side of the Union, directed by an indissoluble community of interest as one nation. Any other tenure by which the West can hold this essential advantage, whether derived from its own separate strength, or from an apostate and unnatural connexion with any foreign power, must be intrinsically precarious.

While, then, every part of our country thus feels an immediate and particular interest in union, all the parts combined cannot fail to find in the united mass of means and efforts greater strength, greater resource, proportionably greater security from external danger, a less frequent interruption of their peace by foreign nations; and, what is of inestimable value, they must derive from union an exemption from those broils and wars between themselves, which so frequently afflict neighboring countries not tied together by the same governments, which their own rivalships alone would be sufficient to produce, but which opposite foreign alliances, attachments, and intrigues would stimulate and embitter. Hence, likewise, they will avoid the necessity of those overgrown military establishments, which, under any form of government, are inauspicious to liberty, and which are to be regarded as particularly hostile to republican liberty. In this sense it is, that your union ought to be considered as a main prop of your liberty, and that the love of the one ought to endear to you the preservation of the other.

These considerations speak a persuasive language to every reflecting and virtuous mind, and exhibit the continuance of the Union as a primary object of patriotic desire. Is there a doubt whether a common government can embrace so large a sphere? Let experience solve it. To listen to mere speculation in such a case were criminal. We are authorized to hope, that a proper organization of the whole, with the auxiliary agency of governments for the respective subdivisions, will afford a happy issue to the experiment. It is well worth a fair and full experiment. With such powerful and obvious motives to union, affecting all parts of our country, while experience shall not have demonstrated its impracticability, there will always be reason to distrust the patriotism of those, who in any quarter may endeavor to weaken its bands.

In contemplating the causes which may disturb our Union, it occurs as matter of serious concern, that any ground should have been furnished for characterizing parties by geographical discriminations, northern and southern, Atlantic and western; whence designing men may endeavor to excite a belief that there is a real difference of local interests and views. One of the expedients of party to acquire influence, within particular districts, is to misrepresent the opinions and aims of other districts. You cannot shield yourselves too much against the jealousies and heart-burnings, which spring from these misrepresentations; they tend to render alien to each other those, who ought to be bound together by fraternal affection. The inhabitants of our western country have lately had a useful lesson on this head;

they have seen, in the negotiation by the Executive, and in the unanimous ratification by the Senate, of the treaty with Spain, and in the universal satisfaction at that event, throughout the United States, a decisive proof how unfounded were the suspicions propagated among them of a policy in the General Government and in the Atlantic States unfriendly to their interests in regard to the Mississippi; they have been witnesses to the formation of two treaties, that with Great Britain, and that with Spain, which secure to them every thing they could desire, in respect to our foreign relations, towards confirming their prosperity. Will it not be their wisdom to rely for the preservation of these advantages on the Union by which they were procured? Will they not henceforth be deaf to those advisers, if such there are, who would sever them from their brethren and connect them with aliens?

To the efficacy and permanency of your Union, a Government for the whole is indispensable. No alliances, however strict, between the parts can be an adequate substitute; they must inevitably experience the infractions and interruptions, which all alliances in all times have experienced. Sensible of this momentous truth, you have improved upon your first essay, by the adoption of a Constitution of Government better calculated than your former for an intimate Union, and for the efficacious management of your common concerns. This Government, the offspring of our own choice, uninfluenced and unawed, adopted upon full investigation and mature deliberation, completely free in its principles, in the distribution of its powers, uniting security with energy, and containing within itself a provision for its own amendment, has a just claim to your confidence and your support. Respect for its authority, compliance with its laws, acquiescence in its measures, are duties enjoined by the fundamental maxims of true Liberty. The basis of our political systems is the right of the people to make and to alter their constitutions of government. But the constitution which at any time exists, till changed by an explicit and authentic act of the whole people, is sacredly obligatory upon all. The very idea of the power and the right of the people to establish Government presupposes the duty of every individual to obey the established Government.

All obstructions to the execution of the laws, all combinations and associations, under whatever plausible character, with the real design to direct, control, counteract, or awe the regular deliberation and action of the constituted authorities, are destructive of this fundamental principle, and of fatal tendency. They serve to organize faction, to give it an artificial and extraordinary force; to put, in the place of the delegated will of the nation, the will of a party, often a small but artful and enterprising minority of the community; and, according to the alternate triumphs of different parties, to make the public administration the mirror of the ill-concerted and incongruous projects of faction, rather than the organ of consistent and wholesome plans digested by common counsels, and modified by mutual interests.

However combinations or associations of the above description may now and then answer popular ends, they are likely, in the course of time and things, to become potent engines, by which cunning, ambitious, and unprincipled men will be enabled to subvert the power of the people, and to usurp for themselves the reins of government; destroying afterwards the very engines which have lifted them to unjust dominion.

Towards the preservation of your government, and the permanency of your present happy state, it is requisite, not only that you steadily discountenance irregular oppositions to its acknowledged authority, but also that you resist with care the spirit of innovation upon its principles, however specious the pretexts. One method of assault may be to effect, in the forms of the constitution, alterations, which will impair the energy of the system, and thus to undermine what cannot be directly overthrown. In all the changes to which you may be invited, remember that time and habit are at least as necessary to fix the true character of governments, as of other human institutions; that experience is the surest standard, by which to test the real tendency of the existing constitution of a country; that facility in changes, upon the credit of mere hypothesis and opinion, exposes to perpetual change, from the endless variety of hypothesis and opinion; and remember, especially, that, for the efficient management of your common interests, in a country so extensive as ours, a government of as much vigor as is consistent with the perfect security of liberty is indispensable. Liberty itself will find in such a government, with powers properly distributed and adjusted, its surest guardian. It is, indeed, little else than a name, where the government is too feeble to withstand the enterprises of faction, to confine each member of the society within the limits prescribed by the laws, and to maintain all in the secure and tranquil enjoyment of the rights of person and property.

I have already intimated to you the danger of parties in the state, with particular reference to the founding of them on geographical discriminations. Let me now take a more comprehensive view, and warn you in the most solemn manner against the baneful effects of the spirit of party, generally.

This spirit, unfortunately, is inseparable from our nature, having its root in the strongest passions of the human mind. It exists under different shapes in all governments, more or less stifled, controlled, or repressed; but, in those of the popular form, it is seen in its greatest rankness, and is truly their worst enemy.

The alternate domination of one faction over another, sharpened by the spirit of revenge, natural to party dissension, which in different ages and countries has perpetrated the most horrid enormities, is itself a frightful despotism. But this leads at length to a more formal and permanent despotism. The disorders and miseries, which result, gradually incline the minds of men to seek security and repose in the absolute power of an individual; and sooner or later the chief of some prevailing faction, more able or more fortunate than his competitors, turns this disposition to the purposes of his own elevation, on the ruins of public liberty.

Without looking forward to an extremity of this kind (which nevertheless ought not to be entirely out of sight), the common and continual mischiefs of the spirit of party are sufficient to make it the interest and duty of a wise people to discourage and restrain it.

It serves always to distract the public councils, and enfeeble the public administration. It agitates the community with ill-founded jealousies and false alarms; kindles the animosity of one part against another, foments occasionally riot and insurrection. It opens the door to foreign influence and corruption, which find a facilitated access to the government itself through the channels of party passions. Thus the policy and the will of one country are subjected to the policy and will of another.

There is an opinion, that parties in free countries are useful checks upon the administration of the government, and serve to keep alive the spirit of liberty. This within certain limits is probably true; and in governments of a monarchical cast, patriotism may look with indulgence, if not with favor, upon the spirit of party. But in those of the popular character, in governments purely elective, it is a spirit not to be encouraged. From their natural tendency, it is certain there will always be enough of that spirit for every salutary purpose. And, there being constant danger of excess, the effort ought to be, by force of public opinion, to mitigate and assuage it. A fire not to be quenched, it demands a uniform vigilance to prevent its bursting into a flame, lest, instead of warming, it should consume.

It is important, likewise, that the habits of thinking in a free country should inspire caution, in those intrusted with its administration, to confine themselves within their respective constitutional spheres, avoiding in the exercise of the powers of one department to encroach upon another. The spirit of encroachment tends to consolidate the powers of all the departments in one, and thus to create, whatever the form of government, a real depotism. A just estimate of that love of power, and proneness to abuse it, which predominates in the human heart, is sufficient to satisfy us of the truth of this position. The necessity of reciprocal checks in the exercise of political power, by dividing and distributing it into different depositories, and constituting each the guardian of the public weal against invasions by the others, has been evinced by experiments ancient and modern; some of them in our country and under our own eyes. To preserve them must be as necessary as to institute them. If, in the opinion of the people, the distribution or modification of the constitutional powers be in any particular wrong, let it be corrected by an amendment in the way which the constitution designates. But let there be no change by usurpation; for, though this, in one instance, may be the instrument of good, it is the customary weapon by which free governments are destroyed. The precedent must always greatly overbalance in permanent evil any partial or transient benefit, which the use can at any time yield.

Of all the dispositions and habits, which lead to political prosperity, religion and morality are indispensable supports. In vain would that man claim the tribute of patriotism, who should labor to subvert these great pillars of human happiness, these firmest props of the duties of men and citizens. The mere politician, equally with the pious man, ought to respect and cherish them. A volume could not trace all their connexions with private and public felicity. Let it simply be asked, Where is the security for property, for reputation, for life, if the sense of religious obligation desert the oaths, which are the instruments of investigation in courts of justice? And let us with caution indulge the supposition, that morality can be maintained without religion. Whatever may be conceded to the influence of refined education on minds of peculiar structure, reason and experience both forbid us to expect, that national morality can prevail in exclusion of religious principle.

It is substantially true, that virtue or morality is a necessary spring of popular government. The rule, indeed, extends with more or less force to every species of free government. Who, that is a sincere friend to it, can look with indifference upon attempts to shake the foundation of the fabric?

Promote, then, as an object of primary importance, institutions for the general diffusion of knowledge. In proportion as the structure of a government gives force to public opinion, it is essential that public opinion should be enlightened.

As a very important source of strength and security, cherish public credit. One method of preserving it is, to use it as sparingly as possible; avoiding occasions of expense by cultivating peace, but remembering also that timely disbursements to prepare for danger frequently prevent much greater disbursements to repel it; avoiding likewise the accumulation of debt, not only by shunning occasions of expense, but by vigorous exertion in time of peace to discharge the debts, which unavoidable wars may have occasioned, not ungenerously throwing upon posterity the burden which we ourselves ought to bear. The execution of these maxims belongs to your representatives, but it is necessary that public opinion should coöperate. To facilitate to them the performance of their duty, it is essential that you should practically bear in mind, that towards the payment of debts there must be revenue; that to have revenue there must be taxes; that no taxes can be devised which are not more or less inconvenient and unpleasant; that the intrinsic embarrassment, inseparable from the selection of the proper objects (which is always a choice of difficulties), ought to be a decisive motive for a candid construction of the conduct of the government in making it, and for a spirit of acquiescence in the measures for obtaining revenue, which the public exigencies may at any time dictate.

Observe good faith and justice towards all nations; cultivate peace and harmony with all. Religion and morality enjoin this conduct; and can it be, that good policy does not equally enjoin it? It will be worthy of a free, enlightened, and at no distant period, a great nation, to give to mankind the magnanimous and too novel example of a people always guided by an exalted justice and benevolence. Who can doubt, that in the course of time and things, the fruits of such a plan would richly repay any temporary advantages which might be lost by a steady adherence to it? Can it be that Providence has not connected the permanent felicity of a nation with its virtue? The experiment, at least, is recommended by every sentiment which ennobles human nature. Alas! is it rendered impossible by its vices?

In the execution of such a plan, nothing is more essential, than that permanent, inveterate antipathies against particular nations, and passionate attachments for others, should be excluded; and that, in place of them, just and amicable feelings towards all should be cultivated. The nation, which indulges towards another an habitual hatred, or an habitual fondness, is in some degree a slave. It is a slave to its animosity or to its affection, either of which is sufficient to lead it astray from its duty and its interest. Antipathy in one nation against another disposes each more readily to offer insult and injury, to lay hold of slight causes of umbrage, and to be haughty and intractable, when accidental or trifling occasions of dispute occur. Hence, frequent collisions, obstinate, envenomed, and bloody contests. The nation, prompted by ill-will and resentment, sometimes impels to war the Government, contrary to the best calculations of policy. The Government sometimes participates in the national propensity, and adopts through passion what reason would reject; at other times, it makes the animosity of the nation subservient to projects of hostility instigated by pride, ambition, and other sinister and pernicious motives. The peace often, sometimes perhaps the liberty, of nations has been the victim.

So likewise, a passionate attachment of one nation for another produces a variety of evils. Sympathy for the favorite nation, facilitating the illusion of an imaginary common interest in cases where no real common interest exists, and infusing into one the enmities of the other, betrays the former into a participation in the quarrels and wars of the latter, without adequate inducement or justification. It leads also to concessions to the favorite nation of privileges denied to others, which is apt doubly to injure the nation making the concessions; by unnecessarily parting with what ought to have been retained; and by exciting jealousy, ill-will, and a disposition to retaliate, in the parties from whom equal privileges are withheld. And it gives to ambitious, corrupted, or deluded citizens (who devote themselves to the favorite nation), facility to betray or sacrifice the interests of their own country, without odium, sometimes even with popularity; gilding, with the appearances of a virtuous sense of obligation, a commendable deference for public opinion, or a laudable zeal for public good, the base or foolish compliances of ambition, corruption or infatuation.

As avenues to foreign influence in innumberable ways, such attachments are particularly alarming to the truly enlightened and independent patriot. How many opportunities do they afford to tamper with domestic factions, to practice the arts of seduction, to mislead public opinion, to influence or awe the public councils! Such an attachment of a small or weak, towards a great and powerful nation, dooms the former to be the satellite of the latter.

Against the insidious wiles of foreign influence (I conjure you to believe me, fellow-citizens), the jealousy of a free people ought to be constantly awake, since history and experience prove that foreign influence is one of the most baneful foes of republican government. But that jealousy, to be useful, must be impartial; else it becomes the instrument of the very influence to be avoided, instead of a defence against it. Excessive partiality for one foreign nation, and excessive dislike of another, cause those whom they actuate to see danger only on one side, and serve to veil and even second the arts of influence on the other. Real patriots who may resist the intrigues of the favorite, are liable to become suspected and odious; while its tools and dupes usurp the applause and confidence of the people, to surrender their interests.

The great rule of conduct for us, in regard to foreign nations, is, in extending our commercial relations, to have with them as little political connexion as possible. So far as we have already formed engagements, let them be fulfilled with perfect good faith. Here let us stop.

Europe has a set of primary interests, which to us have none, or a very remote relation. Hence she must be engaged in frequent controversies, the causes of which are essentially foreign to our concerns. Hence, therefore, it must be unwise in us to implicate ourselves, by artificial ties, in the ordinary vicissitudes of her politics, or the ordinary combinations and collisions of her friendships or enmities.

Our detached and distant situation invites and enables us to pursue a different course. If we remain one people, under an efficient government, the period is not far off when we may defy material injury from external annoyance; when we may take such an attitude as will cause the neutrality, we may at any time resolve upon, to be scrupulously respected; when belligerent nations, under the impossibility of making acquisitions upon us, will not lightly hazard the giving us provocation; when we may choose peace or war, as our interest, guided by justice, shall counsel.

Why forego the advantages of so peculiar a situation? Why quit our own to stand upon foreign ground? Why, by interweaving our destiny with that of any part of Europe, entangle our peace and prosperity in the toils of European ambition, rivalship, interest, humor or caprice?

It is our true policy to steer clear of permanent alliances with any portion of the foreign world; so far, I mean, as we are now at liberty to do it; for let me not be understood as capable of patronizing infidelity to existing engagements. I hold the maxim no less applicable to public than to private affairs, that honesty is always the best policy. I repeat it, therefore, let those engagements be observed in their genuine sense. But, in my opinion, it is unnecessary and would be unwise to extend them.

Taking care always to keep ourselves, by suitable establishments, on a respectable defensive posture, we may safely trust to temporary alliances for extraordinary emergencies.

Harmony, liberal intercourse with all nations, are recommended by policy, humanity, and interest. But even our commercial policy should hold an equal and impartial hand; neither seeking nor granting exclusive favors or preferences; consulting the natural course of things; diffusing and diversifying by gentle means the streams of commerce, but forcing nothing; establishing, with powers so disposed, in order to give trade a stable course, to define the rights of our merchants, and to enable the government to support them, conventional rules of intercourse, the best that present circumstances and mutual opinion will permit, but temporary, and liable to be from time to time abandoned or varied, as experience and circumstances shall dictate; constantly keeping in view, that it is folly in one nation to look for disinterested favors from another; that it must pay with a portion of its independence for whatever it may accept under that character; that, by such acceptance, it may place itself in the condition of having given equivalents for nominal favors, and yet of being reproached with ingratitude for not giving more. There can be no greater error than to expect or calculate upon real favors from nation to nation. It is an illusion, which experience must cure, which a just pride ought to discard.

In offering to you, my countrymen, these counsels of an old and affectionate friend, I dare not hope they will make the strong and lasting impression I could wish; that they will control the usual current of the passions, or prevent our nation from running the course, which has hitherto marked the destiny of nations. But, if I may even flatter myself, that they may be productive of some partial benefit, some occasional good; that they may now and then recur to moderate the fury of party spirit, to warn against the mischiefs of foreign intrigue, to guard against the impostures of pretended patriotism; this hope will be a full recompense for the solicitude for your welfare, by which they have been dictated.

How far in the discharge of my official duties I have been guided by the principles which have been delineated, the public records and other evidences of my conduct must witness to you and to the world. To myself, the assurance of my own conscience, is, that I have at least believed myself to be guided by them.

In relation to the still subsisting war in Europe, my proclamation of the 22d of April, 1793, is the index of my plan. Sanctioned by your approving voice, and by that of your Representatives in both Houses of Congress, the spirit of that measure has continually governed me, uninfluenced by any attempts to deter or divert me from it.

After deliberate examination, with the aid of the best lights I could obtain, I was well satisfied that our country, under all the circumstances of the case, had a right to take, and was bound in duty and interest to take, a neutral position. Having taken it, I determined, as far as should depend upon me, to maintain it, with moderation, perseverance and firmness.

The considerations which respect the right to hold this conduct, it is not necessary on this occasion to detail. I will only observe, that, according to my understanding of the matter, that right, so far from being denied by any of the belligerent powers, has been virtually admitted by all.

The duty of holding a neutral conduct may be inferred, without any thing more, from the obligation which justice and humanity impose on every nation, in cases in which it is free to act, to maintain inviolate the relations of peace and amity towards other nations.

The inducements of interest for observing that conduct will best be referred to your own reflections and experience. With me a predominant motive has been to endeavor to gain time to our country to settle and mature its yet recent institutions, and to progress without interruption to that degree of strength and consistency, which is necessary to give it, humanly speaking, the command of its own fortunes.

Though, in reviewing the incidents of my administration, I am unconscious of intentional error, I am nevertheless too sensible of my defects not to think it probable that I may have committed many errors. Whatever they may be I fervently beseech the Almighty to avert or mitigate the evils to which they may tend. I shall also carry with me the hope, that my country will never cease to view them with indulgence; and that, after forty-five years of my life dedicated to its service with an upright zeal, the faults of incompetent abilities will be consigned to oblivion, as myself must soon be to the mansions of rest.

Relying on its kindness in this as in other things, and actuated by that fervent love towards it, which is so natural to a man who views in it the native soil of himself and his progenitors for several generations, I anticipate with pleasing expectation that retreat, in which I promise myself to realize, without alloy, the sweet enjoyment of partaking, in the midst of my fellow-citizens, the benign influence of good laws under a free government, the ever favorite object of my heart, and the happy reward, as I trust, of our mutual cares, labors, and dangers.

THE MONROE DOCTRINE

JAMES MONROE

[James Monroe (1758–1831), the fifth President of the United States, was born in Westmoreland County, Virginia. After the Revolutionary War, in which he had served, Monroe entered public life, at first filling minor offices and later serving as governor of Virginia, United States senator, minister to England, minister to France, secretary of state under President Madison, and was twice elected President of the United States. One of the leading events of his administration was the announcement of the principle of foreign policy that has come to be called the Monroe Doctrine. The enunciation of this policy was in the Presidential message of December, 1823, and was made necessary by certain things done by Russia and by Spain. The former had taken possession of Alaska and was extending its settlements down the Pacific Coast. The latter was seeking the aid of other European countries in recovering control of his American colonies which had rebelled and won a temporary freedom. England was desirous for commercial reasons that these new republics should not fall under the power of Spain again, and proposed to the United States that they jointly should help the South American countries to maintain their freedom. Monroe, however, thought it best to make the declaration independent of Great Britain. This doctrine was not new with Monroe. As a matter of fact, it had been a settled policy for years before being proclaimed by Monroe. It was effective at the time in checking the encroachments of Russia and Spain, and since then has been called into operation on several occasions, the most notable being in 1865 against France in Mexico, and in 1895 against England in Venezuela. The statement of the original Monroe Doctrine appears in two passages of the Message, which are as follows:]

At the proposal of the Russian Imperial Government, made through the minister of the Emperor residing here, a full power and instructions have been transmitted to the minister of the United States at St. Petersburg to arrange by amicable negotiation the respective rights and interests of the two nations on the northwest coast of this continent. A similar proposal had been made by His Imperial Majesty to the Government of Great Britain, which has likewise been acceded to. The Government of the United States has been desirous by this friendly proceeding of manifesting the great value which they have invariably attached to the friendship of the Emperor and their solicitude to cultivate the best understanding with his Government.

In the discussions to which this interest has given rise and in the arrangements by which they may terminate, the occasion has been judged proper for asserting, as a principle in which the rights and interests of the United States are involved, that the American continents, by the free and independent condition which they have assumed and maintain, are henceforth not to be considered as subjects for future colonization by any European powers. . . .

It was stated at the commencement of the last session that a great effort was then making in Spain and Portugal to improve the condition of the people of those countries, and that it appeared to be conducted with extraordinary moderation. It need scarcely be remarked that the result has been so far very different from what was then anticipated. Of events in that quarter of the globe, with which we have so much intercourse and from which we derive our origin, we have always been anxious and interested spectators. The citizens of the United States cherish sentiments the most friendly in favor of the liberty and happiness of their fellowmen on that side of the Atlantic. In the wars of the European powers in matters relating to themselves we have never taken any part, nor does it comport with our policy so to do. It is only when our rights are invaded or seriously menaced that we resent injuries or make preparation for our defense.

With the movements in this hemisphere we are of necessity more immediately connected, and by causes which must be obvious to all enlightened and impartial observers. The political system of the allied powers is essentially different in this respect from that of America. This difference proceeds from that which exists in their respective Governments; and to the defense of our own, which has been achieved by the loss of so much blood and treasure, and matured by the wisdom of their most enlightened citizens, and under which we have enjoyed unexampled felicity, this whole nation is devoted.

I

We owe it, therefore, to candor and the amicable relations existing between the United States and those powers to declare that we should consider any attempt on their part to extend their system to any portion of this hemisphere as dangerous to our peace and safety. With the existing colonies or dependencies of any European power we have not interfered and shall not interfere. But with the Governments who have declared their independence and maintained it, and whose independence we have, on great consideration and on just principles, acknowledged, we could not view any interposition for the purpose of oppressing them, or controlling in any other manner their destiny, by any European power, in any other light than as the manifestation of an unfriendly disposition toward the United States. In the war between those new Governments and Spain we declared our neutrality at the time of their recognition, and to this we have adhered, and shall continue to adhere, provided no change shall occur which, in the judgment of the competent authorities of this Government, shall make a corresponding change on the part of the United States indispensable to their security.

The late events in Spain and Portugal show that Europe is still unsettled. Of this important fact no stronger proof can be adduced than that the allied powers should have thought it proper, on any principle satisfactory to themselves, to have interposed by force in the internal concerns of Spain. To what extent such interposition may be carried, on the same principle, is a question in which all independent powers whose governments differ from theirs are interested, even those most remote, and surely none more so than the United States.

Our policy in regard to Europe, which was adopted at an early stage of the wars which have so long agitated that quarter of the globe, nevertheless remains the same, which is, not to interfere in the internal concerns of any of its powers; to consider the government *de facto* as the legitimate government for us; to cultivate friendly relations with it, and to preserve those relations by a frank, firm, and manly policy, meeting in all instances the just claims of every power, submitting to injuries from none.

But in regard to those continents circumstances are eminently and conspicuously different. It is impossible that the allied powers should extend their political system to any portion of either continent without endangering our peace and happiness; nor can any one believe that our southern brethren, if left to themselves, would adopt it of their own accord. It is equally impossible, therefore, that we should behold such interposition in any form with indifference.

If we look to the comparative strength and resources of Spain and those new Governments, and their distance from each other, it must be obvious that she can never subdue them. It is still the true policy of the United States to leave the parties to themselves, in the hope that other powers will pursue the same course.

THE STATES AND THE UNION

DANIEL WEBSTER

[Daniel Webster (1782–1852) was born in New Hampshire, but in his public career is associated with Massachusetts. He was twice senator from that state; was secretary of state under Harrison and Tyler and under Fillmore; and was twice an unsuccessful candidate for the nomination for President. As an orator, Webster was one of the most noted in the history of American politics. In political theories, Webster is the great expounder and defender of the Constitution from the national point of view. His opponents were the states-rights school of political thinkers led by Calhoun. In 1832 Hayne, of South Carolina, and Webster engaged in their memorable debate over the rights of the States and the National Government. Hayne argued for state's rights and nullification; Webster, for nationality and union. Though Hayne was historically correct in his interpretation of the Constitution, he gave utterance to the ideals of the past. Webster, though historically inaccurate at points, spoke the mind of the future, and posterity has given him the greater praise. The extract here given, though but a small portion of the entire speech, indicates Webster's position.]

I must now beg to ask, Sir, whence is this supposed right of the States derived? Where do they find the power to interfere with the laws of the Union? Sir, the opinion which the honorable gentleman maintains is a notion founded in a total misappre-

hension, in my judgment, of the origin of this government, and
of the foundation on which it stands. I hold it to be a popular
government, erected by the people; those who administer it,
responsible to the people; and itself capable of being amended
and modified, just as the people may choose it should be. It
is as popular, just as truly emanating from the people, as the
State governments. It is created for one purpose; the State
governments for another. It has its own powers; they have
theirs. There is no more authority with them to arrest the
operation of a law of Congress, than with Congress to arrest the
operation of their laws. We are here to administer a Constitution emanating immediately from the people, and trusted by
them to our administration. It is not the creature of the State
governments. It is of no moment to the argument, that certain
acts of the State legislatures are necessary to fill our seats in this
body. That is not one of their original State powers, a part of
the sovereignty of the State. It is a duty which the people, by
the Constitution itself, have imposed on the State legislatures,
and which they might have left to be performed elsewhere, if
they had seen fit. So they have left the choice of President with
electors; but all this does not affect the proposition that this
whole government, President, Senate, and House of Representatives, is a popular government. It leaves it still all its popular
character. The governor of a State (in some of the States) is
chosen, not directly by the people, but by those who are chosen
by the people for the purpose of performing, among other duties,
that of electing a governor. Is the government of the State, on
that account, not a popular government? This government, Sir,
is the independent offspring of the popular will. It is not the
creature of State legislatures; nay more, if the whole truth must
be told, the people brought it into existence, established it, and
have hitherto supported it, for the very purpose, amongst
others, of imposing certain salutary restraints on State sover-
eignties. The States cannot now make war; they cannot contract alliances; they cannot make, each for itself, separate regulations of commerce; they cannot lay imposts; they cannot coin
money. If this Constitution, Sir, be the creature of State legis-

latures, it must be admitted that it has obtained a strange control over the volitions of its creators.

The people, then, Sir, erected this government. They gave it a Constitution, and in that Constitution they have enumerated the powers which they bestow on it. They have made it a limited government. They have defined its authority. They have restrained it to the exercise of such powers as are granted; and all others, they declare, are reserved to the States or the people. But, Sir, they have not stopped here. If they had, they would have accomplished but half their work. No definition can be so clear as to avoid possibility of doubt; no limitation so precise as to exclude all uncertainty. Who, then, shall construe this grant of the people? Who shall interpret their will, where it may be supposed they have left it doubtful? With whom do they repose this ultimate right of deciding on the powers of the government? Sir, they have settled all this in the fullest manner. They have left it with the government itself in its appropriate branches. Sir, the very chief end, the main design for which the whole Constitution was framed and adopted, was to establish a government that should not be obliged to act through State agency, or depend on State opinion and State discretion. The people had had quite enough of that kind of government under the Confederation. Under that system the legal action, the application of law to individuals, belonged exclusively to the States. Congress could only recommend; their acts were not of binding force till the States had adopted and sanctioned them. Are we in that condition still? Are we yet at the mercy of State discretion and State construction? Sir, if we are, then vain will be our attempt to maintain the Constitution under which we sit.

But, Sir, the people have wisely provided in the Constitution itself a proper, suitable mode and tribunal for settling questions of constitutional law. There are in the Constitution grants of powers to Congress, and restrictions on these powers. There are, also, prohibitions on the States. Some authority must, therefore, necessarily exist, having the ultimate jurisdiction to fix and ascertain the interpretation of these grants, restrictions, and prohibitions. The Constitution has itself pointed out, ordained, and established that authority. How has it accomplished this great and essential end? By declaring, Sir, that *"the Constitution and the laws of the United States made in pursuance thereof shall be the supreme law of the land, anything in the Constitution or laws of any State to the contrary notwithstanding."*

This, Sir, was the first great step. By this the supremacy of the Constitution and laws of the United States is declared. The people so will it. No State law is to be valid which comes in conflict with the Constitution or any law of the United States passed in pursuance of it. But who shall decide this question of interference? To whom lies the last appeal? This, Sir, the Constitution itself decides also, by declaring, *"that the judicial power shall extend to all cases arising under the Constitution and laws of the United States."* These two provisions cover the whole ground. They are, in truth, the keystone of the arch! With these, it is a government; without them it is a confederation. In pursuance of these clear and express provisions, Congress established at its very first session, in the judicial act, a mode for carrying them into full effect, and for bringing all questions of constitutional power to the final decision of the Supreme Court. It then, Sir, became a government. It then had the means of self-protection; and, but for this, it would, in all probability, have been now among things which are past. Having constituted the government and declared its powers, the people have further said that, since somebody must decide on the extent of these powers, the government shall itself decide; subject always, like other popular governments, to its responsibility to the people. And now, Sir, I repeat, how is it that a State legislature acquires any power to interfere? Who, or what, gives them the right to say to the people: "We, who are your agents and servants for one purpose, will undertake to decide that your other agents and servants, appointed by you for another purpose, have transcended the authority you gave them!" The reply would be, I think, not impertinent: "Who made you a judge over another's servants? To their own masters they stand or fall."

Sir, I deny this power of State legislatures altogether. It cannot stand the test of examination. Gentlemen may say that, in an extreme case, a State government might protect the people from intolerable oppression. Sir, in such a case, the people might protect themselves without the aid of the State governments. Such a case warrants revolution. It must make, when it comes, a law for itself. A nullifying act of a State legislature cannot alter the case, nor make resistance any more lawful. In maintaining these sentiments, Sir, I am but asserting the rights of the people. I state what they have declared, and insist on their right to declare it. They have chosen to repose this power in the general government, and I think it my duty to support it, like other constitutional powers. . . .

But, Sir, what is this danger, and what the grounds of it? Let it be remembered that the Constitution of the United States is not unalterable. It is to continue in its present form no longer than the people who established it shall choose to continue it. If they shall become convinced that they have made an injudicious or inexpedient partition and distribution of power between the State governments and the general government, they can alter that distribution at will.

If anything be found in the national Constitution either by original provision or subsequent interpretation, which ought not to be in it, the people know how to get rid of it. If any construction unacceptable to them be established, so as to become practically a part of the Constitution, they will amend it at their own sovereign pleasure. But while the people choose to maintain it as it is, while they are satisfied with it, and refuse to change it, who has given, or who can give, to the State legislatures a right to alter it either by interference, construction, or otherwise? Gentlemen do not seem to recollect that the people have any power to do anything for themselves. They imagine there is no safety for them, any longer than they are under the close guardianship of the State legislatures. Sir, the people have not trusted their safety, in regard to the general Constitution, to these hands. They have required other security, and taken other bonds. They have chosen to trust themselves, first, to the plain words of the instrument, and to such construction as the government itself, in doubtful cases, should put on its own powers, under its oaths of office, and subject to its responsibility to them; just as the people of a State trust their own State governments with a similar power. Secondly, they have reposed their trust in the efficacy of frequent elections and in their own power to remove their own servants and agents whenever they see cause. Thirdly, they have reposed trust in the judicial power, which, in order that it might be trustworthy, they have made as respectable, as disinterested, and as independent as was practicable. Fourthly, they have seen fit to rely, in case of necessity or high expediency, on their known and admitted power to alter or amend the Constitution peaceably and quietly, whenever experience shall point out defects or imperfections. And, finally, the people of the United States have at no time, in no way, directly or indirectly, authorized any State legislature to construe or interpret their high instrument of government; much less to interfere by their own power to arrest its course and operation.

If, Sir, the people in these respects had done otherwise than they have done, their Constitution could neither have been preserved, nor would it have been worth preserving. And if its plain provisions shall now be disregarded, and these new doctrines interpolated in it, it will become as feeble and helpless a being as its enemies, whether early or more recent, could possibly desire. It will exist in every State but as a poor dependant on State permission. It must borrow leave to be; and will be no longer than State pleasure, or State discretion, sees fit to grant the indulgence and to prolong its poor existence.

But, Sir, although there are fears, there are hopes also. The people have preserved this, their own chosen Constitution, for forty years, and have seen their happiness, prosperity, and renown grow with its growth, and strengthen with its strength. They are now, generally, strongly attached to it. Overthrown by direct assault, it cannot be; evaded, undermined, nullified, it will not be, if we, and those who shall succeed us here as agents and representatives of the people, shall conscientiously and vigilantly discharge the two great branches of our public trust, faithfully to preserve, and wisely to administer it.

Mr. President, I have thus stated the reasons of my dissent to the doctrines which have been advanced and maintained. I am conscious of having detained you and the Senate much too long. I was drawn into the debate with no previous deliberation such as is suited to the discussion of so grave and important a subject. But it is a subject of which my heart is full, and I have not been willing to suppress the utterance of its spontaneous sentiments. I cannot, even now, persuade myself to relinquish it without expressing once more my deep conviction that, since it respects nothing less than the Union of the States, it is of most vital and essential importance to the public happiness. I profess, Sir, in my career hitherto to have kept steadily in view the prosperity and honor of the whole country, and the preservation of our Federal Union. It is to that Union we owe our safety at home, and our consideration and dignity abroad. It is to that Union that we are chiefly indebted for whatever makes us most proud of our country. That Union we reached only by the discipline of our virtues in the severe school of adversity. It had its origin in the necessities of disordered finance, prostrate commerce, and ruined credit. Under its benign influences, these great interests immediately awoke as from the dead, and sprang forth with newness of life. Every year of its duration has teemed with fresh proofs of its utility and its blessings; and although our territory has stretched out wider and wider, and our population spread farther and farther, they have not outrun its protection or its benefits. It has been to us all a copious fountain of national, social, and personal happiness.

I have not allowed myself, Sir, to look beyond the Union to see what might lie hidden in the dark recess behind. I have not coolly weighed the chances of preserving liberty, when the bonds that unite us together shall be broken asunder. I have not accustomed myself to hang over the precipice of disunion, to see whether, with my short sight, I can fathom the depth of the abyss below; nor could I regard him as a safe counsellor in the affairs of this government, whose thoughts should be mainly bent on considering, not how the Union should be best preserved, but how tolerable might be the condition of the people when it should be broken up and destroyed. While the Union lasts, we have high, exciting, gratifying prospects spread out before us—for us and our children. Beyond that, I seek not to penetrate the veil. God grant that, in my day, at least, that curtain may not rise! God grant that on my vision never may be opened what lies behind! When my eyes shall be turned to behold for the last time the sun in heaven, may I not see him shining on the broken and dishonored fragments of a once glorious Union; on States dissevered, discordant, belligerent; on a land rent with civil feuds, or drenched, it may be, in fraternal blood! Let their last feeble and lingering glance rather behold the gorgeous ensign of the Republic, now known and honored throughout the earth, still full high advanced, its arms and trophies streaming in their original lustre, not a stripe erased or polluted, nor a single star obscured; bearing for its motto, no such miserable interrogatory as "What is all this worth?" nor those other words of delusion and folly, "Liberty first, and Union afterwards;" but everywhere, spread all over in characters of living light, blazing on all its ample folds, as they float over the sea and over the land and in every wind under the whole heavens, that other sentiment, dear to every true American heart—Liberty *and* Union, now and forever, one and inseparable!

SECOND INAUGURAL ADDRESS

ABRAHAM LINCOLN

[Abraham Lincoln (1809–1865), the sixteenth President of the United States, was born in Hardin (now Larue) County, Kentucky. As a very young boy, he removed with his parents to Indiana. His early education was scanty; a little reading, writing, and arithmetic was all. But taking hold of the hard facts of life and being stimulated and educated by necessity, Lincoln steadily rose to positions of public trust and usefulness. By middle life he had come to stand high at the Bar and seemed to be becoming more and more interested in his profession. But the slavery agitation drew him into politics, and in the famous debates with Stephen A. Douglas on this question Lincoln rose to be the leader of the Republican party. In 1860 he was nominated and elected to the Presidency, and in 1864 he was reëlected. His career as President was ended by his death at the hand of an assassin, April 14, 1865. His Second Inaugural Address was delivered on March 4, 1865. It is a political document marked by a feeling of mingled hopefulness and determination, and by the absence of sectional bitterness. Lincoln himself thought it would "wear as well" as anything he had produced. For further light on Lincoln's character see the selection, *Lincoln as an American*, by Croly, this volume, page 74.]

Fellow-Countrymen—At this second appearing to take the oath of the Presidential office, there is less occasion for an extended address than there was at the first. Then a statement somewhat in detail of a course to be pursued seemed very fitting and proper. Now, at the expiration of four years, during which public declarations have been constantly called forth on every point and phase of the great contest which still absorbs the attention and engrosses the energies of the nation, little that is new could be presented.

The progress of our arms, upon which all else chiefly depends, is as well known to the public as to myself, and it is, I trust, reasonably satisfactory and encouraging to all. With high hope for the future, no prediction in regard to it is ventured.

On the occasion corresponding to this four years ago, all thoughts were anxiously directed to an impending civil war. All dreaded it, all sought to avoid it. While the inaugural address was being delivered from this place, devoted altogether to saving the Union without war, insurgent agents were in the city, seeking to destroy it with war—seeking to dissolve the Union and divide the effects by negotiation. Both parties deprecated war, but one of them would make war rather than let the nation survive, and the other would accept war rather than let it perish, and the war came. One-eighth of the whole population were colored slaves, not distributed generally over the Union, but localized in the southern part of it. These slaves constituted a peculiar and powerful interest. All knew that this interest was somehow the cause of the war. To strengthen, perpetuate, and extend this interest was the object for which the insurgents would rend the Union by war, while the Government claimed no right to do more than to restrict the territorial enlargement of it.

Neither party expected for the war the magnitude or the duration which it has already attained. Neither anticipated that the cause of the conflict might cease, even before the conflict itself should cease. Each looked for an easier triumph, and a result less fundamental and astounding.

Both read the same Bible and pray to the same God, and each invokes His aid against the other. It may seem strange that any men should dare to ask a just God's assistance in wringing their bread from the sweat of other men's faces, but let us judge not, that we be not judged. The prayer of both could not be answered. That of neither has been answered fully. The Almighty has His own purposes. Woe unto the world because of offences, for it must needs be that offences come, but woe to that man by whom the offence cometh. If we shall suppose that American slavery is one of these offences which, in the providence of God, must needs come, but which having continued through His appointed time, He now wills to remove, and that He gives to both North and South this terrible war as the woe due to those by whom the offence came, shall we discern there any departure from those Divine attributes which the believers in a living God always ascribe to Him? Fondly do we hope, fervently do we pray, that this mighty scourge of war may speedily pass away. Yet if God wills that it continue until all the wealth piled by the bondsman's two hundred and fifty years of unrequited toil shall be sunk, and until every drop of blood drawn with the lash shall be paid by another drawn with the sword, as was said three thousand years ago, so, still it must be said, that the judgments of the Lord are true and righteous altogether.

With malice towards none, with charity for all, with firmness in the right as God gives us to see the right, let us finish the work we are in, to bind up the nation's wounds, to care for him who shall have borne the battle, and for his widow and his orphans, to do all which may achieve and cherish a just and a lasting peace among ourselves and with all nations.

WAR MESSAGE—APRIL 2, 1917

WOODROW WILSON

[Woodrow Wilson (1856————), the twenty-eighth President of the United States, was born in Staunton, Virginia. After graduating from Princeton in 1879, he studied law at the University of Virginia and began practice at Atlanta, Georgia. Later he studied history and politics at Johns Hopkins University, and taught those subjects successively at Bryn Mawr, Wesleyan, and Princeton. In 1902 he became president of Princeton, and continued in this position until his political career began in 1910 with his election as governor of New Jersey. Two years later he was elected President of the United States, and in 1916 he was reëlected. His state papers—especially those dealing with the relations between the United States and Germany—have commanded wide attention for their statesmanlike principles and their forcible style. Of these several papers—all of which are worthy of attention—this one of April 2, 1917, in which he laid before Congress the facts and suggested a declaration of war, will always be memorable.]

I have called the Congress into extraordinary session because there are serious, very serious, choices of policy to be made, and made immediately, which it was neither right nor constitutionally permissible that I should assume the responsibility of making.

On the 3d of February last I officially laid before you the extraordinary announcement of the Imperial German Government that on and after the first day of February it was its purpose to put aside all restraints of law or of humanity and use its submarines to sink every vessel that sought to approach either the ports of Great Britain and Ireland or the western coasts of Europe or any of the ports controlled by the enemies of Germany within the Mediterranean. That had seemed to be the object of the German submarine warfare earlier in the war, but since April of last year the Imperial Government had somewhat restrained the commanders of its undersea craft in conformity with its promise then given to us that passenger-boats should not be sunk, and that due warning would be given to all other vessels which its submarines might seek to destroy where no resistance was offered or escape attempted, and care taken that their crews were given at least a fair chance to save their lives in their open boats.

The precautions taken were meager and haphazard enough, as was proved in distressing instance after instance in the progress of the cruel and unmanly business, but a certain degree of restraint was observed.

The new policy has swept every restriction aside. Vessels of every kind, whatever their flag, their character, their cargo, their destination, their errand, have been ruthlessly sent to the bottom without warning, and without thought of help or mercy for those on board, the vessels of friendly neutrals along with those of belligerents. Even hospital-ships and ships carrying relief to the sorely bereaved and stricken people of Belgium, though the latter were provided with safe conduct through the proscribed areas by the German Government itself and were distinguished by unmistakable marks of identity, have been sunk with the same reckless lack of compassion or of principle.

I was for a little while unable to believe that such things would, in fact, be done by any Government that had hitherto subscribed to the humane practices of civilized nations. International law had its origin in the attempt to set up some law which would be respected and observed upon the seas, where no nation had right of dominion, and where lay the free highways of the world. By painful stage after stage has that law been built up with meager enough results, indeed, after all was accomplished that could be accomplished, but always with a clear view at least of what the heart and conscience of mankind demanded.

This minimum of right the German Government has swept aside under the plea of retaliation and necessity, and because it had no weapons which it could use at sea except these, which it is impossible to employ as it is employing them without throwing to the winds all scruples of humanity or of respect for the understandings that were supposed to underlie the intercourse of the world.

I am not now thinking of the loss of property involved, immense and serious as that is, but only of the wanton and wholesale destruction of the lives of non-combatants, men, women, and children engaged in pursuits which have always, even in the darkest periods of modern history, been deemed innocent and legitimate.

Property can be paid for; the lives of peaceful and innocent people cannot be.

The present German warfare against commerce is a warfare against mankind. It is a war against all nations. American ships have been sunk, American lives taken, in ways which it has stirred us very deeply to learn of, but the ships and people of other neutral and friendly nations have been sunk and overwhelmed in the waters in the same way. There has been no discrimination. The challenge is to all mankind. Each nation must decide for itself how it will meet it. The choice we make for ourselves must be made with a moderation of counsel and a temperateness of judgment befitting our character and our motives as a nation. We must put excited feeling away.

Our motive will not be revenge or the victorious assertion of the physical might of the nation, but only the vindication of right, of human right, of which we are only a single champion.

When I addressed the Congress on the 26th of February last I thought that it would suffice to assert our neutral rights with arms, our right to use the seas against unlawful interference, our right to keep our people safe against unlawful violence. But armed neutrality, it now appears, is impracticable. Because submarines are in effect outlaws when used as the German submarines have been used against merchant shipping, it is impossible to defend ships against their attacks as the law of nations has assumed that merchantmen would defend themselves against privateers or cruisers, visible craft giving chase upon the open sea.

It is common prudence in such circumstances, grim necessity, indeed, to endeavor to destroy them before they have shown their own intention. They must be dealt with upon sight, if dealt with at all.

The German Government denies the right of neutrals to use arms at all within the areas of the sea which it has proscribed, even in the defense of rights which no modern publicist has ever before questioned their right to defend. The intimation is conveyed that the armed guards which we have placed on our merchant-ships will be treated as beyond the pale of law and subject to be dealt with as pirates would be.

Armed neutrality is ineffectual enough at best; in such circumstances and in the face of such pretensions it is worse than ineffectual; it is likely to produce what it was meant to prevent; it is practically certain to draw us into the war without either the rights or the effectiveness of belligerents.

There is one choice we cannot make, we are incapable of making: we will not choose the path of submission and suffer the most sacred rights of our nation and our people to be ignored or violated. The wrongs against which we now array ourselves are not common wrongs; they reach out to the very roots of human life.

With a profound sense of the solemn and even tragical character of the step I am taking and of the grave responsibilities which it involves, but in unhesitating obedience to what I deem my constitutional duty, I advise that the Congress declare the recent course of the Imperial German Government to be in fact nothing less than war against the Government and people of the United States. That it formally accept the status of belligerent which has thus been thrust upon it and that it take immediate steps not only to put the country in a more thorough state of defense, but also to exert all its power and employ all its resources to bring the Government of the German Empire to terms and end the war.

What this will involve is clear. It will involve the utmost practicable coöperation in counsel and action with the Governments now at war with Germany, and as incident to that the extension to those Governments of the most liberal financial credits in order that our resources may so far as possible be added to theirs.

It will involve the organization and mobilization of all the material resources of the country to supply the materials of war and serve the incidental needs of the nation in the most abundant and yet the most economical and efficient way possible.

It will involve the immediate full equipment of the navy in all respects, but particularly in supplying it with the best means of dealing with the enemy's submarines.

It will involve the immediate addition to the armed forces of the United States already provided for by law in case of war at least 500,000 men, who should, in my opinion, be chosen upon the principle of universal liability to service, and also the authorization of subsequent additional increments of equal force so soon as they may be needed and can be handled in training.

It will involve also, of course, the granting of adequate credits to the Government, sustained, I hope, so far as they can equitably be sustained by the present generation, by well-conceived taxation. I say sustained so far as may be equitable by taxation because it seems to me that it would be most unwise to base the credits which will now be necessary entirely on money borrowed.

It is our duty, I most respectfully urge, to protect our people so far as we may against the very serious hardships and evils which would be likely to arise out of the inflation which would be produced by vast loans.

In carrying out the measures by which these things are to be accomplished we should keep constantly in mind the wisdom of interfering as little as possible in our own preparation and in the equipment of our own military forces with the duty—for it

J

will be a very practical duty—of supplying the nations already at war with Germany with the materials which they can obtain only from us or by our assistance. They are in the field and we should help them in every way to be effective there.

I shall take the liberty of suggesting, through the several executive departments of the Government, for the consideration of your committees, measures for the accomplishment of the several objects I have mentioned. I hope that it will be your pleasure to deal with them as having been framed after very careful thought by the branch of the Government upon which the responsibility of conducting the war and safeguarding the nation will most directly fall.

While we do these things, these deeply momentous things, let us be very clear and make very clear to all the world what our motives and our objects are. My own thought has not been driven from its habitual and normal course by the unhappy events of the last two months, and I do not believe that the thought of the nation has been altered or clouded by them.

I have exactly the same thing in mind now that I had in mind when I addressed the Senate on the 22d of January last; the same that I had in mind when I addressed the Congress on the 3d of February and on the 26th of February.

Our object now, as then, is to vindicate the principles of peace and the justice in the life of the world as against selfish and autocratic power and to set up amongst the really free and self-governed peoples of the world such a concert of purpose and of action as will henceforth insure the observance of those principles.

Neutrality is no longer feasible or desirable where the peace of the world is involved and the freedom of its peoples, and the menace to that peace and freedom lies in the existence of autocratic Governments backed by organized force which is controlled wholly by their will, not by the will of their people. We have seen the last of neutrality in such circumstances.

We are at the beginning of an age in which it will be insisted that the same standards of conduct and of responsibility for wrong done shall be observed among nations and their Governments that are observed among the individual citizens of civilized states.

We have no quarrel with the German people. We have no feeling toward them but one of sympathy and friendship. It was not upon their impulse that their Government acted in entering this war. It was not with their previous knowledge or approval.

It was a war determined upon as wars used to be determined upon in the old, unhappy days when peoples were nowhere consulted by their rulers and wars were provoked and waged in the interest of dynasties or little groups of ambitious men who were accustomed to use their fellowmen as pawns and tools.

Self-governed nations do not fill their neighbor states with spies or set the course of intrigue to bring about some critical posture of affairs which will give them an opportunity to strike and make conquest. Such designs can be successfully worked only under cover and where no one has the right to ask questions.

Cunningly contrived plans of deception or aggression, carried, it may be, from generation to generation, can be worked out and kept from the light only within the privacy of courts or behind the carefully guarded confidences of a narrow and privileged class. They are happily impossible where public opinion commands and insists upon full information concerning all the nation's affairs.

A steadfast concert for peace can never be maintained except by a partnership of democratic nations. No autocratic Government could be trusted to keep faith within it or observe its covenants. It must be a league of honor, a partnership of opinion. Intrigue would eat its vitals away, the plottings of inner circles who could plan what they would and render account to no one would be a corruption seated at its very heart. Only free peoples can hold their purpose and their honor steady to a common end and prefer the interests of mankind to any narrow interest of their own.

Does not every American feel that assurance has been added to our hope for the future peace of the world by the wonderful and heartening things that have been happening within the last few weeks in Russia?

Russia was known by those who know it best to have been always in fact democratic at heart, in all the vital habits of her thought, in all the intimate relationships of her people that spoke their natural instinct, their habitual attitude toward life.

Autocracy that crowned the summit of her political structure, long as it had stood and terrible as was the reality of its power, was not in fact Russian in origin, in character or purpose; and now it has been shaken off and the great, generous Russian people have been added, in all their native majesty and might, to the forces that are fighting for freedom in the world, for justice and for peace. Here is a fit partner for a League of Honor.

One of the things that have served to convince us that the Prussian autocracy was not and could never be our friend is that from the very outset of the present war it has filled our unsuspecting communities and even our offices of Government with spies and set criminal intrigues everywhere afoot against our national unity of council, our peace within and without, our industries and our commerce.

Indeed, it is now evident that its spies were here even before the war began, and it is, unhappily, not a matter of conjecture, but a fact proved in our courts of justice, that the intrigues which have more than once come perilously near to disturbing the peace and dislocating the industries of the country have been carried on at the instigation, with the support, and even under the personal direction, of official agents of the Imperial German Government accredited to the Government of the United States.

Even in checking these things and trying to extirpate them we have sought to put the most generous interpretation possible upon them because we knew that their source lay, not in any hostile feeling or purpose of the German people toward us (who were, no doubt, as ignorant of them as we ourselves were), but only in the selfish designs of a Government that did what it pleased and told its people nothing. But they have played their part in serving to convince us at last that that Government entertains no real friendship for us and means to act against our peace and security at its convenience. That it means to stir up enemies against us at our very doors the intercepted note to the German Minister at Mexico City is eloquent evidence.

We are accepting this challenge of hostile purpose because we know that in such a Government, following such methods, we can never have a friend; and that in the presence of its organized power, always lying in wait to accomplish we know not what purpose, there can be no assured security for the democratic Governments of the world.

We are now about to accept the gage of battle with this natural foe to liberty, and shall, if necessary, spend the whole force of the nation to check and nullify its pretensions and its power. We are glad, now that we see the facts with no veil of false pretense about them, to fight thus for the ultimate peace of the world and for the liberation of its peoples, the German people included; for the rights of nations great and small and the privilege of men everywhere to choose their way of life and of obedience. The world must be made safe for democracy. Its peace must be planted upon the trusted foundations of political liberty.

We have no selfish ends to serve. We desire no conquest, no dominion. We seek no indemnities for ourselves, no material compensation for the sacrifices we shall freely make. We are but one of the champions of the rights of mankind. We shall be satisfied when those rights have been made as secure as the faith and the freedom of nations can make them.

Just because we fight without rancor and without selfish objects, seeking nothing for ourselves but what we shall wish to share with all free peoples, we shall, I feel confident, conduct our operations as belligerents without passion and ourselves observe with proud punctilio the principles of right and of fair play we profess to be fighting for.

I have said nothing of the Governments allied with the Imperial Government of Germany because they have not made war upon us or challenged us to defend our right and our honor. The Austro-Hungarian Government has indeed avowed its unqualified indorsement and acceptance of the reckless and lawless submarine warfare adopted now without disguise by the Imperial German Government, and it has therefore not been possible for this Government to receive Count Tarnowski, the ambassador recently accredited to this Government by the Imperial and Royal Government of Austro-Hungary; but that Government has not actually engaged in warfare against citizens of the United States on the seas, and I take the liberty, for the present at least, of postponing a discussion of our relations with the authorities at Vienna.

We enter this war only where we are clearly forced into it because there are no other means of defending our rights.

It will be all the easier for us to conduct ourselves as belligerents in a high spirit of right and fairness because we act without animus, not in enmity toward a people or with the desire to bring any injury or disadvantage upon them, but only in armed opposition to an irresponsible Government which has thrown aside all considerations of humanity and of right and is running amuck.

We are, let me say again, the sincere friends of the German people, and shall desire nothing so much as the early reëstablishment of intimate relations of mutual advantage between us, however hard it may be for them, for the time being, to believe that this is spoken from our hearts. We have borne with their present Government through all these bitter months because of that friendship,—exercising a patience and forbearance which would otherwise have been impossible.

We shall, happily, still have an opportunity to prove that friendship in our daily attitude and actions towards the millions of men and women of German birth and native sympathy who live amongst us and share our life, and we shall be proud to prove it toward all who are, in fact, loyal to their neighbors and to the Government in the hour of test. They are, most of them, as true and loyal Americans as if they had never known any other fealty or allegiance. They will be prompt to stand with us in rebuking and restraining the few who may be of a different mind and purpose. If there should be disloyalty it will be dealt with with a firm hand of stern repression, but, if it lifts its head at all, it will lift it only here and there and without countenance except from a lawless and malignant few.

It is a distressing and oppressive duty, gentlemen of the Congress, which I have performed in thus addressing you. There are, it may be, many months of fiery trial and sacrifice ahead of us. It is a fearful thing to lead this great, peaceful people into war, into the most terrible and disastrous of all wars, civilization itself seeming to be in the balance. But the right is more precious than peace, and we shall fight for the things which we have always carried nearest our hearts—for democracy, for the right of those who submit to authority to have a voice in their own governments, for the rights and liberties of small nations, for a universal dominion of right by such a concert of free peoples as shall bring peace and safety to all nations and make the world itself at last free.

To such a task we can dedicate our lives and our fortunes, everything that we are and everything that we have, with the pride of those who know that the day has come when America is privileged to spend her blood and her might for the principles that gave her birth and happiness and the peace which she has treasured. God helping her, she can do no other.

AMERICAN DEMOCRACY

THE HERITAGE OF LIBERTY[1]

CHARLES MILLS GAYLEY

[Charles Mills Gayley (1858————) is professor of English in the University of California. After graduating from the University of Michigan, he studied in Germany, and on his return to this country, occupied positions in the University of Michigan until 1889 when he went to California. The selection here given is from a book, *Shakspere and the Founders of Liberty in America*, which Professor Gayley published in 1917 to remind Americans how essentially at one with Englishmen they had always been in institutions, love of liberty, and democratic ideals.]

The political freedom that, between 1609 and 1640, our English ancestors of Virginia and New England put into form and practice is the political freedom for which our grand-uncles of old England fought from 1642 to 1649, nay, to 1689; Bradford, and Brewster, Winthrop and Endicott, John Cotton and Roger Williams, Harvard and Thomas Hooker, of New England, Alexander Whitaker, Clayborne, Bennett, and Nathaniel Bacon, of Virginia, belong to the history of English ideals no less than to that of America. And Hampden, Pym, Cromwell, Milton, Bunyan, and the Seven Bishops who defied the second James, were but brothers to our English sires in New England. Brothers of the same blood and ultimate ideal were also the royalists of Virginia. Their conservatism and devotion to a lost cause rendered them none the less certain "in the free air of the New World to develop into uncompromising democrats and fierce defenders of their own privileges."

Of all these Englishmen of the seventeenth century, whether of the Old World or the New, there was a heritage in common.

[1]From *Shakspere and the Founders of Liberty in America* (copyright, 1917; The Macmillan Company). Reprinted by permission.

One language welded of the Old English, Scandinavian, Gallic, and Latin: manly, direct, sober, and natively consistent; unfettered, experimental, acquisitive; from emergency to emergency shaped according to the need, incomparable in riches ever cumulative. One race, one nation, one blood infused of many strains and diverse characteristics: of the Anglo-Saxon, the personal independence and native conservatism; of the Norman, the martial genius, equity, political vision, masterful and unifying authority—and of the Norman, the chivalry, the romance and culture, too; of the Celt, intermingling with these in the centuries that flowed into Shakspere, a current of aspiration, poignant passion, poetic imagination—stirring the blood but not intoxicating the Anglo-Norman reason. One custom, of spiritual ideal but of tried experience—practical rather than speculative, distrustful of veering sentiment, slowly crystallizing into the stability of a national consciousness: a custom of individual prerogative and of obedience to the authority that conserves the prerogative; of fair play and equality of opportunity, of fearless speech for the right, and simple for the common weal; a custom making for popular sovereignty, for allegiance, for national honor in national fair dealing, for the might that is right; one custom, mother of the law. One common law: the progressive expression "of a free people's needs and standards of justice;" the outgrowth of social conditions, deriving its authority not from enactment of sovereign monarch or sovereign legislature but from the aggregate social will—the law of precedent and of the righteous independence of the courts.

Long before Magna Charta features of this law, this conservatively expanding charter of liberties and duties, are distinguishable in the procedure of our forefathers in England. From the days of Ethelbert to those of Alfred, and from Alfred to Edward the Confessor, for four and a half centuries before the Conquest, this law, hardly if at all affected by foreign corpus or code, had been "gathering itself together out of the custom of" the independently developing Anglo-Saxon. This sanction "the Conqueror, who claimed the crown by virtue of English law and professed to rule by English law," repeatedly bound himself to observe, "and he handed down the tradition to all who came after him." This law of national precedent, further developed under Henry II and systematically expounded by Glanvil, or by some clerk under his direction, grew into the Great Charter of King John with its equal distribution of civil rights to all classes of freemen, and its restriction of monarchical prerogative. "The king," writes Bracton in the days of John's successor, Henry III, "must not be subject to any man but to God and the law; for the law makes him king. Let the king therefore give to the law what the law gives to him, dominion and power; for there is no king where will, and not law, bears rule." The relation of this English law of custom to the general nature of law as set forth in the civil code of the Roman system, Bracton expounds; but from that system the peculiar English law is not derived. Expanding through Fortescue and Littleton, this English law is the common law of Coke; and by the Virginia charter of 1606, probably drafted by Coke, the rights of the common law were conferred upon the colonists of the New World.

For these Englishmen of the "sceptered isle" and of the untilled wilderness of the West there had been one spirit energizing toward freedom—civil and religious; one charter of rights and obligations. Of political development there had been a continuous history for eleven hundred years before England was planted in America. There had also been one literature, as ancient and as noble, stirring in embers of racial tradition—a tradition of service and heroism and generous acceptance of fate; kindling to mirth and pity, humanity and reverence; leaping to flame in imagination and power; and, in the decades when first the English peopled "worlds in the yet unformed Occident," attaining full glory in the zenith of Shakspere.

Not with those eleven hundred years ceased the oneness of the English heritage. For a period longer than that which has elapsed since the American branch of the Anglo-Saxon race has been a separate nation, the heritage was one. One hundred and forty years have succeeded our Declaration of Independence. Through the hundred and seventy which preceded, the history of Britain was the continuing property of our forefathers of Vir ginia and New England. Not only Hampden and Cromwell and the Ironsides, but Chatham, Holland, Burke, and Sir Philip Francis were compatriots of the colonials. The admirals of the fleet, Blake, Vernon, Anson, Hawke, were our admirals. It was for the nascent empire of our British and British-American forefathers that they won the supremacy of the sea. The victories of Marlborough, Clive's conquest of India, Wolfe's conquest of Canada—to which the young George Washington contributed the services of his still British sword—were glories not of a foreign race but of our race. For four generations we have been an independent people. But for six generations before that the intellectual and spiritual strivings of our British compatriots toward truth and freedom were those of the British in America. Harrington, Algernon Sidney, Locke, Hume, and Berkeley were ours. And in literature, Milton and Bunyan, Dryden and Pope, Swift, Addison, Gray and Goldsmith were our poets and essayists. Such was the birthright of our British forefathers in the American colonies. True it is that in legal procedure they preferred, during the years of primitive social conditions, the appeal to divine law and the law of reason or of human nature, as expounded by Hooker and his school, to any kind of law positive; and it is true that, within the field of positive law, they took more kindly to the civil which derives authority from enactment than to the common which derives from precedent. But when they reached "the stage of social organization which the common law expressed," they were only too glad to claim that birthright also, as conveyed by various early charters. And upon such right they based their appeal for civil liberty.

Not at all with 1776 did the English heritage cease to be the same for the sons of England at home and over the seas. In their resistance to taxation without representation, to coercion by force, to the Acts of Trade, the colonists in America were supported by Fox and the elder Pitt, by Shelburne, Camden, Burke, Rockingham, and all true patriots at home. Americans were asserting their rights as Englishmen under charter and common law. "Do not break their charter; do not take away rights granted them by the predecessors of the Crown!" cried members

of the English House of Commons. Pitt "pointed out distinctly
that the Americans were upholding those eternal principles of
political justice which should be to all Englishmen most dear,
and that a victory over the colonies would be of ill omen for
English liberty, whether in the Old World or the New." Speaking of the tea-duty, Lord North had asseverated, "I will never
think of repealing it until I see America prostrate at my feet."
To this Colonel Barre retorted, "Does any friend of his country
really wish to see America thus humbled? In such a situation
she would serve only as a monument of your arrogance and your
folly. For my part, the America I wish to see is America increasing and prosperous, raising her head in graceful dignity,
with freedom and firmness asserting her rights at your bar, vin-
dicating her liberties, pleading her services, and conscious of
her merit. This is the America that will have spirit to fight your
battles, to sustain you when hard pushed by some prevailing
foe. . . . Unless you repeal this law you run the risk of losing
America." In the House of Lords, three devoted defenders of
American liberty were the Dukes of Portland, Devonshire, and
Northumberland. They were descended from Henry Wriothes-
ley, third Earl of Southampton, the founder, with Sir Edwin
Sandys, of the charter liberties of Virginia. In that House,
protesting against the "Intolerable Acts" of 1774, the Duke of
Richmond thundered, "I wish from the bottom of my heart that
the Americans may resist, and get the better of the forces sent
against them." Not the historical precedent of England nor the
political wisdom of her best "arrayed her in hostility to every
principle of public justice which Englishmen had from time im-
memorial held sacred," but the perversity of an un-English
prince and of his fatuous advisers. Bent upon thwarting the
policy of reformers who would make the Commons more truly
representative of the English people, upon destroying the system
of cabinet government and resuscitating the theory of divine
right, these unfortunates picked their quarrel with the American
colonies. "For," as John Fiske shrewdly remarks, "if the American position, that there should be no taxation without representation, were once granted, then it would straightway become

necessary to admit the principles of Parliamentary reform," and to call the Liberals to power in England. A representation of the colonies in Westminster, though favored by some great Englishmen, might have been impracticable; but if George III had listened to the elder Pitt and his followers, he would have recognized the right of American freemen to levy their own taxes, and the Revolution would have been obviated. The would-be autocrat forced the issue in America and was defeated. If there had been no revolution in America there would have been a revolution in England, and the monarch would in all probability have been dethroned. The War of Independence reasserted for England as well as for America the political rights for which Englishmen, from the time of King John to that of James I, from the time of Hooker, Shakspere, Sandys, Bradford, Winthrop, Sir Thomas Dale, and Sir Francis Wyatt, to that of Cromwell, had contended. It confirmed the victories of the Great Rebellion and of the Revolution of 1688. The younger Pitt denounced the war against the American colonies as "most accursed, wicked, barbarous, cruel, unnatural, unjust, and diabolical." And when Charles Fox heard that Cornwallis had surrendered at Yorktown, he leaped from his chair and clapped his hands. The victory at Yorktown dissipated once for all the fatal delusion of divine prerogative. Those who conceived and carried through the American Revolution were Anglo-Saxons: Otis, Samuel and John Adams, Hancock, Henry, Richard Henry Lee, Franklin, Jefferson, Washington. The greatest of Americans was the greatest Englishman of his age: Washington was but asserting against a despotic sovereign of German blood and broken English speech the prerogative of the Anglo-Saxon breed, the faith of his liberal brothers in England.

Political history has, indeed, worn its independent channel; but spirit and speech, letters, order of freedom and control in the America of today are of the ancient blood and custom.

THE DECLARATION OF INDEPENDENCE IN THE LIGHT OF MODERN CRITICISM[1]

Moses Coit Tyler

[Moses Coit Tyler (1835–1900) was a distinguished American educator and scholar in literature and history. After graduating from Yale in 1877, he became a Congregational minister, but his health failing from overstudy, he spent four years in England recuperating. On his return to America, he accepted, in 1867, the chair of English literature at the University of Michigan. In 1881 he was called to the professorship of American history at Cornell, a position which he held until his death. His literary histories dealing with the Colonial and the Revolutionary periods of American literature have secured for him a wide reputation for scholarship. In a time when it has become fashionable to sneer at certain features of the Declaration of Independence, it is well for every American to follow Tyler's admirable discussion of the criticisms to which this great document has been subjected. As limitations of space in this volume have made it necessary to abridge Tyler's article, the student should if possible secure it in its entirety and carefully read it.]

It can hardly be doubted that some hindrance to a right estimate of the Declaration of Independence is occasioned by either of two opposite conditions of mind, both of which are often to be met with among us: on the one hand, a condition of hereditary, uncritical awe and worship of the American Revolution, and of that state paper as its absolutely perfect and glorious expression; on the other hand, a later condition of cultivated distrust of the Declaration, as a piece of writing lifted up into inordinate renown by the passionate and heroic circumstances of its origin, and ever since then extolled beyond reason by the blind energy of patriotic enthusiasm. Turning from the former state of mind, which obviously calls for no further comment, we may note, as a partial illustration of the latter, that American confidence in the supreme intellectual merit of this all-famous document received a serious wound some forty years ago from the hand of Rufus Choate, when, with a courage greater than would now be required for such an act, he characterized it as made up of "glittering and sounding generalities of natural

[1]From *North American Review*, vol. clxiii, p. 1 (July, 1896).

right." What the great advocate then so unhesitatingly suggested, many a thoughtful American since then has at least suspected—that our great proclamation, as a piece of political literature, cannot stand the test of modern analysis; that it belongs to the immense class of over-praised productions; that it is, in fact, a stately patchwork of sweeping propositions of somewhat doubtful validity; that it has long imposed upon mankind by the well-known effectiveness of verbal glitter and sound; that, at the best, it is an example of florid political declamation belonging to the sophomoric period of our national life, a period which, as we flatter ourselves, we have now outgrown.

Nevertheless, it is to be noted that whatever authority the Declaration of Independence has acquired in the world, has been due to no lack of criticism, either at the time of its first appearance, or since then; a fact which seems to tell in favor of its essential worth and strength. From the date of its original publication down to the present moment, it has been attacked again and again, either in anger, or in contempt, by friends as well as by enemies of the American Revolution, by liberals in politics as well as by conservatives. It has been censured for its substance, it has been censured for its form, for its misstatements of fact, for its fallacies in reasoning, for its audacious novelties and paradoxes, for its total lack of all novelty, for its repetition of old and threadbare statements, even for its downright plagiarisms; finally, for its grandiose and vaporing style.

Perhaps, however, the most frequent form of disparagement to which Jefferson's great state paper has been subjected among us is that which would minimize his merit in composing it, by denying to it the merit of originality. . . .

By no one, however, has the charge of a lack of originality been pressed with so much decisiveness as by John Adams, who took evident pleasure in speaking of it as a document in which were merely "recapitulated" previous and well-known statements of American rights and wrongs, and who, as late as in the year 1822, deliberately wrote:

"There is not an idea in it but what had been hackneyed in Congress for two years before. The substance of it is contained in the declaration of rights and the violation of those rights, in the Journals of Congress, in 1774. Indeed, the essence of it is contained in a pamphlet, voted and printed by the town of Boston, before the first Congress met, composed by James Otis, as I suppose, in one of his lucid intervals, and pruned and polished by Samuel Adams."

Perhaps nowhere in our literature would it be possible to find a criticism brought forward by a really able man against any piece of writing less applicable to the case, and of less force and value, than is this particular criticism by John Adams and others, as to the lack of originality in the Declaration of Independence. Indeed, for such a paper as Jefferson was commissioned to write, the one quality which it could not properly have had, the one quality which would have been fatal to its acceptance either by the American Congress or by the American people—is originality. They were then at the culmination of a tremendous controversy over alleged grievances of the most serious kind—a controversy that had been steadily raging for at least twelve years. In the course of that long dispute, every phase of it, whether as to abstract right or constitutional privilege or personal procedure, had been presented in almost every conceivable form of speech. At last, they had resolved, in view of all this experience, no longer to prosecute the controversy as members of the empire; they had resolved to revolt, and, casting off forever their ancient fealty to the British crown, to separate from the empire, and to establish themselves as a new nation among the nations of the earth. In this emergency, as it happened, Jefferson was called upon to put into form a suitable statement of the chief considerations which prompted them to this great act of revolution, and which, as they believed, justified it. What, then, was Jefferson to do? Was he to regard himself as a mere literary essayist, set to produce before the world a sort of prize-dissertation—a calm, analytic, judicial treatise on history and politics with a particular application to Anglo-American affairs—one essential merit of which would be its originality as a contribution to historical and political literature? Was he not, rather, to regard himself as, for the time being, the very mouthpiece and prophet of the people whom he represented, and as such required to bring together and to set in order, in their name, not what was new, but what was old; to gather up into his own soul, as much as possible, whatever was then also in their souls, their very thoughts and passions, their ideas of constitutional law, their interpretations of fact, their opinions as to men and as to events in all that ugly quarrel, their notions of justice, of civic dignity, of human rights; finally, their memories of wrongs which seemed to them intolerable, especially of wrongs inflicted upon them during those twelve years by the hands of insolent and brutal men, in the name of the King, and by his apparent command?

Moreover, as the nature of the task laid upon him made it necessary that he should thus state, as the reasons for their intended act, those very considerations both as to fact and as to opinion which had actually operated upon their minds, so did it require him to do so, to some extent, in the very language which the people themselves, in their more formal and deliberate utterances, had all along been using. In the development of political life in England and America, there had already been created a vast literature of constitutional progress—a literature common to both portions of the English race, pervaded by its own stately traditions, and reverberating certain great phrases which formed, as one may say, almost the vernacular of English justice, and of English aspiration for a free, manly and orderly political life. In this vernacular the Declaration of Independence was written. The phraseology thus characteristic of it is the very phraseology of the champions of constitutional expansion, of civic dignity and progress, within the English race ever since Magna Charta; of the great state papers of English freedom in the seventeenth century, particularly the Petition of Right in 1629, and the Bill of Rights in 1789; of the great English Charters for colonization in America; of the great English exponents of legal and political progress—Sir Edward Coke, John Milton, Sir Philip Sidney, John Locke; finally, of the great American exponents of political liberty, and of the chief representative bodies, whether local or general, which had convened in America from the time of Stamp Act Congress until that of the Congress which resolved upon our independence. To say, therefore, that the official declaration of

K

that resolve is a paper made up of the very opinions, beliefs, un-beliefs, the very sentiments, prejudices, passions, even the errors in judgment and the personal misconstructions—if they were such—which then actually impelled the American people to that mighty act, and that all these are expressed in the very phrases which they had been accustomed to use, is to pay to that state-paper the highest tribute as to its fitness for the purpose for which it was framed.

Of much of this, also, Jefferson himself seems to have been conscious; and perhaps never does he rise before us with more dignity, with more truth, than when, late in his lifetime, hurt by the captious and jangling words of disparagement then re-cently put into writing by his old comrade, to the effect that the Declaration of Independence "contains no new ideas, that it is a commonplace compilation, its sentences hackneyed in Congress for two years before, and its essence contained in Otis's pamph-let," Jefferson quietly remarked that perhaps these statements might "all be true: of that I am not to be the judge. . . . Whether I had gathered my ideas from reading or reflection, I do not know. I know only that I turned to neither book nor pamphlet while writing it. I did not consider it as any part of my charge to invent new ideas altogether and to offer no senti-ment which had ever been expressed before."

Before passing from this phase of the subject, however, it should be added that, while the Declaration of Independence lacks originality in the sense just indicated, in another and per-haps in a higher sense, it possesses originality—it is individual-ized by the character and by the genius of its author. Jefferson gathered up the thoughts and emotions and even the character-istic phrases of the people for whom he wrote, and these he per-fectly incorporated with what was already in his mind, and then to the music of his own keen, rich, passionate, and enkindling style, he mustered them into that stately and triumphant pro-cession wherein, as some of us still think, they will go march-ing on to the world's end.

There were then in Congress several other men who could have written the Declaration of Independence, and written it well—notably Franklin, either of the two Adamses, Richard Henry Lee, William Livingston, and, best of all, but for his own opposition to the measure, John Dickinson; but had any one of these other men written the Declaration of Independence, while it would have contained, doubtless, nearly the same topics and nearly the same great formulas of political statement, it would yet have been a wholly different composition from this of Jefferson's. No one at all familiar with his other writings, as well as with the writings of his chief contemporaries, could ever have a moment's doubt, even if the fact were not already notorious, that this document was by Jefferson. He put into it something that was his own, and that no one else could have put there. He put himself into it—his own genius, his own moral force, his faith in God, his faith in ideas, his love of innovation, his passion for progress, his invincible enthusiasm, his intolerance of prescription, of injustice, of cruelty; his sympathy, his clarity of vision, his affluence of diction, his power to fling out great phrases which will long fire and cheer the souls of men struggling against political unrighteousness.

And herein lies its essential originality, perhaps the most precious, and, indeed, almost the only, originality ever attaching to any great literary product that is representative of its time. He made himself no improper claim, therefore, when he directed that upon the granite obelisk at his grave should be carved the words: "Here was buried Thomas Jefferson, author of the Declaration of Independence."

If the Declaration of Independence is now to be fairly judged by us, it must be judged with reference to what it was intended to be, namely, an impassioned manifesto of one party, and that the weaker party, in a violent race-quarrel; of a party resolved, at last, upon the extremity of revolution, and already menaced by the inconceivable disaster of being defeated in the very act of armed rebellion against the mightiest military power on earth. This manifesto, then, is not to be censured because, being avowedly a statement of its own side of the quarrel, it does not also contain a moderate and judicial statement of the opposite side; or because, being necessarily partisan in method, it is likewise both partisan and vehement in tone; or because it bristles with accusations against the enemy so fierce and so unqualified as now to seem in some respects overdrawn; or because it resounds with certain great aphorisms about the natural rights of man, at which, indeed, political science cannot now smile, except to its own discomfiture and shame—aphorisms which are likely to abide in this world as the chief source and inspiration of heroic enterprises among men for self-deliverance from oppression.

Thus, ever since its first announcement to the world, and down almost to the present moment, has the Declaration of Independence been tested by criticism of every possible kind— by criticism intended and expected to be destructive. Apparently, however, all this criticism has failed to accomplish its object.

It is proper for us to remember, also, that what we call criticism is not the only valid test of the genuineness and worth of any piece of writing of great practical interest to mankind: there is, in addition, the test of actual use and service, in direct contact with the common sense and the moral sense of large masses of men, under various conditions, and for a long period. Probably no writing which is not essentially sound and true has ever survived this test.

Neither from this test has the great Declaration any need to shrink. As to the immediate use for which it was sent forth— that of rallying and uniting the friends of the Revolution, and bracing them for their great task—its effectiveness was so great and so obvious that it has never been denied. During the century and a quarter since the Revolution, its influence on the political character and the political conduct of the American people has been great beyond calculation. For example, after we had achieved our own national deliverance, and had advanced into that enormous and somewhat corrupting material prosperity which followed the adoption of the Constitution and the development of the cotton-interest and the expansion of the Republic into a trans-continental power, we fell under an appalling temptation—the temptation to forget, or to repudiate, or to refuse to apply to the case of our human brethren in bondage, the principles which we had once proclaimed as the basis of every rightful government. The prodigious service rendered to us in this awful moral emergency by the Declaration of Independence was, that its public repetition, at least once every year, in the hearing of vast throngs of the American people in every portion of the Republic, kept constantly before our minds, in a form of almost religious sanctity, those few great ideas as to the dignity of human nature, and the sacredness of personality, and the indestructible rights of man as mere man, with which we had so gloriously identified the beginnings of our national existence. It did at last become very hard for us to listen each year to the preamble of the Declaration and still to remain the owners and users and catchers of slaves; still harder, to accept the doctrine that the righteousness and prosperity of slavery was to be accepted as the dominant policy of the nation. The logic of Calhoun was as flawless as usual, when he concluded that the chief obstruction in the way of his system was the preamble of the Declaration of Independence. Had it not been for the inviolable sacredness given by it to those sweeping aphorisms about the natural rights of man, it may be doubted whether Calhoun might not have won over an immense majority of the American people to the support of his compact and plausible scheme for making slavery the basis of the Republic. It was the preamble of the Declaration of Independence which elected Lincoln, which sent forth the Emancipation Proclamation, which gave victory to Grant, which ratified the Thirteenth Amendment.

We shall not here attempt to delineate the influence of this state paper upon mankind in general. Of course, the emergence of the American Republic as an imposing world-power is a phenomenon which has now for many years attracted the attention of the human race. Surely, no slight effect must have resulted from the fact that, among all civilized peoples, the one American document best known is the Declaration of Independence, and that thus the spectacle of so vast and beneficent a political success has been everywhere associated with the assertion of the natural rights of man. "The doctrines it contained," says Buckle, "were not merely welcomed by a majority of the French nation, but even the government itself was unable to withstand the general feeling." "Its effect in hastening the approach of the French Revolution . . . was indeed most remarkable." Elsewhere, also, in many lands, among many peoples, it has been cited again and again as an inspiration to political courage, as a model for political conduct[1]; and if, as the brilliant historian just alluded to has affirmed, "that noble Declaration . . . ought to be hung up in the nursery of every king, and blazoned on the porch of every royal palace," it is because it has become the classic statement of political truths which must at last abolish kings altogether, or else teach them to identify their existence with the dignity and happiness of human nature.

DEMOCRACY

JAMES RUSSELL LOWELL

[James Russell Lowell (1819–1891) added to his fame as poet and essayist the distinction of serving as American ambassador to Spain, 1876–1880, and to Great Britain, 1880–1885. In this last position he performed a particularly useful service in interpreting England and the United States to each other. The famous address on Democracy, of which only the most significant part is here printed, was delivered on the occasion of his assuming the honorary presidency of the Birmingham and Midland Institute, England, October 6, 1884, and expresses Lowell's native Americanism and optimistic faith in democracy at a time when American democracy was still on the defensive in European eyes. The selection gives the latter part of the address, the somewhat rambling and whimsical beginning being omitted.]

Few people take the trouble of trying to find out what democracy really is. Yet this would be a great help, for it is our lawless and uncertain thoughts, it is the indefiniteness of our impressions, that fill darkness, whether mental or physical, with specters and hobgoblins. Democracy is nothing more than an experiment in government, more likely to succeed in a new soil, but likely to be tried in all soils, which must stand or fall on its own merits as others have done before it. For there is no trick

---

[1]The editor of the latest edition of *The Writings of Thomas Jefferson*, vol. i., Introd. xxv., does not shrink from calling it "the paper which is probably the best known that ever came from the pen of an individual." [Tyler's note.]

of perpetual motion in politics any more than in mechanics. President Lincoln defined democracy to be "the government of the people, by the people, for the people." This is a sufficiently compact statement of it as a political arrangement. Theodore Parker said that "Democracy meant not 'I'm as good as you are,' but 'You're as good as I am.'" And this is the ethical conception of it, necessary as a complement of the other; a conception which, could it be made actual and practical, would easily solve all the riddles that the old sphinx of political and social economy who sits by the roadside has been proposing to mankind from the beginning, and which mankind have shown such a singular talent for answering wrongly. In this sense Christ was the first true democrat that ever breathed, as the old dramatist Dekker said He was the first true gentleman. The characters may be easily doubled, so strong is the likeness between them. A beautiful and profound parable of the Persian poet Jellaladeen tells us that "One knocked at the Beloved's door, and a voice asked from within, 'Who is there?' and he answered, 'It is I.' Then the voice said, 'This house will not hold me and thee;' and the door was not opened. Then went the lover into the desert and fasted and prayed in solitude, and after a year he returned and knocked again at the door; and again the voice asked, 'Who is there?' and he said, 'It is thyself;' and the door was opened to him." But that is idealism, you will say, and this is an only too practical world. I grant it; but I am one of those who believe that the real will never find an irremovable basis till it rests on the ideal. It used to be thought that a democracy was possible only in a small territory, and this is doubtless true of a democracy strictly defined, for in such all the citizens decide directly upon every question of public concern in a general assembly. An example still survives in the tiny Swiss canton of Appenzell. But this immediate intervention of the people in their own affairs is not of the essence of democracy; it is not necessary, nor, indeed, in most cases, practicable. Democracies to which Mr. Lincoln's definition would fairly enough apply have existed, and now exist, in which, though the supreme authority reside in the people, yet they can act only indirectly on the national policy. This generation has seen a democracy with an imperial figurehead, and in all that have ever existed the body politic has never embraced all the inhabitants included within its territory, the right to share in the direction of affairs has been confined to citizens, and citizenship has been further restricted by various limitations, sometimes of property, sometimes of nativity, and always of age and sex.

The framers of the American Constitution were far from wishing or intending to found a democracy in the strict sense of the word, though, as was inevitable, every expansion of the scheme of government they elaborated has been in a democratical direction. But this has been generally the slow result of growth, and not the sudden innovation of theory; in fact, they had a profound disbelief in theory, and knew better than to commit the folly of breaking with the past. They were not seduced by the French fallacy that a new system of government could be ordered like a new suit of clothes. They would as soon have thought of ordering a new suit of flesh and skin. It is only on the roaring loom of time that the stuff is woven for such a vesture of their thought and experience as they were meditating. They recognized fully the value of tradition and habit as the great allies of permanence and stability. They all had that distaste for innovation which belonged to their race, and many of them a distrust of human nature derived from their creed. The day of sentiment was over, and no dithyrambic affirmations or fine-drawn analyses of the Rights of Man would serve their present turn. This was a practical question, and they addressed themselves to it as men of knowledge and judgment should. Their problem was how to adapt English principles and precedents to the new conditions of American life, and they solved it with singular discretion. They put as many obstacles as they could contrive, not in the way of the people's will, but of their whim. With few exceptions they probably admitted the logic of the then accepted syllogism,—democracy, anarchy, despotism. But this formula was framed upon the experience of small cities shut up to stew within their narrow walls where the number of citizens made but an inconsiderable fraction of the inhabitants, where every passion was reverberated from house to house and from man to man with gathering rumor till every impulse became gregarious and therefore inconsiderate, and every popular assembly needed but an infusion of eloquent sophistry to turn it into a mob, all the more dangerous because sanctified with the formality of law.

Fortunately their case was wholly different. They were to legislate for a widely scattered population and for States already practiced in the discipline of a partial independence. They had an unequaled opportunity and enormous advantages. The material they had to work upon was already democratical by instinct and habitude. It was tempered to their hands by more than a century's schooling in self-government. They had but to give permanent and conservative form to a ductile mass. In giving impulse and direction to their new institutions, especially, in supplying them with checks and balances, they had a great help and safeguard in their federal organization. The different, sometimes conflicting, interests and social systems of the several States made existence as a Union and coalescence into a nation conditional on a constant practice of moderation and compromise. The very elements of disintegration were the best guides in political training. Their children learned the lesson of compromise only too well, and it was the application of it to a question of fundamental morals that cost us our civil war. We learned once for all that compromise makes a good umbrella but a poor roof; that it is a temporary expedient, often wise in party politics, almost sure to be unwise in statesmanship.

Has not the trial of democracy in America proved, on the whole, successful? If it had not, would the Old World be vexed with any fears of its proving contagious? This trial would have been less severe could it have been made with a people homogeneous in race, language, and traditions, whereas the United States have been called on to absorb and assimilate enormous masses of foreign population heterogeneous in all these respects, and drawn mainly from that class which might fairly say that the world was not their friend, nor the world's law. The previous condition too often justified the traditional Irishman, who, landing in New York and asked what his politics were, inquired if there was a Government there, and on being told that there was, retorted, "Thin I'm agin it!" We have taken from Europe the poorest, the most ignorant, the most turbulent of her people and have made them over into good citizens, who have added to our wealth, and who are ready to die in defence of a country and of institutions which they know to be worth dying for. The exceptions have been (and they are lamentable exceptions) where these hordes of ignorance and poverty have coagulated in great cities. But the social system is yet to seek which has not to look the same terrible wolf in the eyes. On the other hand, at this very moment Irish peasants are buying up the worn-out farms of Massachusetts, and making them productive again by the same virtues of industry and thrift that once made them profitable to the English ancestors of the men who are deserting them. To have achieved even these prosaic results (if you choose to call them so), and that out of materials the most discordant, —I might say the most recalcitrant,—argues a certain beneficent virtue in the system that could do it, and is not to be accounted for by mere luck. Carlyle said scornfully that America meant only roast turkey every day for everybody. He forgot that States, as Bacon said of wars, go on their bellies. As for the security of property, it should be tolerably well secured in a country where every other man hopes to be rich, even though the only property qualification be the ownership of two hands that add to the general wealth. Is it not the best security for anything to interest the largest possible number of persons in its preservation and the smallest in its division? In point of fact, far-seeing men count the increasing power of wealth and its combinations as one of the chief dangers with which the institutions of the United States are threatened in the not distant future. The right of individual property is no doubt the very corner-stone of civilization as hitherto understood, but I am a little impatient of being told that property is entitled to exceptional consideration because it bears all the burdens of the State. It bears those, indeed, which can most easily be borne, but poverty pays with its person the chief expenses of war, pestilence, and famine. Wealth should not forget this, for poverty is beginning to think of it now and then. Let me not be misunderstood. I see as clearly as any man possibly can, and rate as highly, the value of wealth, and of hereditary wealth, as the security of refinement, the feeder of all those arts that ennoble and beautify life, and as making a country worth living in. Many an ancestral hall here in England has been a nursery of that culture which has been of example and benefit to all. Old gold has a civilizing virtue which new gold must grow old to be capable of secreting.

I should not think of coming before you to defend or to criticize any form of government. All have their virtues, all their defects, and all have illustrated one period or another in the history of the race, with signal services to humanity and culture. There is not one that could stand a cynical cross-examination by an experienced criminal lawyer, except that of a perfectly wise and perfectly good despot, such as the world has never seen, except in that white-haired king of Browning's who

> "Lived long ago
> In the morning of the world,
> When Earth was nearer Heaven than now."

The English race, if they did not invent government by discussion, have at least carried it nearest to perfection in practice. It seems a very safe and reasonable contrivance for occupying the attention of the country, and is certainly a better way of settling questions than by push of pike. Yet, if one should ask it why it should not rather be called government by gabble, it would have to fumble in its pocket a good while before it found the change for a convincing reply. As matters stand, too, it is beginning to be doubtful whether Parliament and Congress sit at Westminster and Washington or in the editors' rooms of the leading journals, so thoroughly is everything debated before the authorized and responsible debaters get on their legs. And what shall we say of government by a majority of voices? To a person who in the last century would have called himself an Impartial Observer, a numerical preponderance seems on the whole, as clumsy a way of arriving at truth as could well be devised, but experience has apparently shown it to be a convenient arrangement for determining what may be expedient or advisable or practicable at any given moment. Truth, after all, wears a different face to everybody, and it would be too tedious to wait till all were agreed. She is said to lie at the bottom of a well, for the very reason, perhaps, that whoever looks down in search of her sees his own image at the bottom, and is persuaded not only that he has seen the goddess, but that she is far better looking than he had imagined.

The arguments against universal suffrage are equally unanswerable. "What," we exclaim, "shall Tom, Dick and Harry have as much weight in the scale as I?" Of course, nothing could be more absurd. And yet universal suffrage has not been the instrument of greater unwisdom than contrivances of a more select description. Assemblies could be mentioned composed entirely of Masters of Arts and Doctors in Divinity which have sometimes shown traces of human passion or prejudice in their votes. Have the Serene Highnesses and Enlightened Classes carried on the business of Mankind so well, then, that there is no use in trying a less costly method? The democratic theory is that those Constitutions are likely to prove steadiest which have the broadest base, that the right to vote makes a safety-valve of every voter, and that the best way of teaching a man how to vote is to give him the chance of practice. For the question is no longer the academic one, "Is it wise to give every man the ballot?" but rather the practical one, "Is it prudent to deprive whole classes of it any longer?" It may be conjectured that it is cheaper in the long run to lift men up than to hold them down, and that the ballot in their hands is less dangerous to society than a sense of wrong in their heads. At any rate this is the dilemma to which the drift of opinion has been for some time sweeping us, and in politics a dilemma is a more unmanageable thing to hold by the horns than a wolf by the ears. It is said that the right of suffrage is not valued when it is indiscriminately bestowed, and there may be some truth in this, for I have observed that what men prize most is a privilege, even if it be that of chief mourner at a funeral. But is there not danger that it will be valued at more than its worth if denied, and that some illegitimate way will be sought to make up for the want of it? Men who have a voice in public affairs are at once affiliated with one or other of the great parties between which society is divided, merge their individual hopes and opinions in its safer, because more generalized, hopes and opinions, are disciplined by its tactics, and acquire, to a certain degree, the orderly qualities of an army. They no longer belong to a class, but to a body corporate. Of one thing, at least, we may be certain, that, under whatever method of helping things to go wrong man's wit can contrive, those who have the divine right to govern will be found to govern in the end, and that the highest privilege to which the majority of mankind can aspire is that of being governed by those wiser than they. Universal suffrage has in the United States sometimes been made the instrument of inconsiderate changes, under the notion of reform, and this from a misconception of the true meaning of popular government. One of these has been the substitution in many of the states of popular election for official selection in the choice of judges. The same system applied to military officers was the source of much evil during our civil war, and, I believe, had to be abandoned. But it has been also true that on all great questions of national policy a reserve of prudence and discretion has been brought out at the critical moment to turn the scale in favor of a wiser decision. An appeal to the reason of the people has never been known to fail in the long run. It is, perhaps, true that, by effacing the principle of passive obedience, democracy, ill understood, has slackened the spring of that ductility to discipline which is essential to "the unity and married calm of States." But I feel assured that experience and necessity will cure this evil, as they have shown their power to cure others. And under what frame of policy have evils ever been remedied till they became intolerable, and shook men out of their indolent indifference through their fears?

We are told that the inevitable result of democracy is to sap the foundations of personal independence, to weaken the principle of authority, to lessen the respect due to eminence, whether in station, virtue, or genius. If these things were so, society could not hold together. Perhaps the best forcing-house of robust individuality would be where public opinion is inclined to be most overbearing, as he must be of heroic temper who should walk along Piccadilly at the height of the season in a soft hat. As for authority, it is one of the symptoms of the time that the religious reverence for it is declining everywhere, but this is due partly to the fact that statecraft is no longer looked upon as a mystery, but as a business, and partly to the decay of superstition, by which I mean the habit of respecting what we are told to respect rather than what is respectable in itself. There is more rough and tumble in the American democracy than is altogether agreeable to people of sensitive nerves and refined habits, and the people take their political duties lightly and laughingly, as is, perhaps, neither unnatural nor unbecoming in a young giant. Democracies can no more jump away from their own shadows than the rest of us can. They no doubt sometimes make mistakes and pay honor to men who do not deserve it. But they do this because they believe them worthy of it, and though it be true that the idol is the measure of the worshipper, yet the worship has in it the germ of a nobler religion. But is it democracies alone that fall into these errors? I, who have seen it proposed to erect a statue to Hudson, the railway king, and have heard Louis Napoleon hailed as the savior of society by men who certainly had no democratic associations or leanings, am not ready to think so. But democracies have likewise their finer instincts. I have also seen the wisest states-man and most pregnant speaker of our generation, a man of humble birth and ungainly manners, of little culture beyond what his own genius supplied, become more absolute in power than any monarch of modern times through the reverence of his countrymen for his honesty, his wisdom, his sincerity, his faith in God and man, and the nobly humane simplicity of his char-acter. And I remember another whom popular respect en-veloped as with a halo, the least vulgar of men, the most austerely genial, and the most independent of opinion. Wherever he went he never met a stranger, but everywhere neighbors and friends proud of him as their ornament and decoration. Institutions which could bear and breed such men as Lincoln and Emerson had surely some energy for good. No, amid all the fruitless turmoil and miscarriage of the world, if there be one thing steadfast and of favorable omen, one thing to make optimism distrust its own obscure distrust, it is the rooted instinct in men to admire what is better and more beautiful than themselves. The touchstone of political and social institutions is their ability to supply them with worthy objects of this sentiment, which is the very tap-root of civilization and progress. There would seem to be no readier way of feeding it with the elements of growth and vigor than such an organization of society as will enable men to respect themselves, and so to justify them in respecting others.

Such a result is quite possible under other conditions than those of an avowedly democratical Constitution. For I take it that the real essence of democracy was fairly enough defined by the First Napoleon when he said that the French Revolution meant "la carrière ouverte aux talents"—a clear pathway for merit of whatever kind. I should be inclined to paraphrase this by calling democracy that form of society, no matter what its political classification, in which every man had a chance and knew that he had it. If a man can climb, and feels himself encouraged to climb, from a coalpit to the highest position for which he is fitted, he can well afford to be indifferent what name is given to the government under which he lives. The Bailli of Mirabeau, uncle of the more famous tribune of that name, wrote in 1771: "The English are, in my opinion, a hundred times more agitated and more unfortunate than the very Algerines themselves, because they do not know and will not know till the destruction of their overswollen power, which I believe very near, whether they are monarchy, aristocracy, or democracy, and wish to play the part of all three." England has not been obliging enough to fulfill the Bailli's prophecy, and perhaps it was this very carelessness about the name, and concern about the substance of popular government, this skill in getting the best out of things as they are, in utilizing all the motives which influence men, and in giving one direction to many impulses, that has been a principal factor of her greatness and power. Perhaps it is fortunate to have an unwritten constitution, for men are prone to be tinkering the work of their own hands, whereas they are more willing to let time and circumstance mend or modify what time and circumstances have made. All free governments, whatever their name, are in reality governments by public opinion, and it is on the quality of this public opinion that their prosperity depends. It is, therefore, their first duty to purify the element from which they draw the breath of life. With the growth of democracy grows also the fear, if not the danger, that this atmosphere may be corrupted with poisonous exhalations from lower and more malarious levels, and the question of sanitation becomes more instant and pressing. Democracy in its best sense is merely the letting in of light and air. Lord Sherbrooke, with his usual epigrammatic terseness, bids you educate your future rulers. But would this alone be a sufficient safeguard? To educate the intelligence is to enlarge the horizon of its desires and wants. And it is well that this should be so. But the enterprise must go deeper and prepare the way for satisfying those desires and wants in so far as they are legitimate. What is really ominous of danger to the existing order of things is not democracy (which, properly understood, is a conservative force), but the Socialism, which may find a fulcrum in it. If we cannot equalize conditions and fortunes any more than we can equalize the brains of men—and a very sagacious person has said that "where two men ride of a horse one must ride behind"—we can yet, perhaps, do something to correct those methods and influences that lead to enormous inequalities, and to prevent their growing more enormous. It is all very well to pooh-pooh Mr. George and to prove him mistaken in his political economy. I do not believe that land should be divided because the quantity of it is limited by nature. Of what may this not be said? *A fortiori,* we might on the same principle insist on a division of human wit, for I have observed that the quantity of this has been even more inconveniently limited. Mr. George himself has an inequitably large share of it.

But he is right in his impelling motive; right also, I am convinced, in insisting that humanity makes a part, by far the most important part, of political economy; and in thinking man to be of more concern and more convincing than the longest columns of figures in the world. For unless you include human nature in your addition, your total is sure to be wrong and your deductions from it fallacious. Communism means barbarism, but Socialism means, or wishes to mean, coöperation and community of interests, sympathy, the giving to the hands not so large a share as to the brains, but a larger share than hitherto in the wealth they must combine to produce—means, in short, the practical application of Christianity to life, and has in it the secret of an orderly and benign reconstruction. State Socialism would cut off the very roots in personal character—self-help, forethought, and frugality—which nourish and sustain the trunk and branches of every vigorous Commonwealth.

I do not believe in violent changes, nor do I expect them. Things in possession have a very firm grip. One of the strongest cements of society is the conviction of mankind that the state of things into which they are born is a part of the order of the universe, as natural, let us say, as that the sun should go around the earth. It is a conviction that they will not surrender except on compulsion, and a wise society should look to it that this compulsion be not put upon them. For the individual man there is no radical cure, outside of human nature itself, for the evils to which human nature is heir. The rule will always hold good that you must

"Be your own palace or the world's your gaol."

But for artificial evils, for evils that spring from want of thought, thought must find a remedy somewhere. There has been no period of time in which wealth has been more sensible of its duties than now. It builds hospitals, it establishes missions among the poor, it endows schools. It is one of the advantages of accumulated wealth, and of the leisure it renders possible, that people have time to think of the wants and sorrows of their fellows. But all these remedies are partial and palliative merely.

L

It is as if we should apply plasters to a single pustule of the smallpox with a view of driving out the disease. The true way is to discover and to extirpate the germs. As society is now constituted these are in the air it breathes, in the water it drinks, in things that seem, and which it has always believed, to be the most innocent and healthful. The evil elements it neglects corrupt these in their springs and pollute them in their courses. Let us be of good cheer, however, remembering that the misfortunes hardest to bear are those which never come. The world has outlived much, and will outlive a great deal more, and men have contrived to be happy in it. It has shown the strength of its constitution in nothing more than in surviving the quack medicines it has tried. In the scales of the destinies brawn will never weigh so much as brain. Our healing is not in the storm or in the whirlwind, it is not in monarchies, or aristocracies, or democracies, but will be revealed by the still small voice that speaks to the conscience and the heart, prompting us to a wider and wiser humanity.

THE WORKING OF THE AMERICAN DEMOCRACY[1]

CHARLES WILLIAM ELIOT

[Charles William Eliot (1834——) has been for a great many years one of the foremost figures in American education. During the larger part of his career he was president of Harvard University, a position which he filled with notable distinction until his voluntary retirement in 1909. He has not only written and spoken much on educational matters, but has written and spoken much on civic affairs, his utterances always commanding attention because of their clearness and thoughtfulness. The discussion of the achievements of American democracy, which is here given with some abridgment, was originally delivered in 1888 before the Phi Beta Kappa Society of Harvard University.]

In discussing some parts of our national experience, I intend to confine myself to moral and intellectual phenomena, and shall have little to say about the material prosperity of the

[1]From *American Contributions to Civilization*. (Copyright, 1907, The Century Company.) Reprinted by permission.

country. The rapid growth of the United States in population, wealth, and everything which constitutes material strength is, indeed, marvelous; but this concomitant of the existence of democratic institutions in a fertile land, rich also in minerals, ores, oil, and gas, has often been dilated upon, and may be dismissed with only two remarks: First, that a great deal of moral vigor has been put into the material development of the United States; and, secondly, that widespread comfort ought to promote rather than to hinder the civilizing of a people. Sensible and righteous government ought ultimately to make a nation rich; and although this proposition cannot be directly reversed, yet diffused well-being, comfort, and material prosperity establish a fair presumption in favor of the government and the prevailing social conditions under which these blessings have been secured.

The first question I wish to deal with is a fundamental one: How wisely, and by what process, has the American people made up its mind upon public questions of supreme difficulty and importance? Not how will it, or how might it, make up its mind, but how has it made up its mind? It is commonly said that the multitude, being ignorant and untrained, cannot reach so wise a conclusion upon questions of state as the cultivated few; that the wisdom of a mass of men can only be an average wisdom at the best; and that democracy, which in things material levels up, in things intellectual and moral levels down. Even De Tocqueville says that there is a middling standard of knowledge in a democracy, to which some rise and others descend. Let us put these speculative opinions, which have so plausible a sound, in contrast with American facts, and see what conclusions are to be drawn.

The people of this country have had three supreme questions to settle within the last hundred and thirty years: first, the question of independence of Great Britain; secondly, the question of forming a firm federal union; and thirdly, the question of maintaining that union at whatever cost of blood and treasure. In the decision of these questions, four generations of men took active part. The first two questions were settled by a population mainly English; but when the third was decided, the foreign admixture was already considerable. That graver or more far-reaching political problems could be presented to any people, it is impossible to imagine. Everybody can now see that in each case the only wise decision was arrived at by the multitude, in spite of difficulties and dangers which many contemporary statesmen and publicists of our own and other lands thought insuperable. It is quite the fashion to laud to the skies the second of these three great achievements of the American democracy; but the creation of the Federal Union, regarded as a wise determination of a multitude of voters, was certainly not more remarkable than the other two. No government—tyranny or oligarchy, despotic or constitutional—could possibly have made wiser decisions or executed them more resolutely, as the event has proved in each of the three cases mentioned.

So much for the wisdom of these great resolves. Now, by what process were they arrived at?

In each case the process was slow, covering many years during which discussion and debate went on in pulpits, legislatures, public meetings, newspapers, and books. The best minds of the country took part in these prolonged debates. Party passions were aroused; advocates on each side disputed before the people; the authority of recognized political leaders was invoked; public spirit and selfish interest were appealed to; and that vague but powerful sentiment called love of country, felt equally by high and low, stirred men's hearts and lit the intellectual combat with lofty emotion. In presence of such a protracted discussion, a multitude of interested men make up their minds just as one interested man does. They listen, compare what they hear with their own experience, consider the bearings of the question on their own interests, and consult their self-respect, their hopes, and their fears. Not one in a thousand of them could originate, or even state with precision, the arguments he hears; not one in a thousand could give a clear account of his own observations, processes of thought, and motives of action upon the subject —but the collective judgment is informed and guided by the keener wits and stronger wills, and the collective wisdom is higher and surer in guiding public conduct than that of one mind or of several superior minds uninstructed by million-eyed observation and million-tongued debate. . . .

I shall next consider certain forms of mental and moral activity which the American democracy demands of hundreds of thousands of the best citizens, but which are without parallel in despotic and oligarchic states. I refer to the widely diffused and ceaseless activity which maintains, first, the immense Federal Union, with all its various subdivisions into states, counties, and towns; secondly, the voluntary system in religion; and thirdly, the voluntary system in the higher instruction.

To have carried into successful practice on a great scale the federative principle, which binds many semi-independent states into one nation, is a good work done for all peoples. Federation promises to counteract the ferocious quarrelsomeness of mankind, and to abolish the jealousy of trade; but its price in mental labor and moral initiative is high. It is a system which demands not only vital force at the heart of the state, but a diffused vitality in every part. In a despotic government the intellectual and moral force of the whole organism radiates from the central seat of power; in a federal union political vitality must be diffused throughout the whole organism, as animal heat is developed and maintained in every molecule of the entire body. The success of the United States as a federal union has been and is effected by the watchfulness, industry, and public spirit of millions of men who spend in that noble cause the greater part of their leisure, and of the mental force which can be spared from bread-winning occupations. The costly expenditure goes on without ceasing, all over the country, wherever citizens come together to attend to the affairs of the village, town, county, or state. This is the price of liberty and union. The well-known promptness and skill of Americans in organizing a new community result from the fact that hundreds of thousands of Americans—and their fathers before them—have had practice in managing public affairs. To get this practice costs time, labor, and vitality, which in a despotic or oligarchic state are seldom spent in this direction.

The successful establishment and support of religious institutions—churches, seminaries, and religious charities—upon a purely voluntary system, is another unprecedented achievement of the American democracy. In only three generations American democratic society has effected the complete separation of church and state, a reform which no other people has ever attempted. Yet religious institutions are not stinted in the United States; on the contrary, they abound and thrive, and all alike are protected and encouraged, but not supported, by the state. Who has taken up the work which the state has relinquished? Somebody has had to do it, for the work is done. Who provides the money to build churches, pay salaries, conduct missions, and educate ministers? Who supplies the brains for organizing and maintaining these various activities? This is the work, not of a few officials, but of millions of intelligent and devoted men and women scattered through all the villages and cities of the broad land. The maintenance of churches, seminaries, and charities by voluntary contributions and by the administrative labors of volunteers, implies an enormous and incessant expenditure of mental and moral force. It is a force which must ever be renewed from generation to generation; for it is a personal force, constantly expiring, and as constantly to be replaced. Into the maintenance of the voluntary system in religion has gone a good part of the moral energy which three generations have been able to spare from the work of getting a living; but it is worth the sacrifice, and will be accounted in history one of the most remarkable feats of American public spirit and faith in freedom.

A similar exhibition of diffused mental and moral energy has accompanied the establishment and the development of a system of higher instruction in the United States, with no inheritance of monastic endowments, and no gifts from royal or ecclesiastical personages disposing of great resources derived from the state, and with but scanty help from the public purse. Whoever is familiar with the colleges and universities of the United States knows that the creation of these democratic institutions has cost the life-work of thousands of devoted men. At the sacrifice of other aspirations, and under heavy discouragements and disappointments, but with faith and hope, these teachers and trustees have built up institutions, which, however imperfect, have cherished scientific enthusiasm, fostered piety, literature, art, and maintained the standards of honor and public duty, and steadily kept in view the ethical ideas which democracy cherishes. It has been a popular work, to which large numbers of people in successive generations have contributed of their substance or of their labor. The endowment of institutions of education, including libraries and museums, by private persons in the United States, is a phenomenon without precedent or parallel, and is a legitimate effect of democratic institutions. Under a tyranny—were it that of a Marcus Aurelius—or an oligarchy—were it as enlightened as that which now rules Germany— such a phenomenon would be simply impossible. The University of Strasburg, was lately established by an imperial decree, and is chiefly maintained out of the revenue of the state. Harvard University has been 250 years in growing to its present stature, and is even now inferior at many points to the new University of Strasburg; but Harvard is the creation of thousands of persons, living and dead, rich and poor, learned and simple, who have voluntarily given it their time, thought, or money, and lavished upon it their affection; Strasburg exists by the mandate of the ruling few directing upon it a part of the product of ordinary taxation. Like the voluntary system in religion, the voluntary system in the higher education fortifies democracy; each demands from the community a large outlay of intellectual activity and moral vigor.

There is another direction in which the people of the United States have spent and are now spending a vast amount of intellectual and moral energy—a direction not, as in the three cases just considered, absolutely peculiar to the American republic, but still highly characteristic of democracy. I mean the service of corporations. Within the last hundred years the American people have invented a new and large application of the ancient principle of incorporation. We are so accustomed to corporations as indispensable agents in carrying on great public works and services, and great industrial or financial operations, that we forget the very recent development of the corporation with limited liability as a common business agent. Prior to 1789 there were only two corporations for business purposes in Massachusetts. The English general statute which provides for incorporation with limited liability dates only from 1855. No other nation has made such general or such successful use of corporate powers as the American—and for the reason that the method is essentially a democratic method, suitable for a country in which great individual or family properties are rare, and small properties are numerous. Freedom of incorporation makes possible great combinations of small capitals, and, while winning the advantages of concentrated management, permits diffused ownership. These merits have been quickly understood and turned to account by the American democracy. The service of many corporations has become even more important than the service of the several States of the Union. The managers of great companies have trusts reposed in them which are matched only in the highest executive offices of the nation; and they are relatively free from the numerous checks and restrictions under which the highest national officials must always act. The activity of corporations, great and small, penetrates every part of the industrial and social body, and their daily maintenance brings into play more mental and moral force than the maintenance of all the governments on the Continent combined. . . .

It is easy to see some of the reasons why American corporations command the services of men of high capacity and character, who in other countries or in earlier times would have been in the service of the state. In American democratic society corporations supplement the agencies of the state, and their functions have such importance in determining conditions of labor, diffusing comfort and general well-being among millions of people, and utilizing innumerable large streams and little rills of capital, that the upper grades of their service are reached by merit, are filled, as a rule, upon a tenure during good behavior and efficiency, are well paid, and have great dignity and consideration. Of the enormous material benefits which have resulted from the American extension of the principle of incorporation, I need say nothing. I wish only to point out that freedom of incorporation, though no longer exclusively a democratic agency, has given strong support to democratic institutions; and that a great wealth of intellect, energy, and fidelity is devoted to the service of corporations by their officers and directors.

The four forms of mental and moral activity which I have been considering—that which maintains political vitality throughout the Federal Union; that which supports unsubsidized religious institutions; that which develops the higher instruction in the arts and sciences, and trains men for all the professions; and that which is applied to the service of corporations—all illustrate the educating influence of democratic institutions—an influence which foreign observers are apt to overlook or underestimate. The ballot is not the only political institution which has educated the American democracy. Democracy is a training-school in which multitudes learn in many ways to take thought for others, to exercise public functions, and to bear public responsibilities.

So many critics of the theory of democracy have maintained that a democratic government would be careless of public obligations, and unjust toward private property, that it will be interesting to inquire what a century of American experience indicates upon this important point. Has there been any disposition on the part of the American democracy to create exaggerated public debts, to throw the burden of public debts on posterity rather than on the present generation, or to favor in legislation the poorer sort as against the richer, the debtor as against the creditor?

The answer to the question is not doubtful. With the exception of the sudden creation of the great national debt occasioned by the Civil War, the American communities have been very moderate in borrowing, the State debts being for the most part insignificant, and the city debts far below the English standard. Moreover, these democratic communities, with a few local and temporary exceptions, pay their public debts more promptly than any state under the rule of a despot or a class has ever done. The government of the United States has once paid the whole of its public debt, and is in a fair way to perform that feat again. . . . .

After observing the facts of a full century, one may therefore say of the American democracy that it has contracted public debt with moderation, paid it with unexampled promptness, acquired as good a public credit as the world has ever known, made private property secure, and shown no tendency to attack riches or to subsidize poverty, or in either direction to violate the fundamental principle of democracy, that all men are equal before the law. The significance of these facts is prodigious. They mean that, as regards private property and its security, a government by the many, for the many, is more to be trusted than any other form of government; and that as regards public indebtedness, an experienced democracy is more likely to exhibit just sentiments and practical good judgment than an oligarchy or a tyranny.

An argument against democracy, which evidently had great weight with Sir Henry Maine, because he supposed it to rest upon the experience of mankind, is stated as follows: Progress and reformation have always been the work of the few, and have been opposed by the many; therefore democracies will be obstructive. This argument is completely refuted by the first century of the American democracy, alike in the field of morals and jurisprudence, and the field of manufactures and trade. Nowhere, for instance, has the great principle of religious toleration been so thoroughly put in practice as in the United States; nowhere have such well-meant and persistent efforts been made to improve the legal status of women; nowhere has the conduct of hospitals, asylums, reformatories, and prisons been more carefully studied; nowhere have legislative remedies for acknowledged abuses and evils been more promptly and perseveringly sought. There was a certain plausibility in the idea that the multitude, who live by labor in established modes, would be opposed to inventions which would inevitably cause industrial revolutions; but American experience completely upsets this notion. For promptness in making physical forces and machinery do the work of men, the people of the United States surpass incontestably all other peoples. The people that invented and introduced with perfect commercial success the river steamboat, the cotton-gin, the parlor-car and the sleeping-car, the grain-elevator, the street railway—both surface and elevated—the telegraph, the telephone, the rapid printing-press, the cheap book and news-paper, the sewing-machine, the steam fire-engine, agricultural machinery, the pipe-lines for natural oil and gas, and machine-made clothing, boots, furniture, tools, screws, wagons, firearms, and watches—this is not a people to vote down or hinder labor-saving invention or beneficent industrial revolution. The fact is that in a democracy the interests of the greater number will ultimately prevail as they should. It was the stage-drivers and inn-keepers, not the multitude, who wished to suppress the loco-motive; it is some publishers and typographical unions, not the mass of the people, who wrongly imagine that they have an in-terest in making books dearer than they need be. Furthermore, a just liberty of combination and perfect equality before the law, such as prevail in a democracy, enable men or companies to en-gage freely in new undertakings at their own risk, and bring them to triumphant success, if success be in them, whether the multitude approve them or not. The consent of the multitude is not necessary to the success of a printing-press which prints twenty thousand copies of a newspaper in an hour, or of a ma-chine cutter which cuts out twenty overcoats at one chop. In short, the notion that democracy will hinder religious, political, and social reformation and progress, or restrain commercial and industrial improvement, is a chimera.

There is another criticism of the working of democratic insti-tutions, more formidable than the last, which the American democracy is in a fair way to dispose of. It is said that democ-racy is fighting against the best-determined and most peremp-tory of biological laws, namely, the law of heredity, with which law the social structure of monarchical and oligarchical states is in strict conformity. This criticism fails to recognize the dis-tinction between artificial privileges transmissible without re-gard to inherited virtues or powers, and inheritable virtues or powers transmissible without regard to hereditary privileges.

Artificial privileges will be abolished by a democracy; natural, inheritable virtues or powers are as surely transmissible under a democracy as under any other form of government. Families can be made just as enduring in a democratic as in an oligarchic State, if family permanence be desired and aimed at. The desire for the continuity of vigorous families, and for the reproduction of beauty, genius, and nobility of character is universal. "From fairest creatures we desire increase" is the commonest of sentiments. The American multitude will not take the children of distinguished persons on trust; but it is delighted when an able man has an abler son, or a lovely mother a lovelier daughter. That a democracy does not prescribe the close intermarriage which characterizes a strict aristocracy, so-called, is physically not a disadvantage, but a great advantage for the freer society. The French nobility and the English House of Lords furnish good evidence that aristocracies do not succeed in perpetuating select types of intellect or of character.

From this consideration of the supposed conflict between democracy and the law of heredity the transition is easy to my last topic; namely, the effect of democratic institutions on the production of ladies and gentlemen. There can be no question that a general amelioration of manners is brought about in a democracy by public schools, democratic churches, public conveyances, without distinction of class, universal suffrage, town-meetings, and all the multifarious associations in which democratic society delights; but this general amelioration might exist, and yet the highest types of manners might fail. Do these fail? On this important point American experience is already interesting, and I think conclusive. Forty years ago Emerson said it was a chief felicity of our country that it excelled in women. It excels more and more. Who has not seen in public and in private life American women unsurpassable in grace and graciousness, in serenity and dignity, in effluent gladness and abounding courtesy? Now, the lady is the consummate fruit of human society at its best. In all the higher walks of American life there are men whose bearing and aspect at once distinguish them as gentlemen. They have personal force, magnanimity, moderation, and refinement; they are quick to see and to sympathize; they are pure, brave, and firm. These are also the qualities that command success; and herein lies the only natural connection between the possession of property and nobility of character. In a mobile or free society the excellent or noble man is likely to win ease and independence; but it does not follow that under any form of government the man of many possessions is necessarily excellent. On the evidence of my reading and of my personal observation at home and abroad, I fully believe that there is a larger proportion of ladies and gentlemen in the United States than in any other country. This proposition is, I think, true with the highest definition of the term "lady" or "gentleman;" but it is also true, if ladies and gentlemen are only persons who are clean and well-dressed, who speak gently and eat with their forks. It is unnecessary, however, to claim any superiority for democracy in this respect; enough that the highest types of manners in men and women are produced abundantly on democratic soil.

It would appear then from American experience that neither generations of privileged ancestors, nor large inherited possessions, are necessary to the making of a lady or a gentleman. What is necessary? In the first place, natural gifts. The gentleman is born in a democracy, no less than in a monarchy. In other words, he is a person of fine bodily and spiritual qualities, mostly innate. Secondly, he must have, through elementary education, early access to books, and therefore to great thoughts and high examples. Thirdly, he must be early brought into contact with some refined and noble person—father, mother, teacher, pastor, employer, or friend. These are the only necessary conditions in peaceful times and in law-abiding communities like ours. Accordingly, such facts as the following are common in the United States: One of the numerous children of a small farmer manages to fit himself for college, works his way through college, becomes a lawyer, at forty is a much-trusted man in one of the chief cities of the Union, and is distinguished for the courtesy and dignity of his bearing and speech. The son of a country blacksmith is taught and helped to a small college by his minister; he himself becomes a minister, has a long fight with poverty and ill-health, but at forty-five holds as high a place as his profession affords, and every line in his face and every tone in his voice betoken the gentleman. The sons and daughters of a successful shopkeeper take the highest places in the most cultivated society of their native place, and well deserve the preëminence accorded to them. The daughter of a man of very imperfect education, who began life with nothing and became a rich merchant, is singularly beautiful from youth to age, and possesses to the highest degree the charm of dignified and gracious manners. A young girl, not long out of school, the child of respectable but obscure parents, marries a public man, and in conspicuous station bears herself with a grace, discretion, and nobleness which she could not have exceeded had her blood been royal for seven generations. Striking cases of this kind will occur to every person in this assembly. They are everyday phenomena in American society. What conclusion do they establish? They prove that the social mobility of a democracy, which permits the excellent and well-endowed of either sex to rise and to seek out each other, and which gives every advantageous variation or sport in a family stock free opportunity to develop, is immeasurably more beneficial to a nation than any selective in-breeding, founded on class distinctions, which has ever been devised. Since democracy has every advantage for producing in due season and proportion the best human types, it is reasonable to expect that science and literature, music and art, and all the finer graces of society will develop and thrive in America, as soon as the more urgent tasks of subduing a wilderness and organizing society upon an untried plan are fairly accomplished.

Such are some of the reasons drawn from experience for believing that our ship of state is stout and sound; but she sails—

> " . . . the sea
> Of storm-engendering liberty—"

the happiness of the greatest number her destined haven. Her safety requires incessant watchfulness and readiness. Without trusty eyes on the lookout, and a prompt hand at the wheel, the stoutest ship may be dismantled by a passing squall. It is only intelligence and discipline which carry the ship to its port.

THE SURVIVAL OF CIVIL LIBERTY[1]

FRANKLIN HENRY GIDDINGS

[Franklin Henry Giddings (1855———) is a distinguished American sociologist. He was born in Sherman, Connecticut. After graduating from Union College, he engaged in journalism for several years. In 1888 he became professor of sociology in Bryn Mawr, holding this position until 1894 when he went to Columbia University. He is now professor of sociology and the history of civilization in that institution. The selection here given was first delivered as a commencement address at Oberlin College, June, 1899. Although it was called forth by the Spanish-American War, it is pertinent to the situation of the present day.]

Recent events have raised the question of the stability of American institutions. The war with Spain was bitterly deplored by many educated men, who feared that military activity would necessarily create arbitrary power and curtail the liberties of individual citizens. When our demand for the cession of the Philippine Islands was included in the terms of peace, and the treaty of Paris was followed by the despatch of troops to Manila to put down insurrection, these opponents of the nation's policy, believing that their worst fears were being realized, asserted that the American people, intoxicated with military success, were blindly departing from all the safe traditions of their history to enter upon a hazardous and probably fatal experiment of imperialism. The arguments of these men have disquieted many timid souls, some of whom seem to be already convinced that our republic is verily a thing of history—one more splendid failure added to the long list of glorious, but tragic attempts of earth's bravest sons to build an enduring state upon foundations of equality and self-government. Indeed, so despondent have some of our self-styled anti-imperialists become that, in their bitterness, they do not hesitate to malign the character of their fel-

[1]From *Democracy and Empire*. (Copyright, 1900, The Macmillan Company.) Reprinted by permission.

low-citizens, or to insult the fair fame of the nation that has nurtured and that still defends them. In one lamentable instance, a citizen of honored name has so far lost all sense of reality as to declare in a public address that "we are a great assassin nation," and that "the slaughter of patriots stains our hands."

And yet, these proclamations of doom have failed to arouse the nation. Some seventy millions of people continue their daily vocations in serenity of mind, wholly unconscious of the impending extinction of their liberties. Does this mean that the plain people, the bone and sinew of the nation, who hitherto have shown themselves intelligent enough to deal wisely and fearlessly with the gravest issues of human welfare are, after all, amazingly obtuse? Does it mean that, after a hundred years of level-headed self-government, the American people are now blindly moving toward a ruin which clear-sighted men should plainly foresee? Or, does it rather mean that these millions of plain people, with all their mental limitations, are still, as so often they have been in the past, immeasurably wiser—that they are gifted with a deeper insight, that they are endowed with a truer knowledge and a saner judgment, and that they are fortified with a sturdier faith—than are the prophets of gloom? That the latter is the true explanation I have not the shadow of a doubt, and for a brief hour I ask your attention to reasons in support of this belief.

And, first of all, we have the undeniable fact that the faith itself which the American people feel in their own power, in the stability of their institutions, and in the nobility of their destiny, is at the present moment unbounded. Whatever the pessimists may say, the millions of hard-working, common people do not believe that republican government has failed, or that civil liberty is not to be the heritage of their sons. Never since the Constitution was ratified by the thirteen original commonwealths have the American people, as a whole, felt so confident of their place among the nations, or so sure of the excellence of their polity, and of the vitality of their laws and immunities. Never have they been so profoundly convinced that their greatest work for civilization lies not in the past, but in the future. They stand at the beginning of the twentieth century, in their own minds fully assured that the responsibilities which they are about to face, and that the achievements which they expect to complete, are immeasurably greater than are those which have crowned the century of their experiment and discipline.

What, then, are the sources of this faith? Is it a baseless enthusiasm, a thoughtless confidence born of an ignorant conceit, or is it in reality a substantial and truthful forecast of the future, which we may safely accept, as one that is neither more nor less than a projection into coming years of those lessons that experience has taught us in the past?

The sources of all genuine faith in the future are two. The first is vitality. The second is our knowledge of what already is or has been.

The consciousness of vigorous life, the sense of physical power, imparts to those who have it an unconquerable faith in their ability to achieve; and this mere vitality is undoubtedly the primal source of the American's faith in himself and in the destiny of his country. It is also our best assurance that the faith will find realization. In no other population is there such abounding energy, such inventive ability, such fearless enterprise as in the American people. This vitality has been manifested not only in our industrial enterprise, but also in that very territorial expansion which of late has been under discussion. From the Louisiana purchase to the annexation of Hawaii we have seized, with unhesitating promptness, every opportunity to broaden our national domain and to extend our institutions to annexed populations. Even more convincingly has our vigor been shown in the fearlessness with which the cost of every new responsibility has been met. Whether this cost has been paid in treasure or in blood, the American people have met it without one moment's hesitation. Physical courage is, after all, the elemental factor in a nation's power, the very fountainhead of its moral stability and its faith; and that in such courage we are not lacking, the records of Lexington and Yorktown, of New

M

Orleans and Chapultepec, of Antietam and Gettysburg, of Manila and El Caney, will tell.

Next to vitality, and supplementing it, the basis of faith in the future is a sound, full knowledge of the present and the past. The American people know facts about their own numbers, resources, and activities, which fully justify their belief that they are at the beginning, not approaching the end, of their evolution as a civilized nation. Only in a few spots within our national domain does the density of population yet approach the average density of the older European countries. Notwithstanding the rapidity with which the best lands of the interior and of the Southwest have been appropriated as homesteads, the intensive cultivation of our vast domain has hardly begun. While, according to the census of 1890, the states constituting the north Atlantic division had a population of 107 to the square mile, the United States as a whole had less than 22 to the square mile. The western division had less than 3 to the square mile; the great north central division, comprising some of the most prosperous commonwealths in the Union, had less than 30; and the south Atlantic division, comprising the old slave-owning and cotton-growing states, had less than 33. A population of 300,000,000, instead of 75,000,000, or 80,000,000, would not seriously tax our food-producing capacity.

Into this domain the population of Europe continues to discharge its overflow; and the stream of immigration shows no marked decrease save in the exceptional years of industrial depression. Of chief significance, however, is the fact that the greater part of all the immigration that we have thus far received has consisted of the same nationalities from whose amalgamation the original American stock was produced. England, Ireland, Germany, and Scandinavia have sent to our shores the greater part of our population not descended from the American colonists. Of the foreign-born population enumerated in the United States in 1890, 33.76 per cent were from the United Kingdom, 30.11 per cent were from Germany, 10.61 per cent from Canada, 10.09 per cent from Norway, Sweden, and Denmark, 1.22 per cent from France, leaving only 14.21 per cent from all other countries. The total immigration to the United States from 1821 to the 30th of June, 1898, was 18,490,368, and of this total much more than two-thirds came from the United Kingdom and the Germanic countries. When we remember that it was the crossing of the Germanic and the Celtic stocks that produced the English race itself, we are obliged to assume that the future American people will be substantially the same human stuff that created the English common law, founded parliamentary institutions, established American self-government, and framed the Constitution of the United States.

All our knowledge of social evolution compels us to believe that a nation which has not yet begun to reach the limit of its resources and which is thus still receiving great additions to its population by an immigration of elements that, for the most part, are readily assimilated to the older stock, is one which, if no overwhelming catastrophe prevents, must continue for numberless generations to maintain and to perfect its civilization.

Nevertheless, it may be said, the institutions of civil liberty presuppose something more than a vigorous and growing population that has an unbounded faith in its own abilities and destinies. Great peoples have given themselves over to policies—not to say to crazes—that have resulted in the destruction of their primitive liberties and in the complete transformation of their institutions. An energetic people may devote itself to the production of wealth or to military achievements, and neglect the less alluring task of perfecting and protecting individual rights. Rome conquered the world, but at the cost of her republican simplicity. Florence and Venice achieved wealth and splendor, but bowed to despotism. France overran Europe with her armies, and then enthroned her own military dictator.

These lessons of history are often recalled, and their application to American conditions has often been attempted. I think it is high time to protest that, in scientific strictness, these lessons do not apply to ourselves in any important particular. The historian by this time should understand the truth (which the students of physical science in our generation have so completely mastered) that like antecedents have like consequents *when all conditions remain unchanged*, but that, when all conditions are changed, like antecedents, with unerring certainty, are followed by *unlike* consequents. Very slightly, indeed, do the conditions of American life today reproduce the conditions of Roman, Florentine, Venetian, or Parisian history.

The overwhelming difference is this: In the earlier days, republican institutions were cherished only here and there in exceptional communities, and they were threatened on every hand by the hosts of military despotism; today they are rooted in unnumbered communities, which only now and then are diverted by war from the normal pursuits of peace.

Rome, in the days of her republican freedom, was a single local community practically isolated from any similar social organization. Such was the situation also of each of the Italian republics and of Paris after the Revolution; for, outside of Paris, France was not yet republican. To undermine in a single isolated town or city any given form of government and to substitute for it something totally different, has never been a difficult undertaking. But to offset this fact we have the equally important truth—one of the most important that historical sociology discloses—that nothing is more difficult than to destroy institutions and customs that are rooted in more than one spot, if they admit of being carried from one place to another. The Roman Republic was destroyed, but not the Roman law, which lives today and is applied to the interests of millions more of human beings than in the days of Julius Cæsar. The Roman Empire was overthrown, but not the Roman system of provincial administration, which to this hour, in its essential features, is preserved in the municipal and departmental governments of every European state.

Bearing these truths in mind, let us look at the conditions presented by the United States. Instead of being a single city-state, organized on republican lines, practically isolated from any similar community, and, therefore, defenseless against any influence powerfully tending to undermine or to destroy it, the United States is a strongly organized aggregate of thousands of local republics, each one of which, practically independent in its home affairs, preserves all the traditions of English civil liberty, of democratic custom, and of American constitutional order.

It is true that not all of these self-governing local communities enjoy that perfect form of democratic administration which was developed in the New England town; but whether as towns, counties, or parishes, as incorporated villages, boroughs, or municipalities, practically all the subdivisions of the American commonwealths are self-governing bodies of one type or another. They make ordinances and elect magistrates, they raise and expend revenues. It is true that important modifications of local government are now taking place throughout the nation. The concentration of wealth and of population in the larger cities, the long-continued depression of agriculture, and the consequent abandonment of farming by large numbers of country-bred youth, are bringing about a certain readjustment of functions between state and township administration. It is easy for the state to raise money, increasingly difficult for the rural town. Consequently, we see a disposition to throw upon the state governments a part of the burden of maintaining roads and bridges, of supporting schools, and of caring for the insane and other defective persons. With this transfer of financial responsibility, goes, of course, a transfer of administrative regulation. To this extent, it must be admitted, we are witnessing a certain decay of that local self-government which hitherto has been most immediately bound up with the daily lives and lesser interests of the people. And even in the cities the abuses of popular power have, in some instances, led to a transfer of authority from municipal to state governments; as, for example in cities like Boston, which no longer elect or through their mayors appoint their police commissions, but accept them at the hands of the governor of the commonwealth. Yet, notwithstanding these facts, it is certain that throughout the national domain the lesser local governments still have great vitality, and that no modification of our administrative machinery is likely to strip them altogether of their functions. Far more probable is it, that the limit of addition to the duties of our commonwealth governments will soon be reached. Certain functions which in the past have been performed by townships and counties, or by municipalities, may be given over to the states because they pertain to matters in which all the people of the commonwealth are directly interested, but other matters of purely local interest will be left even more entirely than now to the local administrative organs. States may maintain the more important roads and bridges, but not the lesser ones. They will care for the insane, but probably not for the ordinary poor. They will support some of the higher institutions of learning, but not, to any great extent, the common schools.

Local administration, however, is not the only or, perhaps, the most important means through which the traditions of civil liberty are maintained in our American Republic. Of the greatest educational influence are the local courts and their procedure. So long as every boy is bound to learn, not through books, but through the events that happen year by year in his own township or county, the fundamental traditions of the common law, the immunity from arrest without a warrant, the personal responsibility of the officer of the law, the right of bail and of trial by jury, the right of free speech and of public meeting, there is little danger that the American people will submit tamely to any arbitrary attempt of a central government to abridge these liberties.

If these things are true, then it is further true that from the traditions and existing habits of any one of these thousands of self-governing local communities, together composing the United States of America, could be reproduced the entire fabric of American polity, if in every other one the entire constitutional system were suddenly destroyed. This is a fact unique in the history of civil liberty. It is a guarantee of the perpetuity of our institutions, so tremendous that only the blindest of pessimists can fail to appreciate its significance. Remembering that, as was said before, a form of law or type of institution, or even a custom, once rooted in more than one place on the earth's surface, is practically indestructible, since if destroyed in one it can always be reproduced from another, it is impossible to believe that any modification of our governmental system, whether by territorial expansion or by military activity, whether by the growth of trusts or by any other phenomenon of the pursuit of wealth, can ever, throughout the length and breadth of our vast domain, destroy in all these thousands of local communities the instincts, the habits, and the institutions of Anglo-Saxon civil liberty.

Not only will this civil liberty be preserved, but it will also be developed. The heritage of a nation which, historically speaking, is yet in its most vigorous youth, with generations of active effort for the perfection of civilization yet before it, civil liberty will not be worshipped with passive idolatry, but, continually thought about, worked over, and enlarged by a reflective people of abounding vitality and limitless faith in their own destiny, it will be brought to a perfection of justice, of discrimination, of fairness to all men such as has not yet been achieved under any human government.

To a great extent the task of all government—through its legislation, its interpretation of law, and its administrative activity—is to reconcile equality with liberty. Most of the restraints upon liberty are in the interest of that measure of equality which experience has shown to be necessary to social stability, and which the conscience of mankind declares to be right. The reconciliation, however, is not an easy thing to accomplish, and all systems of law and policy remain imperfect.

The equality to which we here refer, and with which public policy has to do, is not an equality of bodily powers, of mental abilities, or of moral attainments. In these matters men are not and, while biological evolution continues, cannot be equal. Only those writers who are willing to misrepresent their opponents ever attribute to the founders of the republic the absurd notion that in these personal attributes men are born equal and free. The equality which the state should create and cherish is that social condition which prevails when a just government restrains those who, being powerful, are also unscrupulous, from taking any unfair advantage of the weak, and when no artificial distinctions, privileges, or monopolies are created by the state itself to aggrandize the few by the impoverishment of the many. To permit the intelligent and the strong to profit by their superiority, so long as they derive their gain from the bounty of nature, and not from the enslavement or robbery of their brethren, is one thing; to permit or to encourage them to use their superiority at the expense of their fellows is a totally different thing; and it is the latter which is opposed by the notion of equality as a principle of civil government.

This notion, however, is of slow growth in the minds of men, and of slower application to the concrete facts of legal procedure, political status, property, trade, taxation, and the employment of labor. From the earliest days we in America have proclaimed the principle of equality before the law. All men, we say, in natural justice have, and in the courts must secure, substantially equal rights. Yet we have not always in practice faithfully adhered to this high standard. The poor man has not always had the same treatment as the rich man, at the bar of justice. Juries have been bribed, and so occasionally have been prosecuting attorneys and even judges. On the whole, however, our record in these matters has probably been higher than that of any preceding civilization in all human history; and it is certain that the moral forces of the nation are conspiring to make it yet more satisfactory in coming years.

Political equality was not an original principle of American government. Of the adult male citizens comprised within the population of less than four million souls dwelling in the United States a century ago, not one half enjoyed the political suffrage. A majority were disqualified by lack of property or of education. The approach to universal suffrage has been very gradually made by the abolition of the earlier restrictions, until now, in many of the commonwealths, voters need not even pay a poll-tax.

Political equality in the long run means an attempt to set limits to those inequalities of economic condition which rapidly grow up in a prosperous state if the rights of private property are unconditionally extended to all the requisites of production, and if no restraints are placed upon the methods of business competition or of trade combination. It is this question of the relation of the state to economic inequality which is by far the most perplexing one to the conscience and the judgment of the patriotic citizen. One immensely important restriction of liberty in the interest of equality was made at the foundation of our government, largely through the sagacity and fearlessness of Thomas Jefferson, who did not hesitate to antagonize the land-owning aristocracy of Virginia, to which he himself belonged. This was the prohibition of primogeniture and entail. Thanks to this wise restriction, the vast estates that under our present laws may be built up in America can be continued in the same families through successive generations only if their owners have the business ability to use them productively.

To what extent we shall further limit the freedom of bequest and the right of private accumulation, no statesman or economist has at this moment the prescience to foretell. We only know that thousands of thoughtful and conscientious men are asking the question whether the withdrawing of some portion of the land and productive capital of the nation from private ownership—as has been done in Australia and New Zealand—may not ultimately be demanded by natural justice and a due consideration for the highest social welfare. We know that experiments in the redistribution of taxation, with the avowed purpose of placing a larger share of public burdens upon the owners of great wealth, are not likely to cease for many years to come. At the same time, we may repose great confidence in both the Puritan conscience and the Yankee common sense of the American people. Whatever the difficulties of the undertaking, we may expect them to find a practical method for limiting the undue growth of economic inequality without discouraging business enterprise or destroying our prosperity.

The same good sense and sound morality may be expected to solve also the problems arising out of the conflicts of individual liberty with natural justice in our business methods. Legislatures and courts have for many years been earnestly endeavoring to maintain the old common-law rule against combinations in restraint of trade; but just how morality and business expediency are to be identified in practice, we do not yet clearly see. Certain it is that at the present moment the conscience of the people is far in advance of the positive law. The law as yet provides no way to punish a combination that deliberately crushes a legitimate business, not by permanently lowering prices for the benefit of consumers, but by a temporary cut which is not to be maintained after the rival is destroyed. Such conduct is not yet a crime, but an unsophisticated conscience pronounces it blameworthy, from a moral point of view as wrong as were the cattle-raiding and castle-burning exploits of mediæval barons, or as any act of wanton conquest. By one or another means it will ultimately be made impossible in a nation that values honorable dealing above gold.

As among educated men there are some who distrust the vital instincts of the people and the popular sense of justice, so also are there some who deplore the popular demand for equality. Blinded by a culture that is at once too sensitive and too narrow in its sympathies, these men would persuade us that only through the growth of economic inequality can we create a splendid art, develop a profound philosophy, and attain elegance of manners. To all such I would commend the thoughtful conclusions of that most cultivated, most reasonable of modern critics, Mr. Matthew Arnold, whose essays on "Democracy" and "Equality" are, perhaps, the sanest reflections on these great themes that our age has produced. It is not equality, it is rather the unchecked growth of a monstrous inequality that, as Arnold shows, ultimately destroys all fresh enthusiasms, all spontaneous sweetness, all brightness in social intercourse, and that brutalizes the selfish rich no less than the burdened poor. "Can it be denied," he asks, "that a certain approach to equality, at any rate a certain reduction of signal inequalities, is a natural, instinctive demand of that impulse which drives society as a whole—no longer individuals and limited classes only, but the mass of a community—to develop itself with the utmost possible fullness and freedom? Can it be denied, that to live in a society of equals tends in general to make a man's spirits expand, and his faculties work easily and actively; while, to live in a society of superiors, although it may occasionally be very good discipline, yet in general tends to tame the spirits and to make the play of the faculties less secure and active? Can it be denied, that to be heavily overshadowed, to be profoundly insignificant, has, on the whole, a depressing and benumbing effect on the character?" And of the common people in France he truly says, that the economic equality which was created among them by the Revolution and the "Code of Napoleon" has undoubtedly given to the lower classes "a self-respect and an enlargement of spirit, a consciousness of counting for something in their country's action, which has raised them in the scale of humanity." "The common people, in France," he continues, "seem to me the soundest part of the French nation. They seem to me more free from the two opposite degradations of multitudes, brutality and servility, to have a more developed human life, more of what distinguishes elsewhere the cultured classes from the vulgar, than the common people in any other country with which I am acquainted."

That this view of the relation of equality to the highest civilization prevails among the American people, as among the people of France, I presume no one will seriously question. At the same time, the American is more assertive, more self-reliant, more intolerant of an unnecessary limitation of his personal liberty than is the man of Gallic blood. The American is at bottom a Saxon-Norman. After all it is the blood of the old untamable pirates that courses through his veins. Consequently, he will continue to struggle with this practical problem of the conciliation of liberty with equality. This problem will continue to furnish the fundamental questions of his politics; and he will gradually solve it, not by the elaboration of an abstract theory, but by a practical dealing with concrete cases as they arise. Just as our law is developed largely through the evolution of equity, wherein a larger and sounder justice is made to override precedents and technicalities that have ceased to be a true expression of living conditions, so shall our politics also develop through the evolution of a larger equity, which, passing the bounds of the equity known to lawyers and the courts, shall be nothing less than a fundamental policy, expressive of the best conscience and judgment of the nation.

The great task, then, which I foresee for the American people in the coming centuries, and which I believe is to be its supreme contribution to civilization, is the creation of this larger equity, and its perfect expression and guarantee in the institutions of civil liberty. It is to be the task of the American people, rather than of any other nation, because in no other nation are combined so many of the forces and conditions necessary for its perfect achievement. No other great nation is still so young, so vigorous, in possession of so exhaustless a fund of energy for great undertakings. In no other nation are the people in reality so democratic. In no other is the sense of equality in reality so strong. In no other is the individual so assertive, so little likely to surrender his privilege of free initiative, and to make himself a mere creature of the state. But chiefly is this task committed to America because in no other people is so strongly developed that spirit of helpfulness, of human brotherhood, which alone will suffice to make the reconciliation of equality with liberty complete and lasting. As yet no other nation in the world has shown this spirit in such practical and costly forms—no other has made such sacrifices to emancipate the slave, to give education to the poorest and the humblest, to carry the elements of civilization through home and foreign missions to the unenlightened of every land. This spirit, together with the other forces and conditions that I have named, will, in the coming years, find a practical solution of the difficult problem of the right relation of equality and liberty, and will thereby establish a relatively perfect equity.

There is, however, a proviso, a condition. All this will happen, provided the American population, with its abounding vitality, its faith in its own powers, and its heritage of liberal traditions dispersed throughout a wide domain, is composed of individual men of the right moral type. Any failure of character, any breaking away from the highest ideals of manhood, could easily result in the destruction of all our hopes.

And here we are brought to a consideration of the relation of our educational institutions to the future of the American nation, and to the survival of civil liberty.

The duty of schools and colleges cannot be told in a word. They must impart knowledge, they must quicken the love of truth, they must foster scientific research, they must discipline character. But none of these is the supreme obligation. The highest duty of any institution of learning is to present to all its students a noble ideal of manhood and womanhood, and through all the ways of discipline to strive unceasingly to mould them to its perfect image. Never should any student find it possible to pass from the quiet nurture of his college life into the storm and stress of the outer world, without taking with him a distinct notion of what sort of man, merely as a man, apart from all his attainments, the college graduate should be; a notion that he can never efface, even though, through any evil disposition, he should wish to do so; a notion that forever will force itself upon his attention, compelling him through all the years of his life to measure what he is by that image of what he ought to be.

Not, indeed, in all the endless marvel of detail can the ideal of character be drawn. By each human being for himself must the detail be filled in. But in general outlines we can sketch the type of perfect manhood that we ought to require of ourselves and of our fellowmen.

The perfect citizen demanded by our own age and by our own nation can be characterized in a single phrase. The American who is worthy to be so called, the patriot on whom his country may depend in any hour of peril, the voter who will neither take the scoundrel's bribe nor follow the lead of any fool —he is exactly and fully described when we say that he is a rationally conscientious man.

For such a man is, first of all, everything for which the word "man" stands in its truest emphasis. He is virile, a personal force, an organism overflowing with splendid power, alert, fearless, able to carry to perfect fulfilment any undertaking to which he may put his hand. Moreover, he is independent, preserving in his disposition and habits the best traditions of a pioneer manhood, of those Americans of an earlier time who asked little and did much, who made homes and careers for themselves.

He demands not too much of society or of his government. He does not expect to be provided for. He does not ask what ready-made places in the government service or elsewhere he may slip into, to enjoy through life with little bother or anxiety. Rather does he explore, invent, and create opportunities for himself and for others. It is a melancholy thing when numbers of educated men go looking for "jobs," or stand waiting for opportunities to drift their way. The educated man has already had opportunity, and the world rightly expects him to show powers of initiative and leadership. He has no right to be a mere imitator of others; and when he is content to be such, there is something radically wrong either with him or with the college that has trained him.

In the second place, the true American is a conscientious man. He feels as a vital truth—and does not merely say as cant—that no one liveth to himself. When he has provided for his own, he does not think that he has accomplished the whole duty of man. He remembers that, although he has demanded little of society, he has in reality received much. Education, legal protection, the unnumbered benefits flowing from the inventions, the sacrifices, and the patriotism of past generations, he has shared. These benefactions he wishes to repay, and he realizes that most of them he must pay for through the activities of good citizenship. And especially does he realize that no man can pay these debts by merely living justly in private life and kindly within the circle of his immediate family and personal friends. There is no more wretched sophistry than that which excuses unprincipled conduct in politics, on the ground that the wrong-doer has always been a good husband and father, and an honorable man in his private affairs. No nation can endure which draws fine distinctions between public and private morality. There is only one kind of honor, there is only one recognized brand of common honesty. A man who, to serve his party, becomes a liar and a thief, *is* a liar and a thief, through and through, in every fibre of his being, though he never told a falsehood to his wife or robbed an orphan niece of her inheritance.

And, finally, the true American must be a rational man. His

conscientiousness must not be of that narrow, dogmatic type, which degenerates into mere formality or, what is worse, into intolerant fanaticism. We must not suppose that because the future of America is full of promise it is devoid of dangers. Among the dangers that we have to face, none is more grave than that fanatical passion which too often manifests itself in lawless dealings with criminal offenders—in the name of justice destroying the very foundation of legal retribution—which now and then takes the form of a wild destruction of property in a misguided attempt to redress the wrongs of the working man, or which, from time to time, breaks forth in political crazes that sweep thousands of voters into the support of sheer folly and dishonor. To meet these dangers we must have men not only honest and manly, but also cool, deliberate, large-minded, able to deal reasonably with problems that are not easy of solution.

> "Not till the ways of prudence all are tried,
> And tried in vain, the turn of rashness comes."

But let us not be deceived by words. There is rationalism and rationalism. The rationalism which our country demands is the positive, not the merely negative and fault-finding kind. We have quite enough of men whose genius consists in an acute perception of all that is wrong or imperfect. We have quite enough of those critics of our political system who can find nothing good since the fathers fell asleep. The men of the new day must be of tougher fiber than they, of broader views, of more inventive mind. The efficient citizen of the twentieth century must be rational in a positive and constructive sense. A lover of justice, a hater of wrong, he must be also a disciple of wisdom.

> "For to live disobedient to these two, Justice and Wisdom, is no life at all."

In presenting these views of the future of our country and of the type of man which it will demand, to you who are about to go forth from college life into the realities of that future, I feel assured of comprehension and approval; because, in an eminent degree, you have enjoyed the teaching and received the inspiration which foster the manly and womanly character that I have endeavored to describe. Preëminently among our colleges has Oberlin stood for the positive, the helpful, the hopeful spirit. Preëminently has she represented ideals of democracy and equality. No distinctions of race or of nationality have been recognized by her. And not only this, but an inspiration of the rarest kind you have had in the personal history of one from whom this institution took its name. Few, indeed, have been the lives that have so perfectly exemplified the ideal of rationally conscientious manhood as did that of Jean Frédéric Oberlin, the tireless pastor of the Ban de la Roche. That district of the Vosges, when Oberlin began his labors there, was merely nine thousand acres of rocky soil, with only mule paths for roads. It was inhabited by a people desperately poor, and so ignorant that few of them could read, while none spoke any other language than a barbarous patois. Before Oberlin died, sixty years later, the Ban de la Roche, largely through his influence, had been transformed into a productive region, densely populated, exporting agricultural products, traversed by excellent roads, and built up with substantial dwellings. Its people had learned to maintain admirable schools and churches, and to speak the French language with a purity not excelled anywhere in France. Such are the possibilities of one earnest life. What may not you accomplish toward the perfection of our American civilization, if, in the active years upon which you now enter, you are faithful to examples such as this!

Do not, however, be satisfied with any mere following of example, with any mere conformity to standards that have been held before you, in your college days. From you, as from those who have lived before you, the world will rightly demand new thoughts and new achievements. Look back upon your Alma Mater with reverence, but also with a filial care that she do not too early descend "the quiet, mossy track of age." As alumni, let it be your study to discover wherein her discipline can be made more liberal, her teaching sounder and broader, her influence wider, saner, and more enduring.

And carry with you into the larger life of American citizenship the same spirit. Be not satisfied with those achievements of the nation that have passed into history. Do not forget the past, but live and work for the future. If you and those others who, like you, have enjoyed the privileges of a liberal training, as educated men and women, as citizens of our republic, shall do your whole duty rationally, conscientiously, fearlessly, there can be no failure of our experiment in self-government, no diminution of the blessings of civil liberty.

N

CITIZENSHIP AND PATRIOTISM

PATRIOTISM, INSTINCTIVE AND INTELLIGENT[1]

Ira Woods Howerth

[Ira Woods Howerth (1860———) was born in Brown County, Indiana. After attending the Northern Indiana Normal College, he engaged for a time in teaching. He then spent several years in advanced study at Harvard and at the University of Chicago. For several years he was connected as professor with the latter institution, but in 1912 he became professor of education and director of university extension work in the University of California. This essay is a clear presentation of two differing types of patriotism that ought to be well understood by all persons.]

Patriotism cannot be really understood without knowing something of the manner of its development. Primarily it is an identification of the individual with the group to which he belongs—family, tribe, state, or nation. The patriot proudly speaks of "my family," "my tribe," "my state," "my people." This identification is based upon a certain feeling which is the product of group association, and this feeling is instinctive.

Sociology ascribes the origin of patriotism to the family life, the family being the first social group. That this is correct is indicated by the origin of the word patriotism. It is derived from the Greek word πατριος, which means of or belonging to one's father. The Indo-Germanic root of the word is *pa*, from which we have the Latin *pater* and the English words father, paternal, patriarch, patriotism, and many others. Perhaps the root-word itself is but the natural infantile utterance reduplicated in the word papa. At all events the word patriotism has plainly a family origin. The papa, the father, being the providing, protecting, and governing element in the

[1]From *Educational Review*, vol. xliv, p. 13 (June, 1912). Reprinted by permission.

family group, his authority supreme, dignity, protection, and support being personified in him, he was naturally the object of reverence and devotion. Loyalty to the *pater*, the father, the patriarch, was therefore the earliest form of patriotism.

In the course of social evolution the family enlarged into the clan, the gens, or the tribe. The interests of single families were then more or less submerged in the interests of a group of families of which each was a component element. The chief representative of these larger interests was the head man, the chieftain, including later the council. Loyalty to the father and family exclusively was inconsistent with clan or tribal life. Hence patriotism extended itself to the interests of the larger group and their tribal representatives. There was, so to speak, an expansion of patriotism. This new form was represented in the clannishness of the early Scot, "owning no tie but to his clan," the tribal instincts of the American Indian and other primitive peoples, and the partisanship of the early Greeks and Romans. With the formation of the tribe, patriotism passed from fatherism to tribalism.

In the amalgamation of tribes into states and nations the expansion of the feeling now known as patriotism continued. Loyalty to the tribe passed over into loyalty to the state or nation, and the feeling of patriotism became what we ordinarily express as love of country, the feeling which incites the individual to identify his interests more or less with those of his country, and to speak and act in a manner which he supposes will illustrate this identification.

Of course, the feeling of patriotism is not confined alone to the personal group of which the individual is a member. It attaches itself also to the natural surroundings of the group. "I love thy rocks and rills, thy woods and templed hills" is the expression of a truly patriotic sentiment. But we may include in our conception of a social group the natural conditions which surround it, and no misunderstanding need arise from defining patriotism as primarily an instinctive group feeling.

Patriotism, then, like all other things in the universe, like the mind and all its manifestations, has had its origin and its development. It originated in association, and association has been the main factor in its growth. Now the fact of the evolution of patriotism, and the manner in which it has taken place, are the basis of a safe prophecy with respect to what patriotism is to become, if political and social organization and amalgamation continue. The affiliation and federation of countries will enlarge the feeling of patriotism. The "Parliament of man and federation of the world" would as certainly conduce to cosmopolitanism or political humanism as tribal associations conduced to tribalism, and the consolidation of tribes into states and states into nations conduced to the modern patriotic feeling. Love of country must gradually give place to love of kind.

Although patriotism expands with the enlarging composition of the group, it does not necessarily sever itself from any point of attachment. The family feeling may still be strong in the tribe, as with the Montagues and Capulets in Rome, for instance, and devotion to the state may be powerful in the citizens of the nation, as was conspicuously shown in the secession of the Southern States of America. So also the cosmopolitan may retain his love of country. He is not necessarily "a traitor," as some seem to suppose. Neither does this larger patriotism imply a lack of family affection with a Mrs. Jellyby's sentimental interest in the inhabitants of Borrioboola-Gha. In pure cosmopolitanism, however, the spirit of national or racial antagonism must necessarily vanish, and loyalty to one country or race as against another country or race must be controlled and tempered by devotion to humanity. The narrower and selfish interests of the particular country to which the citizen belongs must be held inferior to the interests of mankind. Of course, all these interests may coincide, but the world patriot cannot stand with his country "against the world," unless his country is right and "the world" is wrong. True loyalty and humanity can mean only devotion to the principles upon which the well-being of humanity rests. The world patriot must be loyal to right everywhere against wrong anywhere. He must stand for justice to all against injustice to any. When the action or demands of his country conflict with the rights of humanity he must stand for humanity. Hence he may be called by his compatriots unpatriotic, but he is so only as viewed from the interests of the smaller group. The "politicals" of Russia, for instance, are unpatriotic in the eyes of the Russian Bureaucracy and its supporters. Though they be faithful to universal principles of liberty and equality, they are unfaithful to the principles of Russian despotism; hence, from a certain Russian standpoint, they are unpatriotic.

George Kennan, in the *Outlook* for March 30, 1907, gives an interesting and pathetic account of the attempt of some of these politicals to manifest their devotion to the larger principles of freedom embodied in our own Declaration of Independence. He says: "On the morning of the Fourth of July, 1876, hours before the first daylight cannon announced the beginning of the great celebration in Philadelphia, hundreds of small, rude American flags or strips of red, white, and blue cloth fluttered from the grated windows of the politicals around the whole quadrangle of the great St. Petersburg prison, while the prisoners were faintly hurrahing, singing patriotic songs, or exchanging greetings with one another through the iron pipes which united their cells. The celebration, of course, was soon over. The prison guard, although they had never heard of the Declaration of Independence and did not understand the significance of this extraordinary demonstration, promptly seized and removed the flags and tri-colored streamers. Some of the prisoners, however, had more material of the same kind in reserve, and at intervals throughout the whole day scraps and tatters of red, white, and blue were furtively hung out here and there from cell windows or tied around the bars of the gratings. Late in the evening, at a preconcerted hour, the politicals lighted their bits of tallow candles and placed them in their windows, and the celebration ended with a faint but perceptible illumination of the great prison."

This mournful and touching endeavor to celebrate our Fourth of July did not necessarily indicate a greater love of our country than of Russia, but it did imply a devotion to political principles of universal application. We may conceive that the aspiration and ideal of these politicals were merely that these principles should prevail in their own fatherland. They loved not Russia less, but freedom more. They at least approximated a "higher patriotism."

Thus far we have spoken of patriotism as an instinctive feeling or sentiment. Now, it is characteristic of an instinct that it acts without reflection. Though originally purposive in action, and serving as an agent in individual or group preservation, an instinct takes no consideration of objective circumstances. It is a blind impulse. When the stimulus is provided it operates; and its operation has often led, in the course of biological and social evolution, to the extinction of individuals and of groups. Patriotism, therefore, so far as it is instinctive, is impulsive, blind, unreasoning, and irreflective. It thrills, it hurrahs, it boasts, it fights and dies without calmly considering what it is all about. It resents a fancied insult without stopping to ascertain whether it is real. It flies to the defense of the supposed interests of its group without inquiring whether the interests are worthy or the danger is actual. It is blind patriotism and springs from the emotional side of the mind. It differs in no essential respect from the impulse of the tiger to defend its young, or from that of the wild cattle of the prairie to defend the herd. It is easily aroused and easily "stampeded."

On the other hand, there is a patriotism which may be distinguished from instinctive patriotism by the word intelligent. The emotions are subject to the control of the intellect. It is the function and power of the intellect to inhibit, restrain, sometimes to eliminate, an instinct. Even the instinct of self-preservation, strong as it is, has sometimes been wholly inhibited by a duly informed and reflective mind. The proper intelligence may therefore modify, even reverse, the actions springing from instinctive feeling. Patriotic sentiment may be held subject to a thorough knowledge of political and social conditions and a sense of justice. When so held it becomes intelligent patriotism. Intelligent patriotism, then, is patriotic feeling, instinctive patriotism, under the control and guidance of knowledge and reflection. It is love of country and the disposition to serve it, coupled with a knowledge of how to serve it well. It does not yield to impulse. It looks before and after. It restrains a nation from fighting when there are no real interests at stake.

Now there can be no doubt that the great need of all nations is intelligent patriotism. The modern patriot is too much disposed to act upon impulse. He is "touchy;" he goes off "half-cocked;" he is full of racial prejudice, indulges in national bombast and braggadocio, Chauvinism, Jingoism, and manifests a disposition to whip somebody. His patriotism is chiefly an instinctive patriotism. Such patriotism is a feeling for one's country without the control of intelligence; it is patriotic zeal without patriotic knowledge. Under its promptings the patriotic is sometimes the idiotic. The utterances and actions evoked by it are sometimes illustrative of the fact that a man may be a patriot and still be a fool.

Among the effects of instinctive patriotism is the overweening national egotism manifested by so many "patriots." There is a disease called by the learned megalomania. Its primary symptom is "the delusion of grandeur." So many patriots are megalomaniacs that the disease seems to characterize every nation and every people. It led Israel to regard itself as a "peculiar" people, the favorite of the Almighty. It induced the Greeks to call all other peoples barbarians. The Chinese, according to their own estimate, are "celestials," and both the English and the Americans speak of themselves as divinely commissioned to spread the blessings of civilization among "inferior" peoples, even if they smother them in the process. All this is national egotism, megalomania. It arises from a more or less irreflective instinctive patriotism.

Obviously, great national and social dangers are consequent upon instinctive patriotism. By manifesting itself in antipathy toward another nation, and in irreflective action, it provokes suspicion, jealousy, hatred, and unnecessary war. Washington, in his "Farewell Address," pointed out some of these dangers.

"Antipathy in one nation against another," said he, "disposes each more readily to offer insult and injury, to lay hold of slight causes of umbrage, and to be haughty and intractable, when accidental or trifling occasions of dispute occur. Hence, frequent collisions; obstinate, envenomed, and bloody contests. The nation, prompted by ill-will and resentment, sometimes impels to war the government, contrary to the best calculations of policy. The government sometimes participates in the national propensity, and adopts through passion what reason would reject; at other times it makes the animosity of the nation subservient to projects of hostility instigated by pride, ambition, and other sinister and pernicious motives. The peace often, sometimes perhaps the liberty, of nations has been the victim." Instinctive patriotism forced President McKinley into a war with Spain which, with national intelligence and forbearance, might have been avoided. It inspires irresponsible and mischievous remarks and comments concerning other nations, which tend to provoke hostility. The following is a sample: "I would be in favor of annexing Canada right now, if I thought England would fight. But just to take Canada and have no brush with England would be too tame. There are hundreds of young men in this country who would enjoy a war with England, and some of the young veterans of the war would not be slow in going to the front." This is the language of a former general of the American Army as reported by the Associated Press. The correspondent of the Pittsburgh *Gazette* of December 15, 1903, when our relations with Colombia were somewhat strained, wrote: "There are a lot of young officers in Washington who are hoping that the complications between this country and Colombia will result in war. They do not expect it will be much of a war, even if there is a conflict between the two forces, but at any rate it will open the way to promotion for some of them, and promotion is the sole ambition of the soldiers." Remarks like these are prompted solely by instinctive patriotism, patriotism unrestrained by social intelligence.

Such patriotism not only leads to national bickering and strife, but it also prevents that national receptiveness so essential to progress. "The national egotism which scorns to learn of neighbors," say Brinton, "prepares the pathway to national ruin. . . . That nation today which is most eager to learn from others, which is furthest from the fatal delusion that all wisdom flows from its own springs will surely be in the van of progress."[1] But instinctive patriotism is not eager to learn from other nations, for the very simple reason that it thinks they have nothing superior to teach. To the instinctive patriotism nothing in foreign nations is worthy of emulation or adoption. He speaks without the slightest reverence of "Japs," and "Chinks," and "Dagoes;" of "Wild Irishmen," "rat-eating Frenchmen," and "flat-headed Dutchmen." Such a "patriot" may be a gentleman so far as his more intimate personal relationships are concerned, but as a representative of nationality he is often a braggart, a bully, or a fool. His patriotism is irrational and irresponsible, and consequently a danger to his country.

In spite of the dangers of instinctive patriotism, however, it must be recognized that, like other instincts again, it may serve at times a very useful purpose. Indeed, in the absence of social intelligence, it has been absolutely essential to the preservation of social groups. When the life of a nation, for instance, is endangered, its citizens must rise instantly to its defense. There is no time for serious reflection. To deliberate is to be lost. Hence the disposition to spring to arms is an element of national survival; for it leads the citizens to act in concert, and so more effectively. Without instinctive patriotism, no group in a hostile environment could have survived. On the whole, those groups in which it was highest developed are the ones which have persisted. Instinctive patriotism, then, has unquestionably been an element in social survival, as well as an element in social danger and destruction. But however serviceable this form of patriotism may have been in the past, or however necessary in a critical national exigency, it is not the kind of patriotism which is needed today. It involves governments in needless strife, and it renders the citizens easily susceptible to the pernicious influences of kings, diplomats, and un-

[1] *Basis of Social Relationships* (New York, 1902), p. 60. [Howerth's note.]

scrupulous politicians. Hence, it should be supplanted as rapidly as possible by intelligent patriotism.

Intelligent patriotism implies a particular kind of knowledge, a knowledge of national and social relationships, and of the principles of industrial and political well-being. In the endeavor to develop it in the schools, for instance, we may safely rely upon the existence of patriotic feeling and devote attention exclusively to promoting the right kind of intelligence. Saluting the flag, the singing of patriotic songs, Fourth of July celebrations as heretofore conducted, to say nothing of most of the patriotic appeals from pulpit and rostrum, are directed merely to developing instinctive patriotism. The really needed and difficult thing, however, is to inform the instinct so that it will operate, even under trying circumstances, to the real advantage and safety of the nation. Education should be directed not to the development of patriotic feeling, but to imparting the kind of knowledge by which that feeling is restrained and directed.

The difference between instinctive patriotism and intelligent patriotism, as I have tried to present it, is not, of course, absolute. Feeling is necessary to action, and the two can not be separated. But the difference between impulsive action and national action is obvious, and so, I think, must be the distinction I have drawn between instinctive patriotism and intelligent patriotism. Instinctive patriotism is not be to supplanted by intelligent patriotism; it is, rather, to be transformed into it by knowledge.

With the distinction of the two kinds of patriotism now before us it will be interesting to compare some of the patriotic manifestations in modern political discussion. Instinctive patriotism, with a superficial knowledge of science, justifies war on the ground of the law of the survival of the fittest. Intelligent patriotism analyzes the idea of the fittest, finds that it has no ethical signification, and strives to promote all activities calculated to fit our nation to survive. Instinctive patriotism prates in language which to delicate ears sounds almost blasphemous, of the unpremeditated occurrences in our national life as disclosing the will of Providence. Intelligent patriotism recognizes that safe and permanent progress is the result of human forethought, that the blunders of a nation are no less deplorable and blameworthy than those of an individual, and that unconsidered or ill-considered action on the part of man or nation is quite as likely to disclose the will of the devil as the will of the Lord. Instinctive patriotism melodramatically declares that the flag of our country whenever or wherever, and no matter under what circumstances, it is erected, shall never he hauled down. Intelligent patriotism insists that whenever and wherever the flag is raised in injustice, or as a symbol of oppression and tyranny, the sooner it is hauled down the better; for the intelligent patriot is likely to have a feeling that unless it is lowered by our own hands, the God of Justice will somehow tear it down and make it a mockery and a mournful memory in the minds of men. Instinctive patriotism defiantly proclaims, "My country, right or wrong." Intelligent patriotism says, "My country, when she is right, and when she is wrong, my life to set her right." Instinctive patriotism, nonplused by the arguments of the peace advocates, tries to persuade itself that such advocates are uneducated sentimentalists and mollycoddles. Intelligent patriotism quietly continues to organize its peace leagues, associations, and federations, schools, tribunals, and unions, confident that proper intelligence will make war impossible.

The difference between the two kinds of patriotism is shown in nothing more clearly than the character of the two national ideals now inculcated. Instinctive patriotism has much to say about our becoming a "world power," the inevitableness of war, and of our rightful influence in the council of nations. Intelligent patriotism knows we have long been a world power, that war is neither inevitable nor necessary, and is not so much interested in our rightful influence as that our influence be exercised in the rightful way. The instinctive patriotic ideal is militant; the intelligent, scientific and industrial.

Is it necessary to inquire which is the higher form of patriotism? Which is the nobler national aspiration, which evinces the loftier patriotism, supremacy in war and the arts of destruction, with hundreds of millions of our wealth locked up in ships, forts, and arsenals, and thousands of men withdrawn from the peaceful pursuits to man these instruments of death, and become a burden on the back of labor, or supremacy in industry, in trade, in science, in art, in literature, and in education, with health, wealth, and happiness for all our people; and, because we have charity for all and malice toward none, enjoying the good-will and friendship of all the world? For which should we strive as a nation, to evoke the fear of the weaker nations by the strength of our armaments (and their hatred also, for hate is the child of fear), or to deserve and compel their respect and admiration by fair dealing, justice, modesty, moderation, courtesy, and charity, and by our sincerity in upholding the principles of liberty, equality, and fraternity?

Instinctive patriotism is thrilled by glowing descriptions of America as mighty in battle, or as Mistress of the Seas with hundreds of battleships, those grim leviathans of the deep, plowing the waves of every sea and proudly tossing from their iron manes the ocean foam; or resting unwelcome, it may be, because unbidden, guests in the ports of foreign lands; each bearing witness that in this nation of ours, conceived in liberty and dedicated to the proposition that all men are created equal, there is a disposition to forsake the principles of the fathers in a lust for power, and to follow in the wake of Babylon and Nineveh, Greece, Rome and Spain, the nations whose bloody history reveals to him who will but read that the nation that relies upon force must finally become the victim of force. For it is written, "They that take the sword shall perish by the sword."

Intelligent patriotism, on the other hand, is inspired by the ideal of America as a republic supremely powerful by the force of an enlightened public opinion, and supremely glorious on account of her successful pursuit of the arts of peace, and because of her acknowledged leadership in all that liberates and lifts. The prophet of old declared that there shall come a time when swords shall be beaten into plowshares and spears into pruning-hooks, and men shall learn war no more; and that the earth shall be full of knowledge as the waters cover the sea. When these prophecies are to be fulfilled no one can know—

> "Ah, when shall all men's good be each man's rule,
> And universal peace lie like a shaft of light across mankind;
> Or like a lane of beams athwart the sea
> Thru all the circle of the golden year?"

But these prophecies imply a period of continuous peace and general education involving the diffusion of patriotic knowledge. Who can estimate what this will mean to the advancement of the people? It is not given unto men to foretell what this nation is to become; it doth not yet appear what we shall be; but of this we may be sure, that with continuous peace, universal education, and intelligent patriotism, eye hath not seen, nor ear heard, neither has it entered into the imagination of man to conceive the glorious possibilities of the American Republic.

MESSAGE OF THE FLAG

Franklin Knight Lane

[Franklin Knight Lane (1864———) was born in Canada, but in early childhood removed to California. He studied at the University of California, engaged in newspaper work, studying law later and entering into practice in San Francisco. For eight years he was a member of the Interstate Commerce Commission at Washington. This position he relinquished in 1913 to become secretary of the interior. In his speeches and writings he is always forcible and inspiring. The brief address here given, delivered before the employees of the Department of the Interior on Flag Day, 1914, deserves a place among the classics of patriotism. With imagination and insight, with grace and charm, it interprets what the American flag ought to mean to all who live under it.]

This morning, as I passed into the Land Office, The Flag dropped me a most cordial salutation, and from its rippling folds I heard it say: "Good morning, Mr. Flag Maker."

"I beg your pardon, Old Glory," I said, "aren't you mistaken? I am not the President of the United States, nor a member of Congress, nor even a general in the army. I am only a Government clerk."

"I greet you again, Mr. Flag Maker," replied the gay voice, "I know you well. You are the man who worked in the swelter of yesterday straightening out the tangle of that farmer's homestead in Idaho, or perhaps you found the mistake in that Indian contract in Oklahoma, or helped to clear that patent for the hopeful inventor in New York, or pushed the opening of that new ditch in Colorado, or made that mine in Illinois more safe, or brought relief to the old soldier in Wyoming. No matter; whichever one of these beneficent individuals you may happen to be, I give you greeting, Mr. Flag Maker."

I was about to pass on, when The Flag stopped me with these words:

"Yesterday the President spoke a word that made happier the future of ten million peons in Mexico; but that act looms no larger on the flag than the struggle which the boy in Georgia is making to win the Corn Club prize this summer.

"Yesterday the Congress spoke a word which will open the door of Alaska; but a mother in Michigan worked from sunrise until far into the night to give her boy an education. She, too, is making the flag.

"Yesterday we made a new law to prevent financial panics, and yesterday, maybe, a school-teacher in Ohio taught his first letters to a boy who will one day write a song that will give cheer to the millions of our race. We are all making the flag."

"But," I said impatiently, "these people were only working!"

Then came a great shout from The Flag: "The work that we do is the making of the flag. I am not the flag; not at all. I am but its shadow.

"I am whatever you make me, nothing more.

"I am your belief in yourself, your dream of what a People may become.

"I live a changing life, a life of moods and passions, of heartbreaks and tired muscles.

"Sometimes I am strong with pride, when men do an honest

work, fitting the rails together truly. Sometimes I droop, for then purpose has gone from me, and cynically I play the coward. Sometimes I am loud, garish, and full of that ego that blasts judgment.

"But always I am all that you hope to be and have the courage to try for.

"I am song and fear, struggle and panic, and ennobling hope.

"I am the day's work of the weakest man and the largest dream of the most daring.

"I am the Constitution and the courts, statutes and the statute makers, soldier and dreadnaught, drayman and street sweep, cook, counselor, and clerk.

"I am the battle of yesterday and the mistake of tomorrow.

"I am the mystery of the men who do without knowing why.

"I am the clutch of an idea and the reasoned purpose of resolution.

"I am no more than what you believe me to be, and I am all that you believe I can be.

"I am what you make me, nothing more.

"I swing before your eyes as a bright gleam of color, a symbol of yourself, the pictured suggestion of that big thing which makes this nation. My stars and my stripes are your dream and your labors. They are bright with cheer, brilliant with courage, firm with faith, because you have made them so out of your hearts. For you are the makers of the flag, and it is well that you glory in the making."

GOOD CITIZENSHIP[1]

Henry Cabot Lodge

[Henry Cabot Lodge (1850———) was born in Boston, Massachusetts. He was graduated from Harvard and was for a time lecturer in history in that institution. For three years he was editor of the *North American Review*. Since 1886 he has served continuously in Washington as either representative or senator from Massachusetts. In spite of the exactions of public life, he has found time to write several brilliant volumes on historical and biographical subjects, the most notable perhaps being his *Life of Washington*.]

Assuming at the outset that in the United States all men, young and old, who think at all realize the importance of good citizenship, the first step toward its attainment or its diffusion is to define it accurately; and then, knowing what it is, we shall be able intelligently to consider the best methods of creating it and spreading it abroad. In this case the point of discussion and determination lies in the first word of the title. There is no difficulty in the second. The accident of birth or the certificate of a court will make a man a citizen of the republic, entitled to take part in the government and to have the protection of that government wherever he may be. The qualifying adjective applied to citizenship is the important thing here; for, while the mere word "citizen" settles at once a man's legal status, both under domestic and international law, and implies certain rights on his part, and certain responsibilities on the part of his government toward him, we must go much further if we would define his duties to the state upon the performance of which depends his right to be called either good or worthy. Merely to live without actually breaking the laws does not constitute good citizenship, except in the narrow sense of contrast to those who openly or covertly violate the laws which they have helped to make. The word "good," as applied to citizenship, means something more positive and affirmative than mere passive obedience to statutes, if it has any meaning at all. The good citizen, if he

[1]From *A Frontier Town and Other Essays*. (Copyright, 1906, Charles Scribner's Sons.) Reprinted by permission.

would deserve the title, must be one who performs his duties to the state, and who, in due proportion, serves his country. It is when we undertake to define those duties and determine what the due proportion of service is that we approach the serious difficulty of the subject; and yet the duties and the service to the country must be defined, for in them lies all good citizenship, and failure to render them carries a man beyond the pale. A man may not be a bad citizen—he may pay his taxes and commit no statutory offences—but, if he gives no service to his country, nor any help to the community in which he lives, he cannot properly be called a good citizen.

Assuming, then, that good citizenship necessarily implies service of some sort to the state, the country, or the public, it must be understood, of course, that such service may vary widely in amount or in degree. The man and woman who have a family of children, educate them, bring them up honorably and well, teaching them to love their country, are good citizens, and deserve well of the republic. The man who, in order to care for his family and give his children a fair start in life, labors honestly and diligently at his trade, profession, or business, and who casts his vote conscientiously at all elections adds to the strength as well as to the material prosperity of the country, and thus fulfils some of the primary and most important duties of good citizenship. Indeed, it may be said, in passing, that he who labors in any way, who has any intellectual interest, who employs his leisure for any public end,—even the man who works purely for selfish objects,—has one valuable element of good citizenship to his credit in the mere fact of his industry; for there is nobody so detrimental in a country like ours as the mere idler, the mere seeker for self-amusement, who passes his time in constant uncertainty as to how he shall get rid of the next day or the next hour of that brief life which, however short in some cases, is, from every point of view, too long for him. . . .

Good citizenship demands, therefore, something active; in order to be attained, the man must be useful to his country and to his fellowmen, and on this usefulness all else depends. Fortunately, it is possible to be useful in many ways. "Hold your

o

life, your time, your money," said Lowell, "always ready at the hint of your country." To him it was given to make the last great sacrifice. In time of war, the usefulness of man is plain; he has but the simple duty of offering his services to his country in the field. But the service of war, if more glorious, more dangerous, and larger in peril and sacrifice than any other, is also the most obvious. When the country is involved in war, the first duty of a citizen is clear—he must fight for the flag; or if, because of age or physical infirmity, he is unable to fight, he must support those who do, and sustain, in all ways possible, the nation's cause. Good citizenship implies constant readiness to obey our country's call.

Less dangerous, less glorious, rarely demanding the last sacrifice, the time of peace is no less insistent than the exceptional time of war in its demands for good citizenship. How shall a man, in time of peace, fulfil Lowell's requirement of being a useful citizen? He may do it in many ways, for usefulness as a citizen is not confined, by any means, to public office, although it must, in some form or other, promote the general as distinguished from the individual good. A man may be a good citizen in the ordinary sense by fulfilling the fundamental conditions of honest labor, caring for his family, observing law, and expressing his opinion upon governmental measures at the time of election. But this does not make him a good citizen in the larger sense of usefulness. To be a useful citizen, he must do something for the public service which is over and above his work for himself or his family. It may be performed—this public service—through the medium of the man's profession or occupation, or wholly apart and aside from it. This does not mean that the mere production of a great work of art or literature which may be a joy and benefaction to humanity necessarily involves the idea of public service in the sense in which we are considering it here. It may or it may not do so. Turner's art is a great possession for the world to have, but his bequest to the National Gallery was a public service. Regnault's portrait of Prim was a noble picture, but the artist's death as a soldier in defence of Paris was the highest public service. The literature of the English language would be much poorer if Edgar Allan Poe had not lived,—his verse, his prose, his art could ill be spared when the accounts of the nineteenth century are made up,—yet it would be impossible to say that Poe was a useful citizen, highly as we may rate and ought to rate his strange genius. On the other hand, Walt Whitman, who consecrated so much of his work as a poet to his country, was eminently a useful citizen of high patriotism, for he labored in the hospitals and among the soldiers to help his country and his fellowmen without any thought of self or self-interest, or even of his art. So, Ralph Waldo Emerson was a great and useful citizen, as well as a great writer and poet, giving freely of his time and thought and fame to moulding opinion and to the service of his country. The same may be said of Holmes and of Longfellow, of Whittier and of Lowell, of Bancroft and of Motley. In any event, their work would have taken high place in the literature of the United States and of the English-speaking people; in any event it would have brought pleasure to mankind, and, in Dr. Johnson's phrase, would have helped us to enjoy life or taught us to endure it. But over and above their work, they were useful citizens in a high degree. Their art was ever at the service of their country, of a great cause, and of their fellowmen. They helped to direct and create public opinion, and in the hour of stress they sustained the national cause with all the great strength which their fame and talents gave them. With Winthrop, their watchword was: "Our country,—whether bounded by the St. John's or the Sabine, or however otherwise bounded or described, and, be the measurement more or less,— still our country."

The poet and the artist, the scholar and the man of letters are, perhaps, as remote in their lives and pursuits from the generally recognized paths of public service as any men in a community, yet these few examples show not only what they have done, but also what they can do, and how they have met the responsibilities which their high intellectual gifts and large influence imposed upon them. There are also professions which involve in their pursuit public service of a very noble kind. Clergymen and physicians give freely to the public, to their country, and to the community in which they live, their time, their money, their skill, their influence, and their sympathy. It is all done for others, without hope or thought of self-interest or reward. It is all done so naturally, so much in the usual course of their activities, that the world scarcely notes, and certainly does not stop to realize, that the great surgeon exercising his skill, which will command any sum from the rich, without money and without price for the benefit of the poor in the hospitals, or the clergyman laboring among the miseries of the city slums, is doing public service of the highest kind, and is preëminently the useful citizen who goes beyond the limits of personal or family interest to work for the general good—to promote the public welfare in every possible way.

The man of business who devotes his surplus wealth to the promotion of education or of art, or the alleviation of suffering, is doing public service. So, too, among businessmen and lawyers and journalists, among the men engaged in the most energetic and active pursuits, we find those who are always ready to serve on committees to raise money for charitable or public purposes, to advance important measures of legislation, and to reform the evils which are especially rife in great municipalities. To do this they give their money, as well as their time and strength, which are of more value than money, to objects wholly outside the labors by which they support themselves or their families, or gratify their own tastes or ambitions. In this fashion they meet the test of what constitutes usefulness in a citizen by rendering to the country, to the public, and to their fellow-citizens, service which has no personal reward in it, but which advances the good of others and contributes to the welfare of the community.

Thus, in divers ways, only indicated here, are men of all conditions and occupations able to render service and benefit their fellow-citizens. But all these ways so far suggested are, however beneficial, indirect as compared with those usually associated in everyone's mind with the idea of public service. When we use the word "citizen," or "citizenship," the first thought is of the man in relation to the state, as the very word itself implies. It is in this connection that we first think of service when we speak of a public-spirited or useful citizen. There are many other public services, as has been said, just as valuable, just as desirable, very often more immediately beneficial to humanity than those rendered directly to the state or to public affairs, but there is no other which is quite so imperative, quite so near, quite so obvious in the way of duty as the performance of the functions belonging to each man as a member of the state. In our country this is more acutely the case than anywhere else, for this is a democracy, and the government depends upon the action of the people themselves. We have the government, municipal, state, or national, which we make ourselves. If it is good, it is because we make it so. If it is bad, we may think it is not what we want, and that we are not responsible for it, but it is none the less just what it is simply because we will not take the trouble necessary to improve it. There is no greater fallacy than the comfortable statement so frequently heard, that we owe misgovernment, when it occurs anywhere, to the politicians. If the politicians are bad, and yet have power, it is because we give it to them. They are not a force of nature with which there is no contending; they are of our own creation, and, if we disapprove of them and yet leave them in power, it is because we do not care to take the trouble, sometimes the excessive trouble, needful to be rid of them. People in this country, as in other countries, and as in all periods of history, have, as a rule, the government they deserve. The politicians, so commonly denounced as a class, sometimes justly and sometimes unjustly, have only the advantage of taking more pains than others to get what they want, and to hold power in public affairs. To this the reply is always made that the average man engaged in business, or in a profession, has not the time to give to politics which the professional politician devotes to it. That excuse begs the question. If the average man, active, and constantly occupied in his own affairs, cannot find time to choose the men he desires to represent him and perform his public business for him, then either democracy is a failure, or else he can find time if he chooses; and, if he does not choose, he has no right to complain. But democracy is not a failure. After all allowances and deductions are made, it is the best form of government in the world today, and better than any of its predecessors. The fault is not in the system, even if there are in it, as in all other things human, shortcomings and failures, but in those who operate the system; and, in a democracy, those who in the last analysis operate the system are all the people. It must always be remembered, also, that in representative government all the people, and not some of the people, are to be represented. In a country so vast in area and so large in population as the United States, constituencies are very diverse in their qualities and there are many elements. Some constituencies are truly represented by men very alien to the standards and aspirations of other constituencies. All, however, are entitled to representation, and the aggregate representation stands for the whole people. If the representation in the aggregate is sound, and honestly representative, then the theory of democracy is carried out, and the quality of the representation depends on the people represented.

There are two things, then, to be determined by the people themselves—the general policy of the government, and the persons who are to carry that policy into effect and to perform the work of administration. To attain the first object, those who are pledged to one policy or another must be elected, and the persons thus united in support of certain general principles of policy or government constitute a political party. The second object, the choice of suitable persons as representatives of a given political party, must be reached by all the people who support that party taking part in the selection. In the first case, the general policy is settled by the election of a party to power; in the second, the individual representative is picked out by his fellow-members of the same party.

This, in broad terms, describes the field for the exertions of the citizen in the domain of politics, and the methods by which he can make his exertions most effective. I am aware that in this description I have assumed the existence of political parties as not only necessary but also desirable. This is not the place to enter into a history or discussion of the party system. Suffice it to say here that all experience shows that representative government has been a full success only among the English-speaking people of the world, with whom a system of a party of government and a party of opposition has always prevailed. In other countries the failures or serious shortcomings of representative government are attributed by good judges and observers, both native and foreign, largely to the absence of the party system as practised by us. The alternative of two parties, one carrying on the government and the other in opposition ready to take its place, is the system of groups or factions and consequent coalitions among two or more of the groups in order to obtain a parliamentary majority. Government by group-coalitions has proved to be irresponsible, unstable, capricious, and short-lived. Under the system of two parties, continuity, experience and, best of all, responsibility, without which all else is worthless, have been obtained. That there are evils in the party system carried to the extreme of blind or unscrupulous partisanship, no one denies. But this is a comparative world, and the party system is shown, by the experience of two hundred years, to be the best yet devised for the management and movement of a representative government. Nothing, in fact, can be more shallow, or show a more profound ignorance of history, than the proposition, so often reiterated as if it were a truism, that a political party is something wholly evil, and that to call anyone a party man is sufficient to condemn him. Every great measure, every great war, every great reform, which together have made the history of England since the days of William of Orange, and of the United States since the adoption of the Constitution, have been carried on and carried through by an organized political party. Until some better way is discovered and proved to be better, the English-speaking people will continue to use the party system with which, on the whole, they have done so well so far, and the citizen aiming at usefulness must therefore accept the party system as one of the conditions under which he is to act.

The most effective way in which to act is through the medium of a party, and as a member of one of the two great parties, because in this way a man can make his influence felt, not only in the final choice between parties, but in the selection of candidates and in the determination of party politics as well. This does not mean that a man can be effective only by allying himself with a party, but that he can in that way be most effective, both in action and in influence. Many there must be unattached to either of the parties, whose mental condition is such that they can neither submit to discipline nor yield nor compromise their own views in order to promote the general principles in which they believe, all of which conditions or sacrifices are necessary in order to maintain party organization. These are the voters who shift their votes if not their allegiance; and, if it were not for them, one party, as politics are usually hereditary, would remain almost continually in power, and the results would be extremely unfortunate. It is the necessity of appealing to these voters which exercises a restraining effect upon the great party organizations. But these men who vote as they please at the minute, and yet usually describe themselves by a party name, and as a rule act with one party or the other, must be carefully distinguished from the professional independent, whose independence consists in nothing but bitterly opposing and seeking to defeat one party at all times. This independent is the worst of partisans, for he is guided solely by hatred of a party or of individuals, and never supports anything because he believes in it, but merely as an instrument of destruction or revenge. Equally ineffective, even if less malevolent, is the perpetual fault-finder, whether in conversation or in the newspapers. He calls himself a critic, blandly unaware that unrelieved invective is no more criticism than unrelieved laudation, and that true criticism, whether of a book, a work of art, a public measure, or a public man, seeks to point out merits as well as defects, in order to balance one against the other, and thus assist in the proper conduct of life. The real and honest critic and the genuine independent in politics are most valuable, for they are engaged in the advancement of principles in which they believe, and will aid those and work with those who are laboring toward the same ends. But the professional independent, whose sole purpose is to defeat some one party or certain specified persons whom he hates, no matter what that party or those persons may be doing, the critic who only finds fault, the professional philanthropist or reformer who uses his philanthropy or reform solely to vilify his country or his government, and to bring shame or sorrow to some of his fellow-citizens, so that his personal malice may be gratified,—these men advance nothing, for their attitude is pure negation, and they generally do great harm to any cause which they espouse. They are not useful citizens; but, as a rule, to the extent of their power, which luckily is not great, they are positively injurious.

The serious difficulty, however, is not with those who give a false direction to their political activities, but with the political indifference which most good citizens exhibit, except on rare occasions when some great question is at issue which stirs the entire community to its depths. Yet it is in the ordinary every-day affairs of politics that the attention of good citizens is most necessary. It is then that those who constitute the undesirable and objectionable elements get control, for they are always on the watch, and to defeat them it is essential that those who desire good and honest government should be on the watch, too. The idea that they cannot spare the time without detriment to their own affairs is a mistake. The time actually consumed in going to a caucus or a convention is not a serious loss. What is most needed is to follow the course of public affairs closely, to understand what is being done, and what the various candidates represent; and then, when the time for the vote in the caucus or at the polls arrives, a citizen interested only in good government, or in the promotion of a given policy, knows what he wants and can act intelligently. His weakness arises, almost invariably, from the fact that he does not rouse himself until the last minute, that he does not know just what he wants or with whom to act, and that, therefore, he is taken by surprise and beaten by those who know exactly what they want and precisely what they mean to do. Here, then, is where the useful citizen is most needed in politics, and his first duty is to understand his subject, which a little thought and observation day by day will enable him to do. Let him inform himself, and keep always informed, as to men and measures, and he will find that he has ample time to give when the moment of action arrives.

No man can hope to be a useful citizen in the broadest sense, in the United States, unless he takes a continuous and intelligent interest in politics and a full share, not only in the elections, but also in the primary operations which determine the choice of candidates. For this everyone has time enough, and, if he says that he has not, it is because he is indifferent when he ought to be intensely and constantly interested. If he follows public affairs from day to day, and, thus informed, acts with his friends and those who think as he does at the caucus and the polls, he will make his influence fully felt and will meet completely the test of good citizenship. It is not essential to take office. For not doing so, the excuse of lack of time and the demands of more immediate private interest may be valid. But it would be well if every man could have, for a short period, at least, some experience in the actual work of government in his city, state, or nation, even if he has no intention of following a political career. Such an experience does more to broaden a man's knowledge of the difficulties of public administration than anything else. It helps him to understand how he can practically attain that which he thinks is best for the state, and, most important of all, it enables him to act with other men, and to judge justly those who are doing the work of public life. Public men, it is true, seek the offices they hold in order to gratify their ambition, or because they feel that they can do good work in the world in that way. But it is too often overlooked that the great majority of those who hold public office are governed by a desire to do what is best for the country or the state, as they understand it. Ambition may be the motive which takes most men into public life, but the work which is done by these men after they attain their ambition is, as a rule, disinterested and public-spirited. I have lately seen the proposition advanced that, in the last forty years, American public men, with scarcely an exception, have said nothing important because they were so ignorant of their subject, and have done nothing of moment because the country was really governed by professors, men of business, scientists, presidents of learned societies, and especially by gentlemen who feel that they ought to be in high office, but have never been able to get any sufficient number of their fellow-citizens to agree with them in that feeling. With the exception of the last, all these different classes in the community exercise a strong influence on public opinion, the course of public affairs, and public policy. Yet it is none the less true that the absolute conduct of government is in the hands of those who hold high representative or administrative office.

The personal qualities and individual abilities of public men have a profound effect upon the measures and policies which make the history and determine the fate of the nation. Often they originate the measures or the policies, and they always modify and formulate them. Therefore it is essential that every man who desires to be a useful citizen should not only take part in moulding public sentiment, in selecting candidates, and in winning elections for the party or the cause in which he believes, but he should also be familiar with the characters, abilities, and records of the men who must be the instruments by which the policies are to be carried out and the government administered. There are many ways, therefore, in which men may benefit and aid their fellowmen, and serve the state in which they live, but it is open to all men alike to help to govern the country and direct its course along the passing years. In the performance of this duty in the ways I have tried to indicate, any man can attain to good citizenship of the highest usefulness. It is not too much to say that our success as a nation depends upon the useful citizens who act intelligently and effectively in politics.

WHAT "AMERICANISM" MEANS[1]

THEODORE ROOSEVELT

[Theodore Roosevelt (1858——) was graduated from Harvard University in 1880. In this same year he entered public life as a member of the New York legislature. President Harrison appointed him United States Civil Service Commissioner. Later he became assistant secretary of the navy, a position which he resigned when the Spanish-American War began, to organize the famous cavalry regiment, the "Rough Riders." On his return from Cuba, he was elected governor of New York. In 1900 he was elected Vice-President of the United States, and succeeded to the Presidency on the death of President McKinley. In 1904 he was elected President to succeed himself. In 1912 he was defeated for the Presidency as the candidate of the Progressive party. Among the policies which are associated with his name, such, for instance, as the "square deal" between capital and labor, and "social justice" for the wage-earner, "Americanism" has always been conspicuous.]

Patriotism was once defined as "the last refuge of a scoundrel;" and somebody has recently remarked that when Dr. Johnson gave this definition he was ignorant of the infinite possibilities contained in the word "reform." Of course both gibes were quite justifiable, in so far as they were aimed at people who use noble names to cloak base purposes. Equally, of course, the man shows little wisdom and a low sense of duty who fails to see that love of country is one of the elemental virtues, even though scoundrels play upon it for their own selfish ends; and, inasmuch as abuses continually grow up in civic life as in all other kinds of life, the statesman is indeed a weakling who hesitates to reform these abuses because the word "reform" is often on the lips of men who are silly or dishonest.

What is true of patriotism and reform is true also of Americanism. There are plenty of scoundrels always ready to try to belittle reform movements or to bolster up existing iniquities in the name of Americanism; but this does not alter the fact that the man who can do most in this country is and must be the man whose Americanism is most sincere and intense. Outrag-

[1] From *American Ideals and Other Essays*. (Copyright, 1897, G. P. Putnam's Sons.) Reprinted by permission.

eous though it is to use a noble idea as the cloak for evil, it is still worse to assail the noble idea itself because it can thus be used. The men who do iniquity in the name of patriotism, of reform, of Americanism, are merely one small division of the class that has always existed, and will always exist—the class of hypocrites and demagogues, the class that is always prompt to steal the watchwords of righteousness and use them in the interests of evil-doing.

The stoutest and truest Americans are the very men who have the least sympathy with the people who invoke the spirit of Americanism to aid what is vicious in our government, or to throw obstacles in the way of those who strive to reform it. It is contemptible to oppose a movement for good because that movement has already succeeded somewhere else, or to champion an existing abuse because our people have always been wedded to it. To appeal to national prejudice against a given reform movement is in every way unworthy and silly. It is as childish to denounce free trade because England has adopted it as to advocate it for the same reason. It is eminently proper, in dealing with the tariff, to consider the effect of tariff legislation in time past upon other nations as well as the effect upon our own; but in drawing conclusions it is in the last degree foolish to try to excite prejudice against one system because it is in vogue in some given country, or to try to excite prejudice in its favor because the economists of that country have found that it was suited to their own peculiar needs. In attempting to solve our difficult problem of municipal government it is mere folly to refuse to profit by whatever is good in the examples of Manchester and Berlin because these cities are foreign, exactly as it is mere folly blindly to copy their examples without reference to our own totally different conditions. As for the absurdity of declaiming against civil-service reform, for instance, as "Chinese," because written examinations have been used in China, it would be quite as wise to declaim against gunpowder because it was first utilized by the same people. In short, the man who, whether from mere dull fatuity or from an active interest in misgovernment, tries to appeal to American prejudice against things foreign, so as to induce Americans to oppose any measure for good, should be looked on by his fellow-countrymen with the heartiest contempt. So much for the men who appeal to the spirit of Americanism to sustain us in wrong-doing. But we must never let our contempt for these men blind us to the nobility of the idea which they strive to degrade.

We Americans have many grave problems to solve, many threatening evils to fight, and many deeds to do, if, as we hope and believe, we have the wisdom, the strength, the courage, and the virtue to do them. But we must face facts as they are. We must neither surrender ourselves to a foolish optimism, nor succumb to a timid and ignoble pessimism. Our nation is that one among all the nations of the earth which holds in its hands the fate of the coming years. We enjoy exceptional advantages, and are menaced by exceptional dangers; and all signs indicate that we shall either fail greatly or succeed greatly. I firmly believe that we shall succeed; but we must not foolishly blink the danger by which we are threatened, for that is the way to fail. On the contrary, we must soberly set to work to find out all we can about the existence and extent of every evil, must acknowledge it to be such, and must then attack it with unyielding resolution. There are many such evils, and each must be fought after a separate fashion; yet there is one quality which we must bring to the solution of every problem—that is, an intense and fervid Americanism. We shall never be successful over the dangers that confront us; we shall never achieve true greatness, nor reach the lofty ideal which the founders and preservers of our mighty Federal Republic have set before us, unless we are Americans in heart and soul, in spirit and purpose, keenly alive to the responsibility implied in the very name of American, and proud beyond measure of the glorious privilege of bearing it.

There are two or three sides to the question of Americanism, and two or three senses in which the word "Americanism" can be used to express the antithesis of what is unwholesome and undesirable. In the first place we wish to be broadly American and national, as opposed to being local or sectional. We do not wish, in politics, in literature, or in art, to develop that unwholesome parochial spirit, that over-exaltation of the little community at the expense of the great nation, which produces what has been described as the patriotism of the village, the patriotism of the belfry. Politically, the indulgence of this spirit was the chief cause of the calamities which befell the ancient republics of Greece, the medieval republics of Italy, and the petty states of Germany as it was in the last century. It is this spirit of provincial patriotism, this inability to take a view of broad adhesion to the whole nation that has been the chief among the causes that have produced such anarchy in the South American states, and which have resulted in presenting to us, not one great Spanish-American federal nation stretching from the Rio Grande to Cape Horn, but a squabbling multitude of revolution-ridden states, not one of which stands even in the second rank as a power. However, politically this question of American nationality has been settled once for all. We are no longer in danger of repeating in our history the shameful and contemptible disasters that have befallen the Spanish possessions on this continent since they threw off the yoke of Spain. Indeed there is, all through our life, very much less of this parochial spirit than there was formerly. Still there is an occasional outcropping here and there; and it is just as well that we should keep steadily in mind the futility of talking of a northern literature or a southern literature, an eastern or a western school of art or science. The *Sewanee Review* and the *Overland Monthly*, like the *Century* and the *Atlantic*, do good work, not merely for one section of the country, but for American literature as a whole. Their success really means as much for Americans who happen to live in New York or Boston as for Americans who happen to live in the Gulf States or on the Pacific slope. Joel Chandler Harris is emphatically a national writer; so is Mark Twain. They do not write merely for Georgia or Missouri, any more than for Illinois or Connecticut; they write as Americans and for all people who can read English. It is of very great consequence that we should have a full and ripe literary development in the United States, but it is not of the least consequence whether New York, or

Boston, or Chicago, or San Francisco becomes the literary center of the United States.

There is a second side to this question of a broad Americanism, however. The patriotism of the village or the belfry is bad, but the lack of all patriotism is even worse. There are philosophers who assure us that, in the future, patriotism will be regarded not as a virtue at all, but merely as a mental stage in the journey toward a state of feeling when our patriotism will include the whole human race and all the world. This may be so; but the age of which these philosophers speak is still several æons distant. In fact, philosophers of this type are so very advanced that they are of no practical service to the present generation. It may be that in ages so remote that we cannot now understand any of the feelings of those who will dwell in them, patriotism will no longer be regarded as a virtue, exactly as it may be that in those remote ages people will look down upon and disregard monogamic marriage; but as things now are and have been for two or three thousand years past, and are likely to be for two or three thousand years to come, the words "home" and "country" mean a great deal. Nor do they show any tendency to lose their significance. At present, treason, like adultery, ranks as one of the worst of all possible crimes.

One may fall very far short of treason and yet be an undesirable citizen in the community. The man who becomes Europeanized, who loses his power of doing good work on this side of the water, and who loses his love for his native land, is not a traitor; but he is a silly and undesirable citizen. He is·as emphatically a noxious element in our body politic as is the man who comes here from abroad and remains a foreigner. Nothing will more quickly or more surely disqualify a man from doing good work in the world than the acquirement of that flaccid habit of mind which its possessors style cosmopolitanism.

It is not only necessary to Americanize the immigrants of foreign birth who settle among us, but it is even more necessary for those among us who are by birth and descent already Americans not to throw away our birthright, and, with incredible and contemptible folly, wander back to bow down before the alien gods whom our forefathers forsook. It is hard to believe that there is any necessity to warn Americans that, when they seek to model themselves on the lines of other civilizations, they make themselves the butts of all right-thinking men; and yet the necessity certainly exists to give this warning to many of our citizens who pride themselves on their standing in the world of art and letters, or, perchance, on what they would style their social leadership in the community. It is always better to be an original than an imitation, even when the imitation is of something better than the original; but what shall we say of the fool who is content to be an imitation of something worse? Even if the weaklings who seek to be other than Americans were right in deeming other nations to be better than their own, the fact yet remains that to be a first-class American is fifty-fold better than to be a second-class imitation of a Frenchman or Englishman. As a matter of fact, however, those of our countrymen who do believe in American inferiority are always individuals who, however cultivated, have some organic weakness in their moral or mental make-up; and the great mass of our people, who are robustly patriotic, and who have sound, healthy minds, are justified in regarding these feeble renegades with a half-impatient and half-amused scorn.

We believe in waging relentless war on rank-growing evils of all kinds, and it makes no difference to us if they happen to be of purely native growth. We grasp at any good, no matter whence it comes. We do not accept the evil attendant upon another system of government as an adequate excuse for that attendant upon our own; the fact that the courtier is a scamp does not render the demagogue any the less a scoundrel. But it remains true that, in spite of all our faults and shortcomings, no other land offers such glorious possibilities to the man able to take advantage of them as does ours; it remains true that no one of our people can do any work really worth doing unless he does it primarily as an American. It is because certain classes of our people still retain their spirit of colonial dependence on, and exaggerated deference to, European opinion, that they fail to accomplish what they ought to. It is precisely along the lines

P

where we have worked most independently that we have accomplished the greatest results; and it is in those professions where there has been no servility to, but merely a wise profiting by, foreign experience, that we have produced our greatest men. Our soldiers and statesmen and orators; our explorers, our wilderness-winners and commonwealth-builders; the men who have made our laws and seen that they were executed; and the other men whose energy and ingenuity have created our marvelous material prosperity—all these have been men who have drawn wisdom from the experience of every age and nation, but who have nevertheless thought, and worked, and conquered, and lived, and died, purely as Americans; and on the whole they have done better work than has been done in any other country during the short period of our national life.

On the other hand, it is in those professions where our people have striven hardest to mould themselves in conventional European forms that they have succeeded least; and this holds true to the present day, the failure being of course most conspicuous where the man takes up his abode in Europe; where he becomes a second-rate European, because he is over-civilized, over-sensitive, over-refined, and has lost the hardihood and manly courage by which alone he can conquer in the keen struggle of our national life. Be it remembered, too, that this same being does not really become a European; he only ceases being an American, and becomes nothing. He throws away a great prize for the sake of a lesser one, and does not even get the lesser one. The painter who goes to Paris, not merely to get two or three years' thorough training in his art, but with the deliberate purpose of taking up his abode there, and with the intention of following in the ruts worn deep by ten thousand earlier travelers, instead of striking off to rise or fall on a new line, thereby forfeits all chance of doing the best work. He must content himself with aiming at that kind of mediocrity which consists in doing fairly well what has already been done better; and he usually never even sees the grandeur and picturesqueness lying open before the eyes of every man who can read the book of America's past and the book of America's present. Thus it is with the undersized man of letters, who flees his country because he, with his delicate, effeminate sensitiveness, finds the conditions of life on this side of the water crude and raw; in other words, because he finds that he cannot play a man's part among men, and so goes where he will be sheltered from the winds that harden stouter souls. This *emigré* may write graceful and pretty verses, essays, novels; but he will never do work to compare with that of his brother, who is strong enough to stand on his own feet, and do his work as an American. Thus it is with the scientist who spends his youth in a German university, and can thenceforth work only in the fields already fifty times furrowed by the German plows. Thus it is with that most foolish of parents who sends his children to be educated abroad, not knowing—what every clear-sighted man from Washington and Jay down has known—that the American who is to make his way in America should be brought up among his fellow Americans. It is among the people who like to consider themselves, and, indeed, to a large extent are, the leaders of the so-called social world, especially in some of the northeastern cities, that this colonial habit of thought, this thoroughly provincial spirit of admiration for things foreign, and inability to stand on one's own feet, becomes most evident and most despicable. We thoroughly believe in every kind of honest and lawful pleasure, so long as the getting it is not made man's chief business; and we believe heartily in the good that can be done by men of leisure who work hard in their leisure, whether at politics or philanthropy, literature or art. But a leisure class whose leisure simply means idleness is a curse to the community, and in so far as its members distinguish themselves chiefly by aping the worst—not the best—traits of similar people across the water, they become both comic and noxious elements of the body politic.

The third sense in which the word "Americanism" may be employed is with reference to the Americanizing of the newcomers to our shores. We must Americanize them in every way, in speech, in political ideas and principles, and in their way of looking at the relations between Church and State. We welcome the German or the Irishman who becomes an American.

We have no use for the German or Irishman who remains such. We do not wish German-Americans and Irish-Americans who figure as such in our social and political life; we want only Americans, and, provided they are such, we do not care whether they are of native or of Irish or of German ancestry. We have no room in any healthy American community for a German-American vote or an Irish-American vote, and it is contemptible demagogy to put planks into any party platform with the purpose of catching such a vote. We have no room for any people who do not act and vote simply as Americans, and as nothing else. Moreover, we have as little use for people who carry religious prejudices into our politics as for those who carry prejudices of caste or nationality. We stand unalterably in favor of the public-school system in its entirety. We believe that the English, and no other language, is that in which all the school exercises should be conducted. We are against any division of the school fund, and against any appropriation of public money for sectarian purposes. We are against any recognition whatever by the state in any shape or form of state-aided parochial schools. But we are equally opposed to any discrimination against or for a man because of his creed. We demand that all citizens, Protestant and Catholic, Jew and Gentile, shall have fair treatment in every way; that all alike shall have their rights guaranteed them. The very reasons that make us unqualified in our opposition to state-aided sectarian schools make us equally bent that, in the management of our public schools, the adherents of each creed shall be given exact and equal justice, wholly without regard to their religious affiliations; that trustees, superintendents, teachers, scholars, all alike, shall be treated without any reference whatsoever to the creed they profess. We maintain that it is an outrage, in voting for a man for any position, whether state or national, to take into account his religious faith, provided only he is a good American. When a secret society does what in some places the American Protective Association seems to have done, and tries to proscribe Catholics both politically and socially, the members of such society show that they themselves are as utterly un-American, as alien to our school of political thought, as the worst immigrants who land on our shores. This conduct is equally base and contemptible; they are the worst foes of our public-school system, because they strengthen the hands of its ultramundane enemies; they should receive the hearty condemnation of all Americans who are truly patriotic.

The mighty tide of immigration to our shores has brought in its train much of good and much of evil; and whether the good or the evil shall predominate depends mainly on whether these newcomers do or do not throw themselves heartily into our national life, cease to be European, and become Americans like the rest of us. More than a third of the people of the northern states are of foreign birth or parentage. An immense number of them have become completely Americanized, and these stand on exactly the same plane as the descendants of any Puritan, Cavalier, or Knickerbocker among us, and do their full and honorable share of the nation's work. But where immigrants, or the sons of immigrants, do not heartily and in good faith throw in their lot with us, but cling to the speech, the customs, the ways of life, and the habits of thought of the Old World which they have left, they thereby harm both themselves and us. If they remain alien elements, unassimilated, and with interests separate from ours, they are mere obstructions to the current of our national life, and, moreover, can get no good from it themselves. In fact, though we ourselves also suffer from their perversity, it is they who really suffer most. It is an immense benefit to the European immigrant to change him into an American citizen. To bear the name of American is to bear the most honorable of titles; and whoever does not so believe has no business to bear the name at all, and, if he comes from Europe, the sooner he goes back there the better. Besides, the man who does not become Americanized nevertheless fails to remain a European and becomes nothing at all. The immigrant cannot possibly remain what he was, or continue to be a member of the Old World society. If he tries to retain his old language, in a few generations it becomes a barbarous jargon; if he tries to retain his old customs and ways of life, in a few generations he becomes an uncouth boor. He has cut himself off from the Old

World, and cannot retain his connection with it; and if he wishes ever to amount to anything he must throw himself heart and soul, and without reservation, into the new life to which he has come.

So, from his own standpoint, it is beyond all question the wise thing for the immigrant to become thoroughly Americanized. Moreover, from our standpoint, we have a right to demand it. We freely extend the hand of welcome and of good-fellowship to every man, no matter what his creed or birthplace, who comes here honestly intent on becoming a good United States citizen like the rest of us; but we have a right, and it is our duty, to demand that he shall indeed become so, and shall not confuse the issues with which we are struggling by introducing among us Old-World quarrels and prejudices. There are certain ideas which he must give up. For instance, he must learn that American life is incompatible with the existence of any form of anarchy, or, indeed, of any secret society having murder for its aim, whether at home or abroad; and he must learn that we exact full religious toleration and the complete separation of Church and State. Moreover, he must not bring in his Old-World race and national antipathies, but must merge them into love for our common country, and must take pride in the things which we can all take pride in. He must revere only our flag; not only must it come first, but no other flag should even come second. He must learn to celebrate Washington's birthday rather than that of the Queen or Kaiser, and the Fourth of July instead of St. Patrick's Day. Our political and social questions must be settled on their own merits, and not complicated by quarrels between England and Ireland, or France and Germany, with which we have nothing to do: it is an outrage to fight an American political campaign with reference to questions of European politics. Above all, the immigrant must learn to talk and think and *be* United States.

The immigrant of today can learn much from the experience of the immigrants of the past, who came to America prior to the Revolutionary War. Many of our most illustrious Revolutionary names were borne by men of Huguenot blood—Jay, Sevier, Marion, Laurens. But the Huguenots were, on the whole, the best immigrants we have ever received; sooner than any other, and more completely, they became American in speech, conviction, and thought. The Hollanders took longer than the Huguenots to become completely assimilated; nevertheless they in the end became so, immensely to their own advantage. One of the leading Revolutionary generals, Schuyler, and one of the Presidents of the United States, Van Buren, were of Dutch blood; but they rose to their positions, the highest in the land, because they had become Americans and had ceased being Hollanders. If they had remained members of an alien body, cut off by their speech and customs and belief from the rest of the American community, Schuyler would have lived his life as a boorish, provincial squire, and Van Buren would have ended his days a small tavern-keeper. So it is with the Germans of Pennsylvania. Those of them who became Americanized have furnished to our history a multitude of honorable names, from the days of the Muhlenbergs onward; but those who did not become Americanized form to the present day an unimportant body, of no significance in American existence. So it is with the Irish, who gave to Revolutionary annals such names as Carroll and Sullivan, and to the Civil War men like Sheridan and Shields —all men who were Americans and nothing else: while the Irish who remain such, and busy themselves solely with alien politics, can have only an unhealthy influence upon American life, and can never rise as do their compatriots who become straightout Americans. Thus it has ever been with all people who have come hither, of whatever stock or blood.

But I wish to be distinctly understood on one point. Americanism is a question of spirit, convictions, and purpose, not of creed or birthplace. The politician who bids for the Irish or German vote, or the Irishman or German who votes as an Irishman or German, is despicable, for all citizens of this commonwealth should vote solely as Americans; but he is not a whit less despicable than the voter who votes against a good American, merely because that American happens to have been born in Ireland or Germany. Know-nothingism, in any form, is as utterly un-American as foreignism. It is a base outrage to oppose a man because of his religion or birthplace, and all good citizens will hold any such effort in abhorrence. A Scandinavian, a German, or an Irishman who has really become an American has the right to stand on exactly the same footing as any native-born citizen in the land, and is just as much entitled to the friendship and support, social and political, of his neighbors. Among the men with whom I have been thrown in close personal contact socially, and who have been among my staunchest friends and allies politically, are not a few Americans who happen to have been born on the other side of the water, in Germany, Ireland, Scandinavia; and I know no better men in the ranks of our native-born citizens.

In closing, I cannot better express the ideal attitude that should be taken by our fellow-citizens of foreign birth than by quoting the words of a representative American, born in Germany, the Honorable Richard Guenther, of Wisconsin. In a speech spoken at the time of the Samoan trouble, he said:

"We know as well as any other class of American citizens where our duties belong. We will work for our country in time of peace and fight for it in time of war, if a time of war should ever come. When I say our country, I mean, of course, our adopted country. I mean the United States of America. After passing through the crucible of naturalization, we are no longer Germans; we are Americans. Our attachment to America cannot be measured by the length of our residence here. We are Americans from the moment we touch the American shore until we are laid in American graves. We will fight for America whenever necessary. America, first, last, and all the time. America against Germany, America against the world; America, right or wrong; always America. We are Americans."

All honor to the man who spoke such words as those; and I believe they express the feelings of the great majority of those among our fellow-American citizens who were born abroad. We Americans can only do our allotted task well if we face it steadily and bravely, seeing but not fearing the dangers. Above all we must stand shoulder to shoulder, not asking as to the ancestry or creed of our comrades, but only demanding that they be in very truth Americans, and that we all work together, heart, hand, and head, for the honor and the greatness of our common country.

EDUCATED LEADERSHIP

THE SOCIAL VALUE OF THE COLLEGE-BRED[1]

William James

[William James (1842–1910), a distinguished American psychologist and philosopher, was born in New York City. He studied for a time in the Lawrence Scientific School, and afterward obtained an M.D. degree from Harvard. In 1872 he began to teach at Harvard as an instructor in psychology and later became professor. His published works in his particular field of study have placed him among the foremost thinkers of his generation. This article was originally an address delivered at a meeting of the Association of American Alumni at Radcliffe College, November 7, 1907.]

Of what use is a college training? We who have had it seldom hear the question raised—we might be a little nonplused to answer it offhand. A certain amount of meditation has brought me to this as the pithiest reply which I myself can give: The best claim that a college education can possibly make on your respect, the best thing it can aspire to accomplish for you is this—that it should *help you to know a good man when you see him.* This is as true of women's as of men's colleges; but that it is neither a joke nor a one-sided abstraction I shall now endeavor to show.

What talk do we commonly hear about the contrast between college education and the education which business or technical or professional schools confer? The college education is called higher because it is supposed to be so general and so disinterested. At the "schools" you get a relatively narrow practical skill, you are told, whereas the "colleges" give you the more liberal culture, the broader outlook, the historical perspective, the philosophic atmosphere, or something which phrases of that

[1]From *McClure's Magazine*, vol. xxx, p. 419. (February, 1908.) Reprinted by permission.

sort try to express. You are made into an efficient instrument for doing a definite thing, you hear, at the schools; but, apart from that, you may remain a crude and smoky kind of petroleum, incapable of spreading light. The universities and colleges, on the other hand, although they may leave you less efficient for this or that practical task, suffuse your whole mentality with something more important than skill. They redeem you, make you well-bred; they make "good company" of you mentally. If they find you with a naturally boorish or caddish mind, they cannot leave you so, as a technical school may leave you. This, at least, is pretended; this is what we hear among college-trained people when they compare their education with every other sort. Now, exactly how much does this signify?

It is certain, to begin with, that the narrowest trade or professional training does something more for a man than to make a skilful practical tool of him—it makes him also a judge of other men's skill. Whether his trade be pleading at the bar or surgery or plastering or plumbing, it develops a critical sense in him for that sort of occupation. He understands the difference between second-rate and first-rate work in his whole branch of industry; he gets to know a good job in his own line as soon as he sees it; and getting to know this in his own line, he gets a faint sense of what good work may mean anyhow, that may, if circumstances favor, spread into his judgments elsewhere. Sound work, clean work, finished work; feeble work, slack work, sham work—these words express an identical contrast in many different departments of activity. In so far forth, then, even the humblest manual trade may beget in one a certain small degree of power to judge of good work generally.

Now, what is supposed to be the line of us who have the higher college training? Is there any broader line—since our education claims primarily not to be "narrow"—in which we also are made good judges between what is first-rate and what is second-rate only? What is especially taught in the colleges has long been known by the name of the "humanities," and these are often identified with Greek and Latin. But it is only as literatures, not as languages, that Greek and Latin have

any general humanity value; so that in a broad sense the humanities mean literature primarily, and in a still broader sense,
the study of masterpieces in almost any field of human endeavor.
Literature keeps the primacy; for it not only *consists* of masterpieces, but is largely *about* masterpieces, being little more than
an appreciative chronicle of human master-strokes, so far as it
takes the form of criticism and history. You can give humanistic value to almost anything by teaching it historically. Geol-
ogy, economics, mechanics, are humanities when taught with
reference to the successive achievements of the geniuses to which
these sciences owe their being. Not taught thus, literature
remains grammar, art a catalogue, history a list of dates, and
natural science a sheet of formulas and weights and measures.

The sifting of human creations!—nothing less than this is
what we ought to mean by the humanities. Essentially this
means biography; what our colleges should teach is, therefore,
biographical history, that not of politics merely, but of anything and everything so far as human efforts and conquests are
factors that have played their part. Studying in this way, we
learn what types of activity have stood the test of time; we
acquire standards of the excellent and durable. All our arts
and sciences and institutions are but so many quests of perfection on the part of men; and when we see how diverse the
types of excellence may be, how various the tests, how flexible
the adaptations, we gain a richer sense of what the terms
"better" and "worse" may signify in general. Our critical
sensibilities grow both more acute and less fanatical. We sympathize with men's mistakes even in the act of penetrating them;
we feel that pathos of lost causes and misguided epochs even
while we applaud what overcame them.

Such words are vague and such ideas are inadequate, but their
meaning is unmistakable. What the colleges—teaching humanities by examples which may be special, but which must be
typical and pregnant—should at least try to give us, is a general
sense of what, under various disguises, *superiority* has always
signified and may still signify. The feeling for a good human
job anywhere, the admiration of the really admirable, the dis-

esteem of what is cheap and trashy and impermanent—this is what we call the critical sense, the sense for ideal values. It is the better part of what men know as wisdom. Some of us are wise in this way naturally and by genius; some of us never become so. But to have spent one's youth at college, in contact with the choice and rare and precious, and yet still to be a blind prig or vulgarian, unable to scent out human excellence or to divine it amid its accidents, to know it only when ticketed and labeled and forced on us by others, this indeed should be accounted the very calamity and shipwreck of a higher education.

The sense for human superiority ought, then, to be considered our line, as boring subways is the engineer's line and the surgeon's is appendicitis. Our colleges ought to have lit up in us a lasting relish for the better kind of man, a loss of appetite for mediocrities, and a disgust for cheapjacks. We ought to smell, as it were, the difference of quality in men and their proposals when we enter the world of affairs about us. Expertness in this might well atone for some of our awkwardness at accounts, for some of our ignorance of dynamos. The best claim we can make for the higher education, the best single phrase in which we can tell what it ought to do for us, is, then, exactly what I said: it should enable us to *know a good man when we see him.*

That the phrase is anything but an empty epigram follows from the fact that if you ask in what line it is most important that a democracy like ours should have its sons and daughters skilful, you see that it is this line more than any other. "The people in their wisdom"—this is the kind of wisdom most needed by the people. Democracy is on its trial, and no one knows how it will stand the ordeal. Abounding about us are pessimistic prophets. Fickleness and violence used to be, but are no longer, the vices which they charge to democracy. What its critics now affirm is that its preferences are inveterately for the inferior. So it was in the beginning, they say, and so it will be world without end. Vulgarity enthroned and institutionalized, elbowing everything superior from the highway, this, they tell us, is our irremediable destiny; and the picture-papers of the European continent are already drawing Uncle Sam with the hog instead of the eagle for his heraldic emblem. The privileged aristocracies of the foretime, with all their iniquities, did at least preserve some taste for higher human quality and honor certain forms of refinement by their enduring traditions. But when democracy is sovereign, its doubters say, nobility will form a sort of invisible church, and sincerity and refinement, stripped of honor, precedence, and favor, will have to vegetate on sufferance in private corners. They will have no general influence. They will be harmless eccentricities.

Now, who can be absolutely certain that this may not be the career of democracy? Nothing future is quite secure; states enough have inwardly rotted; and democracy as a whole may undergo self-poisoning. But, on the other hand, democracy is a kind of religion, and we are bound not to admit its failure. Faiths and utopias are the noblest exercise of human reason, and no one with a spark of reason in him will sit down fatalistically before the croaker's picture. The best of us are filled with the contrary vision of a democracy stumbling through every error till its institutions glow with justice and its customs shine with beauty. Our better men *shall* show the way and we *shall* follow them; so we are brought round again to the mission of the higher education in helping us to know the better kind of man whenever we see him.

The notion that a people can run itself and its affairs anonymously is now well known to be the silliest of absurdities. Mankind does nothing save through initiatives on the part of inventors, great or small, and imitation by the rest of us—these are the sole factors active in human progress. Individuals of genius show the way, and set the patterns, which common people then adopt and follow. *The rivalry of the patterns is the history of the world.* Our democratic problem thus is statable in ultra-simple terms: Who are the kind of men from whom our majorities shall take their cue? Whom shall they treat as rightful leaders? We and our leaders are the x and the y of the equation here; all other historic circumstances, be they economical, political, or intellectual, are only the background of occasion on which the living drama works itself out between us.

In this very simple way does the value of our educated class define itself; we more than others should be able to divine the worthier and better leaders. The terms here are monstrously simplified, of course, but such a bird's-eye view lets us immediately take our bearings. In our democracy, where everything else is so shifting, we alumni and alumnæ of the colleges are the only permanent presence that corresponds to the aristocracy in older countries. We have continuous traditions, as they have; our motto, too, is *noblesse oblige:* and, unlike them, we stand for ideal interests solely, for we have no corporate selfishness and wield no powers of corruption. We ought to have our own class-consciousness. "Les intellectuels!" What prouder club-name could there be than this one, used ironically by the party of "red blood," the party of every stupid prejudice and passion, during the anti-Dreyfus craze, to satirize the men in France who still retained some critical sense and judgment! Critical sense, it has to be confessed, is not an exciting term, hardly a banner to carry in processions. Affections for old habit, currents of self-interest, and gales of passion are the forces that keep the human ship moving; and the pressure of the judicious pilot's hand upon the tiller is a relatively insignificant energy. But the affections, passions, and interests are shifting, successive, and distraught; they blow in alternation while the pilot's hand is steadfast. He knows the compass, and, with all the leeways he is obliged to tack toward, he always makes some headway. A small force, if it never lets up, will accumulate effects more considerable than those of much greater forces if these work inconsistently. The ceaseless whisper of the more permanent ideals, the steady tug of truth and justice, give them but time, *must* warp the world in their direction.

This bird's-eye view of the general steering function of the college-bred amid the driftings of democracy ought to help us to a wider vision of what our colleges themselves should aim at. If we are to be the yeast-cake for democracy's dough, if we are to make it rise with culture's preferences, we must see to it that culture spreads broad sails. We must shake the old double reefs out of the canvas into the wind and sunshine, and let in every modern subject, sure that any subject will prove humanistic, if its setting be kept only wide enough.

Stevenson says somewhere to his reader: "You think you are just making this bargain, but you are really laying down a link in the policy of mankind." Well, your technical school should enable you to make your bargain splendidly; but your college should show you just the place of that kind of bargain—a pretty poor place, possibly—in the whole policy of mankind. That is the kind of liberal outlook, of perspective, of atmosphere, which should surround every subject as a college deals with it.

We of the colleges must eradicate a curious notion which numbers of good people have about such ancient seats of learning as Harvard. To many ignorant outsiders, that name suggests little more than a kind of sterilized conceit and incapacity for being pleased. In Edith Wyatt's exquisite book of Chicago sketches called *Every One His Own Way*, there is a couple who stand for culture in the sense of exclusiveness, Richard Elliot and his feminine counterpart—feeble caricatures of mankind, unable to know any good thing when they see it, incapable of enjoyment unless a printed label gives them leave. Possibly this type of culture may exist near Cambridge and Boston, there may be specimens there, for priggishness is just like painter's colic or any other trade-disease. But every good college makes its students immune against this malady, of which the microbe haunts the neighborhood-printed pages. It does so by its general tone being too hearty for the microbe's life. Real culture lives by sympathies and admirations, not by dislikes and disdains—under all misleading wrappings it pounces unerringly upon the human core. If a college, through the inferior human influences that have grown regnant there, fails to catch the robuster tone, its failure is colossal, for its social function stops; democracy gives it a wide berth, turns toward it a deaf ear.

"Tone," to be sure, is a terribly vague word to use, but there is no other, and this whole meditation is over questions of tone. By their tone are all things human either lost or saved. If democracy is to be saved it must catch the higher, healthier tone. If we are to impress it with our preferences, we ourselves must use the proper tone, which we, in turn must have caught from our own teachers. It all reverts in the end to the action of innumerable imitative individuals upon each other and to the question of whose tone has the highest spreading power. As a class, we college graduates should look to it that *ours* has spreading power. It ought to have the highest spreading power.

In our essential function of indicating the better men, we now have formidable competitors outside. *McClure's Magazine,* the *American Magazine, Collier's Weekly* and, in its fashion, the *World's Work,* constitute together a real popular university along this very line. It would be a pity if any future historian were to have to write words like these: "By the middle of the twentieth century the higher institutions of learning had lost all influence over public opinion in the United States. But the mission of raising the tone of democracy, which they had proved themselves so lamentably unfitted to exert, was assumed with rare enthusiasm and prosecuted with extraordinary skill and success by a new educational power; and for the clarification of their human sympathies and elevation of their human preferences, the people at large acquired the habit of resorting exclusively to the guidance of certain private literary adventures, commonly designated in the market by the affectionate name of 'ten-cent magazines.'"

Must not we of the colleges see to it that no historian shall ever say anything like this? Vague as the phrase of knowing a good man when you see him may be, diffuse and indefinite as one must leave its application, is there any other formula that describes so well the result at which our institutions *ought* to aim? If they do that, they do the best thing conceivable. If they fail to do it, they fail in very deed. It surely is a fine synthetic formula. If our faculties and graduates could once collectively come to realize it as the great underlying purpose toward which they have always been more or less obscurely groping, a great clearness would be shed over many of their problems; and, as for their influence in the midst of our social system, it would embark upon a new career of strength.

THE RELATION BETWEEN A LIBERAL EDUCATION AND TRUE AMERICANISM[1]

HENRY CABOT LODGE

[For biographical note, see page 224. This selection was originally an oration delivered before the Phi Beta Kappa Society at Harvard University, June, 1892. The title then used, "True Americanism," has been here changed to one which indicates more clearly that the writer was discussing how a liberal education should be productive of a high type of Americanism.]

One of the best known and least read of Queen Anne's men is Sir Richard Steele. His good and evil fortune, his kind heart, his ready wit, his attractive but somewhat imperfect character, are all familiar to a large posterity with whom he has ever been popular. But his writings, in which he took so much simple pride, are, it is to be feared, largely unread. The book of quotations contains only two sentences of his writing, and one of these can hardly be called familiar. But the other fully deserves the adjective, for it is perhaps the finest compliment ever paid by a man to a woman. Steele wrote of Lady Elizabeth Hastings that "to love her was a liberal education," and thus rescued her forever from the oblivion of the British Peerage. He certainly did not mean by this that to love the Lady Elizabeth was as good as a knowledge of Latin and Greek, for that would have been no compliment at all, unless from Carlyle's friend Dryasdust, a very different personage from the gallant and impecunious husband of "Prue." No, Steele meant something very far removed from Latin and Greek, and everybody knows what he meant, even if one cannot put it readily into words.

To the mind of the eighteenth century, a liberal education entirely classical, if you please, so far as books went, meant the education which bred tolerance and good manners and courage,

[1]From *Harvard Graduates' Magazine*, vol. iii, p. 9. (September, 1892.) Reprinted by permission.

Q

which taught a man to love honor and truth and patriotism and all things of good report. Like the history of Sir John Froissart, it was the part of a liberal education "to encourage all valorous hearts and to show them honourable examples." Such, I think, we all believe a liberal education to be today, in its finest and best sense. But yet this is not all, nor are the fields of learning, which a great university opens to its students, all. Besides the liberal education of Steele and the ample page of knowledge which a university unrolls, there is still something more, and this something is the most important part. . . .

Ordinarily we think of a college simply as a place where men receive their preliminary training for the learned professions, where they lay the foundations for a life of scientific or historical investigation, for classical scholarship, or for the study of modern languages or literature, and where they gather that general knowledge which constitutes the higher education, even if the student leaves learning behind him at the college gate to enter on a life of action or of business. Yet in reality these are but the details of a liberal education, and we do not want to lose sight of the city on account of the number of houses immediately around us.

The great function of a liberal education is to fit a man for the life about him, and to prepare him, whatever profession or pursuit he may follow, to be a useful citizen of the country which gave him birth. This is of vast importance in any country, but in the United States it is of peculiar moment, because here every man has imposed upon him the duties of sovereignty, and in proportion to his capacity and his opportunities are the responsibilities of that sovereignty. . . .

If a man is not a good citizen it boots little whether he is a learned Grecian or a sound Latinist. If he is out of sympathy with his country, his people, and his time, the last refinement and the highest accomplishments are of slight moment. But it is of the last importance that every man, and especially every educated man, in the United States, no matter what his profession or business, should be in sympathy with his country, with its history in the past, its needs in the present, and its aspirations for the future. If he has this, all the rest will follow, and it is precisely at this point that there seems to be a real danger in our university life and in our liberal education. The peril, moreover, is none the less real because the wrong influence is subtle.

We are apt to gather here at the end of each college year in a kindly and very natural spirit of mutual admiration. Those of us who come from the busy outside world come to renew old memories, and to brighten, if only for a moment, the friendships which time and separation would darken and rust. We are in no mood for criticism. Yet it is perhaps as well not to let the mutual congratulations go too far, for we have the advantage of coming from without, and are not likely to mistake the atmosphere which gathers about a university for that of the world at large. A Lord Chancellor of England on one occasion at Oxford said that he had listened with delight to the general admiration which everyone had expressed for everybody else, and for the university in particular, and that he was glad to see the great advances that had come since his time, and to know that Oxford could boast that the tide of thought and civilization had risen in the university as high almost as that which flowed without the college walls. The sting of the satire lay as usual in its leaven of truth. The danger of every university lies in its losing touch with the world about it. This is bad anywhere. It is worse in a republic than anywhere else.

We must, however, be more definite again if we would reach any result. "Losing touch" is a vague expression, "lack of sympathy" is little better. It is not easy to put my meaning in one word, but perhaps to say that the first duty of an American university and its liberal education should be to make its students good Americans comes as near to it as anything. Still we must go a step further, for many persons are prone to sneer at the demand for Americanism, as if it meant merely a blatant and boastful Chauvinism, employed only for the baser political uses. There is always an attempt to treat it as if it were something like the utterances which Dickens satirized long ago in the persons of Jefferson Brick and Elijah Pogram. That was certainly neither an agreeable nor creditable form of national self-assertion. Yet it was infinitely better, coarse and bragging as it was, than the opposite spirit which turns disdainfully even from the glories of nature because they are American and not foreign, and which looks scornfully at the Sierras because they are not the Alps. The Bricks and the Pograms may have been coarse and vulgar, yet the spirit which they caricatured was at least strong, and capable of better things. But the other spirit is pitifully weak, and has no future before it except one of further decay.

True Americanism is something widely different from either of these. It is really only another word for intelligent patriotism. Loud self-assertion has no part in it, and mere criticism and carping, with their everlasting whine because we are not as others are, cannot exist beside it. Americanism in its right sense does not tend in the least to repress wholesome criticism of what is wrong, on the contrary it encourages it. But this is the criticism which is made only as the first step toward a remedy, and is not mere snarling for snarling's sake. Such Americanism as this takes pride in what we have done and in the men we have bred, and knows not the eternal comparison with other people which is the sure sign of a tremulous little mind, and of a deep doubt of one's own position.

To all of which the answer is constantly made that this is merely asserting a truism and a commonplace, and that of course everyone is intelligently patriotic. Of the great mass of our people this is true beyond question. They are thoroughly patriotic in the best sense. Theoretically it is true of all. Practically there is still much left to be desired among our liberally educated men. It is this precise defect among those who have a liberal education of which I wish to speak.

The danger of the higher education of a great university is that it may in widening the horizon destroy the sense of proportion so far as our own country is concerned. The teachings of a university open to us the literature, the art, the science, the learning, and the history of all other nations. They would be quite worthless if they did not do so. These teachings form, and necessarily form, the great mass of all that we study here. That which relates to our own country is inevitably only a small part, comparatively speaking, of the great whole. This is quite natural. Our own nation is comparatively new. Its history is not long, and it is not set off by the glitter of a court, or of an ancient aristocracy. Our literature is young. Our art is just developing. In the broad sweep of a liberal education, that which relates to the United States is but one of many parts. Hence there is a tendency to lose the sense of proportion, to underrate our own place in the history and life of the world, and to forget that knowledge of our own country, while it excludes nothing else, is nevertheless more important to each of us than that of all other countries, if we mean to play a man's part in life. There is no danger that liberally educated men will overvalue their own country, there is great danger that they will undervalue it. This does not arise from any lack of opportunity here to learn our history, or to know what we have done as a people. It comes from a failure rightly to appreciate our history and our achievements. We are too apt to think of ourselves as something apart and inferior, and to fail to see our true place in the scale of nations. Many men of liberal education either expect too much of the United States, or value too little what has been accomplished here. As has just been said, we are a young nation. Certain fruits of a high civilization require time to ripen. It is foolish to criticise the absence of those things which time alone can bring to perfection, and their coming is retarded, not hastened, by fault-finding. On the other hand, we are apt to overlook what really has been done, and we often fail to judge rightly because we use superficial comparisions with some other contemporary people, instead of measuring ourselves by the just standards of the world's history.

Let us look for a moment at the last hundred years which cover our history as a nation. In that time we have conquered a continent, won it from the wilderness and the savages, by much privation, and much desperate and heroic fighting, unrecorded for the most part, with nature and with man. Where else in the nineteenth century will you find such a conquest as that? And this empire that we have conquered we have saved also from being rent asunder. That work of salvation cost us four years of gigantic war. Look again over the nineteenth century and see where you can find a war of like magnitude, equal to ours in its stake, its fighting, its sacrifices, or in the noble spirit that it evoked among our people. As the French traveler said, standing among the graves at Arlington, "only a great people is capable of a great civil war."

I will not touch upon the material development, unequaled in history, which has gone hand in hand with this conquest of waste places and fighting tribes of Indians. It is enough here to count only those higher things which show the real greatness of a nation.

Turn to the men. In our hundred years we have given to the world's roll of statesmen Washington and Lincoln. You cannot match them elsewhere in the same period. Are there any better, or purer, or greater than they to be found in the tide of time? Take up the list of great soldiers. Setting aside Napoleon, who stands all apart with Cæsar and Hannibal, what nation has made a larger gift to the leaders of men in battle than the country which added to the list the names of Washington, Grant, and Lee? Since Nelson fell at Trafalgar, where in naval warfare will you find a greater chief than Farragut?

In those great inventions which have affected the history and development of man, the country which has given to the world the cotton-gin, the telegraph, the sewing-machine, the steamship, the telephone, and the armored ship holds a place second to none.

Turn now to those fields which exact the conditions of an old civilization,—wealth, leisure, and traditions. Even here, despite the adverse circumstances of national youth, there is much to record, much to give fair promise, much in which to rejoice.

From the time of Franklin and his kite, we ever have done our share in scientific work. We have developed a literature of our own, and made it part of the great literature of the English-speaking race. The Luxembourg has opened its jealously guarded doors to give space and place to four American painters, and the chisel of St. Gaudens has carved statues which no contemporary elsewhere can rival. The buildings at the Chicago Fair came as a beautiful surprise and a great achievement. They showed that we had the full capacity to take rank among the great building races of the earth.

It is a great record for a hundred years. Even if we glance only at the mountain tops, it is a marvelous story of conquest and growth. If our universities do not teach us to value it rightly, they are of little worth, for to know the present and to act in it we must have a just knowledge of our place in history. If we have that knowledge, we shall realize that a nation which, whatever its shortcomings, has done so much and bred such men, has a promise for the future and a place in the world which brings a grave responsibility to those who come to the inheritance.

The first step, then, for our universities, if in the true spirit of a liberal education they seek to fit men for the life about them, is to make them Americans and send them forth in sympathy with their country. And the second step is like the first: A university should aim to put a man in sympathy with his time, and make him comprehend it if we would have him take effective part in the life of his time. As the danger on the first point of patriotism is that the many-sided teachings of a university will prevent a just sense of the place of our country, so on the second point the danger is that dealing largely with the past, the university will alienate its students from the present. The past is a good schoolhouse but a bad dwelling-place. We cannot really understand the present without the fullest knowledge of the past, but it is the present with which we are to deal, and the past must not be allowed to hide it.

There is a very visible tendency in universities to become in their teachings *laudatores temporis acti*, and this tendency is full of peril. The world was never made better, the great march of humanity was never led by men whose eyes were fixed upon the past. The leaders of men are those who look forward, not backward.

> "For not through eastern windows only,
>   When daylight comes, comes in the light;
>   In front the sun climbs slow, how slowly,
>   But westward look—the land is bright."

As I say do not undervalue your own country, so I say do not undervalue your own time. The nineteenth century is dying. It has been a great century. It has seen Waterloo, and Sedan, and Gettysburg. As it has passed along it has beheld the settlement of Australia and South Africa, and the conquest of the American continent. It has replaced the stage-coach with the locomotive, and united the continents with electric cables. It has been the century of Lincoln and Bismarck, of Wellington and Grant, and Lee and Moltke. Scott and Thackeray, Dickens and Hawthorne, have woven stories to rejoice it; and Browning and Tennyson and Victor Hugo, Longfellow, Lowell, Holmes and Poe have been among its later poets. It has been a time richly worth living in. Now in its closing years, with the new and unknown century hard upon us, it is more than ever a time worth living in, full of marvelous voices to those who will listen with attentive ears, full of opportunity to anyone who will take part in its strifes, fullest of all of profound interest to those who will look upon it with considerate eyes.

How, then, is a university to reach the results we ought to have from its teachings in this country and this period? How is it to inspire its students with sympathy for their country and their time as the most important of all its lessons? Some persons may reply that it can be obtained by making the university training more practical. Much has been said on this point first and last, but the theory, which is vague at best, seems to me to have no bearing here. It is not a practical education which we seek in this regard, even if it was the business of a university to give one, but a liberal education, which shall foster certain strong qualities of heart and head. Our search now and here is not for an education which shall enable a man to earn his living with the least possible delay, but for a training which shall develop character and mind along certain lines.

To one man Harvard gives the teaching which fits him to be an engineer, to another that which opens to him law or medicine or theology. But to all her students alike it is her duty to give that which will send them out from her gates able to understand and to sympathize with the life of the time. This cannot be done by rules or systems or textbooks. It can come and can only come from the subtle, impalpable, and yet powerful influences which the spirit and atmosphere of a great university can exert upon those within its care. It is not easy to define or classify those influences, although we all know their general effect. Nevertheless it is, I think, possible to get at something sufficiently definite to indicate what is lacking, and where the peril lies. It all turns on the spirit which inspires the entire collegiate body, on the mental attitude of the university as a whole. This brings us at once to the danger which I think confronts all our large universities today, and which I am sure confronts that university which I know and love best. We are given over too much to the critical spirit, and we are educating men to become critics of other men, instead of doers of deeds themselves. This is all wrong. Criticism is healthful, necessary, and desirable, but it is always abundant, and is infinitely less important than performance. There is not the slightest risk that the supply of critics will run out, for there are always enough middle-aged failures to keep the ranks full, if every other resource should fail. But even if we were short of critics, it is a sad mistake to educate young men to be mere critics at the outset of life. It should be the first duty of a university to breed in them far other qualities. Faith and hope, and belief, enthusiasm, and courage, are the qualities to be trained and developed in young men by a liberal education. Youth is the time for action, for work, not for criticism. A liberal education should encourage the spirit of action, not deaden it. We want the men whom we send out from our universities to count in the battle of life and in the history of their time, and to count more and not less because of their liberal education. They will not count at all, be well assured, if they come out trained only to look coldly and critically on all that is being done in the world, and on all who are doing it. Long ago Emerson pointed the finger of scorn at this type when he said: "There is my fine young Oxford gentleman, who says there is nothing new and nothing true and no matter." We cannot afford to have that type, and it is the true product of that critical spirit which says to its scholars, "See how badly the world is governed; see how covered with dust and sweat the men are who are trying to do the world's business, and how many mistakes they make; let us sit here in the shade with Amaryllis and add up the errors of these bruised, grimy fellows, and point out what they ought to do, while we make no mistakes ourselves by sticking to the safe rule of attempting nothing." This is a very comfortable attitude, but it is the one of all others which a university should discourage instead of inculcating. Moreover, with such an attitude of mind toward the world of thought and action is always allied a cultivated indifference, than which there is nothing more enervating.

And these things are no pale abstractions because they are in their nature purely matters of sentiment and thought. When Cromwell demanded the New Model, he said, "A set of poor tapsters and town apprentices would never fight against men of honor." They were of the same race and the same blood as the cavaliers, these tapsters and apprentices; they had the same muscles and the same bodily form and strength. It was the right spirit that was lacking, and this Cromwell with the keen eye of genius plainly saw. So he set against the passion of loyalty the stern enthusiasm of religion, and swept resistance from his path. One sentiment against another, and the mightier conquered. Come nearer to our own time. Some six thousand ill-armed American frontiersmen met ten thousand of the unconquered army of Wellington's veterans hard by New Orleans. They beat them in a night attack, they got the better of them in an artillery duel, and finally they drove back with heavy slaughter the onset of these disciplined troops who had over and over again carried by storm defenses manned by the soldiers of Napoleon. These backwoodsmen were of the same race as their opponents, no stronger, no more inured to hardships, than Wellington's men, but they had the right spirit in them. They did not stop to criticise the works, and to point out that cotton-bales were not the kind of rampart recognized in Europe. They did not pause to say that a properly constituted army ought to have bayonets and that they had none. Still less did they set about finding fault with their leader. They went in and did their best, and their best was victory. One example is as good as a hundred. It is the spirit, the faith, the courage, the determination of men, which have made the world move. These are the qualities which have carried the dominion of the English-speaking people across continents and over wide oceans to the very ends of the earth. It is the same in every field of human activity. The men who see nothing but the lions in the path, who fear ridicule and dread mistakes, who behold the faults they may commit more plainly than the guerdon to be won, win no battles, govern no states, write no books, carve no statues, paint no pictures. The men who do not fear to fall are those who rise. It is the men who take the risks of failure and mistakes who win through defeats to victory.

If the critical spirit govern in youth, it chokes action at its very source. We must have enthusiasm, not indifference, willingness to subordinate ourselves to our purpose, if we would reach results, and an imperfect result is far better than none at all. Abraham Lincoln said once, speaking of Henry Clay: "A free people in times of peace and quiet, when pressed by no common danger, naturally divide into parties. At such times the man who is of neither party, is not, cannot be, of any consequence. Mr. Clay was therefore of a party." This which Lincoln said of politics merely expresses in a single direction the truth that a man cannot succeed who is a mere critic. He must have the faith and enthusiasm which will enable him to do battle whether with sword or pen, with action or thought, for a cause in which he believes. This does not imply any lack of independence, any blind subservience to authority or prejudice. Far from it. But it does imply the absence of the purely critical spirit with no purpose but criticism, which dries up the very springs of action.

> "That is the doctrine simple, ancient, true;
> Such is life's trial, as old Earth smiles and knows.
> Make the low nature better by your throes;
> Give earth yourself, go up for gain above."

There is nothing fanciful in all this. It is very real, very near, very practical. You cannot win a boat-race, or a football match unless you have the right spirit. Thews and sinews are common enough. They can be had for the asking. But the best will not avail if they are not informed with the right spirit. You must have more than trained muscles; you must have enthusiasm, determination, brains, and the capacity for organization and subordination. If the critical spirit prevails, and everyone is engaged in criticising, analyzing, and declaring how much better things would be if they were only different, you will not, you cannot win, other things being equal. Differences in physical qualities may often determine results, but such differences come and go like luck at a game of cards. But if the critical, indifferent spirit reigns, it means sure and continued defeats, for it saps the very roots of action and success.

As it is in the struggles of the playground or the river, so it is in the wider fields of serious life. If a university breeds a race of little critics, they will be able to point out other men's faults and failures with neatness and exactness, but they will accomplish nothing themselves. They will make the world no better for their presence, they will not count in the conflict, they will not cure a single one of the evils they are so keen to detect. Worst of all, they will bring reproach on a liberal education, which will seem to other men to be a hindrance when it should be a help.

The time in which we live is full of questions of the deepest moment. There has been, during the century now ending, the greatest material development ever seen, greater than that of all preceding centuries together. The condition of the average man has been raised higher than ever before, and wealth has been piled up beyond the wildest fancy of romance. We have built up a vast social and industrial system, and have carried civilization to the highest point it has ever touched. That system and that civilization are on trial. Grave doubts and perils beset them. The economic theories of fifty years ago stand helpless and decrepit in their immobility before the social questions which face us now. Everywhere today there is an ominous spirit of unrest. Everywhere there is a feeling that all is not well when wealth abounds and none the less dire poverty ranges by its side, when the land is not fully populated and yet the number of the unemployed reaches to the millions. One is not either an alarmist or a pessimist because he recognizes these facts, and it would be worse than folly to try to blink them out of sight. I believe that we can deal with them successfully if we will but set ourselves to the grave task, as we have to the trials and dangers of the past. I am sure that, if these great social problems can be solved anywhere, they can be solved here in the United States. But the solution will tax to the utmost all the wisdom and courage and learning that the country can provide. What part are our universities, with their liberal education, to play in the history that is now making and is still to be written? They are the crown and glory of our civilization, but they can readily be set aside if they fall out of sympathy with the vast movements about them. I do not say whether they should seek to resist, or to sustain, or to guide and control those movements. But if they would not dry up and wither, they must at least understand them. A great university must be in touch with the world about it, with its hopes, its passions, its troubles, and its strivings. If it is not, it must be content

"For aye to be in shady cloister mewed,
Chanting faint hymns to the cold, fruitless moon."

LIBERTY AND DISCIPLINE[1]

Abbott Lawrence Lowell

[Abbott Lawrence Lowell (1856———) has been, since 1909, president of Harvard University. He is distinguished as an authority on the science of government, and is the author of many books and articles in this field.]

We are living in the midst of a terrific war in which each side casts upon the other the blame for causing the struggle; but in which each gives the same reason for continuing it to the bitter end—that reason being the preservation from destruction of the essential principle of its own civilization. One side claims to be fighting for the liberty of man; the other for a social system based

[1]From *Yale Review*, vol. v, p. 741. (July, 1916.) Reprinted by permission.

on efficiency and maintained by discipline. Of course the difference is one of degree. No one believes in permitting every man to do whatever he pleases, no matter how it may injure his neighbor or endanger the community; and no country refuses all freedom of action to the individual. But although the difference is only of degree and of emphasis, it is none the less real. Our own people have always asserted their devotion to the principle of personal liberty, and in some ways they have carried it farther than any other nation. It is not, therefore, useless to compare the two principles that we may understand their relative advantages, and perceive the dangers of liberty and the conditions of its fruitfulness.

Americans are more familiar with the benefits of discipline, in fact, than conscious of them in theory. Anyone who should try to manage a factory, a bank, a railroad, a ship, a military company, or an athletic team, on the principle of having every employee or member of the organization take whatever part in the work, and do it in whatever way seemed best in his own eyes, would come to sudden grief and be mercilessly laughed at. We all know that any enterprise can be successful only if there is coördination of effort, or what for short we call team play; and that this can happen only if the nature of each man's work, and the way he is to perform it, is arranged with a view to the whole, so that each part fitting into its place contributes its proper share to the total result. Experience has taught us that the maximum efficiency is attained where the team play is most nearly perfect, and therefore, the subordination of the individual to the combined action is most nearly complete. Then there is the greatest harmony of action, and the least waste by friction or working at cross purposes. But everyone is aware that such a condition does not come about of itself. Men do not fit into their places in a team or organization spontaneously. Until they have become experts they do not appreciate the relation of their particular work to the plan as a whole; and even when they have become familiar with the game or the industry, they are apt to overestimate their own part in it, or disagree about the best method of attaining the result. Everyone likes to rule, and when Artemus Ward suggested that all the men in a regiment should be made Brigadier Generals at once to avoid jealousy, he touched a familiar weakness in human nature. He was not obliged to explain the joke, because no one fails to see the absurdity of having everybody in command. But that would be exactly the situation if nobody were in command. If there is to be a plan for combined action, somebody must have power to decide what that plan shall be; and if the part of every performer is to be subordinated to the common plan, somebody must have authority to direct the action of each in conformity with the plan. Moreover, that authority must have some means of carrying its directions into effect. It must be maintained by discipline; either by forcing those who do not play their parts rightly to conform to the general plan, or by eliminating them from the organization.

This principle of coördinated effort maintained by discipline applies to every combination of men where the maximum efficiency for a concrete object is desired, be it a business, a charity, or a whole state. It is a vitally important principle which no people can afford to lose from sight, but it is not everything. Whether it conduces to the greatest happiness or not is a question I leave on one side, for I am now discussing only effectiveness. Yet even from that standpoint we have left something out of account. The principle would be absolutely true if men were machines, or if the thing desired were always a concrete object to be attained by coöperation, such as the building of a railroad, the production of wealth, the winning of victory in war or on a playing field. But men are human beings and the progress of civilization is a thing far too complex to be comprised within any one concrete object or any number of such objects depending on combined effort. This is where the advantages of liberty come in.

Pasteur, one of the greatest explorers of nature and benefactors of the age, remarked that the value of liberty lay in its enabling every man to put forth his utmost effort. In France under the ancient monarchy men were very nearly born to trades and professions, or at least large portions of the people were virtually excluded from many occupations. The posts of officers in the army were generally reserved for men of noble rank. The places of judges were purchased, and were in fact largely hereditary, and so on through much of the higher grade of employments. The Revolution broke this system down, and Napoleon insisted that the true principle of the French Revolution was the opening of all careers to talent; not so much equality as freedom of opportunity. Under any system of compulsion or restraint a man may be limited to duties unsuited to his qualities, so that he cannot use the best talents he possesses. The opportunities in a complex modern civilization are of infinite variety, subtle, elastic, incapable of being compassed by fixed regulations for attaining definite objects. The best plan for perfecting the post office, if strictly followed, would not have produced the telegraph; the most excellent organization of the telegraph would not have created the telephone; the most elaborate system of telephone wires and switchboards would not have included the wireless. The greatest contributions to knowledge, to the industrial arts, and to the comforts of life have been unforeseen, and have often come in unexpected directions. The production of these required something more than a highly efficient organization maintained by discipline.

Moreover—what is nearer to our present purpose—believers in the principle of liberty assert that a man will put forth more effort, and more intelligent effort, if he chooses his own field, and works in his own way, than if he labors under the constant direction of others. The mere sense of freedom is stimulating in a high degree to vigorous natures. The man who directs himself is responsible for the consequences. He guarantees the result, and stakes his character and reputation on it. If after selecting his own career he finds that he has chosen wrongly, he writes himself down a fool. The theory of liberty, then, is based upon the belief that a man is usually a better judge of his own aptitudes than anyone else can be, and that he will put forth more and better effort if he is free than if he is not.

Both these principles, of discipline and of liberty, contain much truth. Neither is absolutely true, nor can be carried to its logical extreme, for one by subjecting all a man's actions to the control of a master would lead to slavery, the other by leaving every man free to disregard the common welfare would lead to anarchy. In America we are committed, as it were, to err on the side of liberty; and it is my purpose to consider here what are the dangers and conditions of liberty in the American college. It is in college that young men first enjoy the pleasure of liberty and assume its responsibilities. They sometimes think themselves still under no little restriction, because they cannot leave the college during term time without permission, and must attend the lectures, examinations, and other duties; but these are slight compared with the restraints which will surround any busy man in after life. There is no better place than college to learn to use freedom without abusing it. This is one of the greatest opportunities of college life, the thing that makes strong men stronger and sometimes weak men weaker than before.

Liberty means a freedom of choice in regulating one's conduct. If you are free to attend a lecture, but not free to stay away from it, then it is compulsory. You have no liberty whatever in the matter. A man of wealth has no freedom about paying taxes. He is obliged to pay them. But he has freedom about giving money away to relieve distress, or for other charitable purposes, because he may give or not as he pleases. A man is at liberty to be generous or mean, to be kindly or selfish, to be truthful or tricky, to be industrious or lazy. In all these things his duty may be clear, but he is free to disregard it. In short, liberty means freedom to do wrong as well as to do right, else it is no freedom at all. It means freedom to be foolish as well as to be wise, to prefer immediate self-indulgence to future benefit for oneself or others, liberty to neglect as well as to perform the duties of the passing hour that never comes again. But if liberty were used exclusively to do wrong, it would be intolerable, and good sense would sweep it from the earth. The supposition on which liberty is based, the condition on which it exists, is that men will use it for right more than for wrong; that in the long run they will do right more often, and do more that is good, than under a system of restraint.

R

Mark this, liberty and discipline are not mutually exclusive. Liberty does not mean that good results can ever be attained without discipline. If rightly used it means only that regulation by others is replaced by self-discipline no less severe and inexorable. The man who does not force himself to work when he is disinclined to do so will never achieve anything worth doing. Some really industrious men affect to do only what they like, never working save when the spirit moves them; and occasionally such men deceive themselves in trying to deceive others. If not, they have usually schooled themselves to want what they ought to want. Self-discipline has brought their inclinations as well as their conduct into a happy subjection to their will. But, in fact, labor carried anywhere near the point of maximum productivity, the point where a man puts forth his utmost effort, is never wholly pleasureable, although the moral force required to drive oneself at top speed varies much in different people. An idle disposition, however, is no sufficient excuse for shirking. Many years ago a stingy old merchant in Boston lay dying. The old miser turned to the brother sitting by his bedside and said: "John, I wish I had been more generous in giving away money in my life. But it has been harder for me than for most men to give money; and, John, I think the Lord will make allowance for differences in temperament." Thus do we excuse ourselves for self-indulgence.

How many men in every American college make an effort to get through with little to spare, win a degree, and evade an education? Not an insignificant number. How many strive earnestly to put forth their utmost effort to obtain an education that will develop their intellectual powers to the fullest extent, and fit them in the highest possible degree to cope with the problems they will face as men and as citizens? Again not an insignificant number, but are they enough to satisfy Pasteur's aspirations, or even to justify his idea of the object of liberty?

Everywhere in the higher education of Europe, whether the system is one of freedom or restraint, whether as in Germany a degree is conferred only on men who have real proficiency, or as in Oxford and Cambridge a mere pass degree is given for very little real work, everywhere the principle of competition is dominant for those who propose to make a marked success in life. Let us take the countries which claim to be fighting in this war for liberty. A student at Oxford or Cambridge knows that his prospects, not only of a position in the university, but at the bar, in permanent public employment and political life, are deeply influenced by, and in many cases almost dependent upon, his winning a place in the first group of scholars at graduation. The man who gets it plays thereafter with loaded dice. It gives him a marked advantage at the start, and to some extent follows him ever afterwards. Of course, there are exceptional men who by ability come to the front rank without it, but on the whole they are surprisingly few. Mr. Balfour is sometimes referred to as a man who did not distinguish himself at Cambridge, and Sir Edward Grey is said to have been an incorrigibly poor scholar at Balliol in Oxford, yet both of them won third-class honors, which is not far from what we should consider Φ B K rank. To mention only men who have been prominent in public life, Peel, Cardwell, Sherbrooke, Gladstone, Harcourt, Bryce, Trevelyan, Asquith, Haldane, Milner, Simon, Ambassador Spring-Rice, and many more won honors of the first class at one of the two great English universities; while a number of other men distinguished in public life, such as Disraeli, Chamberlain, and Lloyd-George, did not go to Oxford or Cambridge. It would not be difficult to add a long list of judges, and in fact, as an Oxford man once remarked to me, high honors at the university have been almost a necessity for reaching the bench. No doubt the fact that men have achieved distinction at their universities is a test of their ability; but also the fact that they have done so is a direct help at the outset of their careers.

If we turn to France we find the same principle of competition in a direct form though working in other channels. The *Ecole Centrale*, the great school of engineering, and the *Beaux Arts*, the great school of architecture and art, admit only a limited number of students by competitive examination; and the men who obtain the highest prizes at graduation are guaranteed public employment for life. Europeans believe that preëminence in those things for which higher education exists is a measure of intellectual and moral qualities; and the fact that it is recognized as such tends to make it so, for the rewards attached to it make ambitious and capable young men strive for it, and put forth their utmost effort in the competition. Let us hope that some day our colleges, and the public at large, will recognize more fully than they do today the value of excellence in college work as a measure of capacity, as a promise of future achievement, and thereby draw out more effort among the undergraduates. It is already the case to a large extent in our professional schools, and ought to be the case in our colleges, if a college education is really worth the money and labor expended on it.

At present the college is scholastically democratic. The world rarely asks how a man got in, or how he graduated. It is enough that he did graduate somehow. Bachelor degrees, whether indicating high scholarship or a minimum of work, are treated by the public as free and equal; and what is worse they are far too much so treated by the colleges and universities themselves. Now, the requirement for a college degree cannot be more than a minimum, and in the nature of things a rather low minimum, requiring on the part of men with more than ordinary ability a very small amount of work; far less than is needed to call forth their utmost effort.

This is one of many illustrations of the well-known fact that education moves slowly, and follows rather than leads the spirit of the time. We live in a strenuous age, a time of activity and energy. I think it was Bagehot who remarked that the change of habits was evident even in the casual greeting of friends. He says that we ask a man whom we have not met for some time, "What have you been doing since I saw you last?" as if we expected him to have been doing something. I remember some time ago reading a story in a magazine about travelers in a railroad train, who were stopped at a custom house to have their baggage examined, and found, that, instead of holding clothes, their bags and trunks contained the works they had done in life. It was the last judgment, and several well-meaning persons found their many pieces of luggage sadly empty. A gentleman among the number came forward to explain that they had supposed their duty to consist in avoiding sin, and they had done so; that their lives had been spent in pleasures, for the most part wholly innocent, and that this was all they had understood to be required of them.

The story illustrates a change of attitude which has come over the world, and men who have passed fifty have seen it come in, comparing the generation that went before them with that which has followed them. Thou shalt is quite as important as thou shalt not. Professor Munro in speaking in a college chapel some time ago on the importance of positive as well as negative morality remarked that most people if asked the meaning of the fourth commandment would think only of its forbidding work on Sunday; whereas its opening words are "Six days shalt thou labor." We live not only in a strenuous world, but in the most strenuous part of the world. Innocent leisure is no longer quite respectable here, except in college; and it is getting not to be respectable there—except in study.

Most of us feel that the American college is a very precious thing. It is a clean and healthy place, morally, intellectually, and physically. I believe that no large body of young men anywhere in the world live on the whole such clean lives, or are cleaner or more honorable in thought. The college is a place where a man may, and where many a man does, develop his character and his mental force to an almost indefinite extent; where he may, and often does, acquire an inspiration that sustains him through life; where he is surrounded by influences that fit him, if he will follow them, for all that is best in the citizen of a republic. The chief defect in the American college today is that it has not yet been stirred by the strenuous spirit of the age, the spirit that dignifies the principle of liberty, or at least it has been stirred mainly in the line of what are called student activities. These are excellent things in themselves, to be encouraged in full measure, but they do not make up for indolence and lack of effort in the studies which are, after all, the justification for the existence of the college. Let us put this matter perfectly plainly. The good sense of the community would never approve of having young men devote the whole of their best four years to the playing field, or to those other accessories of college life, the management of athletic or other organizations, or writing for college papers. These, as I have said, are excellent as accessories, but if they were the whole thing, if instruction and study were abolished, the college would soon be abolished also. What, then, in a land of restless activity and energy is likely to be the future of a college in which a large part of the undergraduates regard extra-curriculum activities as the main interest, and education as an accessory; and where a smaller, but not inconsiderable fraction regard all activity as irksome? If our young men cannot answer that question themselves, let them ask some man who is not himself a college graduate but has worked his way up in the world by his diligence, perseverance, pluck, and force of character.

The danger that under a system of liberty men will fail to put forth their utmost effort lies not merely, or perhaps mainly, in a lack of moral force. It is due quite as much to a lack of moral and intellectual vision, an inability to see any valuable result to be accomplished by the effort. This is particularly true in college. Many a man who intends to work hard thereafter in his profession or business, tries to get through college with a small amount of study. He is fully aware that in his future career he will make no use of a knowledge of the force of the Greek aorist, of the properties of a regular parallelopipedon, or of the effect of the reign of Edward the First on English constitutional history; and hence he is inclined to think these things of no great practical consequence to him. In no form of human productivity of far-reaching importance is the direct practical utility of every step in the process visible to the man who takes it. The workman in a factory may not know why he mixes certain ingredients in prescribed proportions, why he heats the mixture to a certain temperature, or why he cools it slowly. It might be difficult to explain it to him; and he does these things because they are ordered by the boss.

The difficulty of perceiving the connection between the means and the end is greater in the case of education, as distinguished from mechanical training, than in almost anything else, because the processes are more subtle, more intangible, less capable of accurate analysis. In fact the raw material that is being worked up is not the subject matter of the work but the mind of the worker himself; and the effect on his mind is not from day to day perceptible. His immediate task is to learn something, and he asks himself whether it is really worth learning; whereas the knowledge he acquires is not of the first importance, the vital question being how much he has improved in the ability to acquire and use it. At school the process is equally obscure, but the boy learns his lessons because he is obliged to do so. If he is a good boy he learns them well, because, although blind to the meaning of it all, he knows it is his duty. He does not seek to understand the process; and I recall now with amusement the ridiculous attempts we sometimes made in our school days to explain to our girl friends why it was worth while to study Latin. Many a boy who has ranked high at school, without asking himself the use of studying at all, does little work in college, because he asks himself why he should make the effort and cannot answer the question. The contrast illustrates the difference between a system of discipline and one of liberty. In both the relation of the work of the day and the result to be attained is invisible, but the motive power is not the same.

Under a system of external discipline the motive power is supplied by the habit of obedience, enforced where necessary by penalties. For the good man the habit or duty of blind obedience is enough. As Colonel Mudge expressed it when he received a mistaken order to charge and sprang forward to lead his regiment at Gettysburg, "It is murder, but it is the order." Some of the greatest examples of heroism in human history have been given in this way. But blind obedience cannot be the motive power where liberty applies, and a man must determine his own conduct for himself. In the vast number of actions where the direct utility of each step cannot be seen, he must act on general principles, on a conviction that the particular step is part of a long process which leads forward to the end. The motive power of liberty is faith. All great enterprises, all great lives, are built upon and sustained by an overmastering faith in something.

Faith is based upon imagination which can conceive things the eye cannot behold. Young people are prone to think of imagination as fantastic, the creation by the mind of impossible forms and events, distortions of nature, or caricatures of man. But it is a higher imagination which pictures invisible things as they are, or as they might really be. Historic imagination does not people the past with impossible beings doing senseless acts, but with living men who thought and acted as men do not think and act today, but actually did under conditions that have long passed away. The true reformer is not he who portrays an ideal commonwealth which could never be made to work, but the man whose imagination has such a grasp on the springs of human nature that he can foresee how people would really conduct themselves in conditions yet untried, and whose plans work out as he designed them.

If faith is thus based upon imagination, its fruition requires a steadfastness of purpose that is not weakened by discouragements or turned aside by obstacles that shut out the view and cast dark shadows across the path. The doubter, who asks himself at every stage whether the immediate effort is really worth while, is lost. Prophesy confidently of him that he will never reach his goal.

President Pritchett in a walking tour in Switzerland asked a mountaineer about the road to the place whither he was bound. The man replied that he had never been there, but he knew that was the path which led to it. Such is the pathway to the ventures of life. None of us has ever been over the road we intend to travel in the world. If we believe that the way we take leads to our destination we must follow it, not stopping or turning back because a curve in the mountain trail obscures the distant scene, or does not at the moment seem to lead in the right direction. We must go on in faith that every step along the road brings us nearer, and that the faster we walk the farther we shall go before night falls upon us. The man who does not feel any reason for effort because he cannot see the direct utility of the things he learns has no faith in a college education; and if he has no faith in it he had better not waste time on it, but take up something else that he has faith in, or that is better suited to men of little faith.

Every form of civilization is, not only at its inception and in critical times, but always and forever, on trial. If it proves less effective than others it will be eliminated, peacefully or forcibly, by a gradual process of change or by a catastrophe. Now the test of a civilization based on liberty is the use men make of the liberty they enjoy, and it is a failure not only if men use it to do wrong, but also if they use it to do nothing, or as little as is possible to maintain themselves in personal comfort. This is true of our institutions as a whole and of the American college in particular. A student who has no sustaining faith in the education he can get there; who will not practise the self-discipline needed to obtain it; who uses his liberty to put forth not his utmost, but the least possible, effort; who uses it not to acquire, but to evade, a thorough education, fails to that extent in his duty to himself, to his college, to his country, and to the civilization he inherits. The man who uses his liberty to put forth his utmost effort in college and throughout his life, not only does his duty, but is helping to make freedom itself successful. He is working for a great principle of human progress. He is fighting the battle of liberty and securing its victory in the civilization of mankind.

Never have I been able to understand—and even less than ever in these terrible days, when young men, on whom the future shone bright with hope, sacrifice from a sense of duty their lives, the welfare of those dearest to them, and everything they care for—less than ever can I understand how any man can stand in safety on a hillside and watch the struggle of life in the plain below without longing to take part therein; how he can see the world pass by without a craving to make his mark, however small, on his day and generation. Many a man who would be eager to join a deadly charge if his country were at war, lacks the insight or imagination to perceive that the warfare of civilization is waged not more upon the battlefield than in the workshop, at the desk, in the laboratory, and the library. We have learned in this stress of nations that men cannot fight without ammunition well made in abundance; but we do not see that the crucial matter in civilization is the preparedness of young men for the work of the world; not only an ample supply of the best material, but a product moulded on the best pattern, tempered and finished to the highest point of perfection. Is this the ideal of a dreamer that cannot be realized; or is it a vision which young men will see and turn to a virile faith?

NATIONALIZING EDUCATION[1]

John Dewey

[John Dewey (1859———) was born at Burlington, Vermont. After completing his college work at the University of Vermont, he did post-graduate work at Johns Hopkins University. From 1884–1904 he was a member of the department of philosophy in the University of Michigan, being head of the department during the latter part of this period. In 1902–4 he was director of the school of education of the University of Chicago. Since 1904 he has been professor of philosophy in Columbia University.]

The words "nation" and "national" have two quite different meanings. We cannot profitably discuss the nationalizing of education unless we are clear as to the difference between the two. For one meaning indicates something desirable, something to be cultivated by education, while the other stands for something to be avoided as an evil plague. The idea which has given the movement toward nationality, which has been such a feature of the last century, its social vitality, is the consciousness of a community of history and purpose larger than that of the family, the parish, the sect, and the province. The upbuilding of national states has substituted a unity of feeling and aim, a freedom of intercourse, over wide areas, for earlier local isolations, suspicions, jealousies, and hatreds. It has forced men out of narrow sectionalism into membership in a larger social unit,

[1]From *Proceedings, National Education Association*, 1916. Reprinted by permission.

and created loyalty to a state which subordinates petty and selfish interests.

One cannot say this, however, without being at once reminded that nationalism has had another side. With the possible exception of our own country, the national states of the modern world have been built up through conflict. The development of a sense of unity within a charmed area has been accompanied by dislike, by hostility, to all without. Skilful politicians and other self-seekers have always known how to play cleverly upon patriotism and upon ignorance of other peoples, to identify nationalism with latent hatred of other nations. Without exaggeration, the present world war may be said to be the outcome of this aspect of nationalism, and to present it in its naked unloveliness.

In the past our geographical isolation has largely protected us from the harsh, selfish, and exclusive aspect of nationalism. The absence of pressure from without, the absence of active and urgent rivalry and hostility of powerful neighbors, has perhaps played a part in the failure to develop an adequate unity of sentiment and idea for the country as a whole. Individualism of a go-as-you-please type has had too full swing. We have an inherited jealousy of any strong national governing agencies and we have been inclined to let things drift rather than to think out a central, controlling policy. But the effect of the war has been to make us aware that the days of geographical isolation are at an end, and also to make us conscious that we are lacking in an integrated social sense and policy for our country as a whole, irrespective of classes and sections.

We are now faced by the difficulty of developing the good aspect of nationalism without its evil side—of developing a nationalism which is the friend and not the foe of internationalism. Since this is a matter of ideas, of emotions, of intellectual and moral disposition and outlook, it depends for its accomplishment upon educational agencies, not upon outward machinery. Among these educational agencies, the public school takes first rank. When some time in the remote future the tale is summed up and the public, as distinct from the private and merely personal, achievement of the common school is recorded, the question which will have to be answered is, What has the American public school done toward subordinating a local, provincial, sectarian, and partisan spirit of mind to aims and interests which are common to all the men and women of the country—to what extent has it taught men to think and feel in ideas broad enough to be inclusive of the purposes and happiness of all sections and classes? For unless the agencies which form the mind and morals of the community can prevent the operation of those forces which are always making for a division of interests, class and sectional ideas and feelings will become dominant, and our democracy will fall to pieces.

Unfortunately at the present time one result of the excitement which the war has produced is that many influential and well-meaning persons attempt to foster the growth of an inclusive nationalism by appeal to our fears, our suspicions, our jealousies, and our latent hatreds. They would make the measure of our national preparedness our readiness to meet other nations in destructive war rather than our fitness to coöperate with them in the constructive tasks of peace. They are so disturbed by what has been revealed of internal division, of lack of complete national integration, that they have lost faith in the slow policies of education. They would kindle a sense of our dependence upon one another by making us afraid of peoples outside of our border; they would bring about unity within by laying stress upon our separateness from others. The situation makes it all the more necessary that those concerned with education should withstand popular clamor for a nationalism based upon hysterical excitedness or mechanical drill, or a combination of the two. We must ask what a real nationalism, a real Americanism, is like. For unless we know our own character and purpose, we are not likely to be intelligent in our selection of the means to further them.

I want to mention only two elements in the nationalism which our education should cultivate. The first is that the American nation is itself complex and compound. Strictly speaking, it is interracial and international in its make-up. It is composed of a multitude of peoples speaking different tongues, inheriting diverse traditions, cherishing varying ideals of life. This fact is basic to our nationalism as distinct from that of other peoples. Our national motto, "One from Many," cuts deep and extends far. It denotes a fact which doubtless adds to the difficulty of getting a genuine unity. But it also immensely enriches the possibilities of the result to be attained. No matter how loudly anyone proclaims his Americanism, if he assumes that any one racial strain, any one component culture, no matter how early settled it was in our territory, or how effective it has proved in its own land, is to furnish a pattern to which all other strains and cultures are to conform, he is a traitor to an American nationalism. Our unity cannot be a homogeneous thing like that of the separate states of Europe from which our population is drawn; it must be a unity created by drawing out and composing into a harmonious whole the best, the most characteristic, which each contributing race and people has to offer.

I find that many who talk the loudest about the need of a supreme and unified Americanism of spirit really mean some special code or tradition to which they happen to be attached. They have some pet tradition which they would impose upon all. In thus measuring the scope of Americanism by some single element which enters into it they are themselves false to the spirit of America. Neither Englandism nor New Englandism, neither Puritan nor Cavalier, any more than Teuton or Slav, can do anything but furnish one note in a vast symphony.

The way to deal with hyphenism, in other words, is to welcome it, but to welcome it in the sense of extracting from each people its special good, so that it shall surrender into a common fund of wisdom and experience what it especially has to contribute. All of these surrenders and contributions taken together create the national spirit of America. The dangerous thing is for each factor to isolate itself, to try to live off its past, and then to attempt to impose itself upon other elements, or, at least, to keep itself intact and thus refuse to accept what other cultures have to offer, so as thereby to be transmuted into authentic Americanism.

In what is rightly objected to as hyphenism, the hyphen has become something which separates one people from other peoples, and thereby prevents American nationalism. Such terms as Irish-American or Hebrew-American or German-American are false terms because they seem to assume something which is already in existence called America, to which the other factor may be externally hitched on. The fact is, the genuine American, the typical American, is himself a hyphenated character. This does not mean that he is part American and that some foreign ingredient is then added. It means that, as I have said, he is international and interracial in his make-up. He is not American plus Pole or German. But the American is himself Pole-German-English-French-Spanish-Italian-Greek-Irish-Scandinavian-Bohemian-Jew and so on. The point is to see to it that the hyphen connects instead of separates. And this means at least that our public schools shall teach each factor to respect every other, and shall take pains to enlighten all as to the great past contributions of every strain in our composite make-up. I wish our teaching of American history in the schools would take more account of the great waves of migration by which our land for over three centuries has been continuously built up, and made every pupil conscious of the rich breadth of our national make-up. When every pupil recognizes all the factors which have gone into our being, he will continue to prize and reverence that coming from his own past, but he will think of it as honored in being simply one factor in forming a whole, nobler and finer than itself.

In short, unless our education is nationalized in a way which recognizes that the peculiarity of our nationalism is its internationalism, we shall breed enmity and division in our frantic efforts to secure unity. The teachers of the country know this fact much better than do many of its politicians. While too often politicians have been fostering a vicious hyphenatedism and sectionalism as a bid for votes, teachers have been engaged in transmuting beliefs and feelings once divided and opposed, into a new thing under the sun—a national spirit inclusive not exclusive, friendly not jealous. This they have done by the influence of personal contact, coöperative intercourse, and sharing in common tasks and hopes. The teacher who has been an active agent in furthering the common struggle of native-born, African, Jew, Italian, and perhaps a score of other peoples, to attain emancipation and enlightenment will never become a party to a conception of America as a nation which conceives of its history and its hopes as less broad than those of humanity—let politicians clamor for their own ends as they will.

The other point in the constitution of a genuine American nationalism to which I invite attention is that we have been occupied during the greater part of our history in subduing nature, not one another or other peoples. I once heard two foreign visitors coming from different countries discuss what had been impressed upon them as the chief trait of the American people. One said vigor, youthful and buoyant energy. The other said it was kindness, the disposition to live and let live, the absence of envy at the success of others. I like to think that while both of these ascribed traits have the same cause back of them, the latter statement goes deeper. Not that we have more virtue, native or acquired, than others, but that we have had more room, more opportunity. Consequently, the same conditions which have put a premium upon active and hopeful energy have permitted the kindlier instincts of man to express themselves. The spaciousness of a continent not previously monopolized by man has stimulated vigor and has also diverted activity from the struggle against fellowman into the struggle against nature. When men make their gains by fighting in common a wilderness, they have not the motive for mutual distrust which comes when they get ahead only by fighting one another. I recently heard a story which seems to me to have something typical about it. Some manufacturers were discussing the problem of labor. They were loud in their complaints. They were bitter against the exactions of unions, and full of tales of an inefficiency which seemed to them calculated. Then one of them said: "Oh, well! Poor devils! They haven't much of a chance and have to do what they can to hold their own. If we were in their place, we should be just the same." And the others nodded assent and the conversation lapsed. I call this characteristic, for if there was not an ardent sympathy, there was at least a spirit of toleration and passive recognition.

But with respect to this point as well as with respect to our composite make-up, the situation is changing. We no longer have a large unoccupied continent. Pioneer days are past, and natural resources are possessed. There is danger that the same causes which have set the hand of man against his neighbor in other countries will have the same effect here. Instead of sharing in a common fight against nature, we are already starting to fight against one another, class against class, haves against have-nots. The change puts a definite responsibility upon the schools to sustain our true national spirit. The virtues of mutual esteem, of human forbearance, and well-wishing, which in our earlier days were the unconscious products of circumstances, must now be the conscious fruit of an education which forms the deepest springs of character.

Teachers, above all others, have occasion to be distressed when the earlier idealism of welcome to the oppressed is treated as a weak sentimentalism, when sympathy for the unfortunate and those who have not had a fair chance is regarded as a weak indulgence fatal to efficiency. Our traditional disposition in these respects must now become a central motive in public education, not as a matter of condescension or patronizing, but an essential to the maintenance of a truly American spirit. All this puts a responsibility upon the schools which can be met only by widening the scope of educational facilities. The schools have now to make up to the disinherited masses by conscious instruction, by the development of personal power, skill, ability, and initiative, for the loss of external opportunities consequent upon the passing of our pioneer days. Otherwise power is likely to pass more and more into the hands of the wealthy, and we shall end with this same alliance between intellectual and artistic culture and economic power due to riches, which has been the curse of every civilization in the past, and which our fathers in their democratic idealism thought this nation was to put an end to.

Since the idea of the nation is equal opportunity for all, to nationalize education means to use the schools as a means for making this idea effective. There was a time when this could be done more or less well simply by providing schoolhouses, desks, blackboards, and perhaps books. But that day has passed. Opportunities can be equalized only as the schools make it their active serious business to enable all alike to become masters of their own industrial fate. That growing movement which is called industrial or vocational education now hangs in the scales. If it is so constructed in practice as to produce merely more competent hands for subordinate clerical and shop positions, if its purpose is shaped to drill boys and girls into certain forms of automatic skill which will make them useful in carrying out the plans of others, it means that, instead of nationalizing education in the spirit of our nation, we have given up the battle, and decided to refeudalize education.

I have said nothing about the point which my title most naturally suggests—changes in administrative methods which will put the resources of the whole nation at the disposition of the more backward and less fortunate portions, meaning by resources not only money but expert advice and guidance of every sort. I have no doubt that we shall move in the future away from a merely regional control of the public schools in the direction of a more central regulation. I say nothing about this phase of the matter at this time, not only because it brings up technical questions, but because this side of the matter is but the body, the mechanism of a nationalized education. To nationalize American education is to use education to promote our national idea, which is the idea of democracy. This is the soul, the spirit, of a nationalized education, and, unless the administrative changes are executed so as to embody this soul, they will mean simply the development of red tape, a mechanical uniformity and a deadening supervision from above.

Just because the circumstances of the war have brought the idea of the nation and the national to the foreground of everyone's thoughts, the most important thing is to bear in mind that there are nations and nations, this kind of nationalism and that. Unless I am mistaken, there are some now using the cry of an

S

American nationalism, of an intensified national patriotism, to further ideas which characterize the European nations, especially those most active in the war, but which are treasonable to the ideal of our nation. Therefore, I have taken this part of your time to remind you of the fact that our nation and democracy are equivalent terms; that our democracy means amity and good will to all humanity (including those beyond our border), and equal opportunity for all within. Since as a nation we are composed of representatives of all nations who have come here to live in peace with one another and to escape the enmities and jealousies which characterize Old World nations, to nationalize our education means to make it an instrument in the active and constant suppression of the war spirit and in the positive cultivation of sentiments of respect and friendship for all men and women, wherever they live. Since our democracy means the substitution of equal opportunity for all for the Old World ideal of unequal opportunity for different classes, and the limitation of the individual by the class to which he belongs, to nationalize our education is to make the public school an energetic and willing instrument in developing initiative, courage, power, and personal ability in each individual. If we can get our education nationalized in spirit in these directions, the nationalizing of the administrative machinery will in the end take care of itself. So I appeal to teachers in the face of every hysterical wave of emotion, and of every subtle appeal of sinister class interest, to remember that they, above all others, are the consecrated servants of the democratic ideas in which alone this country is truly a distinctive nation—ideas of friendly and helpful intercourse between all and the equipment of every individual to serve the community by his own best powers in his own best way.

CHANGES AND ADJUSTMENTS

EXPERIMENTS IN GOVERNMENT[1]

ELIHU ROOT

[Elihu Root (1845——) was born in Clinton, New York. After being graduated from Hamilton College, he studied law and has practised his profession during the greater part of his life in New York City. He entered public life as secretary of war under President McKinley, and was secretary of state during President Roosevelt's administration. After serving one term as senator from New York, he resumed the practice of law. He has distinguished himself signally both as a lawyer and a publicist. His lectures at Princeton University in 1913 under the Stafford Little Endowment—from which the selection here given is taken—were forcible pleas for caution in adopting innovations in government.]

There are two separate processes going on among the civilized nations at the present time. One is an assault by Socialism against the individualism which underlies the social system of western civilization. The other is an assault against existing institutions upon the ground that they do not adequately protect and develop the existing social order. It is of this latter process in our own country that I wish to speak, and I assume an agreement that the right of individual liberty and the inseparable right of private property which lie at the foundation of our modern civilization ought to be maintained.

The conditions of life in America have changed very much since the Constitution of the United States was adopted. In 1787 each state entering into the Federal Union had preserved the separate organic life of the original colony. Each had its center of social and business and political life. Each was separated from the others by the barriers of slow and difficult com-

[1]From *Experiments in Government*. (Copyright, 1913, Princeton University Press.) Reprinted by permission.

munication. In a vast territory, without railroads or steamships or telegraph or telephone, each community lived within itself.

Now, there has been a general social and industrial rearrangement. Production and commerce pay no attention to state lines. The life of the country is no longer grouped about state capitals, but about the great centers of continental production and trade. The organic growth which must ultimately determine the form of institutions has been away from the mere union of states toward the union of individuals in the relation of national citizenship.

The same causes have greatly reduced the independence of personal and family life. In the eighteenth century life was simple. The producer and consumer were near together and could find each other. Everyone who had an equivalent to give in property or service could readily secure the support of himself and his family without asking anything from government except the preservation of order. Today almost all Americans are dependent upon the action of a great number of other persons, mostly unknown. About half of our people are crowded into the cities and large towns. Their food, clothes, fuel, light, water—all come from distant sources, of which they are in the main ignorant, through a vast, complicated machinery of production and distribution with which they have little direct relation. If anything occurs to interfere with the working of the machinery, the consumer is individually helpless. To be certain that he and his family may continue to live, he must seek the power of combination with others, and in the end he inevitably calls upon that great combination of all citizens which we call government to do something more than merely keep the peace—to regulate the machinery of production and distribution and safeguard it from interference so that it shall continue to work.

A similar change has taken place in the conditions under which a great part of our people engage in the industries by which they get their living. Under comparatively simple industrial conditions the relation between employer and employee was mainly a relation of individual to individual, with individual freedom of contract and freedom of opportunity essential to equality in the commerce of life. Now, in the great manufacturing, mining, and transportation industries of the country, instead of the free give and take of individual contract, there is substituted a vast system of collective bargaining between great masses of men organized and acting through their representatives, or the individual on the one side accepts what he can get from superior power on the other. In the movement of these mighty forces of organization the individual laborer, the individual stockholder, the individual consumer, is helpless.

There has been another change of conditions through the development of political organization. The theory of political activity which had its origin approximately in the administration of President Jackson, and which is characterized by Marcy's declaration that "to the victors belong the spoils," tended to make the possession of office the primary and all-absorbing purpose of political conflict. A complicated system of party organization and representation grew up under which a disciplined body of party workers in each state supported one another, controlled the machinery of nomination, and thus controlled nominations. The members of state legislatures and other officers, when elected, felt a more acute responsibility to the organization which could control their renomination than to the electors, and therefore became accustomed to shape their conduct according to the wishes of the nominating organization. Accordingly the real power of government came to be vested to a high degree in these unofficial political organizations, and where there was a strong man at the head of an organization his control came to be something very closely approaching dictatorship. Another feature of this system aggravated its evils. As population grew, political campaigns became more expensive. At the same time, as wealth grew, corporations for production and transportation increased in capital and extent of operations and became more dependent upon the protection or toleration of government. They found a ready means to secure this by contributing heavily to the campaign funds of political organizations, and therefore their influence played a large part in determining who should be nominated and elected to office. So that in many states political organizations controlled the operations of government, in accordance with the wishes of the managers of the great corporations. Under these circumstances our governmental institutions were not working as they were intended to work, and a desire to break up and get away from this extra constitutional method of controlling our constitutional government has caused a great part of the new political methods of the last few years.

It is manifest that the laws which were entirely adequate under the conditions of a century ago to secure individual and public welfare must be in many respects inadequate to accomplish the same results under all these new conditions; and our people are now engaged in the difficult but imperative duty of adapting their laws to the life of today. The changes in conditions have come very rapidly, and a good deal of experiment will be necessary to find out just what government can do and ought to do to meet them.

The process of devising and trying new laws to meet new conditions naturally leads to the question whether we need not merely to make new laws, but also to modify the principles upon which our government is based and the institutions of government designed for the application of those principles to the affairs of life. Upon this question it is of the utmost importance that we proceed with considerable wisdom.

By institutions of government I mean the established rule or order of action through which the sovereign (in our case the sovereign people) attains the ends of government. The governmental institutions of Great Britain have been established by the growth through many centuries of a great body of accepted rules and customs which, taken together, are called the British Constitution. In this country we have set forth in the Declaration of Independence the principles which we consider to lie at the basis of civil society "that all men are created equal; that they are endowed, by their Creator, with certain unalienable rights; that among these are life, liberty, and the pursuit of happiness. That to secure these rights, governments are instituted among men, deriving their just powers from the consent of the governed."

In our Federal and state constitutions we have established the institutions through which these rights are to be secured. We have declared what officers shall make the laws, what officers shall execute them, what officers shall sit in judgment upon claims of right under them. We have prescribed how these officers shall be selected and the tenure by which they shall hold their offices. We have limited them in the powers which they are to exercise, and, where it has been deemed necessary, we have imposed specific duties upon them. The body of rules thus prescribed constitute the governmental institutions of the United States.

When proposals are made to change these institutions there are certain general considerations which should be observed.

The first consideration is that free government is impossible except through prescribed and established governmental institutions, which work out the ends of government through many separate human agents, each doing his part in obedience to law. Popular will cannot execute itself directly except through a mob. Popular will cannot get itself executed through an irresponsible executive, for that is simple autocracy. An executive limited only by the direct expression of popular will cannot be held to responsibility against his will, because, having possession of all the powers of government, he can prevent any true, free, and general expression adverse to himself, and unless he yields voluntarily he can be overturned only by a revolution. The familiar Spanish-American dictatorships are illustrations of this. A dictator once established by what is or is alleged to be public choice never permits an expression of public will which will displace him, and he goes out only through a new revolution because he alone controls the machinery through which he could be displaced peaceably. A system with a plebiscite at one end and Louis Napoleon at the other could not give France free government; and it was only after the humiliation of defeat in a great war and the horrors of the Commune that the French people were able to establish a government which would really execute their will through carefully devised institutions in which they gave their chief executive very little power indeed.

We should, therefore, reject every proposal which involves the idea that the people can rule merely by voting, or merely by voting and having one man or group of men to execute their will.

A second consideration is that in estimating the value of any system of governmental institutions due regard must be had to the true functions of government and to the limitations imposed by nature upon what it is possible for government to accomplish. We all know, of course, that we cannot abolish all the evils in this world by statute or by the enforcement of statutes, nor can we prevent the inexorable law of nature which decrees that suffering shall follow vice, and all the evil passions and folly of mankind. Law cannot give to depravity the rewards of virtue, to indolence the rewards of industry, to indifference the rewards of ambition, or to ignorance the rewards of learning. The utmost that government can do is measurably to protect men, not against the wrong they do themselves, but against wrong done by others, and to promote the long, slow process of educating mind and character to a better knowledge and nobler standards of life and conduct. We know all this, but when we see how much misery there is in the world and instinctively cry out against it, and when we see some things that government may do to mitigate it, we are apt to forget how little, after all, it is possible for any government to do, and to hold the particular government of the time and place to a standard of responsibility which no government can possibly meet. The chief motive power which has moved mankind along the course of development which we call the progress of civilization has been the sum total of intelligent selfishness in a vast number of individuals, each working for his own support, his own gain, his own betterment. It is that which has cleared the forests and cultivated the fields and built the ships and railroads, made the discoveries and inventions, covered the earth with commerce, softened by intercourse the enmities of nations and races, and made possible the wonders of literature and of art. Gradually, during the long process, selfishness has grown more intelligent, with a broader view of individual benefit from the common good, and gradually the influences of nobler standards of altruism, of justice, and human sympathy have impressed themselves upon the conception of right conduct among civilized men. But the complete control of such motives will be the millennium. Any attempt to enforce a millennial standard now by law must necessarily fail, and any judgment which assumes government's responsibility to enforce such a standard must be an unjust judgment. Indeed, no such standard can ever be forced. It must come, not by superior force, but from the changed nature of man, from his willingness to be altogether just and merciful.

A third consideration is that it is not merely useless, but injurious for government to attempt too much. It is manifest that to enable it to deal with the new conditions I have described we must invest government with authority to interfere with the individual conduct of the citizen to a degree hitherto unknown in this country. When government undertakes to give the individual citizen protection by regulating the conduct of others toward him in the field where formerly he protected himself by his freedom of contract, it is limiting the liberty of the citizen whose conduct is regulated and taking a step in the direction of paternal government. While the new conditions of industrial life make it plainly necessary that many such steps shall be taken, they should be taken only so far as they are necessary and are effective. Interference with individual liberty by government should be jealously watched and restrained, because the habit of undue interference destroys that independence of character without which in its citizens no free government can endure.

We should not forget that while institutions receive ·their form from national character, they have a powerful reflex influence upon that character. Just so far as a nation allows its institutions to be moulded by its weaknesses of character rather than by its strength, it creates an influence to increase weakness at the expense of strength.

The habit of undue interference by government in private

affairs breeds the habit of undue reliance upon government in private affairs at the expense of individual initiative, energy, enterprise, courage, independent manhood.

The strength of self-government and the motive power of progress must be found in the characters of the individual citizens who make up a nation. Weaken individual character among a people by comfortable reliance upon paternal government and a nation soon becomes incapable of free self-government and fit only to be governed: the higher and nobler qualities of national life that make for ideals and effort and achievement become atrophied and the nation is decadent.

A fourth consideration is that in the nature of things all government must be imperfect because men are imperfect. Every system has its shortcomings and inconveniences; and these are seen and felt as they exist in the system under which we live, while the shortcomings and inconveniences of other systems are forgotten or ignored.

It is not unusual to see governmental methods reformed and after a time, long enough to forget the evils that caused the change, to have a new movement for a reform which consists in changing back to substantially the same old methods that were cast out by the first reform.

The recognition of shortcomings or inconveniences in government is not by itself sufficient to warrant a change of system. There should be also an effort to estimate and compare the shortcomings and inconveniences of the system to be substituted, for although they may be different they will certainly exist.

A fifth consideration is that whatever changes in government ought to be made, we should follow the method which undertakes as one of its cardinal points to hold fast that which is good. Francis Lieber, whose affection for the country of his birth equaled his loyalty to the country of his adoption, once said:

"There is this difference between the English, French, and Germans: That the English only change what is necessary and as far as it is necessary; the French plunge into all sorts of novelties by whole masses, get into a chaos, see that they are fools, and retrace their steps as quickly, with a high degree of practical sense in all this unpracticability; the Germans attempt no change without first recurring to first principles and metaphysics beyond them, systematizing the smallest details in their minds; and when at last they mean to apply all their meditation, opportunity, with its wide and swift wings of a gull, is gone."

This was written more than sixty years ago, before the present French Republic and the present German Empire, and Lieber would doubtless have modified his conclusions in view of those great achievements in government if he were writing today. But he does correctly indicate the differences of method and the dangers avoided by the practical course which he ascribes to the English and in accordance with which the great structure of British and American liberty has been built up generation after generation and century after century. Through all the seven hundred years since Magna Charta we have been shaping, adjusting, adapting our system to the new conditions of life as they have arisen, but we have always held on to everything essentially good that we have ever had in the system. We have never undertaken to begin over again and build up a new system under the idea that we could do it better. We have never let go of Magna Charta or the Bill of Rights or the Declaration of Independence or the Constitution. When we take account of all that governments have sought to do and have failed to do in this selfish and sinful world, we find that as a rule the application of new theories of government, though devised by the most brilliant constructive genius, have availed but little to preserve the people of any considerable regions of the earth for any long periods from the evils of despotism on the one hand or of anarchy on the other, or to raise any considerable portion of the mass of mankind above the hard conditions of oppression and misery. And we find that our system of government which has been built up in this practical way through so many centuries, and the whole history of which is potent in the provisions of our Constitution, has done more to preserve liberty, justice, security, and freedom of opportunity for many people for a long period and over a great portion of the earth, than any other system of government ever devised by man. Human nature does not change very much. The forces of evil are hard to control now as they always have been. It is easy to fail and hard to succeed in reconciling liberty and order. In dealing with this most successful body of governmental institutions the question should not be what sort of government do you or I think we should have. What you and I think on such a subject is of very little value indeed. The question should be:

How can we adapt our laws and the workings of our government to the new conditions which confront us without sacrificing any essential element of this system of government which has so nobly stood the test of time and without abandoning the political principles which have inspired the growth of its institutions? For there are political principles, and nothing can be more fatal to self-government than to lose sight of them under the influence of apparent expediency. . . .

The Constitution of the United States deals in the main with essentials. There are some non-essential directions such as those relating to the methods of election and of legislation, but in the main it sets forth the foundations of government in clear, simple, concise terms. It is for this reason that it has stood the test of more than a century with but slight amendment, while the modern state constitutions, into which a multitude of ordinary statutory provisions are crowded, have to be changed from year to year. The peculiar and essential qualities of the government established by the Constitution are:

First, it is representative.

Second, it recognizes the liberty of the individual citizen as distinguished from the total mass of citizens, and it protects that liberty by specific limitations upon the power of government.

Third, it distributes the legislative, executive, and judicial powers, which make up the sum total of all government, into three separate departments, and specifically limits the powers of the officers in each department.

Fourth, it superimposes upon a federation of state governments a national government with sovereignty acting directly not merely upon the states, but upon the citizens of each state, within a line of limitation drawn between the powers of the national government and the powers of the state governments.

Fifth, it makes observance of its limitations requisite to the validity of laws, whether passed by the nation or by the states, to be judged by the courts of law in each concrete case as it arises.

Every one of these five characteristics of the government established by the Constitution was a distinct advance beyond the ancient attempts at popular government, and the elimination of any one of them would be a retrograde movement and a reversion to a former and discarded type of government. In each case it would be the abandonment of a distinctive feature of government which has succeeded, in order to go back and try again the methods of government which have failed. Of course we ought not to take such a backward step except under the pressure of inevitable necessity.

THE LIBERATION OF A PEOPLE'S VITAL ENERGIES[1]

WOODROW WILSON

[For biographical note regarding author, see page 141. The volume from which this selection was taken is a compilation of the more significant portions of President's Wilson's campaign speeches delivered previous to his election the first time. Throughout the speeches there is a fine tone of unselfish public service and of a new spirit of social justice in politics and national life.]

No matter how often we think of it, the discovery of America must each time make a fresh appeal to our imaginations. For centuries, indeed from the beginning, the face of Europe had been turned toward the east. All the routes of trade, every impulse and energy, ran from west to east. The Atlantic lay at the world's back door. Then, suddenly, the conquest of Constantinople by the Turk closed the route to the Orient. Europe had either to face about or lack any outlet for her energies; the unknown sea at the west at last was ventured upon, and the earth learned that it was twice as big as it had thought. Columbus did not find, as he had expected, the civilization of Cathay; he

[1] From *The New Freedom*. (Copyright, 1913, Doubleday, Page & Co.) Reprinted by permission.

found an empty continent. In that part of the world, upon that new-found half of the globe, mankind, late in its history, was thus afforded an opportunity to set up a new civilization; here it was strangely privileged to make a new human experiment.

Never can that moment of unique opportunity fail to excite the emotion of all who consider its strangeness and richness; a thousand fanciful histories of the earth might be contrived without the imagination daring to conceive such a romance as the hiding away of half the globe until the fulness of time had come for a new start in civilization. A mere sea captain's ambition to trace a new trade route gave way to a moral adventure for humanity. The race was to found a new order here on this delectable land, which no man approached without receiving, as the old voyagers relate, you remember, sweet airs out of woods aflame with flowers and murmurous with the sound of pellucid waters. The hemisphere lay waiting to be touched with life—life from the old centers of living, surely, but cleansed of defilement, and cured of weariness, so as to be fit for the virgin purity of a new bride. The whole thing springs into the imagination like a wonderful vision, an exquisite marvel which once only in all history could be vouchsafed.

One other thing only compares with it; only one other thing touches the springs of emotion as does the picture of the ships of Columbus drawing near the bright shores—and that is the thought of the choke in the throat of the immigrant of today as he gazes from the steerage deck at the land where he has been taught to believe he in his turn shall find an earthly paradise, where, a free man, he shall forget the heartaches of the old life, and enter into the fulfilment of the hope of the world. For has not every ship that has pointed her prow westward borne hither the hopes of generation after generation of the oppressed of other lands? How always have men's hearts beat as they saw the coast of America rise to their view! How it has always seemed to them that the dweller there would at last be rid of kings, of privileged classes, and of all those bonds which had kept men depressed and helpless, and would there realize the full fruition of his sense of honest manhood, would there be one of a great body of brothers, not seeking to defraud and deceive one another, but seeking to accomplish the general good!

What was in the writings of the men who founded America—to serve the selfish interests of America? Do you find that in their writings? No; to serve the cause of humanity, to bring liberty to mankind. They set up their standards here in America in the tenet of hope, as a beacon of encouragement to all the nations of the world; and men came thronging to these shores with an expectancy that never existed before, with a confidence they never dared feel before, and found here for generations together a haven of peace, of opportunity, of equality.

God send that in the complicated state of modern affairs we may recover the standards and repeat the achievements of that heroic age!

For life is no longer the comparatively simple thing it was. Our relations one with another have been profoundly modified by the new agencies of rapid communication and transportation, tending swiftly to concentrate life, widen communities, fuse interests, and complicate all the processes of living. The individual is dizzily swept about in a thousand new whirlpools of activities. Tyranny has become more subtle, and has learned to wear the guise of mere industry, and even of benevolence. Freedom has become a somewhat different matter. It cannot,—eternal principle that it is,—it cannot have altered, yet it shows itself in new aspects. Perhaps it is only revealing its deeper meaning.

What is liberty?

I have long had an image in my mind of what constitutes liberty. Suppose that I were building a great piece of powerful machinery, and suppose that I should so awkwardly and unskilfully assemble the parts of it that every time one part tried to move it would be interfered with by the others, and the whole thing would buckle up and be checked. Liberty for the several parts would consist in the best possible assembling and adjustment of them all, would it not? If you want the great piston of the engine to run with absolute freedom, give it absolutely perfect alignment and adjustment with the other parts of the machine, so that it is free, not because it is let alone or isolated, but because it has been associated most skilfully and carefully with the other parts of the great structure.

What is liberty? You say of the locomotive that it runs free. What do you mean? You mean that its parts are so assembled and adjusted that friction is reduced to a minimum, and that it has perfect adjustment. We say of a boat skimming the water with light foot, "How free she runs," when we mean, how perfectly she is adjusted to the force of the wind, how perfectly she obeys the great breath out of the heavens that fills her sails. Throw her head up into the wind and see how she will halt and stagger, how every sheet will shiver and her whole frame be shaken, how instantly she is "in irons," in the expressive phrase of the sea. She is free only when you have let her fall off again and have recovered once more her nice adjustment to the forces she must obey and cannot defy.

Human freedom consists in perfect adjustments of human interests and human activities and human energies.

Now, the adjustments necessary between individuals, between individuals and the complex institutions amidst which they live, and between those institutions and the government, are infinitely more intricate today than ever before. No doubt this is a tiresome and roundabout way of saying the thing, yet perhaps it is worth while to get somewhat clearly in our mind what makes all the trouble today. Life has become complex; there are many more elements, more parts, to it than ever before. And, therefore, it is harder to keep everything adjusted—and harder to find out where the trouble lies when the machine gets out of order.

You know that one of the interesting things that Mr. Jefferson said in those early days of simplicity which marked the beginnings of our government was that the best government consisted in as little governing as possible. And there is still a sense in which that is true. It is still intolerable for the government to interfere with our individual activities except where it is necessary to interfere with them in order to free them. But I feel confident that if Jefferson were living in our day he would see what we see: that the individual is caught in a great confused nexus of all sorts of complicated circumstances, and that to let him alone is to leave him helpless as against the obstacles with which he has to contend; and that, therefore, law in our day must come to the assistance of the individual. It must come to his assistance to see that he gets fair play; that is all, but that is much. Without the watchful interference, the resolute interference, of the government, there can be no fair play between individuals and such powerful institutions as the trusts. Freedom today is something more than being let alone. The program of a government of freedom must in these days be positive, not negative merely.

Well, then, in this new sense and meaning of it, are we preserving freedom in this land of ours, the hope of all the earth?

Have we, inheritors of this continent and of the ideals to which the fathers consecrated it—have we maintained them, realizing them, as each generation must, anew? Are we, in the consciousness that the life of man is pledged to higher levels here than elsewhere, striving still to bear aloft the standards of liberty and hope, or, disillusioned and defeated, are we feeling the disgrace of having had a free field in which to do new things and of not having done them?

The answer must be, I am sure, that we have been in a fair way of failure—tragic failure. And we stand in danger of utter failure yet except we fulfil speedily the determination we have reached, to deal with the new and subtle tyrannies according to their deserts. Don't deceive yourselves for a moment as to the power of the great interests which now dominate our development. They are so great that it is almost an open question whether the government of the United States can dominate them or not. Go one step further, make their organized power permanent, and it may be too late to turn back. The roads diverge at the point where we stand. They stretch their vistas out to regions where they are very far separated from one another; at the end of one is the old tiresome scene of government tied up with special interests; and at the other shines the liberating light of individual initiative, of individual liberty, of in-

T

dividual freedom, the light of untrammeled enterprise. I believe that that light shines out of the heavens itself that God has created. I believe in human liberty as I believe in the wine of life. There is no salvation for men in the pitiful condescensions of industrial masters. Guardians have no place in a land of freemen. Prosperity guaranteed by trustees has no prospect of endurance. Monopoly means the atrophy of enterprise. If monopoly persists, monopoly will always sit at the helm of the government. I do not expect to see monopoly restrain itself. If there are men in this country big enough to own the government of the United States, they are going to own it; what we have to determine now is whether we are big enough, whether we are men enough, whether we are free enough, to take possession again of the government which is our own. We haven't had free access to it, our minds have not touched it by way of guidance, in half a generation, and now we are engaged in nothing less than the recovery of what was made with our own hands, and acts only by our delegated authority.

I tell you, when you discuss the question of the tariffs and of the trusts, you are discussing the very lives of yourselves and your children. I believe that I am preaching the very cause of some of the gentlemen whom I am opposing when I preach the cause of free industry in the United States, for I think they are slowly girding the tree that bears the inestimable fruits of our life, and that if they are permitted to gird it entirely nature will take her revenge and the tree will die.

I do not believe that America is securely great because she has great men in her now. America is great in proportion as she can make sure of having great men in the next generation. She is rich in her unborn children; rich, that is to say, if those unborn children see the sun in a day of opportunity, see the sun when they are free to exercise their energies as they will. If they open their eyes in a land where there is no special privilege, then we shall come into a new era of American greatness and American liberty; but if they open their eyes in a country where they must be employees or nothing, if they open their eyes in a land of merely regulated monopoly, where all the conditions of industry are determined by small groups of men, then they will see an America such as the founders of this Republic would have wept to think of. The only hope is in the release of the forces which philanthropic trust presidents want to monopolize. Only the emancipation, the freeing and heartening of the vital energies of all the people will redeem us. In all that I may have to do in public affairs in the United States I am going to think of towns such as I have seen in Indiana, towns of the old American pattern, that own and operate their own industries, hopefully and happily. My thought is going to be bent upon the multiplication of towns of that kind and the prevention of the concentration of industry in this country in such a fashion and upon such a scale that towns that own themselves will be impossible. You know what the vitality of America consists of. Its vitality does not lie in New York, nor in Chicago; it will not be sapped by anything that happens in St. Louis. The vitality of America lies in the brains, the energies, the enterprise of the people throughout the land; in the efficiency of their factories and in the richness of the fields that stretch beyond the borders of the town; in the wealth which they extract from nature and originate for themselves through the inventive genius characteristic of all free American communities.

That is the wealth of America, and if America discourages the locality, the community, the self-contained town, she will kill the nation. A nation is as rich as her free communities; she is not as rich as her capital city or her metropolis. The amount of money in Wall Street is no indication of the wealth of the American people. That indication can be found only in the fertility of the American mind and the productivity of American industry everywhere throughout the United States. If America were not rich and fertile, there would be no money in Wall Street. If Americans were not vital and able to take care of themselves, the great money exchanges would break down. The welfare, the very existence of the nation, rests at last upon the great mass of the people; its prosperity depends at last upon the spirit in which they go about their work in their several communities throughout the broad land. In proportion as her towns and her countrysides are happy and hopeful will America realize the high ambitions which have marked her in the eyes of all the world.

The welfare, the happiness, the energy and spirit of the men and women who do the daily work in our mines and factories, on our railroads, in our offices and ports of trade, on our farms and on the sea, is the underlying necessity of all prosperity. There can be nothing wholesome unless their life is wholesome; there can be no contentment unless they are contented. Their physical welfare affects the soundness of the whole nation. How would it suit the prosperity of the United States, how would it suit business, to have a people that went every day sadly or sullenly to their work? How would the future look to you if you felt that the aspiration had gone out of most men, the confidence of success, the hope that they might improve their condition? Do you not see that just so soon as the old self-confidence of America, just so soon as her old boasted advantage of individual liberty and opportunity, is taken away, all the energy of her people begins to subside, to slacken, to grow loose and pulpy, without fiber, and men simply cast about to see that the day does not end disastrously with them?

So we must put heart into the people by taking the heartlessness out of politics, business, and industry. We have got to make politics a thing in which an honest man can take his part with satisfaction because he knows that his opinion will count as much as the next man's, and that the boss and the interests have been dethroned. Business we have got to untrammel, abolishing tariff favors, and railroad discrimination, and credit denials, and all forms of unjust handicaps against the little man. Industry we have got to humanize,—not through the trusts but through the direct action of law guaranteeing protection against dangers and compensation for injuries, guaranteeing sanitary conditions, proper hours, the right to organize, and all the other things which the conscience of the country demands as the workingman's right. We have got to cheer and inspirit our people with the sure prospects of social justice and due reward, with the vision of the open gates of opportunity for all. We have got to set the energy and the initiative of this great people absolutely free, so that the future of America will be greater than the past, so that the pride of America will grow with achievement, so that America will know as she advances from generation to generation that each brood of her sons is greater and more enlightened than that which preceded it, know that she is fulfilling the promise that she has made to mankind.

Such is the vision of some of us who now come to assist in its realization. For we Democrats would not have endured this long burden of exile if we had not seen a vision. We could have traded; we could have got into the game; we could have surrendered and made terms; we could have played the role of patrons to the men who wanted to dominate the interests of the country—and here and there gentlemen who pretended to be of us did make those arrangements. They couldn't stand privation. You never can stand it unless you have within you some imperishable food upon which to sustain life and courage, the food of those visions of the spirit where a table is set before us laden with palatable fruits, the fruits of hope, the fruits of imagination, those invisible things of the spirit which are the only things upon which we can sustain ourselves through this weary world without fainting. We have carried in our minds, after you had thought you had obscured and blurred them, the ideals of those men who first set their foot upon America, those little bands who came to make a foothold in the wilderness, because the great teeming nations that they had left behind them had forgotten what human liberty was, liberty of thought, liberty of religion, liberty of residence, liberty of action.

Since their day the meaning of liberty has deepened. But it has not ceased to be a fundamental demand of the human spirit, a fundamental necessity for the life of the soul. And the day is at hand when it shall be realized on this consecrated soil—a New Freedom—a Liberty widened and deepened to match the broadened life of man in modern America, restoring to him in very truth the control of his government, throwing wide all gates of lawful enterprise, unfettering his energies, and warming the generous impulses of his heart—a process of release, emancipation, and inspiration, full of a breath of life as sweet and wholesome as the airs that filled the sails of the caravels of Columbus and gave the promise and boast of magnificent Opportunity in which America *dare not fail.*

A PLEA FOR THE AMERICAN TRADITION[1]

WINSTON CHURCHILL

[Winston Churchill (1871———) was born in St. Louis, Missouri. He was graduated from the United States Naval Academy in 1894, but resigned from the Navy in order to devote himself to writing. He has produced some ten novels of distinction, several of them dealing with problems of American life and politics. He has himself taken an active part in politics in New Hampshire, the state in which he is now living.]

It has been the complacent custom of the average man to despise systems of philosophy, to think of them as harmless speculations made for arm-chairs and leisure. Every once in a while the world undergoes a rude awakening from this fallacy, as when it is shaken by a French Revolution. The unrest of the masses in the eighteenth century, becoming conscious in the philosophy of the rights of man, lighted a conflagration that took a quarter of a century to quench and left a transformed world behind it. And recently we have had once more a terrifying proof that philosophies, that cultures, may be dynamic.

Those who had seen and studied the German Empire before the war beheld the spectacle of a nation which, though not without internal dissensions and party strife, had achieved a remarkable degree of efficiency and individual contentment; a nation in which waste had been largely eliminated, in which poverty was less prevalent than in the Anglo-Saxon democracies. Prosperity was more widely diffused. The industrial problem, hanging menacingly over England and America like an evil genie above the smoke, in Germany was apparently far on its way toward solution. The transformation from a loosely knit,

[1]From *Harper's Monthly Magazine*, vol. cxxxii, p. 299 (January, 1916). Reprinted by permission.

over-populated group of states in which there was much misery and poverty into a rich, self-confident, and aggressive empire had taken place within a comparatively few years.

It was not until the war broke out that we of the Anglo-Saxon democracies began to inquire why and how, only to find to our amazement that this growth was due to a principle at work among the German people, a philosophy, a Kultur, a leaven with which they had become saturated. It is not necessary here to enter into an analysis of this Kultur, or to attempt to pass judgment upon it; apparently it is a development from an odd combination of the systems of many thinkers; it has been shaped by the needs and environment of a people and is in harmony with the temperament of that people. Nor is it needful to inquire to what extent this national philosophy or culture was intellectually conscious. In the early days of our republic the American was imbued with a racial tradition whose origin goes back to the Magna Charta; a tradition laying emphasis on individual initiative and individual freedom. It was in our blood, and it made the British Colonies and the United States of America. The average Scotch-Irish settler, the western farmer, did not know any more of Locke or Adam Smith than the German peasant of today knows of Fichte and Hegel, Nietzsche, von Treitschke, or Bernhardi. But this American tradition, because of the change from a simple agricultural and a complex industrial society, has gradually become obscured.

It is difference in ideas, in views of life, that arouses suspicions and antagonisms, that leads to conflict between individuals as well as nations. The emotions, the longings, and aspirations of a people are expressed by their thinkers in ideas, and ideas lead to action. Whatever may be the merits or demerits of the German culture, the revelation of its existence and nature has sharply aroused thinking Americans to the realization that it is not for us. Both our traditions and temperament are opposed to it. We are beginning to grasp the fact that democracy is at stake—whatever democracy has come to mean.

The opening of the present war found the Anglo-Saxon democracies in a state of muddle and chaos. Our houses were not in order. And that we might have to defend our institutions, such as they were, never seems to have occurred to us. We had evolved no system of defense in harmony with the nature of our government, with our traditions—we had no system of defense worthy of the name. And England, save for her navy, was in the same plight. Prosperity had made many of us smug and selfish, ready to reap profits out of other people's misfortunes; we had mistaken the pursuit of wealth for the pursuit of happiness; we were wasteful, and riddled with political corruption. The rise of modern industry with its introduction of the machine had changed the face of our civilization, largely swept away the democracy we had, created a class of economic dependents; established, indeed, an economic slavery—a slavery no less real than that in which the master was individualized. And that equality of opportunity, so prevalent when land and resources were plentiful, had dwindled amazingly. Serious writers agree that it is growing increasingly difficult for men to rise from the ranks of the workers, partly because of increasing class solidarity, partly because of the great denial necessary to acquire sufficient funds—a denial that reacts on the family. Those who do rise become recruits of a hostile camp—the camp of the employer; and those who do rise seem to be possessed more markedly than ever of those characteristics—so hostile to democratic ideals— hinted at by the author of the "Spoon River Anthology:"

> "Beware of the man who rises to power
> From one suspender."

We are in the throes of industrial strife, class strife, the very condition our forefathers who founded this nation hoped to obviate. We have a large element of our population burning with a sense of injustice and dependence—feelings that partially die down only to flare up again; an element for the most part uneducated in any real sense of the word; an element imbued with crude and non-American ideas as to how this injustice is to be righted. Their solution is one of class solidarity and revolution, and they cannot be blamed for advocating it. We must make up our minds that we shall not have peace or order until equality of opportunity tends to become restored and dependence eliminated.

We shall have to find and put in practice, if democracy is to endure, a democratic solution of the industrial problem.

It is curious, but true, that it does not seem to have occurred to us to examine the traditions of our race to see whether these might not be developed and made as applicable to the problem of industrial democracy as they had been to that of political democracy. Our statesmen, in their despair, attempted to solve the problem by a tendency to adopt a collectivism borrowed from Central Europe. Indeed, many of the measures passed in England and America during the past dozen years are in principle alien to the American tradition and temperament. Pensions, for instance, are not compatible with Anglo-Saxon independence and respect; nor do we take kindly to laws, however benevolent, that hamper the freedom and development of the individual. Coercion is repugnant to us.

It has been said that the United States of America is no longer Anglo-Saxon. But I believe that I am in accord with experience and modern opinion when I say that environment is stronger than heredity, and that our immigrants become imbued with our racial individualism—at present largely instructive and materialistic in quality. Whether our immigration problem is at present being handled with wisdom and efficiency is quite another matter.

Professor Dewey quotes a sentence from Heine declaring that nations have an instinctive presentiment of what is required to fulfil their missions, and it is quite true that we in America have such a presentiment, although we have not translated it into a conscious creed or culture; with us it is little more than a presentiment, but the war has served to make us realize, that, if our democracy is to be preserved, its survival must be justified, it must be efficient. The first essential to such efficiency is that our philosophy, our spirit and ideals, should be defined, and secondly that our citizens from the early years of childhood should be saturated and animated with these principles and ideals. In short, we must have a culture of American democracy, and that culture must be in harmony with the character and temperament and traditions of the nation.

For this reason it becomes essential to examine our character and traditions, for nations as well as men must first arrive at a thorough comprehension of their characters before a scheme of life can be made to fit them. The "presentiment of destiny" lies hidden in character. The leopard cannot change his spots: men and nations cannot change their inherent characteristics, but they can develop and transform these, direct them from material toward spiritual ends.

Only a little reflection is required to convince any one that the Anglo-Saxon, and particularly the American, is an individualist. It is said with much truth that we are lawless by nature, and we have, indeed, very little respect for laws. We are jealous of control; we are not and never have been a submissive people, and we could not live under a benevolent government that would teach us what is good for us. Our forefathers came over here to live unto themselves, to exercise their own opinions and work out their own destinies. However unattractive such individualism may appear, we have to make the best of it, to make virtue out of necessity. All good people—contrary to Sunday-school traditions—are not alike. And if we are going to become good, we must become good in our own way.

When certain American colonists, impatient with British interference, rebelled against England, they wrote down in the Declaration of Independence a creed, a philosophy, that was quite in keeping with Anglo-Saxon temperament, with Anglo-Saxon ideals as far back as the Magna Charta. Every man is entitled to life, liberty, and the pursuit of happiness. A government was necessary, but they were determined to have as little government as possible, to give the individual the greatest amount of liberty consistent with any government at all; they laid stress on individual initiative and development, on self-realization.

Our forefathers were neither saints nor dreamers. They also were not averse to the accumulation of wealth, and undoubtedly they had an eye to the main chance. But there is one truth that cannot be too emphatically affirmed, that in human affairs the material and the spiritual are inextricably mixed together, though one or the other may be preponderant.

In spite of—perhaps because of—the fact that the American creed was a magnificent declaration of faith in man, it was received with derision and laughter in Europe, regarded as Utopian. Yet we are pledged to it, both by our temperament and traditions. We cannot do otherwise. We shall have to work out our destiny along these lines.

But instead of spiritualizing this creed we have steadily materialized it, we have mistaken the pursuit of happiness for the pursuit of wealth; we have failed to grasp the truth that happiness lies—and lies alone—in self-realization; that the acquisition of wealth, that the triumph of man over nature, is merely accessory to happiness.

The creed is deeply religious in its sublime trust in man, its confidence that he will not pursue false gods forever, that he will come at length to a realization of the futility of the purely material, and that he will turn at last voluntarily and make his contribution to the whole. I should like to emphasize that word *voluntarily*, because it is the most significant in democracy. We are a nation of volunteers; we do not wish to be forced into serving our government, but to do so of our own free will. This does not mean that voluntary service is unorganized service.

Our creed infers also that before we can have efficiency in government we must have self-control in individuals. It differs from the German culture in that it implies development and ultimate unity through differentiation, and a belief that that nation is the richest nation which contains the most highly developed and richest individuals. National wealth, both material and spiritual, grows out of the self-realization of citizens and their voluntary contributions to the nation.

American democracy, then, as I have said, confesses its trust in mankind, and if we open our eyes we may see about us no lack of experiments throughout the republic in which this trust in humanity is being more or less justified. Many of our universities and some of our public schools have adopted a qualified system of self-government, and our faith is such that we are even applying it, and not without encouragement, to the prison system. Trust is the despair of politicians.

Democracy must, from its very nature, evolve its own truths from experience and traditions, and can accept no external authority. It is an adventure. It is never safe—otherwise the element of faith would be eliminated from it. It grows as the soul grows, through mistakes and suffering. Nevertheless, there is in it some guiding principle of progress that is constant, and with which its citizens should be imbued and inspired. I am speaking of an American culture, using it in the German sense of Kultur. To quote Professor Dewey again: Culture, according to Kant, differs from civilization in this, that civilization is a natural and largely unconscious or involuntary growth, the by-product of the needs engendered when people live close together, while culture is deliberate and conscious, the fruit not of men's natural motives, but of natural motives transformed by the inner spirit. Observe the word *transformed*.

The spirit of democracy, the philosophy of democracy, needs to be developed and made conscious in order that we may gradually transform our material individualism into a spiritual individualism. Thus the pursuit of happiness becomes the struggle for self-realization; thus the riches and the gifts developed are devoted, voluntarily, to the good of the whole. There is no coercion, but a spirit. Competition becomes emulation, such as we see now among scientists, or in that finer element of the medical profession that bends all its energies for the benefit of humanity. Trust is the order of the day. Individual initiative is stimulated rather than paralyzed, and the citizen contributes to government rather than attempts to compel government to contribute to him.

All this does not make organization any the less necessary. It does not mean that the volunteer must not be trained. Quite the contrary. But it does mean that the volunteer must grow up conscious of the traditions of his country, instilled with the spirit of its institutions.

As has been said, it would seem of late years that there has been a tendency to lose faith in the virtue of the principles of American democracy to right wrongs, to cure the evils that modern industrialism has brought in its train. A marked sentiment has arisen, demanding that government be given strong coercive powers to be exercised on behalf of and for the protection of the economically dependent. Such legislation is class legislation—it either takes for granted that an economically dependent class is inevitable, or else that the members of the dependent order will gradually be emancipated, not as individuals, but as a class. From the point of view of our traditions it is quite as subversive as legislation in favor of the economically powerful. Vicious as this undoubtedly is, it has been to a large extent extra-legal and therefore within the bounds of cure.

That an ounce of prevention is worth a pound of cure may be taken as a cardinal motto of our democracy. We are, of course, face to face at present with a condition and not a theory, and we have today the anomalous situation of a political quasi-democracy upon which an economic oligarchy has been superimposed —we have an economically dependent class that has only the choice between masters, as Herbert Croly in his *Progressive Democracy* points out; a class whose members as individuals have no command over the conditions in which they shall work; and the fact that these conditions are often dictated by labor unions does not emancipate the individual. In such a case we are as far from American democracy as ever. Old-age pensions, minimum-wage laws, workingmen's compensation acts, may, in the muddle we have got into, be necessary to secure a temporary measure of justice, but fundamentally they are not American. Conscription was necessary in our Civil War, but conscription is not in harmony with Anglo-Saxon democracy. The laws I have mentioned are poultices and not cures, inasmuch as they do not go to the root of the evil. These laws confess no ultimate trust in human nature; they assume that a situation will always exist wherein the powerful will take advantage over the weak unless a strong government steps in to restrain them.

Democracy is contributive; it does not receive favors from its government, but confers them. And the tendency to throw the onus of support on government is not to create a self-reliant people, nor a self-respecting, resourceful, and inventive people. Labor tends to become routine; there is no pride in it. Unless labor is emancipated from its condition of dependence, unless we restore dignity and pride in work, and begin to reëstablish that comparative equality of opportunity that once existed when this country had wide, empty lands and unclaimed resources, our republic will go on the rocks. Of this we may be sure. It cannot continue to exist half slave and half free. Unless our citizens without distinction of class are awakened to the danger and instilled with the spirit of our traditions, we shall have a class revolution, and that means collectivism with all its leveling influences. Collectivism does not tend to produce the rich individual, because initiative is destroyed. Class solidarity in a class struggle against injustice has indeed its ennobling influence, but it is a very different thing from what Americans understand as patriotism. Moreover, the characteristics of this class struggle in its earlier stages is that of the barter of one kind of property for another—and so long as labor is regarded as property it can never have any true dignity or distinction. The struggle, in spite of the heights in sacrifice often attained to by working men and women on strike, in spite of their physical and moral sufferings, is founded fundamentally on material issues. The great mass of working people are at present uneducated in any true sense, and therefore their ambitions, once gained, are apt to be satisfied with purely material comforts. A proof of this may be found in the fact that in times of prosperity, when work is plentiful and wages high, the labor agitator generally preaches to deaf ears unless the employees can be convinced that the employer is taking too large a share of the profits.

What, then, is the American solution? It depends absolutely upon the elimination of the class spirit from our body politic.

Let us examine once more the theory of our state. We find in it certain fundamental principles in harmony with our national and racial character, and our general conclusion is, therefore, that we shall achieve no progress by breaking with traditions, but on the other hand these traditions must be developed to cope with new conditions that arise and confront us, conditions for which no man or set of men are to blame. One of these new conditions is this, that instead of a sparsely settled land fabulously rich in resources, with plenty of room for all who might come, we have today a population of a hundred million and the resources largely taken up and exploited. The day of the pioneer is past; the day of the administrator is at hand; husbandry and efficiency must take the place of waste. In former times, when lands and resources were plentiful, a large equality of opportunity existed, and equality of opportunity is the very foundation stone of American individualism. Indeed, it may be said that the state did guarantee this equality in not seizing the lands and resources for herself, but in throwing them open to her citizens.

A logical development, therefore, of the American doctrine, if indeed it be a development rather than application to new conditions, is that the state should guarantee equality of opportunity in a modern industrial commonwealth. And this guarantee of a fair start may be said to be the one *positive* function in the theory of the American state. All other adjustments, the righting of injustices and wrongs, must be left to the workings of the American democratic spirit in the citizens themselves, must depend upon the extent to which the body politic is saturated with this spirit. It is in truth what may be called a big order. But there is no other way out for us.

It is a fact of profound significance that American democracy from its very beginning instinctively laid stress on universal education, and foreign travelers who came a hundred years ago to study our curious institutions were struck by the extent to which cultivation had permeated our citizenship. A self-governing people must be intelligent. And—be it noted— what was largely meant by education was the adequate preparation of the young for intelligent participation in the life and affairs of the nation as it then existed.

An almost incredible change has taken place since then. Our simple republic has become a complex commonwealth. And we must bear in mind that the final justification for the existence of this commonwealth must be that of creating material wealth for spiritual ends. An industrial commonwealth does not imply mere utilitarianism; the analogy of the bee and the hive does not hold. Life is not without its graces; existence is a rounded thing. Literature and art are not alone for the privileged, but are made more and more democratic, are part and parcel of the education of all, while religion is inherent in government itself, in harmony with it—the contributive spirit of the whole.

A new system of education based on psychology, on scientific principles, an education for life in a modern industrial democracy, is being put into practice in various parts of the United States, and is destined ultimately to supplant the old system. Education in its very nature is selective, but what may be called the new education is not that which we know as vocational, which is class education. It does not undertake to educate the workman *for* a workman. It is based on the American theory that every citizen, whatever his future calling may be, must be made familiar with the development of industry, with the development of government, of art and literature and religion, from the earliest times up to the present. This is not so difficult as it seems. It is an education in the principles of growth, in the social development of humanity. It is analogous to the physical and individual development of humanity from the egg. It is an education in truth, in science, and in straight thinking.

Industrially the modern steel-mill is an evolution from the village blacksmith's shop and foundry, just as a modern textile-mill is an evolution from the home spinning-wheel and loom on the farm. These industries have been taken out of the home, the blacksmith-shop and the foundry are no longer familiar village spectacles. What was a part of the education of the individual outside of the school has now, perforce, become a part of the general educational task.

The new education is based on the sound principle of the direct application of thought to action, of passing from the concrete to the abstract rather than from the abstract to the concrete. The uses of knowledge are held up as incentives to its acquirement. The child learns to read because he loves stories;

he learns arithmetic and weights and measures because he wishes to build a house; while the practice of a measure of self-government in school leads to a grasp of its value in democracy.

Presently the future citizen discovers what he can do best, to select the particular service in life for which nature has fitted him. It may not be an important service, he may not be equipped by nature for a leader. But he has had his opportunity. The state has given it to him. The opportunity does not necessarily cease when his early education has been finished, since some individuals develop late. But under such a system no citizen is able to say that he has not had a chance to develop what is in him, and thus the element of discontent is removed at its source. He is, so far as the state can make him such, a *rounded* individual; he has learned to use his hands and his head, and to appreciate the finer things in life.

It is quite true that men will not work except for a prize; the personal possession of property is essential, but if the prize has not a spiritual aspect it is dross. In so far as work itself is the prize, in so far as the achieved gift is a contribution, and a voluntary contribution, to humanity it is worthy of individual effort.

Education founded on these principles instills patriotism instead of class feeling, and strikes at the very root of the tendency toward class solidarity and class strife. And it implies, furthermore, a truer conception of democracy than that held in Jackson's day—a democracy of leadership combined with responsibility. The choice individuals are developed with the least possible resentment.

Guaranteed education is therefore a fundamental principle in American democracy, but before leaving the subject, it is well, in addition to dwelling upon the significance of experiments such as the Gary schools, to call attention to another experiment, that of education in detail, which is being tried along traditional American lines at Schenectady and Cincinnati and other places in this country. Here, at Union College and the University of Cincinnati, education is directly connected with industry, the theoretical knowledge acquired in the college or university

U

immediately applied by the students in the great manufacturing establishments whose properties lie adjacent. Thus students who prove their ability are actually in the industry and in line for rapid advancement. They are familiar with its theory as well as with its processes.

Lastly, students learn in the schools and universities to value the principles of American democracy to such an extent that they are willing to defend them, to fight if necessary for the right of self-development that is the American heritage. Even as the industrial army of the future must be recruited from educated citizens rather than from raw and ignorant masses, so must the military forces of the republic. It is a question whether militarism ever was or ever will be an American trait; but those who fear it, who are apprehensive that a large army will create a dangerous, high-handed ruling caste, need have no dread of such a caste if our army is organized in harmony with democratic principles.

The American democratic state, then, has but the one *positive* function, that of guaranteeing to each of its citizens a fair start —since the protection of rights is merely negative. The emphasis is laid on the spirit, the trust is put in the spirit, not in the law. *Enlightened self-interest* is the old and much-ridiculed phrase; an illuminating phrase, nevertheless; individual initiative and the satisfaction of individual achievement remain; the self-interest remains also, but transformed by enlightenment and made contributory to the interests of the whole. Here is precisely the paradox of Christianity: "He that findeth his life shall lose it, and he that loseth his life for My sake shall find it."

It is no wonder, indeed, that such a political creed as our forefathers composed seemed to Europe impractical and Utopian. Thus analyzed, it must seem to many Utopian today. That our Anglo-Saxon theory of democracy is no short cut to the millennium is quite evident, and if democracy is to have any approach to perfection, that comparative perfection must be one of *growth*, not of achievement. A satisfaction in development rather than in achievement seems to be the principle of life.

Congress and state legislatures may pass coercive laws in the hope of securing a crude justice, but it has been well said that there never was a law that a coach and four couldn't be driven through. We Americans are skilful coach-drivers, and coach-driving through laws as obstacles has been the pastime and delight of many corporation lawyers. Public opinion must precede laws and not follow them. The truth may as well be faced that our salvation depends absolutely on what is called public opinion, and public opinion is only another name for the democratic spirit or culture with which our electorate must be saturated.

For those who have eyes to see, however, there are signs in various quarters of the growth of this spirit, and these may be taken as concrete illustrations of its workings. There is a sentiment, for instance, in favor of what we call "prohibition"— an example of the extreme that is apt to precede moderation. The moderate term, of course, is temperance, for temperance implies self-control. Wave after wave of "prohibition" has swept over the country, leaving some states—to use the vivid expression—high and dry. Whatever of value there is in this sentiment is the result of a conviction dawning on our people that alcoholic beverages are what modern economics aptly call *illth*, in contradistinction to *wealth*. The educated citizen of a democracy must become familiar with the deteriorating effects of alcohol, its influence on hand and brain and the consequent loss in individual service, as well as the degeneracy and insanity that follow its excessive use. A people who have been deprived of alcohol by a benevolent government will undoubtedly be a saner and healthier people, but they will neither be as intelligent nor as efficient nor as developed as that people which ultimately arrives at the knowledge as to why alcohol is harmful and paralyzing to efficiency, and which voluntarily deprives itself of it. Here is the principle of democracy in a nutshell. A public opinion is gradually created by an educative process, and laws follow it as a matter of course. On the other hand, "prohibition" that has not an educated public opinion behind it is a laughing-stock, as the experience of some of our states in New England and elsewhere has proved.

There is a new spirit in the universities, a healthier and sounder public opinion than existed at the end of the nineteenth century; a new interest in and knowledge of government and enthusiasm for democracy, with a desire to share its tasks and responsibilities. The response to the call of the training-camps at Plattsburg and elsewhere is an encouraging indication of it.

Peculiarly significant, however, is the birth of this new spirit among employers of labor—an indication that *emulation* may replace competition. There is no need to be cynical on this score, to insist that the men who control great corporations and combinations of capital have been frightened out of many practices in which they hitherto have indulged. There can be no question that the public attitude toward these practices has changed, and it would be stupid and un-American to maintain that this opinion has not permeated the element that employs labor, and made them more American also. This emulative spirit, this indication of the dawning of *enlightened* self-interest, this willingness to put a shoulder to the wheel, is at present more marked among employers of the large corporations. But it will spread, and is spreading. Even as we have today in the medical profession an association, an emulative body of medical opinion purifying that profession of quackery and fraud and strictly commercial practice, even as we have among the lawyers bar associations, so we shall have among business men and employers a growing element that sets its face against practices hitherto indulged in, making these practices more and more difficult of accomplishment by the remnant. When employers of their own initiative take steps to insure the safety and health of their employees, and at their own risk make experiments that tend toward the ultimate establishment of industrial democracy, toward giving the working man a share and interest in the industry, labor must respond. Little by little individual animosities are broken down and class animosity is weakened. It makes no difference if these experiments with a view to industrial democracy do not meet the demands of extremists; it makes no difference whether motives are mixed if the good be predominant. If the spirit is there, we may trust to its working. Our watchwords must be patience and faith, faith that our great problem of industrial democracy will one day be solved by the same principle of equality of opportunity, by the same trust in man that solved for us the problem of political democracy.

A nation saturated with the conviction that all should have an equal chance, imbued with this volunteer, emulative spirit instilled by education and growing out of experience, cannot ultimately go wrong. Let us therefore make our individual contributions, and be assured that it is better to give than to receive.

CAN DEMOCRACY BE ORGANIZED?[1]

EDWIN ANDERSON ALDERMAN

[Edwin Anderson Alderman (1861———) was born in Wilmington, North Carolina. He was educated at the University of North Carolina, and was for several years a teacher in the public schools of North Carolina. He has been successively professor of pedagogy at the University of North Carolina, president of the University of North Carolina, president of Tulane University, and, since 1904, president of the University of Virginia. He has been strongly interested in political and social questions, and his addresses, delivered with the accomplishments of a finished orator, have been brilliant discussions of many important questions. The selection here given was originally an address before the North Carolina Literary and Historical Society in 1915.]

The United States of America is one of the oldest governments on earth. England and Russia alone, among the nations of Europe, equal it in age, and even England has undergone such radical changes in the past century, as compared with the United States, as to constitute us, with our unchanged government since 1789, the most stable of modern nations. Our nearness to the perspective and our absorption in our own life have blinded us to the inspiring National panorama, as it has unfolded itself before the world. First, a group of rustic communities, making common cause in behalf of ancient guarantees of English freedom; then suspicious colonies, unused to the ways of democracies, striving after some bond amid the clash of jealous interests; then a wonderful paper-writing, compact of high sense and

[1]From *Proceedings of the North Carolina Literary and Historical Society, 1915.* Reprinted by permission.

human foresight and tragic compromise; then a young republic, lacking the instinct of unity, but virile, unlovely, raw, wayward, in its confident young strength. Some confused decades of sad, earnest effort to pluck out an evil growth planted in its life by the hard necessities of compromise by the fathers, but which needs must blossom into the flower of civil war before it could be plucked out and thrown to the void. Then young manhood, nursing its youth, whole and indivisible, proven by trial of fire and dark days, opening its eye upon a new world of steam and force, and seizing greedily and selfishly every coign of vantage; and today the most venerable republic, the richest of nations, the champion and exemplar of world democracy.

No nation, I venture to assert, was ever born grounded on so definite and fixed a principle and with so conscious a purpose. Such a wealth of hope for humanity never before gathered about a mere political experiment, and such a mass of pure idealism never before suffused itself into the framework of a state. How can such a nation so begun, so advanced, so beset, be so guided, that all of its citizens shall indeed become free men, entering continually into the possession of intellectual, material, and moral benefits? How can a people devoted to individualism and freedom retain that individualism which guarantees freedom and yet engraft upon their social order that genius for coöperation which alone insures power and progress? These are the final interrogatories of democracy as a sane vision glimpses it, robbed of its earlier illusions. The fathers of this republic did not understand the present mould of democracy. The very word was obnoxious to them. Their ideal was a state the citizens of which chose their leaders and then trusted them. They did not foresee the socialized state. They did not envisage a minute and paternal organization of society which may be achieved alike by Prussian absolutism or mere socialism, which is chronologically, if not logically, the child of democracy. The fear that tugged at their hearts was the fear of tyranny, the dread of kings, the denial of self-direction, which prevented a man from speaking his opinion or going his way as he willed. Their democracy was a working government which should give effect to the will of the people and at the same time provide sufficient safeguard for individual liberty. The emphasis of the time was everywhere upon the rights of the individual rather more than upon the duties of the citizen. When their theories, as Mr. Hadley points out, seemed likely to secure this result, the fathers published them boldly; when they seemed likely to interfere, they ignored them. The creed, then, which had a religious sanction in an age of moral imagination to men of superb human enthusiasm like Washington, Franklin, Jefferson, and Adams, was the belief that democracy, considered as individual freedom, was the final form of human society. It is idle to deny that a century of trial has somewhat dulled the halo about this ancient concept of democracy, but in my judgment only to men of little faith. It is quite true that our democracy of today is not what Rousseau thought it would be, nor Lord Byron, nor Shelley, nor Karl Marx. But as we meditate about it and conclude that it has not realized all of its hopes, we ought to try to settle first what it has done and then place that to its credit. Here are some things that I think democracy has done, or helped to do. It has abated sectarian fury. Sectarian fury is ridiculous in this age; it was not always so. It has abolished slavery. It has protected and enlarged manhood suffrage, and has gone far toward womanhood suffrage. It has mitigated much social injustice. It has developed a touching and almost sublime faith in the power of education, illustrating it by expending six hundred million dollars a year in the most daring thing that democracy has ever tried to do: namely, to fit for citizenship every human being born within its borders. It has increased kindness and gentleness, and thus diminished the fury of partisanship. It has preserved the form of the Union through the storm of a civil war, and yet has had power to touch with healing unity and forgiveness its passions and tragedies. It has conquered and civilized a vast continent. It has developed great agencies of culture and has somehow made itself a symbol of individual prosperity. It has developed a common consciousness and a volunteer statesmanship among its free citizens as manifested more strikingly than elsewhere in the world in great educational, religious, scientific and philanthropic societies, which profoundly influence and mould society. Out of what other state could have issued as a volunteer movement so efficient an agency as the Commission for the Relief of Belgium or the Rockefeller Sanitary Commission? It has permitted and fostered the growth of a public press of gigantic power reflecting the crudities and impulses of a vast and varied population, but charged with a fierce idealism and staunch patriotism that have almost given it a place among the coördinate branches of our organized government. It has stimulated inventive genius and business enterprise to a point never before reached in human annals. It has brought to American-mindedness millions of men of all races, creeds, and ideals. I do not, therefore, think that democracy as it has evolved among us has failed. What autocracy on earth has done as much? It has justified itself of the sufferings and sacrifices and the dreams of the men who established it in this new land. But it has also without doubt, by the very trust that it places in men, developed new shapes of temptations and wrong-doing. Democracy, like a man's character, is never clear out of danger. The moral life of men, said Froude, is like the flight of a bird in the air; he is sustained only by effort, and when he ceases to exert himself he falls. And the same, it seems to me, is impressively true of institutional and governmental life.

Patriotism—which is hard to define and new with every age—and public spirit—which is hard to define and new with every age—must constantly redefine themselves. Patriotism meant manhood's rights when Washington took it to his heart. It somehow spelled culture, refinement and distinction of mind when Emerson in his Phi Beta Kappa address besought the sluggish intellect of his country to look up from under its iron lids. It signified national ideals and theories of government to the soldiers of Lee and to the soldiers of Grant. It meant industrial greatness and a splendid desire to annex nature to man's uses when the great business leaders of this generation and of the last generation built up their great businesses and tied the Union together in a unity of steel and steam more completely than all the wars could do, and did it with a patriotism and a statesmanship and an imagination that no man can deny. The honest businessman needs somebody to praise him. He has done a great service in this country, and when he is steady and honest there is no greater force in all our life. A decade ago patriotism in America meant a reaction from an unsocial and selfish individualism to restraint and consideration for the general welfare, expressing itself in a cry for moderation and fairness and justice and sympathy in the use of power and wealth as the states of spirit and mind that alone can safeguard republican ideals. The emphasis, as I have said, was formerly on the rights of man; it is getting to be placed, as Mazzini preached, upon the duties of man. If in our youth and feverish strength there had grown up a spirit of avarice and a desire for quick wealth, and a theory of life in lesser minds that estimated money as everything and was willing to do anything for money, that very fact served to define the patriotic duty and mood of the national mind. This reawakened patriotism of the common good had the advantage of appeal to a sound public conscience, and of being supported by a valid public opinion. The part that vulgar cunning has played in creating great fortunes has been made known to this democracy and they are coming to know the genuine from the spurious, and some who were once looked at with admiration and approval as great ones, are not now seen in that light.

This very growth in discernment gave us power to see in a nobler and truer light, for the people of America, the names of those upright souls in business and in politics—and there are many noble men in business and politics—who have held true in a heady time and who have kept clean and kept human their public sympathies and their republican ideals and by so doing have kept sweet their country's fame. Democracy simply had met and outfaced one of the million moral crises that are likely to assail free government, and I believe that it is cleaner today in ruling passion, in motive, and in practice than it has been in fifty years.

It is now clear to all minds that the movement of our business operations in this republic, unregulated and proceeding along individualistic lines, had come perilously near to developing a scheme of monopoly and a union of our political machinery with the forces of private gain that might easily have transformed our democracy into some ugly form of tyranny and injustice. We have halted this tendency somewhat tardily, but resolutely, and the nerves of the Nation were somewhat shaken by the very thought of what might have been, very much as a man gazes with gratitude and yet with fear upon a hidden precipice over which his pathway led. We had been saying over and over to ourselves with fierce determination that this nation should remain democratic, and should not become plutocratic or autocratic or socialistic; and we should find the way to guarantee this. All about us were heard the voices of those who thought they saw the way and who were beckoning men to follow, but new dangers faced us, however, even as we left the ancient highway and attempted to cut new paths, for in endeavoring to make it possible for democracy, as we understood it, and a vast industrialism, as we had developed it, to live together justly under the same political roof, we had plainly come to a point where there was danger of our government developing into a system of state socialism in conflict with our deepest traditions and convictions. The leadership of the future, therefore, would have a triple problem—to protect the people against privilege, to raise the levels of democratic living, and to preserve for the people the ancient guarantees and inestimable advantages of representative government and individual initiative.

You will observe that I have thus far spoken as a citizen preoccupied with the thoughts of that ancient world which ended on August 1, 1914, and I have not permitted myself to align and examine in full the perils and weaknesses of democratic society as they had manifested themselves under conditions of peace and apparent prosperity. These weaknesses had already begun, under the strain of ordinary industrial life, to reveal themselves under five general aspects, each aspect being in essence a sort of revulsion or excess of feeling from what were considered definite political virtues:—

1. A contempt of obedience as a virtue too closely allied to servility.

2. A disregard of discipline as smacking too much of docility.

3. An impatience with trained technical skill as seeming to affirm that one man is not so good as another.

4. A failure to understand the value of the common man as a moral and political asset and an inability to coördinate education to daily life as a means of forwarding national ends and ideals.

5. A crass individualism which exalted self and its rights above society and the solemn social obligation to coöperate for the common good.

The theory of democracy which alone among great human movements had known no setback for a century of time, was fast becoming self-critical and disposed to self-analysis, and especially in America these fundamental weaknesses were being assailed in practical forms. The liberal or progressive movement in our politics was striking at the theory of crass individualism, and after the unbalanced fashion of social reform was moving toward pure democracy of state socialism in the interest of communal welfare. Our old, original, intense American individualism, shamed by its ill-governed cities and lack of concern for popular welfare, had passed forever. Socialism, considered as a paternal form of government, exercising strict regulation over men's lives and destroying individual energy and initiative, was still feared and resisted; but the social goal of democracy was becoming even by the most conservative, to be considered the advancement and improvement of society by a protection of life and health, by a reformation of educational methods and by a large amount of governmental control of fundamentals for the common good. A multitude of laws, ranging from laws governing milk for babies, to public parks and free dispensaries and vast corporations, attested the vigor of this new attitude. And strange to say this new spirit was not wholly self-begotten. Plutocracy, with its common sense, its economies and hatred of waste, its organization and its energy, had taught us much. We, too, had caught a spirit from what we used to call effete

Europe. Australia taught us how to vote; Belgium, Germany, and England that there was a democracy adapted to city and factory as well as to the farm and countryside.

The forces of education were pleading the cause of team work in modern life, scientifically directed, not by amateurs and demagogues, but by experts and scientists, whether in city government or public hygiene or scientific land culture, while seriousness and self-restraint were everywhere the themes of public teachers, pleading for order and organization as an ideal of public welfare, nearly as vital as liberty and self-direction. And then, without warning, fell out this great upheaval of the world, so vast, so fundamental, despite its sordid and stupid beginnings, that the dullest among us must dimly realize that a new epoch has registered itself in human affairs. War is a great pitiless flame. It sweeps its fiery torch along the ways of men, destroying but renovating, killing but quickening, and even amid its horrors of corruption and death leaving white ashes cleanly and fertile. War is also a ghastly mirror in which actualities and ideals and tendencies reflect themselves in awful vividness. Who caused this war, who will be aggrandized by this war—its triumphs and humiliations—are important and moving, but not vital questions. The fundamental question is what effect will its reactions have upon that movement of the human spirit called democracy, begun so simply, advanced so steadfastly, yesterday acclaimed as the highest development of human polity, but today already being sneered at and snarled at by a host of enemies. Will war, the harshest of human facts, destroy, weaken, modify, or strengthen essential democracy? It is my conviction that the Allies in this struggle are fighting for democracy—at least for the brand of democracy with which my spirit is familiar and which my soul has learned to love. Once more in the great human story, the choice is being made between contrasting civilizations, between ideals and institutions, between liberty and the lesser life. Every drop of my blood leaps to sympathy with those peoples who, heedless of inexorable efficiency, dream a mightier dream of an order directed by justice, invigorated by freedom, instinct with the higher hap-

piness of individual liberty, self-directed to reason and coöperation. "For what avail the plough or sail, or land or life if freedom
fail?" The very weaknesses of democratic government under
the crucial test of war appeal to me. The tutelage of democracy
breeds love of justice, the methods of persuasion and debate,
and a conception of life which makes it sweet to live and in a
way destroys the temperament for war, until horror and wrong
and reversion to type create anew the savage impulse. Whatever
way victory falls, democracy is destined to stand its trial, and to
be submitted to a merciless cross-examination by the mind and
spirit of man. It may and will yield up some of its aspirations;
it will seize and adapt some of the weapons of its foes; it may
relinquish some of its ancient theories and methods; it will shed
some of its hampering weaknesses; but it will still remain democracy, and it is the king, the autocrat, and the mechanical state
which will suffer in the end rather than the common man who,
in sublime loyalty to race and flag, is now reddening the soul of
Europe with his blood, or the great principle which has fascinated
every generous thinking soul since freedom became the heritage
of man.

The Germans are a mighty race, fecund in physical force and
organizing genius. Like the French of 1789, they are now more
possessed with a group of passionate creative impulses than any
other nation. This grandiose idealism, for such it is, seems to me
reactionary, but it is held with a sort of thrilling devotion and
executed with undoubted genius. Nineteen hundred and fourteen
is for the Prussians a sort of Prussian Elizabethan age, in which
vast dreams and ideas glow in the hearts and minds of Teutonic
Raleighs, Drakes, and Grenvilles, ready to die for them. The
ideal of organization, the thought of a great whole uniting its
members for effective work in building a powerful state, and the
welding of a monstrous federal union of nations akin in interest
and civilizations possess the Germanic mind. For the German
the individual exists for the state, and his concept of the state
is far more beautiful and spiritual than we Americans generally
imagine. The state is to be the resultant of the best thought
and efforts of all its units. They have a glorious concept of com-

munal welfare, but to them parliamentarism is frankly a disease and suffrage a menace. To them, and I am quoting a notable German scholar, "democracy is a thing, infirm of purpose, jealous, timid, changeable, unthorough, without foresight, blundering along in an age of lucidity guided by confused instincts." On the whole Germany is probably better governed in external forms than the United States or England. The material conditions of her people are better, her cities cleaner, her economies finer, her social life better administered, and her power to achieve amazing results under the fiercest of tests nearly marvelous. The world cannot and probably will not reject as vile all this German scholarship, concentration, and scientific power. The world may either slavishly imitate Germany, or wisely modify or set up a contrary system overtopping the German ideal in definite accomplishment, according to the inclination of the scales of victory. The fatality of the German nation is that it does not behold the world as it is. It beholds its ideals and is logic-driven to their achievement. It has gone from the sand waste of Brandenburg to world-power by force and the will to do, and by force and will it seeks its will and hacks its way through. It is enslaved by the majesty of plan and precision—the power of concert. Napoleon, "that ablest of historic men," as Lord Acton called him, tried all this once and failed. But here it all is again, with its weapons of flame and force. Germany, apparently, does not understand the fair doctrine of live and let live. Pride sustains its soul, and ambition directs its energy. In spite of all these concrete achievements Germany does not seem to me a progressive nation, but rather a Giant of Reaction—a sort of mixture, as someone has called it, of Ancient Sparta and Modern Science. And it is well to hold in mind that this mass-efficiency is brought to pass by subjecting even in the minutest particulars the individual to the supreme authority of the state. This subjection is scientific, well-meant, but very minute.

The flaw of democracy is that it does understand and sympathize with the soul of man, but is so sympathetic with his yearning for free self-government and self-direction, so opposed to force as a moulding agent, so jealous of initiative, that it has not yet found the binding thread of social organization by which self-government and good government become one and the same thing. Let us confess that *"Les mœurs de la liberté"* cannot be the manners of absolutism. Debate, political agitation, bold, popular expression, are not the methods of smooth precision and relentless order. Napoleon revealed to the world the democratic passion and passed off the stage. Perhaps it is the destiny of the Prussian to teach us administration and order and to put us in the way of finding and achieving it without sacrificing our liberties, and then he, too, will pass.

To work out a free democratic, socialized life, wherein the individual is not lost in a metaphysical super-state, nor sunk in inaction and selfishness, by inducing desire for such life, by applying trained intelligence to its achievement, and by subjecting ourselves to the tests and disciplines that will bring it to pass—that is the task of American democracy and indeed of a fuller, deeper world-wide democracy. The center of gravity of the autocratic state is in the state itself, and in such ideals as self-anointed leaders suggest. The effect of the democracy has been to shift the center of gravity too much to the individual self and his immediate welfare.

There must be a golden mean somewhere and we must find it. When the great readjustment dawns, when the gaping wounds of war have healed, all the world will be seeking this golden mean. The social democrat of Germany, who is silent now in his splendid National devotion, will be seeking it; the Russian peasant, inarticulate, mystic, reflective; the Frenchman with his clear brain and forward-looking soul; the Englishman wrapped in his great tradition. Perhaps in our untouched and undreamed vigor, we shall become the champions of the great quest.

There would be fitness in such a result. Here continental democracy was born; here it has grown great upon an incomparable soil and with enormous waste. Let us prepare for our colossal moral and practical responsibilities in the world life, therefore, not alone by preparing commonsense establishments of force on land and sea, until such time as human reason shall deem them not needed, but by the greater preparedness of self-restraint, self-analysis, and self-discipline. Let us not surrender our age-long dream of good, just self-government to any mechanical ideal of quickly obtaining material results erected into a crude dogma of efficiency. Democracy must know how to get material results economically and quickly. Democracy must and can be organized to that end, and this organization will undoubtedly involve certain surrenders, certain social and political self-abnegations in the interests of collectivism. But I hold the faith that all this can be done yet, retaining in the family of freedom that shining jewel of individual liberty which has glowed in our life since the beginning. The great democratic nations—America, England, France, Switzerland—have before them, therefore, the problem of retaining their standards of individual liberty, and yet contriving juster and finer administrative organs. Certainly the people that have built this Union can learn how to coördinate the activities of its people and obtain results as definite as those obtained under systems of mere authority.

Since my college days I have been hearing about and admiring the German genius for research, for adaptation of scientific truth and for organization. Now the whole world stands half astonished and half envious of their creed of efficiency. In so far as this creed is opposed to slipshodness and waste, it is altogether good, but the question arises, Is the ability to get things done well deadly to liberty, or is it consistent with personal liberty? In examining German progress, I do not find as many examples of supreme individual efficiency or independent spirit as I find in the democratic nations. The steam engine, the factory system, telegraph, telephone, wireless, electric light, the gasoline engine, aëroplane, machine gun, the submarine, uses of rubber, dreadnaught, the mighty names of Lister and Pasteur, come out of the democratic nations. The distinctive German genius is for administration and adaptation, rather than for independent creation. His civil service is the finest in the world. He knows what he wants. He decides what training is necessary to get that result. He universalizes that training. He enforces obedience to its discipline. A man must have skill; he must obey; he must work; he must coöperate. The freer nations desire the same results, but neglect to enforce their realization. Their theory of government forces them to plead for its attainment. Certain classes and individuals heed this persuasion, and in an atmosphere of precious freedom great personalities spring into being. In the conflict between achievement based on subjection and splendid obedience, and that based on political freedom, my belief is that the system of political and social freedom will triumphantly endure. In essence, it is the conflict between the efficiency of adaptation and organization and the efficiency of invention and creation. What autocracy needs is the thrill and push of individual liberty, and the continental peasant will get it as the result of this war, for the guns of autocracy are celebrating the downfall of autocracy, even in its most ancient fastness—Russia. These autocracies will realize their real greatness when they substitute humility for pride, freedom for accomplishment, as compelling national motives. What democracy needs is the discipline of patient labor, of trained skill, of thoroughness in work, and a more socialized conception of public duty. As President Eliot has pointed out, the German theory of social organization is very young, and her literature, philosophy, and art are fairly new. It is a bit premature to concede the supreme validity of her Kultur and of her political organization until she can point to such names as Dante and Angelo, Shakspere and Milton, Newton and Darwin and Pasteur, and until such names appear in her political history as Washington and Jefferson and Burke. This is not meant to deny the surpassing greatness of her music and her philosophy, nor to minimize the glory of her Goethes or Schillers or Lessings or Steins, but to suggest that she has not yet reached the superlative. It is not yet quite sure that with all their genius for organization and efficiency, they may not be self-directed to ruin. Certainly the German has as much to learn from the freer nations as we have to learn from the Teutonic genius. Switzerland has organized her democracy and kept her personal liberty, and there is no finer spectacle on

v

earth today than the spectacle of France, seed-sowing, torch-bearing France; France, that has touched the heights and sounded the depths of human experience and national tragedy; "*La belle France*," that has substituted duty for glory as a national motive, and has kept her soul free in the valley of humiliation; grim, patient, silent, far-seeing France, clinging to her republican ideals and reorganizing her life from hovel to palace in the very impact of conflict and death, so that it is enabled to present to the world the finest example of organized efficiency and military glory that the world has seen in some generations. In order to organize an autocracy, the rulers ordain that it shall get in order and provide the means to bring about that end. To organize a democracy, we must organize its soul, and give it power to create its own ideals. It is primarily a peace organization, and that is proof that it is the forward movement of the human soul and not the movement of scientific reaction. It is through a severe mental training in our schools and a return to the conception of public duty which guided the sword and uplifted the heart of the Founder of the Republic that we shall find strength to organize the democracy of the future, revolutionized by science and by urban life. The right to vote implies the duty to vote right; the right to legislate, the duty to legislate justly; the right to judge about foreign policy, the duty to fight if necessary; the right to come to college, the duty to carry one's self hand-somely at college. Our youth must be taught to use their senses, to reason simply and correctly, from exact knowledge thus brought to them to attain to sincerity in thought and judgment through work and patience. In our home and civic life, we need some moral equivalent for the training which somehow issues out of war—the glory of self-sacrifice, obedience to just authority, contempt of ease, and a realization that through thoughtful, collective effort great results will be obtained. A great spiritual glory will come to these European nations through their sorrow and striving, which will express itself in great poems and great literature. They are preparing new shrines at which mankind will worship. Let us take care that prosperity be not our sole national endowment. War asks of men self-denials and sacrifice for ideals. Peace must somehow do the same. Autocracy orders men to forget self for an over-self called the state. Democracy must inspire men to forget self for a still higher thing called humanity.

There stands upon the steps of the Sub-Treasury building, in Wall Street, the bronze figure of an old Virginia country gentleman looking out with his honest eyes upon the sea of hurrying, gain-getting men. This statue is a remarkable allegory, for in his grave, thoughtful person, Washington embodies that form of public spirit, that balance of character, that union of force and justice that redefines democracy. Out of his lips seems to issue the great creed which is the core of democratic society, and around which this finer organization shall be solidly built. Power rests on fitness to rule. Fitness to rule rests on trained minds and spirits. You can trust men if you will train them. The object of power is the public good. The ultimate judgment of mankind in the mass is a fairly good judgment

IN ARMS FOR DEMOCRACY

THE WORLD CONFLICT IN ITS RELATION TO AMERICAN DEMOCRACY[1]

Walter Lippmann

[Walter Lippmann (1889———) was born in New York City. He was graduated from Harvard in 1910, and for a time was assistant in philosophy in that institution. Later he formed editorial connections in New York, writing much for the periodical press. He is the author of several books dealing with politics and kindred subjects. The article here reprinted, which gives a comprehensive review of the conditions leading to America's entering the world war, was originally read before a meeting of the American Academy of Political and Social Science, in the summer of 1917, shortly after this step had been taken.]

I

The way in which President Wilson directed America's entrance into the war has had a mighty effect on the public opinion of the world. Many of those who are disappointed or pleased say they are surprised. They would not be surprised had they made it their business this last year to understand the policy of their government.

In May, 1916, the President made a speech which will be counted among the two or three decisive utterances of American foreign policy. The Sussex pledge had just been extracted from the German government, and on the surface American neutrality seemed assured. The speech was an announcement that American isolation was ended, and that we were prepared to join a League of Peace. This was the foundation of all that followed, and it was intended to make clear to the world that America would not abandon its traditional policy for imperialistic adven-

[1]From *Annals of the American Academy of Social and Political Science*, vol. lxxii, p. 1 (July, 1917.)

ture, that if America had to fight it would fight for the peace and order of the world. It was a great portent in human history, but it was overshadowed at the time by the opening of the presidential campaign.

Through the summer the President insisted again and again that the time had come when America must assume its share of responsbility for a better organization of mankind. In the early autumn very startling news came from Germany. It was most confusing because it promised peace maneuvers, hinted at a separate arrangement with the Russian court party, and at the resumption of unlimited submarine warfare. The months from November to February were to tell the story. Never was the situation more perplexing. The prestige of the Allies was at low ebb, there was treachery in Russia, and, as Mr. Lansing said, America was on the verge of war. We were not only on the verge of war, but on the verge of a bewildering war which would not command the whole-hearted support of the American people.

With the election past, and a continuity of administration assured, it became President Wilson's task to make some bold move which would clarify the muddle. While he was preparing this move, the German chancellor made his high-handed proposal for a blind conference. That it would be rejected was obvious. That the rejection would be followed by the submarine war was certain. The danger was that America would be drawn into the war at the moment when Germany appeared to be offering the peace for which the bulk of American people hoped. We know now that the peace Germany was prepared to make last December was the peace of a conqueror. But at the time Germany could pose as a nation which had been denied a chance to end the war. It was necessary, therefore, to test the sincerity of Germany by asking publicly for a statement of terms. The President's circular note to the powers was issued. This note stated more precisely than ever before that America was ready to help guarantee the peace, and at the same time it gave all the belligerents a chance to show that they were fighting for terms which could be justified to American opinion. The note was very much misunderstood at first because the President had said that, since both sides claimed to be fighting for the same thing, neither could well refuse to define the terms. The misunderstanding soon passed away when the replies came. Germany brushed the President aside, and showed that she wanted a peace by intrigue. The Allies produced a document which contained a number of formulas so cleverly worded that they might be stretched to cover the wildest demands of the extremists or contracted to a moderate and just settlement. Above all, the Allies assented to the League of Peace which Germany had dismissed as irrelevant.

The war was certain to go on with America drawn in. On January 22, after submarine warfare had been decided upon but before it had been proclaimed, the President made his address to the Senate. It was an international program for democracy. It was also a last appeal to German liberals to avert a catastrophe. They did not avert it, and on February 1, Germany attacked the whole neutral world. That America would not submit was assured. The question that remained to be decided was the extent of our participation in the war. Should it be merely defensive on the high seas, or should it be a separate war? The real source of confusion was the treacherous and despotic Russian government. By no twist of language could a partnership with that government be made consistent with the principles laid down by the President in his address to the Senate.

The Russian Revolution ended that perplexity and we could enter the war with a clear conscience and a whole heart. When Russia became a republic and the American republic became an enemy, the German empire was isolated before mankind as the final refuge of autocracy. The principle of its life is destructive of the peace of the world. How destructive that principle is, the everwidening circle of the war has disclosed.

II

Our task is to define that danger so that our immense sacrifices shall serve to end it. I cannot do that for myself without turning to the origins of the war in order to trace the logical steps by which the pursuit of a German victory has enlisted the enmity of the world.

We read statements by Germans that there was a conspiracy against their national development, that they found themselves encircled by enemies, that Russia, using Serbia as an instrument, was trying to destroy Austria, and that the Entente had already detached Italy. Supposing that all this were true, it would remain an extraordinary thing that the Entente had succeeded in encircling Germany. Had that empire been a good neighbor in Europe, by what miracle could the old hostility between England and France and Russia have been wiped out so quickly? But there is positive evidence that no such conspiracy existed.

Germany's place in the sun is Asia Minor. By the Anglo-German agreement of June, 1914, recently published, a satisfactory arrangement had been reached about the economic exploitation of the Turkish empire. Professor Rohrbach has acknowledged that Germany was given concessions "which exceeded all expectations," and on December 2, 1914, when the war was five months old, von Bethmann-Hollweg declared in the Reichstag that "this understanding was to lessen every possible political friction." The place in the sun had been secured by negotiation.

But the road to that place lay through Austria-Hungary and the Balkans. It was this highway which Germany determined to control absolutely; and the chief obstacle on that highway was Serbia backed by Russia. Into the complexities of that Balkan intrigue I am not competent to enter. We need, however, do no more than follow Lord Grey in the belief that Austria had a genuine grievance against Serbia, a far greater one certainly than the United States has ever had against Mexico. But Britain had no stake in the Austro-Serbian quarrel itself.

It had an interest in the method which the central powers took of settling the quarrel. When Germany declared that Europe could not be consulted, that Austria must be allowed to crush Serbia without reference to the concert of Europe, Germany proclaimed herself an enemy of international order. She preferred a war which involved all of Europe to any admission of the fact

that a coöperative Europe existed. It was an assertion of unlimited national sovereignty which Europe could not tolerate.

This brought Russia and France into the field. Instantly
Germany acted on the same doctrine of unlimited national
sovereignty by striking at France through Belgium. Had
Belgium been merely a small neutral nation the crime would
still have been one of the worst in the history of the modern
world. The fact that Belgium was an internationalized state
has made the invasion the master tragedy of the war. For
Belgium represented what progress the world had made towards
coöperation. If it could not survive then no internationalism
was possible. That is why through these years of horror upon
horror, the Belgian horror is the fiercest of all. The burning, the
shooting, the starving, and the robbing of small and inoffensive
nations is tragic enough. But the German crime in Belgium is
greater than the sum of Belgium's misery. It is a crime
against the bases of faith at which the world must build or
perish.

The invasion of Belgium instantly brought the five British
democracies into the war. I think this is the accurate way to
state the fact. Had the war remained a Balkan war with France
engaged merely because of her treaty with Russia, had the
fighting been confined to the Franco-German frontier, the British
empire might have come into the war to save the balance of
power and to fulfil the naval agreements with France but the
conflict would probably never have become a people's war in
all the free nations of the empire. Whatever justice there may
have been in Austria's original quarrel with Serbia and Russia
was overwhelmed by the exhibition of national lawlessness in
Belgium.

This led to the third great phase of the war, the phase which
concerned America most immediately. The Allies directed by
Great Britain employed sea power to the utmost. They barred
every road to Germany, and undoubtedly violated many commercial rights of neutrals. What America would do about this
became of decisive importance. It if chose to uphold the rights
it claimed, it would aid Germany and cripple the Allies. If

it refused to do more than negotiate with the Allies, it had, whatever the technicalities of the case might be, thrown its great weight against Germany. It had earned the enmity of the German government, an enmity which broke out into intrigue and conspiracy on American soil. Somewhere in the winter of 1915, America was forced to choose between a policy which helped Germany and one which helped the Allies. We were confronted with a situation in which we had to choose between opening a road to Germany and making an enemy of Germany. With the proclamation of submarine warfare in 1915 we were told that either we must aid Germany by crippling sea power or be treated as a hostile nation. The German policy was very simple: British mastery of the seas must be broken. It could be broken by an American attack from the rear or by the German submarine. If America refused to attack from the rear, America was to be counted as an enemy. It was a case of he who is not for me is against me.

To such an alternative there was but one answer for a free people to make. To become the ally of the conqueror of Belgium against France and the British democracies was utterly out of the question. Our choice was made and the supreme question of American policy became: how far will Germany carry the war against us and how hard shall we strike back? That we were aligned on the side of Germany's enemies no candid man, I think, can deny. The effect of this alignment was to make sea power absolute. For mastery of the seas is no longer the possession of any one nation. The supremacy of the British navy in this war rests on international consent, on the consent of her allies and of the neutrals. Without that consent the blockade of Germany could not exist, and the decision of America not to resist allied sea power was the final blow which cut off Germany from the world. It happened gradually, without spectacular announcement, but history, I think, will call it one of the decisive events of the war.

The effect was to deny Germany access to the resources of the neutral world, and to open these resources to the Allies. Poetic justice never devised a more perfect retribution. The nation which had struck down a neutral to gain a military advantage found the neutral world a partner of its enemies.

That partnership between the neutral world and Germany's enemies rested on merchant shipping. This suggested a new theory of warfare to the German government. It decided that since every ship afloat fed the resources of its enemies, it might be a good idea to sink every ship afloat. It decided that since all the highways of the world were the communications of the Allies, those communications should be cut. It decided that if enough ships were destroyed, it didn't matter what ships or whose ships, England and France would have to surrender and make a peace on the basis of Germany's victories in Europe.

Therefore, on the 31st of January, 1917, Germany abolished neutrality in the world. The policy which began by denying that a quarrel in the Balkans could be referred to Europe, went on to destroy the internationalized state of Belgium, culminated in indiscriminate attack upon the merchant shipping of all nations. The doctrine of exclusive nationalism had moved through these three dramatic phases until those who held it were at war with mankind.

III

The terrible logic of Germany's policy had a stupendous result. By striking at the bases of all international order, Germany convinced even the most isolated of neutrals that order must be preserved by common effort. By denying that a society of nations exists, a society of nations has been forced into existence. The very thing Germany challenged Germany has established. Before 1914 only a handful of visionaries dared to hope for some kind of federation. The orthodox view was that each nation had a destiny of its own, spheres of influence of its own, and that it was somehow beneath the dignity of a great state to discuss its so-called vital interests with other governments. It was a world almost without common aspiration, with few effective common ideals. Europe was split into shifting alliances, democracies and autocracies jumbled together. America lay apart with a budding imperialism of its own   China was marked as the helpless victim of exploitation. That old political system was one in which the German view was by no means altogether disreputable. Internationalism was half-hearted and generally regarded somewhat cynically.

What Germany did was to demonstrate *ad nauseam* the doctrine of competitive nationalism. Other nations had applied it here and there cautiously and timidly. No other nation in our time had ever applied it with absolute logic, with absolute preparation, and with absolute disregard of the consequences. Other nations nad dallied with it, compromised about it, muddled along with it. But Germany followed through, and Germany taught the world just where the doctrine leads.

Out of the necessities of defense men against it have gradually formulated the ideals of a coöperative nationalism. From all parts of the world there has been a movement of ideals working slowly towards one end, towards a higher degree of spiritual unanimity than has ever been known before. China and India have been stirred out of their dependence. The American republic has abandoned its isolation. Russia has become something like a republic. The British empire is moving towards closer federation. The Grand Alliance called into existence by the German aggression is now something more than a military coalition. Common ideals are working through it—ideals of local autonomy and joint action. Men are crying that they must be free and that they must be united. They have learned that they cannot be free unless they coöperate, that they cannot coöperate unless they are free.

I do not wish to underestimate the forces of reaction in our country or in the other nations of the Alliance. There are politicians and commercial groups who see in this whole thing nothing but opportunity to secure concessions, manipulate tariffs and extend the bureaucracies. We shall know how to deal with them. Forces have been let loose which they can no longer control, and out of this immense horror ideas have arisen to possess men's souls. There are times when a prudent statesman must build on a contracted view of human nature. But there are times when new sources of energy are tapped, when the impossible becomes

possible, when events outrun our calculations. This may be such
a time. The Alliance to which we belong has suddenly grown hot
with the new democracy of Russia and the new internationalism
of America. It has had an access of spiritual force which opens
a new prospect in the policies of the world. We can dare to
hope for things which we never dared to hope for in the past.
In fact if those forces are not to grow cold and frittered they
must be turned to a great end and offered a great hope.

IV

That great end and that great hope is nothing less than the
Federation of the World. I know it sounds a little old-fashioned
to use that phrase because we have abused it so long in empty
rhetoric. But no other idea is big enough to describe the alliance.
It is no longer an offensive-defensive military agreement among
diplomats. That is how it started, to be sure. But it has grown,
and is growing, into a union of peoples determined to end forever
that intriguing, adventurous nationalism which has torn the
world for three centuries. Good democrats have always believed
that the common interests of men were greater than their special
interests, that ruling classes can be enemies, but that the nations
must be partners. Well, this war is being fought by nations. It
is the nations who were called to arms, and it is the force of
nations that is now stirring the world to its foundations.

The war is dissolving into a stupendous revolution. A few
months ago we still argued about the Bagdad corridor, strategic
frontiers, colonies. Those were the stakes of the diplomat's war.
The whole perspective is changed today by the revolution in
Russia and the intervention of America. The scale of values is
transformed, for the democracies are unloosed. Those democracies have nothing to gain and everything to lose by the old
competitive nationalism, the old apparatus of diplomacy, with
its criminal rivalries in the backward places of the earth. The
democracies, if they are to be safe, must coöperate. For the old
rivalries mean friction and armament and a distortion of all
the hopes of free government. They mean that nations are

organized to exploit each other and to exploit themselves. That is the life of what we call autocracy. It establishes its power at home by pointing to enemies abroad. It fights its enemies abroad by dragooning the population at home.

That is why practically the whole world is at war with the greatest of the autocracies. That is why the whole world is turning so passionately towards democracy as the only principle on which peace can be secured. Many have feared, I know, that the war against Prussian militarism would result the other way, that instead of liberalizing Prussia the outcome would be a Prussianization of the democracies. That would be the outcome if Prusso-Germany won. That would be the result of a German victory. And that is why we who are the most peaceful of democracies are at war. The success of the submarine would give Germany victory. It was and is her one great chance. To have stood aside when Germany made this terrible bid for victory would have been to betray the hope cf free government and international union.

V

There are two ways now in which peace can be made. The first is by political revolution in Germany and Austria-Hungary. It is not for us to define the nature of that revolution. We cannot dictate liberty to the German people. It is for them to decide what political institutions they will adopt, but if peace is to come through revolution we shall know that it has come when new voices are heard in Germany, new policies are proclaimed, when there is good evidence that there has, indeed, been a new orientation. If that is done the war can be ended by negotiation.

The other path to peace is by the definite defeat of every item in the program of aggression. This will mean, at a minimum, a demonstration on the field that the German army is not invincible; a renunciation by Germany of all the territory she has conquered; a special compensation to Belgium; and an acknowledgment of the fallacy of exclusive nationalism by an application for membership in the League of Nations.

Frontier questions, colonial questions, are now entirely secondary, and beyond this minimum program the United States has no direct interest in the territorial settlement. The objects for which we are at war will be attained if we can defeat absolutely the foreign policy of the present German government. For a ruling caste which has been humiliated abroad has lost its glamor at home. So we are at war to defeat the German government in the outer world, to destroy its prestige, to deny its conquests, and to throw it back at last into the arms of the German people marked and discredited as the author of their miseries. It is for them to make the final settlement with it.

If it is our privilege to exert the power which turns the scale, it is our duty to see that the end justifies the means. We can win nothing from this war unless it culminates in a union of liberal peoples pledged to coöperate in the settlement of all outstanding questions, sworn to turn against the aggressor, determined to erect a larger and more modern system of international law upon a federation of the world. That is what we are fighting for, at this moment, on the ocean, in the shipyard and in the factory, later perhaps in France and Belgium, ultimately at the council of peace.

If we are strong enough and wise enough to win this victory, to reject all the poison of hatred abroad and intolerance at home, we shall have made a nation to which free men will turn with love and gratitude. For ourselves we shall stand committed as never before to the realization of democracy in America. We who have gone to war to insure democracy in the world will have raised an aspiration here that will not end with the overthrow of the Prussian autocracy. We shall turn with fresh interests to our own tyrannies—to our Colorado mines, our autocratic steel industries, our sweatshops and our slums. We shall call that man un-American and no patriot who prates of liberty in Europe and resists it at home. A force is loose in America as well. Our own reactionaries will not assuage it with their Billy Sundays or control through lawyers and politicians of the Old Guard.

AMERICAN AND ALLIED IDEALS[1]

Stuart Pratt Sherman

[Stuart Pratt Sherman (1881———) was born at Anita, Iowa. After graduating at Williams College, he studied at Harvard, and became, in 1906, an instructor in English in the Northwestern University. In the following year he went to the University of Illinois where he is now professor of English. In his writings, especially in the field of literary criticism, he has shown himself one of the most brilliant of the younger men of letters in the United States.]

I have heard one of our prophets declaring that either Germany or America is destined to rule the world, and that on the whole he hopes it will be America. If I may speak out of my own convictions, there is one thing more abhorrent to my conscience than that Germany should dominate the world by force of arms. That one more abhorrent thing is that America should dominate the world by force of arms. When a man execrates on the part of a foreign nation a course which he praises on the part of his own nation; when a man curses Germany because it is militaristic and then rebukes America because it is not militaristic; when a man reviles the Germans for crying, "On to Calais" and then turns to his fellow countrymen crying, "On to Panama;" when a man ridicules the Germans for calling themselves God's chosen people, and then turns to the Americans and calls them God's chosen people; when a man upbraids the Germans for shouting right or wrong my country, and then turns to the Americans shouting right or wrong my country— confronted by this bull-headed preposterous nationalism the experienced Muse of history bursts into scornful laughter; he that sitteth in the heavens turns away his face; and Americans in the midst of this horrible slaughter are properly admonished to prepare for the next war!

Nor can we escape from the derisive laughter of the Immortals by talking about the Anglo-Saxons. Only one degree removed from the preposterous nationalist is the preposterous Anglo-

[1]From *American and Allied Ideals*. (No. 12, War Information Series, February, 1918, issued by the Committee on Public Information.) Reprinted by permission.

Saxon. I feel fairly intimate with the ideals of America; they are mine. I know something of the ideals of England; they are allied to America's. But what are the Anglo-Saxon ideals? Do they include Disraeli's, Mr. Lloyd-George's, or Mr. Wilson's? For that matter, who are the Anglo-Saxons—other than those Germanic tribes that drove back the Celtic and Pictish ancestors of our Scotch-Irish presidents? I do not see how the American scholar's sympathies can be strongly enlisted in a feud in behalf of the Anglo-Saxon blood. What stake have the countrymen of Lafayette in a blood feud of the Anglo-Saxons? Or the countrymen of Garibaldi? Or the countrymen of Kerensky? Or the Japanese? Or the Brazilians? Or the Portuguese? Or the people of China and Siam? The ties of blood and race count for next to nothing in this conflict. The English-speaking peoples have no monopoly in the ideals of the Allies. The American who now raises the flag of Anglo-Saxonism raises a meaningless symbol which insults the pride of millions of his fellow countrymen and most of the Allies, and may well challenge the Orient to muster and drill her millions for the next war.

Appeals to race prejudice, to a purely self-regarding patriotism, to the old-fashioned nationalism, happily do not nowadays always carry conviction to the intellectual class to which educated men are alleged to belong. Many of them have banished race prejudice as a relic of tribal days. Many of them are convinced that national pride needs a schoolmaster; and are glad that it has one! They have studied the world upheaval in which the nations now quake; they have searchingly scrutinized their own consciences; and many of them have reached the conclusion that the master cause of this tragedy, of which all the world's the stage, is precisely the old self-regarding nationalism—the nationalism which glorifies power and has no principle of contraction to oppose to its principle of expansion. When they hear Germans shouting *"Deutschland über Alles,"* and Americans shouting *"America über Alles,"* their hearts refuse to rally to either call.

They say that the only way to avoid brutal and hideous clashes of international strife for national expansion is to stop this barbaric shouting; and to set up and establish supernational ideals and principles which shall impose an effective check upon the indefinitely expansive principle of nationality. Some of our statesmen tell us that it cannot be done. They declare that they are too stupid to contrive the machinery of international government. We do not altogether believe them. We have a very great confidence in both the ingenuity and the power of statesmen; and it is based upon experience. We believe that statesmen can do anything that they have a mind to do. We believe in the ingenuity and power of statesmen, because we see them all around the world accomplishing much more difficult and incredible things, such, for example, as persuading great nations to pledge their last dollar and their last man and to walk through the valley of the shadow of hideous death to support a statesman's word, plighted perhaps without their knowledge or consent. From that spectacle we derive our belief that when statesmen heartily apply their ingenuity to contriving what the hearts of all the plain people of the world desire, they will be not a little surprised to discover the easiness of the task and the inexhaustible power behind them.

Where shall we find the supernational principles and powers which we wish our statesmen to establish, which we demand that they shall establish? We shall find them in the cause for which America and her associates are now fighting. Cynics may say that each of the Allies is fighting for its own special interest, its own peculiar culture, its trade, to recover this or that bit of territory, to annex this or that province or port. Doubtless selfish motives do enter to some extent into the practical considerations of most of the governments, just as brutal and selfish men enter into the armies. But unless the leading spokesmen of the Allies are black-hearted liars, they are about a nobler business than national buccaneering. And whatever the governments are about, we are profoundly convinced that the great mass of the people of the Allies are not cynics and *do not intend to be dupes;* that they are not fighting for ports and provinces and trade; that they are fighting for the common interests of the whole family of civilized nations—for nothing less than

W

the cause of mankind. They can unite from the ends of the earth as one people, sinking their national peculiarities, because they are drawn by a bond deeper than language or nationality or race; they are drawn by the bond that unites the commonwealth of nations. They are not fighting for French or English or American law, justice, truth, and honor, but for international law, international truth, international justice, international honor.

The new national pride and patriotism developed by this conflict finds its basis in the service which each nation renders to the cause above all nations, the cause of civilized society, the cause of civilized man. The new type of patriot no longer cries, "my country *against* the world," but "my country *for* the world." The moment that he takes that attitude he finds no more hostility between the idea of nationalism and the idea of internationalism than between the idea of a company and the idea of a regiment, or the idea of a state and the idea of a nation. As each good citizen's loyalty to his state accepts a principle of control in his loyalty to his nation, so his loyalty to his nation accepts a principle of control in his loyalty to the general family of nations.

Here is the great fact which challenges the loyalty of every humane man. Propaganda for America and the Allies is not to be urged to the disadvantage of any nation whatsoever, provided only that each nation is willing to behave like a member of a family of nations, provided only that it will accept for its conduct outside its borders the fundamental principles of civilization. Our propaganda is not for separatism and exclusion. It is rather our profound conviction that there is no room left in the world for barbarians, for heathen tribes without the law. Humanity is not safe while any nation professes inhumanity. We are not fighting to put the Germans out but to get them in. Furthermore we have got to take the Orient in, frankly and fully; or in all probability we or our children, or our children's children, will have to fight the Orient. To some of us the influence upon the Orient of the German rebellion against the Family of Nations appears as not the least ominous and dreadful aspect of the present war.

If out of the infinite travail of this war there is to come a new birth of national freedom under international law, if these our numberless dead are not to have died in vain, we must keep our great war aims ever vividly before us. We must not merely defeat our adversaries but also establish the principles for which we drew the sword. If in the day of victory the apathy of enlightened men permits reactionaries and old-fashioned statesmen to arrange a peace under which the nations revert to the former state of international anarchy and competitive preparations for fresh conflicts, the spirits of millions of bemocked and victimized young dead men should rise from their graves to protest against the great betrayal. To insure that the war shall end as a purging tragedy and not as an empty farce we need now and shall need for a long time to come impassioned expositors of the laws of man and God, profaned by the enemy and defended by America and the Allies.

The first duty of the propagandist is to determine what the ideals and principles of the Allies are; and this involves determining what they are not. One can best discover what they are not by reading modern German literature, German newspapers, German ethics and politics, the works of Schopenhauer, Nietzsche, Treitschke, Bernhardi, Hartmann, etc. If time is short, one can quickly sharpen one's consciousness of what our ideals are not by reading daily one or two selections from an anthology of German thought, such as is contained in *Conquest and Kultur*, published by the Committee on Public Information. In this literature one will make acquaintance with the Kaiser's tribal god who has merited the iron cross for his able support of the strategy of the German General Staff, the god who is to stand arm in arm with the Kaiser reviewing his Uhlans on the Day of Judgment. There one will find the leaders of German thought deifying a state with no aspect of deity but power; denying the right of small nations to live; reviving old and instituting new forms of slavery; affirming that might is right; defending the ravishment of Belgium; rejoicing in the *Lusitania* massacre; glorifying *Schrecklichkeit;* recommending that ships of friendly neutrals should be *spurlos versenkt;* advocating keeping subject peoples in ignorance and misery; chanting the holiness of war and hoping that it may last forever; extolling war as the prime element of their *Kultur;* and proudly declaring their opposition to the establishment on earth of the kingdom of righteousness and peace. There one will find the ideals and principles of a government which has covenanted with death and agreed with hell.

The propagandist can do good service by holding these ideas up to execration, not because they are German ideas but because they are ideas hostile to the commonwealth of man. And if by chance any spokesman of the Allied nations falls into the error of saying anything resembling these ideas, the propagandist may perform equally good service by pointing out with emphasis that he speaks like one of the depraved leaders of German thought and an enemy of the Allies.

His happiest occupation, however, should be the discovery, collection, and enthusiastic promulgation on every proffered occasion of the ideals of the Allies. This kind of propaganda has not yet received the attention it deserves. The tendency has been to expose the perversity and iniquity of the enemy's aims and to take for granted the righteousness and justice of our own. As the war proceeds, the Allied nations are steadily drawn by necessity to fight fire with fire; to parry the blow of an autocratic government, they have had to make their own governments temporarily autocratic; to meet the rush of a nation in arms, they have had to put their own nations in arms; to resist the assault of a people trained to sacrifice all to the state, they have been compelled for the nonce to demand a similar sacrifice. As all the participants in this dreadful mêlée become more and more deeply imbrued in the blood and wrath of combat, it grows increasingly difficult to distinguish by their external aspects the victim from the assassin. This hour when his hands are subdued to the dark color of the bleeding mire wherein he grapples with the foe is the bitter hour for the idealist. It is the hour of sinister opportunity for the man who builds his philosophy upon the incorrigible baseness of our human natures. It is then that the cynic and the reactionary croak and shout:

"You are all tarred with the same brush. We bet on the black-est. Fall to! and the devil take the hindmost." This is the hour when it tremendously concerns us to be reminded who began the war and what it is about. This is the hour when it behooves us to remember that our soldiers are defending the causes which our statesmen define. It is the business of the strategists of international idealism to demand that the armies of the Allies shall never fight for a cause unworthy of the com-monwealth of man.

Where shall we look for the ideals of the Allies? Primarily, perhaps, in the utterances of the Allied statesmen at the present time and in the vast literature of the conflict. Take, if you like, Siam's statement of its reasons for entering the war, to "uphold the sanctity of international rights against nations showing a contempt of humanity." Or take Mr. Wilson's statement that our motive is not "revenge or the victorious assertion of the physical might of the nation, but only the vindication of right, of human right, of which we are only a single champion;" or his other statement that we fight "for a universal dominion of right by such a concert of free peoples as shall bring peace and safety to all nations and make the world itself at last free."

It should be a great source of inspiration and confidence to recognize that the ideals of the Allies have been the ideals of just men in all ages; so that we may find them, most of them, expressed in all the great literatures of the world, ancient and modern, including the literature of the great Germans of the eighteenth century. Contemporary German thought is pre-historic, reversionary, paradoxical. It seeks to fly against the great winds of time, to row against the deep current of human purposes, to ignore the grand agreements of civilized men, and to seek its sanction in the unconscious law of the jungle. The Allies are seeking to coöperate with the power not ourselves which has been struggling for righteousness through the entire history of man; and their cause will be borne forward by the confluent moral energies of all times and peoples.

It was to Goethe that Arnold generously gave credit for the idea of an international republic of intellectual men, an idea precious to every scholar and man of letters. "Let us conceive," said Arnold, "of the whole group of civilized nations as being, for intellectual and spiritual purposes, one great confederation whose members have a due knowledge both of the past out of which they all proceed, and of one another. This was the idea of Goethe, and it is an ideal which will impose itself upon the thoughts of our modern societies more and more." It was Goethe who said: "National hatred is something peculiar. You will always find it strongest where there is the lowest degree of culture. And there is a degree where it vanishes altogether and where one stands to a certain extent above nations." These are ideals of the Allies, now scoffed at by the depraved leaders of the thought of Goethe's countrymen.

Mr. Roosevelt has discovered the cause of the Allies in the words of Micah: "What more doth the Lord require of thee than to do justice and love mercy and to walk humbly with thy God?" Another of the Prophets, as if foreseeing the advice given by the German General Staff to the God of the German armies, expressed an ideal of the Allies when he said: "Who hath directed the Spirit of the Lord, or being his Counsellor hath taught him? . . . Behold, the nations are as a drop of a bucket, and are counted as the small dust of the balance. . . . All nations before Him are as nothing; and they are counted to Him less than nothing and vanity. . . . [When His spirit is poured from on high] judgment shall dwell in the wilderness, and righteousness remain in the fruitful field. And the *work of righteousness shall be peace;* and the *effect of righteousness, quietness and assurance forever.*"

Confucius expressed an ideal of the Allies, very dear to the heart of all Americans, when he said: "People despotically governed and kept in order by punishment may avoid infraction of the law, but they will lose their moral sense. People virtuously governed and kept in order by the inner law of self-control will retain their moral sense, and moreover become good."

Cicero expressed a majestic ideal of the Allies, when he said: "True law is right reason conformable to nature, universal, unchangeable, eternal, whose commands urge us to duty, and whose prohibitions restrain us from evil. . . . Neither the senate nor the people can give us any dispensation for not obeying this universal law of justice. . . . It is not one thing at Rome, and another at Athens; one thing today, and another tomorrow; but in all times and nations this universal law must forever reign, eternal and imperishable. It is the sovereign master and emperor of all things. God himself is its author, its promulgator, its enforcer. And he who does not obey it flies from himself, and does violence to the very nature of man."

English literature, especially since the seventeenth century when the divine right of kings received its death blow, is full of expressions of Allied ideals. Milton implies one in *Paradise Regained*

> "They err who count it glorious to subdue
> By conquest far and wide, to overrun
> Large countries, and in field great battles win,
> Great cities by assault; what do these worthies
> But rob and spoil, burn, slaughter, and enslave
> Peaceable nations, neighboring or remote
> Made captive, yet deserving freedom more
> Than those their conquerors, who leave behind
> Nothing but ruin wheresoe'er they rove
> And all the flourishing works of peace destroy."*

And Milton expresses an ideal of the Allies for the period following the war: "If after being released from the toils of war, you neglect the arts of peace . . . if you think it is a more grand, or a more beneficial, or a more wise policy, to invent subtle expedients for increasing the revenue, to multiply our naval and military force, to rival in craft the ambassadors of foreign states, to form skillful treaties and alliances, than to administer unpolluted justice to the people, to redress the injured, to succor the distressed, and speedily to restore to every one his own, you are involved in a cloud of error, and too late you will perceive, when the illusion of *those* mighty benefits has vanished,

---

*Quoted by E. de Sélincourt in *English Poets and the National Ideal*. [Sherman's note.]

that in neglecting these, you have only been precipitating your own ruin and despair."

The literature of France, especially since the French Revolution, is full of the ideals of the Allies. For France I will quote a few lines from the essay by Victor Giraud on French civilization, recently published in this country by the Department of Romance Languages of the University of Michigan:

"France has never been able to believe that force alone, the force of pride and brute strength, could be the last word in the affairs of this world. She has never admitted that science could have for its ultimate purpose to multiply the means of destruction and oppression, and it was one of her old writers, Rabelais, who pronounced these memorable words: 'Science without conscience is the ruin of the soul.' She has not been able to conceive that an ethnic group, a particular type of mind, should have the right to suppress others: instead of a rigid and mechanical uniformity of thought and life, the ideal to which she aspires is that of the free play, spontaneous development, and the living harmony of the nations of the world."

In the response of the South American states to the appeal of the cause of the Allies, deep has called unto deep. No novel circumstance, no momentary impulse, no revelation of yesterday has revealed to the Latin-American peoples their essential community of interest with France, with England, with the United States of the North. Through all temporary misunderstandings and estrangements, they have remembered that they are kindred offspring of one great emancipative idea, inheritors of a common political purpose, pilgrims to a common goal. Through the confusions of desperate wars Simon Bolívar, the Washington of their revolutions, led them a hundred years ago to the threshold of the new world of national independence, civic equality, liberty, popular sovereignty and justice. He, man of strife though he had to be, cherished lifelong his fond dream of a parliament of man, and in the evening of his life summoned on the Isthmus of Panama a congress of nations, which he intended should present a united front to imperial aggression, become the perpetual source and guarantor of public law, and establish concord among all peace-loving peoples. From that day to this the statesmen of South America have been with increasing earnestness and effectiveness the friends of arbitral justice and the architects of international peace.

What shall I say of America but that the ideals for which the Allies are now every day more consciously fighting presided over her birth as a nation and have been her guiding stars in all the high moments of her history? I mean that the American nation, established at an epoch of intellectual expansion, was to a remarkable degree founded upon international principles by men of international outlook and sympathies. Our founders in general claimed nothing for Americans but what they were willing and anxious to concede to all men; so that it has ever been a splendid tradition of the American Government, when about to take a momentous step, frankly to state its case, and openly to invite the considerate judgment—not of Americans—but of mankind, thus checking the expansive principle of nationalism by the contractive principle of a supernational allegiance.

America, furthermore, has never established the worship of a tribal or national deity. The God invoked by the framers of our Declaration of Independence, our Constitution, our Congress, our Courts, and by our great presidents, has quite obviously, I think, been approached as the Father of Mankind. The eighteenth century deists—men like Paine, Franklin, and Jefferson—had indeed thoroughly repudiated the idea of a warlike tribal Jehovah; the qualities which they habitually attributed to the deity were justice and benevolence; and these characteristics have remained, I believe, the leading ones in what we may call our national conceptions of divinity. And how has our national faith in a Father of all Mankind been reflected in our political conceptions? Well, Benjamin Franklin said in the midst of a great war: "Justice is as strictly due between neighbour Nations as between neighbour citizens . . . and a Nation which makes an unjust war is only a *great Gang*." And our Declaration of Independence holds that the God of nature has made it self-evident that *all men* are created equal and endowed with inalienable rights to life, liberty, and the pursuit of happiness. Washington, in his "Farewell Address," expresses his faith that Providence has connected the permanent felicity of a nation with its virtue; accordingly he urges his countrymen to forego temporary national advantages, and to try the novel experiment of always acting nationally on principles of "exalted justice and benevolence." Jefferson, in his first inaugural, felicitates his countrymen on the fact that religion in America, under all its various forms, inculcates "honesty, truth, temperance, gratitude, and the love of man." Liberty, equality, justice, benevolence, truth—these are not tribal ideals.

All these ideals which our national fathers derived from the Father of all Nations, Lincoln received and cherished as a sacred heritage, and he added something precious to them. He took them into his great heart and quickened them with his own warm sense of human brotherhood, with his instinctive gentleness and compassion for all the children of men. "With malice towards none; with charity for all; with firmness for the right, as God gives us to see the right, let us strive on to finish the work we are in; to bind up the nation's wounds; to care for him who shall have borne the battle, and for his widow, and his orphan—to do all which may achieve and cherish a just and lasting peace among ourselves, and with all nations." Why do these words, uttered near the bitter end of a long war, touch us so deeply, and thrill us year after year? Because in them the finest morality of the individual American is identified at last with the morality of the nation. The words consecrate the loftiest of all American ideals, namely, that the conduct of the nation shall be inspired by a humanity so pure and exalted that the humanest citizen may realize his highest ideals in devotion to it.

That ideal still animates the American people. We are not sending out our young men today to fight for a state which acknowledges no duty but the extension of its own merciless power. We are sending them out to fight for a state which finds its highest duty in the defense and extension of justice and mercy. Our national purpose has been solemnly rededicated to the objects of the canonized Father and the Preserver of the Republic. We are not to break with our great traditional aspiration towards the expression in the state of the civility, morality, and responsibility of the humanest citizens. In the noble words of Mr. Wilson's recent address: "The hand of God is laid upon the nations. He will show them favor, I devoutly believe, only if they rise to the clear heights of his own justice and mercy." So believe all just men.

Here then let us close our appeal to those who have drawn apart from this our war and have sought for their emotions a neutral place of refuge above the conflict. The cause of America and the Allies is the defense of the common culture of the family of civilized nations. It is the cause of the commonwealth of man. The ideals and principles which we wish to take hold of character and govern conduct are the best principles and ideals that men have. We need not fear the perils that beset the propagandist if we have once a clear vision of the object of our propaganda. We need not fear lest we become wily liars, for our very object is that central human truth which is the object of all knowledge. We need not fear lest we become venomous haters, for our very object is the inculcation of the sense of human brotherhood and human compassion. We need not fear lest we become besotted nationalists, for our very object is the inculcation of a sense for those common things which should be precious to all men, everywhere, at all times. We have drawn the sword to defend what Cicero beautifully called, "the country of all intelligent beings."

ETHICAL PROBLEMS OF THE WAR[1]

Gilbert Murray

[Gilbert Murray (1866———) is regius professor of Greek, Oxford University. He was born in Sydney, New South Wales. After being graduated from St. John's College, Oxford, he was for a year Fellow of New College, Oxford, and then became professor of Greek in Glasgow University (1889–1899). While in his present position he has several times visited the United States to lecture on Greek literature. Since the beginning of the war, he has spoken and written in a very thoughtful way upon the problems of the war. Some of these have been brought together in book form under the title, *Faith, War, and Policy*. This selection was originally delivered as an address to the Congress of Free Churches, England, in October, 1915, and represents the reaction toward the war on the part of a representative Englishman.]

Curiously enough I remember speaking in this hall, I suppose about fifteen years ago, against the policy of the war in South Africa. I little imagined then that I should live to speak in favor of the policy of a much greater and more disastrous war, but that is what, on the whole, I shall do. But I want to begin by facing certain facts. Don't let us attempt to bind ourselves or be blinded by phrases into thinking that the war is anything but a disaster, and an appalling disaster. Don't let us be led away by views which have some gleam of truth in them into believing that this war will put an end to war—that it will convert Germany, and certainly convert Russia to liberal opinions, that it will establish natural frontiers throughout Europe or that it will work a moral regeneration in nations which were somehow sapped by too many years of easy living in peace. There is some truth, and very valuable truth, in all those considerations, but they do not alter the fact that the war is, as I said, an appalling disaster. We knew when we entered upon it that it was a disaster—we knew that we should suffer, and that all Europe would suffer.

Now let us run over very briefly the ways in which it is doing evil. Let us face the evil first. There is, first, the mere suffering, the leagues and leagues of human suffering, that is now spreading

[1]From *The War of Democracy: the Allies' Statement*, edited by James Bryce. (Copyright, 1917, Doubleday, Page & Company.) Reprinted by permission.

across Europe, the suffering of the soldiers, the actual wounded combatants, and, behind them, the suffering of non-combatants, the suffering of people dispossessed, of refugees, of people turned suddenly homeless into a world without pity. Behind that you have the sufferings of dumb animals. We are not likely to forget that. There is another side which we are even less likely to forget, and that is our own personal losses. There are very few people in this room who have not suffered in that direct, personal way; there will be still fewer by the end of the war. I don't want to dwell upon that question; the tears are very close behind our eyes when we begin to think of that aspect of things, and it is not for me to bring them forward. Think, again, of the state's loss, the loss of all those chosen men, not mere men taken haphazard, but young, strong men, largely men of the most generous and self-sacrificing impulses who responded most swiftly to the call for their loyalty and their lives. Some of them are dead, some will come back injured, maimed, invalided, in various ways broken. There is an old Greek proverb which exactly expresses the experience that we shall be forced to go through, "The spring is taken out of your year." For a good time ahead the years of England, of most of Europe, will be without a spring. In that consideration I think it is only fair, and I am certain that an audience like this will agree with me, to add all the nations together. It is not only we and our allies who are suffering the loss there; it is a loss to humanity. According to the Russian proverb, "They are all sons of mothers," the wildest Senegalese, the most angry Prussian. And that is the state that we are in. We rejoice, of course we rejoice, to hear of great German losses; we face the fact. We do rejoice; yet it is terrible that we should have to; for the loss of these young Germans is also a great and a terrible loss to humanity. It seems almost trivial after these considerations of life and death, but think, too, of our monetary losses; of the fact that we have spent 1,595 millions and that we are throwing away money at the rate of nearly five millions a day. Yet just think what it means, that precious surplus with which we meant to make England finer in every way—that surplus is gone.

From a rich, generous, sanguine nation putting her hopes in the future, we shall emerge a rather poverty-stricken nation, bound to consider every penny of increased expenditure; a harrassed nation, only fortunate if we are still free. Just think of all our schemes of reform and how they are blown to the four winds—schemes of social improvement, of industrial improvement; a scheme like Lord Haldane's great education scheme which was to begin by caring for the health of the small child, and then lead him up by a great ladder from the primary school to the university! How some of us who were specially interested in education revelled in the thought of that great idea; but it was going to cost such a lot of money. It would cost nearly as much as half a week of the war! Think what riches we had then, and, on the whole, although we are perhaps the most generous nation in Europe, what little use we made of them. We speak of spiritual regeneration as one of the results of war, but here, too, there is the spiritual evil to be faced. I do not speak merely of the danger of reaction. There will be a grave danger of political reaction and of religious reaction, and you will all have your work cut out for you in that matter. The political reaction, I believe, will not take the form of a mere wave of extreme Conservatism; the real danger will be a reaction against anything that can be called mellow and wise in politics; the real danger will be a struggle between crude militarist reaction and violent unthinking democracy. As for religion, you are probably all anxious as to what is going to happen there. Every narrow form of religion is lifting up its horns again; rank superstition is beginning to flourish. I am told that fortune-tellers and crystal-gazers are really having now the time of their lives. It will be for bodies like yourselves to be careful about all that. But besides that there is another more direct spiritual danger. We cannot go on living an abnormal life without getting fundamentally disorganized. We have seen that, especially in Germany; with them it seems to be a much stronger tendency, much worse than it is with us; but clearly you cannot permanently concentrate your mind on injuring your fellow creatures without habituating yourself to evil thoughts. In Germany, of course, there is a deliberate cult of hatred. There is a process, which I won't stop to analyze, a process utterly amazing, by which a highly civilized and ordinarily humane nation has gone on from what I can only call atrocity to atrocity. How these people have ever induced themselves to commit the crimes in Belgium which are attested by Lord Bryce's Commission, even to organizing the flood of calculated mendacity that they pour out day by day, and, last of all, to stand by passive and apparently approving, while deeds like the new Armenian massacres are going on under their egis, and in the very presence of their consuls, all this passes one's imagination. Now we do not act like that; there is something or other in the English nature which will not allow it. We shall show anger and passion, but we are probably not capable of that organized cruelty, and I hope we never shall be. Yet the same forces are at work. I do not want to dwell upon this subject too long, but when people talk of national regeneration or the reverse, there is one very obvious and plain test which one looks at first and that is the drink bill. We have made a great effort to restrain our drinking; large numbers of people have given up consuming wine and spirits altogether, following the King's example. We have made a great effort and what is the result? The drink bill is up seven millions as compared with the last year of peace! That seven millions is partly due to the increased price; but at the old prices, it would still be up rather over two millions. And ahead, at the end of all this, what prospect is there? There is sure to be poverty and unemployment, great and long continued, just as there was after 1815. I trust we shall be better able to face it; we shall have thought out the difficulties more; we who are left with any reasonable margin of subsistence will, I hope, be more generous and more clear-sighted than our ancestors a century earlier. But in any case there is coming a time of great social distress and very little money indeed to meet it with. We shall achieve, no doubt, peace in Europe; we shall have, probably, some better arrangement of frontiers, but underneath the place there will be terrific hatred. And in the heart of Europe, instead of a treacherous and grasping neighbor, we shall be left with a deadly enemy, living for revenge.

Now, ladies and gentlemen, I do not think that I have shirked the indictment of this war. It is a terrible indictment; and you will ask me, perhaps, after that description, if I still believe that our policy in declaring war was right. Yes; I do. Have I any doubt in any corner of my mind that the war was right? I have none. We took the path of duty and the only path we could take. Some people speak now as if going on with the war was a kind of indulgence of our evil passions. The war is not an indulgence of our evil passions; the war is a martyrdom.

Now, let us not exaggerate here. It is not a martyrdom for Christianity. I saw a phrase the other day that we were fighting for the nailed hand of One crucified, against the "mailed fist." That description is an ideal a man may carry in his own heart, but, of course, it is an exaggeration to apply to our national position, to the position of any nation in international politics. We are not saints; we are not a nation of early Christians. Yet we are fighting for a great cause. How shall I express it? We are a country of ripe political experience, of ancient freedom; we are, with all our faults, I think, a country of kindly record and generous ideals, and we stand for the established tradition of good behavior between the nations. We stand for the observance of treaties and the recognition of mutual rights, for the tradition of common honesty and common kindliness between nation and nation; we stand for the old decencies, the old human-ities, "the old ordinance," as the King's letter put it, "the old ordinance that has bound civilized Europe together." And against us there is a power which, as the King says, has changed that ordinance. Europe is no longer held together by the old decencies as it was. The enemy has substituted for it some rule which we cannot yet fathom to its full depth. You can call it militarism or *Realpolitik* if you like; it seems to involve the domination of force and fraud; it seems to involve organized ruthlessness, organized terrorism, organized mendacity. The phrase that comes back to my mind when I think of it is Mr. Gladstone's description of another evil rule—it is the negation of God erected into a system of government. The sort of thing for which we are fighting, the old ordinance, the old kindliness, and the old humanities—is it too much to say that, if there is God in man, it is in these things, after all, that God in man speaks?

The old ordinance is illogical. Of course it is illogical. It means that civilized human beings in the midst of their greatest passions, in the midst of their angers and rages, feel that there is something deeper, something more important than war or victory—that at the bottom of all strife there are some remnants of human brotherhood. Now, I do not want to go into a long list of German atrocities; much less do I want to denounce the enemy. As Mr. Balfour put it in his whimsical way: "We take our enemy as we find him." But it has been the method throughout this war—the method the enemy has followed—to go at each step outside the old conventions. We have sometimes followed. Sometimes we have had to follow. But the whole history of the war is a history of that process. The peoples fought according to certain rules, but one people got outside the rules right from the beginning. The broken treaty; the calculated ferocity in Belgium and northern France; the killing of women and non-combatants by sea and land and air; the shelling of hospitals; the treatment of wounded prisoners in ways they had never expected; all the doctoring of weapons with a view to cruelty; explosive bullets: the projectile doctored with substances which would produce a gangrenous wound; the poisoned gases; the infected wells. It is the same method throughout. The old conventions of humanity, the old arrangements which admitted that beneath our cruelties, beneath our hatreds there was some common humanity and friendliness between us, these have been systematically broken one after another. Now observe: these things were done, not recklessly, but to gain a specific advantage; they were done, as Mr. Secretary Zimmermann put it in the case of Miss Cavell, "to inspire fear." And observe that in many places they have been successful. They have inspired fear. Only look at what has recently happened and what is happening now in the Balkans. Every one of these Balkan states has looked at Belgium. The German agents have told them to look at Belgium. They have looked at Belgium and their courage has failed

x

them. Is that the way in which we wish the government of the world to be conducted in future? It is the way it will be unless we and our Allies stand firm to the end.

All these points, terrible as they are, seem to me to be merely consequences from what happened at the very beginning of the war. There are probably some people here who differ from what I am saying, and I am grateful to them for the patient way in which they are listening to me. To all these I would earnestly say: "Do not despise the diplomatic documents." Remember carefully that the diplomacy of July and August, 1914, is a central fact. Remember that it is the one part of the history antecedent to this war which is absolutely clear as daylight. Read the documents and read the serious studies of them. I would recommend specially the book by Mr. William Archer, called "Thirteen Days." There is also Mr. Headlam's admirable book, "The History of Twelve Days," and the equally admirable book by the American jurist, Mr. Stowell. There the issue is clear and the question is settled. The verdict of history is already given in these negotiations. There was a dispute, a somewhat artificial dispute, which could easily have been settled by a little reasonableness on the part of the two principals. If that failed, there was the mediation of friends, there was a conference of the disinterested nations—there was appeal to the concert of Europe. There was the arbitration of The Hague— an arbitration to which Serbia appealed on the very first day and to which the Czar appealed again on the very last. All Europe wanted peace and fair settlement. The governments of the two Central Powers refused it. Every sort of settlement was overridden. You will all remember that, when every settlement that we could propose had been shoved aside, one after another, Sir Edward Grey made an appeal to Germany to make any proposal herself—any reasonable proposal—and we bound ourselves to accept it, to accept it even at the cost of deserting our associates. No such proposal was made. All Europe wanted peace and fair dealing except one Power, or one pair of Powers, if you so call it, who were confident, not in the justice of their cause, but in the overpowering strength of their war machine.

As the semi-official newspaper said: "Germany does not enter conferences in which she is likely to be in a minority." By fair dealing they might have got their rights or a little more than their rights. By war they expected to get something like the supremacy of Europe. In peace, with their neighbors reasonable, in no pressing danger, Germany deliberately preferred war to fair settlement; and thereby, in my judgment, Germany committed the primal and fundamental sin against the brotherhood of mankind. Of course, all great historical events have complicated causes, but on that fact almost alone I should base the justice and the necessity of our cause in this war. Other objects have been suggested; that we are fighting lest Europe should be subject to the hegemony of Germany. If Germany naturally, by legitimate means, grows to be the most influential power, there is no reason for anyone to fight her. It is said we are fighting for democracy against autocratic government. I prefer democracy myself, but one form of government has no right to declare war because it dislikes another form. It is suggested that we are fighting to prevent the break-up of the Empire. In that case, from motives of loyalty, of course we should have to fight, and I think the break-up of the Empire would be a great disaster to the world. But not for any causes of that description would I use the phrase I have used, or say that in this war we were undergoing a martyrdom. I do use it deliberately now, for I believe no greater evil could occur than that mankind should submit, or should agree to submit, to the rule of naked force.

Now I would ask again those who are following me, as I say, with patience, but I have no doubt with difficulty, to remember that this situation, in spite of particular details, is, on the whole, an old story. The Greeks knew all about it when they used the word "Hubris"—that pride engendered by too much success which leads to every crime. Many nations, after a career of extraordinary success, have become mad or drunk with ambition. "By that sin fell the angels." They were not so wicked to start with but afterward they became devils. We should never have said a word against the Germans before this madness entered into them. We liked them. Most of Europe rather liked and admired them. But, as I said, it is the old story. There have been tyrants. Tyrants are common things in history. Bloody aggression is a common thing in history in its darker periods. But nearly always where there have been tyrants and aggressors there have been men and peoples ready to stand up and suffer and to die rather than submit to the tyrant; the voice of history speaks pretty clearly about these issues, and it says that the men who resisted were right. So that, ladies and gentlemen, as, with our eyes open, we entered into this struggle, I say, with our eyes open, we must go on with it. We must go on with it a united nation, trusting our leaders, obeying our rulers, minding each man his own business, refusing for an instant to lend an ear to the agitated whispers of faction or of hysteria. It may be that we shall have to traverse it until the cause of humanity is won.

And now, ladies and gentlemen, that being the cause, we are girt up in this war to the performance of a great duty; and there are many things in it which, evil as they are, can in some way be turned to good. It lies with us to do our best so to turn them.

If we take the old analogy from biology we are a community, a pack, a herd, a flock. We have realized our unity. We are one. I think most of us feel that our lives are not our own; they belong to England. France has gone through the same process to an even greater degree. Mr. Kipling, who used certainly to be no special lover of France, has told us that there "the men are wrought to an edge of steel, and the women are a line of fire behind them." Our divisions before the war it is a disgrace to think of. They were so great that the enemy calculated upon them, and judged that we should not be able to fight. These divisions have not been killed as we hoped; the remnants of them are still living. I cannot bear to speak of them. Let us think as little as possible about them, and lend no ear, no patience to the people who try to make them persist. As for the division of class and class, I think there, at least, we have made a great gain. I would ask you to put to yourselves this test. Remember how before the war the ordinary workman spoke of his employer and the employer of his workmen, and think now how the average soldier speaks of his officer and how the officer speaks of his

men. The change is almost immeasurable. Inside the country
we have gained that unity; outside, in our relations with foreign
countries, we have also made a great gain. Remember, we have
allies now, more allies, and far closer allies than we have ever
had. We have learned to respect and to understand other nations.
You cannot read those diplomatic documents of which I spoke
without feeling respect for both the French and Russian diplo-
matists for their steadiness, their extreme reasonableness, their
entire loyalty, and, as you study them, you are amused to see
the little differences of national character all working to one end.
Since the war has come on we have learned to admire other
nations. There is no man in England who will ever again in his
heart dare to speak slightingly or with contempt of Belgium or
Serbia. It is something that we have had our hearts opened;
that we, who were rather an insular people, welcome other
nations as friends and comrades. Nay, more, we made these
alliances originally about a special principle on which I would like
to say a sentence or two. That is the principle of *entente*, or
cordial understanding, which is specially connected with the
name of our present Foreign Secretary, and, to a slighter extent,
with that of his predecessor. The principle of entente has been
explained by Sir Edward Grey several times, but I take two
phrases of his own particularly. It began because he found that
all experience had shown that any two great empires who were
touching each other, whose interests rubbed one against another
frequently in different parts of the world, had no middle course
open to them between continual liability to friction and cordial
friendship. He succeeded in establishing that relation of perfect frankness and mutual friendship with the two great empires
with whom our interests were always rubbing. Instead of friction, instead of suspicion and intrigue, we established with our
two old rivals a permanent habit of fair dealing, frankness and
good will. The second great principle of entente was this, that
there is nothing exclusive in these friendships. We began it
with France, we continued it with Russia, we achieved it in
reality, although not in actual diplomatic name, with the
United States, and practically also with Italy, and anyone who

has read the diplomatic history will see the effort upon effort we made to establish it with our present enemies. I think we have here some real basis for a sort of Alliance of Europe—that sort of better concert for which we all hope. One cannot guess details. It is very likely indeed that at the beginning Germany will stay outside and will refuse to come into our kind of concert. If so we must "take our enemies as we find them." The fact of there being an enemy outside will very likely make us inside hold together all the better for the first few years. When we are once thoroughly in harness, and most nations have the practice of habitually trusting one another and never intriguing against one another, then, no doubt, the others will come in.

Now I spoke at the beginning about the possible dangers of reaction, but there is a very good side also in the reaction. Part of it is right. It is a reaction against superficial things, superficial ways of feeling, and perhaps also superficial ways of thought. We have gone back in our daily experience to deeper and more primitive things. There has been a deepening of the quality of our ordinary life. We are called upon to take up a greater duty than ever before. We have to face more peril; we have to endure greater suffering; death itself has come close to us. It is intimate in the thoughts of every one of us, and it has taught us in some way to love one another. For the first time for many centuries this "unhappy but not inglorious generation," as it has been called, is living and moving daily, waking and sleeping, in the habitual presence of ultimate and tremendous things. We are living now in a great age.

A thing which has struck me, and I have spoken of it elsewhere, is the way in which the language of romance and melodrama has now become true. It is becoming the language of our normal life. The old phrase about "dying for freedom," about "death being better than dishonor"—phrases that we thought were fitted for the stage or for children's stories, are now the ordinary truths on which we live. A phrase which happened to strike me was recorded of a Canadian soldier who went down, I think in the *Arabic*, after saving several people; before he sank he turned and said, "I have served my King and country and this is my end." It was the natural way of expressing the plain fact. I read yesterday a letter from a soldier at the front about the death of one of his fellow-soldiers, and the letter ended quite simply: "After all he has done what we all want to do—die for England." The man who wrote it has since then had his wish. Or, again, if one wants a phrase to live by, which would a few years ago have seemed somewhat unreal, or "high falutin'," he can take those words that are now in everybody's mind: "I see now that patriotism is not enough—I must die without hatred or bitterness toward anyone."

Romance and melodrama were a memory, broken fragments living on of heroic ages of the past. We live no longer upon fragments and memories; we ourselves have entered upon a heroic age. As for me, personally, there is one thought that is always with me, as it is with us all, I expect—the thought that other men are dying for me, better men, younger, with more hope in their lives, many of them men whom I have taught and loved. I hope you will allow me to say, and will not be in any way offended by the thought I want to express to you. Some of you will be orthodox Christians and will be familiar with that thought of One who loved you dying for you. I would like to say that now I seem to be familiar with the feeling that something innocent, something great, something that loves me has died, and is dying daily, for me. That is the sort of community that we are now—a community in which one man dies for his brother—and underneath all our hatreds, all our little angers and quarrels, we are brothers who are ready to seal our brotherhood with blood. It is for us that these men are dying, for us, the women, the old men, and the rejected men, and to preserve the civilization and the common life which we are keeping alive and reshaping toward wisdom or unwisdom, toward unity or discord. Well, ladies and gentlemen, let us be worthy of these men; let us be ready, each one, with our sacrifice when it is asked. Let us try, as citizens, to live a life which shall not be a mockery to the faith these men have placed in us. Let us build up an England for which these men, lying in their scattered graves over the face of the green world, would have been proud to die.

AFTER THE CONFLICT

A LEAGUE TO ENFORCE WORLD PEACE[1]

WILLIAM HOWARD TAFT

[William Howard Taft (1857———), twenty-seventh President of the
United States, was born in Cincinnati, Ohio. After graduating from Yale
University, he entered upon the practice of law in his native city, rising
steadily into positions of public trust and usefulness. Among the most notable of these were judge of the Sixth United States District, the first civil
governor of the Philippine Islands, secretary of war in the cabinet of President
Roosevelt. In November, 1908, he was elected to the Presidency, and was
renominated at the close of his term. He was, however, defeated by Woodrow
Wilson, and has been, since 1913, Kent professor of law in Yale University.
He has always taken a great interest in the questions of arbitration and world-
wide peace. This selection gives an account of one of the most widely discussed schemes for reducing the probability of war as much as possible.]

This is an assembly of those who direct the forming of character of the youth of the country and who, because of their intelligence and attention to the issues of the day and their standing in the community, exercise a substantial influence in fram-
ing and making effective the popular will. This meeting, therefore, gives an exceptional opportunity to spread to the four
corners of the United States the consideration of a constructive
plan for national and human betterment. I seize this chance to
bring before you the program of an association already organized and active to promote a league to enforce world peace.

Our program is limited to the establishment of such a league
after the present world war shall close. We are deeply interested
in bringing this war to a close, and we would rejoice much in
successful mediation, but, in order to be useful, we limit our
plan to the steps to be taken when peace comes, and to an international arrangement between the powers after war ceases.

[1] From *Proceedings of the National Education Association*, 1916.

The league was organized on Bunker Hill Day, a year ago, in Independence Hall, at Philadelphia. Its program contemplates a treaty between the great powers of the world, by which the signatories agree to be bound to four obligations: the first is that all questions arising between the members of the league shall be submitted to a judicial tribunal for hearing and judgment; the second, that all questions which cannot be settled on principles of law and equity shall be submitted to a council of conciliation for hearing and a recommendation of compromise; the third, that if any member of the league commits acts of hostility against another member before the question between them shall be submitted as provided in the first two articles the remainder of the members of the league shall jointly use forthwith their economic and military forces against the member prematurely resorting to war and in favor of the member prematurely attacked; the fourth, that congresses between the members of the league shall be held from time to time to formulate and codify rules of international law to govern the relations between the members of the league, unless some member of the league shall signify its dissent within a stated period.

1. Considering the fourth clause first, the question arises: What is international law? It is the body of rules governing the conduct of the nations of the world toward one another, acquiesced in by all nations. It lacks scope and definiteness. It is found in the writings of international jurists, in treaties, in the results of arbitration, and in the decisions of those municipal courts which apply international law, like the Supreme Court of the United States and courts that sit in prize cases to determine the rules of international law governing the capture of vessels in naval warfare. It is obvious that a congress of the league, with quasi-legislative powers, could greatly add to the efficacy of international law by enlarging its application and codifying its rules. It would be greatly in the interest of the world and of world peace to give to such a code of rules the express sanction of the family of nations.

2. Coming now to the first proposal, involving the submission of all questions at issue, of a legal nature, to a permanent inter-

national court, it is sufficient to point out that the proposal is practical and is justified by precedent. The Supreme Court of the United States, exercising the jurisdiction conferred on it by the Constitution, sits as a permanent international tribunal to decide issues between the states of the Union. The law governing the settlement of most of the controversies between the states cannot be determined by reference to the Constitution, to statutes of Congress, nor to the legislation of the states. Should Congress in such cases attempt to enact laws, they would be invalid. The only law which applies is that which applies between independent governments, to wit, international law. Take the case of Kansas against Colorado, heard and decided by the Supreme Court. Kansas complained that Colorado was using more of the water of the Arkansas River which flowed through Colorado into Kansas than was equitable, for purposes of irrigation. The case was heard by the Supreme Court and decided, not by a law of Congress, not by the law of Kansas, not by the law of Colorado, for the law of neither applied. It was decided by principles of international law.

Many other instances of similar decisions by the Supreme Court could be cited. But it is said that such a precedent lacks force here because the states are restrained from going to war with each other by the power of the National Government. Admitting that this qualifies the precedent to some extent, we need go no farther than Canada to find a complete analogy and a full precedent. There is now sitting, to decide questions of boundary waters (exactly such questions as were considered in Kansas versus Colorado), a permanent court, consisting of three Americans and three Canadians, to settle the principles of international law that apply to the use of rivers constituting a boundary between the two countries and of rivers crossing the boundary. The fact is that we have got so into the habit of arbitration with Canada that no reasonable person expects that any issue arising between us and that country, after a hundred years of peace, will be settled otherwise than by arbitration. If this be the case between ourselves and Canada, and England, why may it not be practicable with every well-established and ordered government of the great powers? The second Hague conference, attended by all nations, recommended the establishment of a permanent international court to decide questions of a legal nature arising between nations.

3. The second proposal involves the submission to a commission of conciliation of all questions that cannot be settled in court on principles of law or equity. There are such questions which may lead to war, and frequently do, and there are no legal rules for decision. We have such questions giving rise to friction in our domestic life. If a lady who owns a lawn permits children of one neighbor to play upon that lawn and refuses to admit the children of another neighbor, because she thinks the latter children are badly trained and will injure her lawn or her flowers, it requires no imagination to understand that there may arise a neighborhood issue that will lead to friction between the families. The issue is, however, a non-justiciable one. Courts cannot settle it, for the reason that the lady owning the lawn has the right to say who shall come on it and who shall be excluded from it. No justiciable issue can arise, unless one's imagination goes to the point of supposing that the husbands of the two differing ladies came together and clashed, and then the issue in court will not be as to the comparative training of the children of the families.

We have an analogous question in our foreign relations, with reference to the admission of the Chinese and Japanese. We discriminate against them in our naturalization and immigration laws and extend the benefit of those laws only to whites and persons of African descent. This discrimination has caused much ill-feeling among the Japanese and Chinese. We are within our international right in excluding them, but it is easy to understand how resentment because of such discrimination might be fanned into a flame, if, through lawless violence or unjust state legislation, the Japanese might be mistreated within the United States.

We have had instances of the successful result of commissions of conciliation where the law could not cover the differences between the two nations. Such was the case of the Behring Sea controversy. We sought to prevent the killing of female seals in the Behring Sea and asserted our territorial jurisdiction over that sea for this purpose. The question was submitted to international arbitrators, and the decision was against us, but the arbitrators, in order to save to the world the only valuable and extensive herd of fur seals, recommended a compromise by treaty between the nations concerned, and, accordingly, treaties have been made between the United States, Great Britain, Russia, and Japan, which have restored the herd to its former size and value. So much, therefore, for the practicable character of the first two proposals.

The third proposal is more novel than the others, and gives to the whole plan a more constructive character. It looks to the use of economic means first, and military forces if necessary, to enforce the obligation of every member of the league to submit any complaint it has to make against another member of the league, either to the permanent international court or to the commission of conciliation, and to await final action by that tribunal before beginning hostilities. It will be observed it is not the purpose of this program to use the economic boycott or the jointly acting armies of the league to enforce the judgment declared or the compromise recommended. These means are used only to prevent the beginning of war before there has been a complete submission, hearing of evidence, argument, and decision or recommendation. We sincerely believe that in most cases, with such a delay, such a winnowing out of the issues, and such an opportunity for the peoples of the differing countries to understand one another's positions, war would generally not be resorted to. Our ambition is not to propose a plan, the perfect working out of which will absolutely prevent war, first, because we do not think such a plan could perfectly work, and, secondly, because we are willing to concede that there may be governmental and international injustice which cannot be practically remedied except by force. If, therefore, after a full discussion and decision by impartial judges or a recommendation by earnest, sincere, and equitable compromisers, a people still thinks that it must vindicate its rights by war, we do not attempt in this plan to prevent it by force.

Having thus explained what the plan is, let us consider the objections which have been made to it.

The first objection is that, in a dispute between two members of the league, it would be practically difficult to determine which one was the aggressor and which one, therefore, in fact began actual hostilities. There may be some trouble in this, I can see, but what we are dealing with is a working hypothesis, a very general plan. The details are not worked out. One can suggest that an international council engaged in an attempt to mediate the differences might easily determine for the league which nation was at fault in beginning hostilities. It would doubtless be necessary, where some issues arise, to require a maintenance of the *status quo* until the issues were submitted and decided in one tribunal or the other; but it does not seem to me that these suggested difficulties are insuperable or may not be completely governed by a detailed procedure that of course must be fixed before the plan of the league shall become operative.

The second objection is to the use of the economic boycott and of the army and the navy to enforce the obligations entered into by the members of the league upon the recalcitrant member. I respect the views of pacifists and those who advocate the doctrine of non-resistance as the only Christian doctrine. Such is the view of that Society of Friends which, with a courage higher than that of those who advocate forcible means, are willing to subject themselves to the injustice of the wicked in order to carry out their ideal of what Christian action should be. They have been so far in advance of the general opinions of the world in their history of three hundred years, and have lived to see so many of their doctrines recognized by the world as just, that I always differ with them with reluctance. Still it seems to me that in the necessity of preserving our civilization and saving our country's freedom and individual liberty, maintained now for one hundred and twenty-five years, we have no right to assume that we have passed beyond the period in history when nations are affected by the same frailties and the same temptations to cupidity, cruelty, and injustice as men. In our domestic communities we need a police force to protect the innocent and the just against the criminal and the unjust, and to maintain the guaranty of life, liberty, and property. The analogy between the domestic community and that of nations is sufficiently close to justify and require what is, in fact, an international police force. The attitude of those who oppose using force or a threat of force to compel nations to keep the peace is really like that of the modern school of theoretical anarchists, who maintain that if all restraint were removed and there were no government, and the children and youth and men and women were trained to self-responsibility, every member of society would know what his or her duty was and would perform it. They assert that it is the existence of restraint that leads to the violation of right. I may be permitted to remark that with modern fads of education we have gone far in the direction of applying this principle of modern anarchy in the discipline and education of our children and youth, but I do not think the result can be said to justify the theory, if we can judge from the strikes of school children or from the general lack of discipline and respect for authority that the rising generation manifests. The time has not come when we can afford to give up the threat of the police and the use of force to back up and sustain the obligation of duty.

The third objection is that it would be unconstitutional for the United States, through its treaty-making power, to enter into such a league. The objection is based on the fact that the Constitution vests in Congress the power to declare war. It is said that this league would transfer the power to declare war away from Congress to some foreign council, in which the United States would have only a representative. This objection grows out of a misconception of the effect of a treaty and a confusion of ideas. The United States makes its contract with other nations under the Constitution through the President and two-thirds of the Senate, who constitute the treaty-making power. The President and the Senate have a right to bind the United States to any contract with any other nation covering a subject-matter within the normal field of treaties. For this purpose the President and the Senate are the United States. When the contract comes to be performed, the United States is to perform it through that department of the government which by the Constitution should perform it, and which should represent the government and should act for it. Thus, the treaty-making power may bind the United States to pay to another country under certain conditions a million dollars. When the conditions are fulfilled, then it becomes the duty of the United States to pay the million dollars. Under the Constitution only Congress can appropriate the million dollars from the treasury. Therefore it becomes the duty of Congress to make that appropriation. It may refuse to make it. If it does so, it dishonors the written obligation of the United States. It has the power either to perform the obligation or to refuse to perform it. That fact, however, does not make the action of the treaty power in binding the United States to pay the money unconstitutional. So the treaty-making power may bind the United States under certain conditions to make war. When the conditions arise requiring the making of war, then it becomes the duty of Congress honorably to perform the obligation of the United States. Congress may violate this duty and exercise its power to refuse to declare war. It thus dishonors a binding obligation of the United States. But the obligation was entered into in the constitutional way and it is to be performed in the constitutional way. We are not lacking in precedent. In order to secure the grant of the Canal Zone and the right to finish the canal, the treaty-making power of the United States agreed to guarantee the integrity of Panama. The effect of this obligation is that if any other nation attempts to subvert the government of the Republic of Panama or to take any of her territory, the United States must make war against the nation thus invading Panama. Now, Congress may refuse to make war against such a nation, but if it does so, it violates the honor of the United States in breaking its promise. The United States cannot make such a war unless its Congress declares war. That does not make the guaranty of the integrity of Panama entered into by the treaty-making power of the United States unconstitutional. So here, when conditions arise under this league to enforce peace which would require the United States to lend its economic means and military force to resist the hostile action of one member of the league against another, it would become the duty of Congress to declare war. If Congress did not discharge that duty, as it has the power not to do under the Constitution, it merely makes the United States guilty of violating its plighted faith.

Again, it is said that to enter into such a league would require us to maintain a standing army. I do not think this follows at all. If we become, as we should become, reasonably prepared to resist unjust military aggression, and have a navy sufficiently large, and coast defenses sufficiently well equipped to constitute a first line of defense, and an army which we could mobilize into a half-million trained men within two months, we would have all the force needed to do our part of the police work in resisting the unlawful aggression of any one member of the league against another.

Fourthly, it has been urged that for us to become a party to this league is to give up our Monroe Doctrine, under which we ought forcibly to resist any attempt on the part of European or Asiatic powers to subvert an independent government in the Western Hemisphere, or to take from such a government any substantial part of its territory. It is a sufficient answer to this objection to say that a question under the Monroe Doctrine would come under that class of issues which must be submitted to a council of conciliation. Pending this, of course, the *status quo* must be maintained. An argument and recommendation of compromise would follow. If we did not agree to the compromise and proceeded forcibly to resist violation of the Doctrine, we would not be violating the terms of the league by hostilities entered upon thereafter. More than this, as Professor Wilson of Harvard, the well-known authority upon international law, has pointed out, we are already under a written obligation to delay a year before beginning hostilities, in respect to any question arising between us and most of the great powers, and this necessarily includes a violation of the Monroe Doctrine. It is difficult to see, therefore, how the obligation of such a league as this would put us in any different position from that which we now occupy in regard to the Monroe Doctrine.

Finally, I come to the most formidable objection, which is that the entering into such a league by the United States would be a departure from the policy that it has consistently pursued since the days of Washington, in accordance with the advice of his "Farewell Address," that we enter into no entangling alliances with European countries. Those of us who support the proposals of the league believe that were Washington living today he would not consider the league an entangling alliance. He had in mind such a treaty as that which the United States made with France, by which we were subjected to great embarrassment when France attempted to use our ports as bases of operation against England when we were at peace with England. He certainly did not have in mind a union of all the great powers of the world to enforce peace, and while he did dwell, and properly dwelt, on the very great advantage that the United States had in her isolation from European disputes, it was an isolation which does not now exist. In his day we were only three and a half millions of people, with thirteen states strung along the Atlantic seaboard. We were five times as far from Europe as we are now in respect to speed of transportation, and we were twenty-five times as far away in respect to speed of communication. We are now one hundred millions of people between the two oceans and between the Canadian line and the Gulf. We face the Pacific with California, Oregon, and Washington, which alone make us a Pacific power. We own Alaska, the northwestern corner of our continent, a dominion of immense extent, with natural resources as yet hardly calculable, and with a country capable of supporting a considerable body of population. It makes us a close neighbor of Russia across the Behring Straits; it brings us close to Japan with the islands of the Behring Sea. We own Hawaii, two thousand miles out to sea from San Francisco, with a population including seventy-five thousand Japanese laborers, the largest element of that population. We own the Philippine Islands, one hundred and forty thousand square miles, with eight millions of people under the eaves of Asia. We are properly anxious to maintain an open door to China and to share equally in the enormous trade which that

Y

country, with her four hundred teeming millions, is bound to furnish when organized capital and her wonderful laboring populations shall be intelligently directed toward the development of her naturally rich resources. Our discrimination against the Japanese and the Chinese presents a possible cause of friction in the resentment that they now feel, which may lead to untoward emergencies. We own the Panama Canal in a country which was recently a part of a South American confederation. We have invested four hundred millions in that great world enterprise to unite our eastern and western seaboards by cheap transportation, to increase the effectiveness of our navy, and to make a path for the world's commerce between the two great oceans.

We own Porto Rico with a million people, fifteen hundred miles out at sea from Florida, and we owe to those people protection at home and abroad, as they owe allegiance to us.

We have guaranteed the integrity of Cuba, and have reserved the right to enter and maintain the guaranty of life, liberty, and property, and to repress insurrection in that island. Since originally turning over the island to its people, we have had once to return there and restore peace and order. We have on our southern border the international nuisance of Mexico, and nobody can foresee the complications that will arise out of the anarchy there prevailing. We have the Monroe Doctrine still to maintain. Our relations to Europe have been shown to be very near, by our experience in pursuing lawfully our neutral rights in our trade upon the Atlantic Ocean with European countries. Both belligerents have violated our rights and, in the now nearly two years which have elapsed since the war began, we have been close to war in the defense of those rights. Contrast our present world relations with those which we had in Washington's time. It would seem clear that the conditions have so changed as to justify a seeming departure from advice directed to such a different state of things. One may reasonably question whether the United States, by uniting with the other great powers to prevent the recurrence of a future world war, may not risk less in assuming the obligations of a member of the league than by refusing to become such a member in view of her world-wide interests. But even if the risk of war to the United States would be greater by entering the league than by staying out of it, does not the United States have a duty as a member of the family of nations to do its part and run its necessary risk to make less probable the coming of such another war and such another disaster to the human race?

We are the richest nation in the world, and, in the sense of what we could do were we to make reasonable preparation, we are the most powerful nation in the world. We have been showered with good fortune. Our people have enjoyed a happiness known to no other people. Does not this impose upon us a sacred duty to join the other nations of the world in a fraternal spirit and with a willingness to make sacrifice if we can promote the general welfare of men?

At the close of this war the governments and the people of the belligerent countries, under the enormous burdens and suffering from the great losses of the war, will be in a condition of mind to accept and promote such a plan for the enforcement of future peace. President Wilson, at the head of this administration and the initiator of our foreign policies under the Constitution, and Senator Lodge, the senior Republican member of the Committee on Foreign Relations, and therefore the leader of the opposition on such an issue, have both approved of the principles of the league to enforce peace. Sir Edward Grey and Lord Bryce have indicated their sympathy and support of the same principles, and we understand that M. Briand, of France, has similar views. We have found the greatest encouragement in our project on every hand among the people. We have raised a large fund to spread our propaganda. I ask your sympathy and support.

GOOD TEMPER IN THE PRESENT CRISIS[1]

LAWRENCE PEARSALL JACKS

[Lawrence Pearsall Jacks (1860————) was born in Nottingham, England. Since 1903 he has been professor of philosophy, Manchester College, Oxford. He is also editor of the *Hibbert Journal*. During the war he has contributed to English and American magazines a number of notable war articles.]

Ethical reconstruction does not require the invention of a new system of ethics. The old systems contain enough and more than enough to serve our purpose, if people would only put them into practice. These old systems are not all of equal value or of equal truth, but the least true of them stands for something in advance of the actual practice of the world. If any of them were to be adopted and loyally carried out by mankind—any one of them from the Chinese system of Lao-Tse to the idealism of T. H. Green—we should see an immense improvement in the conduct of men. I was reading the other day about Epicureanism, a much discredited system. But I could not resist the impression that if we were all good Epicureans we should behave ourselves much better than we do. The trouble about ethics is not that the systems are wrong—though many of them are—but that people don't follow them even where they are right.

There is no department of thought where the distinction between teaching and learning is of more importance. To teach ethics is one thing; to get the ethics learned which is taught is quite another—though the two are very often confused. A vast amount of ethics has been taught which mankind has never learned: and we may well ask ourselves whether a world which has refused to hear Moses and the Prophets will be more attentive to our improvements of their doctrine. Let us remember that the moral reformers of our time are not the first to attempt ethical reconstruction. The Ten Commandments were an ethical reconstruction of great importance. And yet many generations

[1]From *The Yale Review*, vol. vii, p. 512 (April, 1918). Reprinted by permission.

of men have been taught them without learning them. What better fate have we to expect?

So then, though I believe ethical reconstruction to be much needed today as a result of the great social upheaval of recent times, I doubt if it is to be brought about by the invention of a new system of ethics. Nor need we invent so much as a new virtue. Here again the old virtues are sufficient. What we should try to do, in the interests of ethical reconstruction, is to study the old virtues more closely and fix our attention on that one which is the mother of them all. Perhaps "the mother" is too strong a term. Some of the virtues are climatic—by which I mean that they furnish the climate, the atmosphere, the soil in which all the other virtues grow. As moral reformers—not as moral philosophers only, but as moral reformers anxious for a reconstruction of ethics—we should fix our attention on these climatic virtues. We may be sure that if only we can get the climate right, the atmosphere right, the soil right, the rest will be comparatively easy; whereas if the climate is wrong all our labors will be in vain.

The climatic virtue I am about to name as the basis of ethical reconstruction is one which is hardly mentioned in any textbook of moral philosophy. Its name lacks the dignity which would entitle it to a place in a philosophical treatise. It is simply good temper. But though good temper is a very homely expression, it is certainly not more vague, nor more likely to be misunderstood, than any of the great moral terms which we spell with capital letters, such as Justice, Liberty, or Truth. Suppose a group of people were asked these two questions in rapid succession: first, What is truth?—then, What is good temper? I venture to say that most of them would find the truth question the harder of the two. They would agree more rapidly about good temper than they would about truth. William James, not to speak of others, devoted a considerable part of his philosophical gifts to defining truth. But no philosopher, so far as I am aware, has found it necessary to write a treatise on the meaning of good temper. The reason is that the term is sufficiently well understood by everybody who hears it.

Assured of that I name good temper as the basic virtue of ethical reconstruction.

If the reader is not satisfied with this and insists on having a proper definition of the term I will do my best to meet him. Fortunately I am able to quote a very high authority, if not for a definition of good temper at least for a most accurate description of it. It may be found in the thirteenth chapter of St. Paul's First Epistle to the Corinthians. That we may have them before us, here are a few of the statements:

"Though I speak with the tongues of men and of angels and have not charity I am become as sounding brass or a tinkling cymbal."

"If I should bestow all my goods to feed the poor, and if I give my body to be burned and have not charity it profiteth me nothing."

"Charity never faileth; but whether there be prophecies they shall fail, whether there be tongues they shall cease, whether there be knowledge it shall vanish away."

It is plain that St. Paul has here got hold of one of those "mother-truths" to which Goethe attached so much importance. He is describing a climatic virtue—a virtue, that is, which provides the air, the light, the soil in which all the other virtues grow. It is quite easy to translate his language into modern phraseology—and to bring it home to this modern question of ethical reconstruction. "If you want a new moral world," St. Paul says to us, "improve your temper. Do not put your trust in mere arrangements of one kind or another. So long as your temper remains bad no good arrangement can do itself justice. Even a league of peace would not work if the parties to it were in a bad temper. Unless the charity that never faileth is present the league of peace will spend its time in quarreling. Do not trust in knowledge, for knowledge can be perverted to bad ends, and always is so perverted when temper is bad. Then as to social problems—poverty, distress, and the others. By all means let public money be raised for these objects; let the public tax itself that the poor may be fed. But don't spoil your temper in the process, or it will profit nothing. Above all, place no final confidence in tongues. Ethical reconstruction is not to be effected by making speeches about it, nor by writing books about it, nor by passing laws about it, nor by spelling it with capital letters. Tongues shall cease, partly because the speakers grow tired, partly because the hearers grow tired of listening to them. But good temper is never tiresome either to itself or to others."

Such then is good temper; and I submit that it is the greatest ethical need of the present time. No matter where you look, to international morals, to state morals, to political morals, to private morals—the need stands out as one and the same. If we take the evils that exist in any of these departments, and the crimes that are committed, we shall find ultimately that bad temper is at the root of them all.

First as to the international situation. When we look at this in a broad light what must strike us all is the utter un-reasonableness of it, the sheer, stark, flagrant unreasonable-ness—all signs of bad temper! If any dozen individuals were to take up the reciprocal attitudes in which the leading states of the world now stand, if they were to do the same things to one another and to say the same things of one another, how should we judge those dozen individuals? These men, we should say, have lost their tempers and their heads. They are beside themselves. They have got into such a rage with one another that they literally don't know what they are doing nor what they are talking about. They are all mad together.

Let us go to the mother-truth of things—even though it was a German who gave us that advice. What was the origin of the present war? Bad temper. What has maintained it for three years and more? Bad temper. What has given it a char-acter of ferocity which has no parallel in the recorded wars of history? Bad temper. What threatened the peace of the world for generations before the war? Bad temper. What, unless we are very careful, will continue to threaten the peace of the world after the war has come to an end? Bad temper.

Turn next to the ethical conditions as they exist within the national boundaries of the British Empire—I am writing from England—or at least as they did exist before the war.

What was the outstanding feature of those conditions? Again, I answer, bad temper. Bad temper was hindering all round. It was preventing a working accommodation between labor and capital. It was preventing a settlement of the Irish question and is preventing it now. It was keeping a whole multitude of groups, parties, and sects at loggerheads with one another. It was actually dividing the sexes, and England was threatened with a woman's war. Everybody was in a rage with somebody. Reform was being discussed all around; but it was not being discussed amicably, and the reformers, instead of helping one another, were hindering one another and getting in one another's way. There were many of them abroad, and their temper was not good.

I have just been reading Mr. Bertrand Russell's book on social reconstruction; and I confess to finding in it a certain oversight, and that at the point where most people are apt to be similarly blind. Mr. Russell speaks of the strife that always goes on in democratic communities between the supporters of established order on one side and the innovators, the friends of progress, on the other. He shows how these two tendencies by operating together may be made to work out to a good result. Now, all that is very important, but it is by no means the whole of the story. In addition to this strife between established order and innovation, there is the more active strife that goes on among the innovators themselves. One of the commonest mistakes we make is to speak of progress as though it had a unitary aim, as though all innovators, all advocates of change, from the nature of the case, formed a like-minded band of brothers, agreed on the changes that ought to take place, agreed on the order in which they ought to come, and agreed as to the manner in which they ought be to carried out. This is seldom or never the case when progressive tendencies are at work. On the contrary, a severe struggle for existence goes on among these tendencies themselves. This is why so many promising revolutions have come to nothing. It is not so much because the old order was wrong as because the new tendencies became weak by exhausting their strength in mutual quarrels.

In this way the French Revolution ended in the military despotism of Napoleon; and we all can see how a like danger threatens the Russian Revolution at the present moment.

These things suggest to us the immense importance of good temper in a democratic community. Of all the forms of government man has devised, democracy is the one which requires the largest amount of sweet reasonableness. It is required in order to adjust the immense diversities of opinion and policy which inevitably arise where thought is free and where an open field is offered for the proposals of the innovator. *Per contra,* bad temper is never so disastrous as it is under democratic conditions. Once let it prevail, and the forces of progress, instead of working together, fall upon one another, hinder one another, thwart and paralyze one another; intelligence is expended in party or sectional warfare, strength goes into quarreling, and there is an immense wastage of good ideas. Under these circumstances democratic government is not self-government—of the people, by the people, and for the people—and it is only by a fiction that we can call it even representative. For what is then done by legislators does not represent what the people want, but only so much as is left over of what they want after the various quarreling sections have settled their accounts and exhausted their spleen and their rhetoric.

Now, this was the condition toward which all classes in England were drifting before the war. Some people might say they had actually arrived at it; I will content myself with saying they were drifting toward it. The good of democracy was in danger of being spoilt and undone by the abominable ebullitions of bad temper which had broken out among the various parties and sections in the progressive movement. It was not merely that the old was arrayed against the new, but the new was arrayed against itself.

One of the effects of freedom, as we all know, is to breed strong individualities. Freedom allows men to develop on their own lines; and when they have developed, the result is an immense diversity of strongly marked individuals with opinions of their own as to what ought to be done, and how it ought to be done. This is what we all want; the best society is precisely that which includes the largest variety of character and type. But the danger is this: that strongly marked individuals are apt to be intolerant of one another. That danger can be avoided only when the spirit of accommodation, the spirit of sweet reasonableness—I had almost said the spirit of good humor—is in the ascendant. If the opposite spirit prevails, democracy becomes a mere clash and struggle ot the divergent types it has created; and often it has gone to pieces from that very cause and has been replaced by some form of autocracy.

The terms I have just used—the spirit of accommodation, and the rest—are only other names for what St. Paul calls "the charity that never faileth." And again I name it as the basis of reconstruction. As time goes on, the strong individualities which liberty produces will grow stronger, and the differences among them will become more and more numerous. I see no prospect whatever of uniformity of type; all the tendencies of the time are toward diversities of type.

Let us turn back for a moment to the international situation. The Allies are fighting for the right of nationalities to develop on their own lines. If that ideal is realized, what may we expect? We shall have a large number of nations, a larger number than ever, each of them developing a culture and character of its own, becoming a strong and distinct individual with opinions and ideals of its own—diversity of type. But suppose these nations, each with its own strongly marked character, should be intolerant of each other. Suppose they lack the spirit of accommodation, of sweet reasonableness, of tolerance, of good humor. Will you have peace? No, you will have war. Dangerous as bad temper is when a dozen distinct nationalities are involved, it will become far more dangerous when there are a hundred of them. Once more, all depends on the charity that never faileth.

Or consider the state of affairs in any one country, say, England, after the war. Think of the immense number of reconstructions of all sorts that have been already planned out. Two pictures arise before the mind. One is a picture of jostle and chaos in which all these schemes are fighting for front place, nobody willing to give way, or to make room, each section insisting on the immediate realization of its own demand, and threatening this and that if it is refused. If that picture comes true, there will result an atmosphere as unfavorable as it well could be to any kind of ethical improvement. The other picture is more difficult to paint. It is the picture of a good-tempered community animated by a spirit of give and take, accommodating, reasonable, considerate, abounding in good fellowship, ready to treat, and to make the best of things until something better can be provided. In such an atmosphere ethical improvement would have a favorable climate. Nay, more. The advent of this social and political good temper, in place of the bad temper to which we have been accustomed, would itself be a real step of progress. It would do more to improve the value of human life than any law that could be put on the statute book. Indeed, it would do the work of law to a very great extent. For we should then see that many of the changes we seek to effect by means of law are far better effected by the exercise of common-sense and kind feeling as between man and man.

The general conclusion is that if we are to have a real ethical reconstruction—actual improvement of conduct—we must have a basis for it, or rather an atmosphere and climate, in the temper of the community. The question then arises, How are we to secure good temper? What are the causes of it? Perhaps it would be well to frame the question rather differently. What are the causes of bad temper in a community? I rather think if we could keep bad temper out good temper would come in of itself.

Bad temper inevitably arises whenever material wealth is the main object of social pursuit. This is so much of a commonplace that I need hardly pause to prove it. Some people, however, hold it in a rather half-hearted way. They hold that wealth causes bad temper only when it is unfairly distributed. As an abstract proposition I daresay that is true. The trouble lies in the application of it. In practice it is extremely difficult to convince anybody that his share of wealth is a fair one. It may be a liberal share, it may be a large share, but what is to prevent him from thinking and claiming that it ought to be much larger? People are not easily satisfied on this point, especially when they are inclined to be suspicious of one another. Far be it from me, however, to belittle the importance of fair distribution. Its importance cannot be exaggerated. But no scheme of that kind, even though it is worked and backed by the authority of the state, will be successful unless certain conditions are present. The conditions are that the parties concerned in the distribution shall be on good terms with one another; that the various trades, and the various ranks of labor, from the most skilled to the least, shall have confidence in each other's good faith, and be ready to take a generous view of each other's merits. Only in such an atmosphere can anybody be got to accept his share as a fair one. If the opposite conditions are present, if the spirit of suspiciousness is abroad, if bad blood is in circulation, if groups and parties have no confidence in one another, if men think their neighbors are trying to take advantage of them, if the habit is to assume that every man is a rascal until he has proved the contrary, then the scheme of distribution, no matter what it is, will satisfy nobody. "Fairness" will be treated as a dodge, and if the state backs the scheme up, the cry will be raised that the state has been captured by villains. We are fond of talking of the economic basis of society. I venture to say that society has no basis in economics either good or bad. The basis of society is human; it consists in the mutual trust of man in man, which no economic scheme can ever replace.

The same holds true of international relations. So long as the great states of the world base their greatness on material possessions they will never love one another, and there will be mighty little of the charity that never faileth in their mutual dealings. Rich states will always be objects of envy to those less rich than themselves. We shall always have one state complaining that it hasn't got its fair share—a sufficiently large place in the sun—and pointing to some other state which has more than its fair share—which is exactly what Germany, a very rich state, has been doing for years. It is impossible to exaggerate the amount of international bad temper which arises from this very cause—and at times it becomes so bad that nations are perfectly irrational, and the very elements of ethics are cast to the winds. Of course, the state which is the richest of all, and has no cause to envy the others, may be in the best possible temper; but this will not protect it from the evil temper of the others who envy its supremacy. Its riches will expose it not only to envy but to robbery; and no sooner does that start than all the evil passions are let loose. So long as civilization is based on wealth the outlook for international good temper is very black.

Looking now to the inner life of the community, can we name any other cause of bad temper, besides that connected with the pursuit of wealth? I believe we can. There is a tendency in all democratic communities to over-legislate, to produce more laws than are needed. Jeremy Bentham, who knew all that was to be known in his time about law-making, regarded all legislation as a necessary evil. Every law provokes a certain amount of bad temper in the process of making it. It irritates the community for the time being. In plain language there is always "a row." Can we name an important law about the making of which there was not a row? Well, these rows may be necessary, and even wholesome up to a point, but don't let us multiply them to such a point that we get into the row-habit. Instead of trying how many laws we can make, let us rather try how many we can do without, if only for the sake of checking the habit of quarrelsomeness; because, if quarrelsomeness becomes chronic, if it becomes the normal temper of the community then unreasonableness will be general, and ethical reconstruction will be out of the question. Remember that ethical reconstruction is always reconstruction by consent. But we shall never get that consent out of a nasty-tempered community. One of the main conditions of ethical reconstruction is that we shall keep legislation within proper bounds, that we shall avoid having so much of it that our tempers become permanently spoiled.

Putting all this together, it is evident that ethical reconstruction depends on certain profound changes in the structure of civilization. They indicate a time when wealth will no longer be the basis of civilization; and when people will trust one another more than they do and rely less on the arm of the law. Such changes will not come about suddenly, and any attempt to make them sudden would only lead to disaster. We have before us no more than an object of gradual endeavor. Yet to have even that in these times of rocking confusion is no small thing, and we can begin at once.

A civilization not based upon wealth; a democracy whose ideal is not the maximum of legislation but the minimum. Such is the dream. Can it be realized? In answer let me remind the reader of Plato's conception of the invisible state. The true state, according to Plato, is not only invisible now, but remains invisible forever. Its nature is to be invisible; it can never be otherwise. "I do not believe it is to be found anywhere on earth," says Glaucon at the end of the ninth book of the *Republic*. "Ah well," answers Socrates, "the pattern of it is perhaps laid up in heaven for him who wishes to behold it. . . . And the question of its present or future existence on earth is quite unimportant."

But many persons are not content with that. They insist on turning the invisible state into a visible one. They appear to think that so long as the state is invisible it is not real and doesn't work. It never occurs to them that in trying to make it visible they may do violence to its nature; so that it becomes not more real but less real, and gets into a condition where it works badly or doesn't work at all. And yet I believe that such is often the case.

We see exactly the same process at work in the history of religion. The mind of man has always kicked against the notion that the deity is invisible. The notion has been that a real deity, an effective deity, must be a deity that can be seen; that an invisible deity, if I may say so, is no good. Hence in the history of all religions we can trace a process of turning the invisible deity into the visible one, and the process ends in setting up some wooden idol of the god, a thing one can see and feel and handle—a thing of which one can say "there it is." Then it is discovered that by making the god visible men have done violence to his nature. The visible wooden idol won't work. It can neither save nor help nor deliver. By becoming visible it has lost the attributes of God—and when that is discovered the idol is smashed.

Most of our current notions of the state, even as they are sometimes expounded by philosophers, are at the stage of idolatry. They lead to a worship of visible institutions. Now, I have nothing to say against visible institutions. The need of them is obvious—parliaments, laws, highly trained departments, systems of town arrangements, and perhaps armies and navies—though of these last I am not so sure. What I object to is the worship of them. Nothing will ever persuade me that these visible things, either singly or together, are the state; while, as to worshipping them, I would as soon think of falling down on the pavement of Whitehall and saying my prayers to the War Office. These things I can see; but the true state is something which cannot be seen and which I for one do not expect to see and do not want to see. I agree with Socrates: the question of its present or future existence on this earth is quite unimportant.

The coming changes in social structure will take the form of a fuller recognition of the claims of the invisible state—unless indeed the war end in such a way as to set them back for the time being—as would unquestionably happen if Germany were to win. We may expect a gradual decline of emphasis on the visible state, and a gradual increase of emphasis on the invisible. The change will come without violence, and there will be nothing in it to offend the supporters of established order. Little by little it will be discovered that what is now entrusted to the visible forces can be much better done by the invisible. It will be seen that human nature contains immense reserves of invisible force which have never yet been made use of. The world's resources of common sense and kind feeling have hardly been tapped up to now; but we shall tap them more and more, and by using them we shall build up the true, invisible state.

What the new basis will be is hard to say. Perhaps Mr. Russell has got the right word—creativeness. Quality must take the place of quantity. The ideal will no longer be to produce as much as possible, nor to get as large a share as you can of what has been produced. The ideal will rather be that every man shall enjoy his day's work and that a good article shall come out at the end of it. Beauty, which we have banished from our common life, with such dreadful consequences to us all, so that many of us have almost lost the taste for excellence; beauty, which cannot be bought for gold and riches and is so shy of the places where men make money, will return with healing on its wings.

The creation of beauty—by which I do not mean mere pictures to hang in our drawing-rooms or ornaments to place on the chimney piece—but excellent articles of every description, things which it will be a delight to make, a delight to have, a delight to use—things which plainly declare that the workman has enjoyed his day's work and that a good article has come out at the end of it—this will provide a slowly widening field for human intelligence and human energy. It will not do away with competition: but instead of competing as heretofore as to who can produce most, we shall compete as to who can produce best— a very different thing—a kind of competition in which men can freely indulge without the least danger that they will learn to hate one another in the process. It will teach them to love one another. Meanwhile the true state will remain just as invisible as it now is. But wherever two or three are gathered together, there it will be in the midst of them.

In conclusion I will add one word more in the hope of persuading the reader that the invisible state is the real state. Who are the members of the state? What are they? Where are they? Shall we say that the members of the state are the sum total of the persons who happen to be alive at the moment? Shall we say that a man remains a member of the state only so long as he draws the breath of life and ceases to be a member the moment that breath goes out of his body? What then of the thousands, of the tens of thousands of men, who have laid down their lives for the state in these three years? When the bullet struck them down, when the bursting shell blew them to fragments, did they cease then and there to be members of the state for which they had sacrificed their lives? I trow not. I claim them as the dearest and the closest and the most influential of all my fellow-citizens in the great commonwealth. And yet they have no votes, and yet they are invisible! Votes? If votes could be given to those who have most influence, to whom would they be given first? They would be given to the invisible multitudes of the mighty dead—not to these recent dead alone, but to millions behind them, rank behind rank in the long tale of the buried generations. That is not the language of psychical research. It is the language of severe political philosophy. It is the statement of a fact.

WHAT SHALL WE WIN WITH THE WAR?[1]

ERNEST HUNTER WRIGHT

[Ernest Hunter Wright (1882———) was born in Virginia and prepared for college in the schools of that state. He was graduated from Columbia University in 1905, and received the Doctor's degree from the same institution in 1910. Since 1910 he has been a member of the English Department of Columbia University, and now holds the rank of Assistant Professor. The article here reprinted is an interesting forecast of some of the consequences of the war.]

In material gain we do not ask a groat's worth from the war; that is understood. We shall give billions for freedom, but do not want a cent in booty. We are ready to pour out our blood that the world may be rescued, but we would not barter a drop of it for patches of territory. If the words in which we renounce the spoils in advance have grown common with us to the point of triteness, that very fact is truly remarkable. Except that we would avoid the semblance of satisfaction, at present, of all times, we might pause to wonder how often hitherto such an ideal as this, now commonplace, has moved a people of free choice to an equal strife and sacrifice. What nation before has offered all the gold and all the lives that may be needed solely

[1]From *The Century*, vol. xcvi, p. 339 (July, 1918).

Z

that an idea may prevail? But let the question be anything except a boast. It implies a mere fact, accepted as self-evident among us, and we have not thought to plume ourselves upon it. Not we, but the world, has learned it. It is one great thing that we have already won out of the war.

Of immaterial things there are also a number that we do not ask. We crave no vengeance. Less than twenty years ago millions of us made patriotism vocal in the cry, "Remember the *Maine!*" Now, despite hymns of hate turned finally against ourselves especially, no one is urging us to remember the *Lusitania*. We are not trying to forget it, but we have no need to spur our zeal with slogans clamoring for penalties unpayable for deeds irreparable, done to us or done to others. Nor are we in the lists to win mere honor. We would not lose it; we dearly hope that when the clouds of battle pass we shall have as ample a measure of it as our friends in the struggle have already gained. Yet we should never have plunged into a national duel, any more than our citizens engage in private ones, to settle a point of honor solely, however important that may be. On the contrary, even in humiliation we were willing to endure, as in settlement we stand ready to propose "any unprecedented thing" that promises to make the world safer. It is solely because safety will come in no other way that we commit ourselves to fight to the last ounce of our manhood for its preservation. Whoever hopes for less than that, or whoever lusts for more, is not of us. Of that we are certain.

And yet it may be that, if we fight like men for that cause, we shall win much more. That we do not demand more is the best reason for believing that we may receive it. Mainly the gain may come, as is usual with immaterial gains, unsought, inevitably; but we may possibly do much to speed its coming and assure its permanency if we form some anticipation of it. Changes of vast extent are certainly coming upon us. The body social cannot be stirred and shaken in unprecedented action only to relapse into its former habitudes. Ancient questions reviewed by us in this crisis will, some of them, receive new answers, and new questions will arise. We shall have need more than ever to "Prove all things; hold fast that which is good." May we, then, with our eyes still fastened on the one goal that must be won, consider for a moment, even thus early, what other winnings may be ours?

We may win unity. To many of the more discerning among us, of whatever social creed, the lack of it has long seemed one of our failings. "*La France,*" in Michelet's appealing phrase, "*est une personne;*" and lovers of that land have always felt the term as something more than a figure of speech. Hardly could the warmest admirer of the United States have used it of his own country a year ago. America was not a "person;" she was an aggregation. We had begun as disunited colonies uncommonly diverse in social or religious or economic aims, and the crisis that made us free came far short of making us one. Contrarieties persisted through the years when each state was going its own precarious way, and, when the intolerable result forced a closer federation, burst into flames of antagonism that were smothered with difficulty, and only partly, by the compromises of the Constitution. For two more generations they smoldered on, and then flared up in a wall of fire searing its wide way between the two camps of hatred into which it had parted the land. The first of our crises failed to unite us, and the second was disastrously divisive.

All that is over now, we say, and thank Heaven. Well, yes, if we mean that the notion of secession is dead and that the memory of Mosby on the one hand, or of the march through Georgia on the other, is all but obliterated. But if we mean that, in the mass of the people especially, no prejudice hangs over from the ancient time, that none arises out of the still different social ideals of New York and Charleston, or out of the far more different interests of the Southern planter and the Northern banker and merchant, we might be nearer to the truth.

Whatever was happening in Massachusetts, south of the Potomac boys even of the second generation after Appomattox were brought up in considerable distrust of the offspring of the Yankee. I can vouch for it that the scion of the new-comer from the North had a hard time in school in my day in the nineties.

Many a day we sent him home blubbering his r's to his mother, and the principal was not very hard on us for it. One morning we had a holiday to see the soldiers go off to Cuba. We sped them on their way with clamorous patriotism, and when the train was out of sight we turned our surplus energy to pummeling the little carpet-bagger from Vermont. A few months later the President passed through our town, and in a speech gave thanks that a common cause had at last made us into "one country and one people." But it was not quite true, as the little carpet-bagger had reason to know later; the cause had not been great enough, the struggle intense enough, to bring unison. There was still a North and a South.

More strikingly there is an East and a West, or several Easts and several Wests. A land so vast and so diversified has enforcedly developed different types and clashing interests, and its rapid growth has left its people little leisure to reason themselves into like-mindedness. And state governments have aided physical geography in this matter. In one state you may do business for which in another you would go to jail; in one you may be married and crazy, in another single and sane. In the intelligent society of certain regions a young man who has no socialistic leaning is in danger of being considered unthinking, while in another region to confess to socialism would be to court the estate of outcast.

However little we may habitually think of it, the differences between the Californian and the Vermonter, the Mormon and the South Carolinian, are rather extreme for a country so young and perfectly at peace with itself. Think of the charges and countercharges we have heard recently from one part of the country accusing another part of apathy toward the Great War, think of the campaigns launched in one region with the purpose of "waking up" another. The spectacle of a prominent author in New York challenging a Kansas bishop to raise a thousand dollars for a war charity, and offering in that glad case to retract her charges against Kansan hebetude, is a case in point.

The more disquieting sight of many delegates in Washington representing one region of the country as against or at the expense of the whole, with the pork-barrel as their perfect work, is only too familiar. Just as these words are being written, the morning paper brings a pronouncement from a congressman that clamors for quotation. The legislator points out that ten southern states are now controlling thirty-one out of sixty chairmanships in the House, that four of these states alone control eighteen chairmanships, and that the South should keep this power at great costs.

He continues:

> But it won't be able to do so if these ten southern states vote almost solidly against the Federal Suffrage Amendment. The South has everything to lose by such a short-sighted policy. . . . I speak as a southern Democrat. . . . The Democratic party is now in control of all branches of the Federal Government. Almost every committee assignment, so far as the chairmanships are concerned, is held by southern Democrats. . . . For the southern Democrats in Congress to say to the millions of patriotic women of the nation that suffrage shall not be given them would bring down upon our heads such condemnation from the suffrage states that we would be driven from power.

No pleading for or against suffrage here, no inquiry as to whether even the South wants it, nothing but unashamed nudity of sectional grasping—in the ninth month of the war! Our illustration happens to be furnished by a Kentuckian, but others as impressive might be quoted from deputies of every state. The thing would be amazing if it were not so American.

But even such differences are unimportant, most people will agree, in comparison with those of social or of economic class. Oregonian and New Yorker can get along together when they meet, though we must remember that the vast majority of them never do meet; but what about the miner and the coal baron, the I. W. W. in the lumber camp and the broker on the exchange? The piece-worker in Allen Street and the negro bent over the cotton in Mississippi have about as little as is possible in common with the manufacturer who more or less directly pays them both.

Of course we share class problems with every other nation, and with some for whom they are more perplexing than for us; but the rapidity of their growth in this land of plenty is rather remarkable. The contrast here between the four hundred and the four million, between dollars and muscle or inheritance and brains, has grown apace for a country where nature left much for all. Twenty or so years ago Coxey's Army was a joke; today it would be at least a symptom, and the difference measures a development of class consciousness. With us, also, the contrast is likely to be between inordinate wealth and dire poverty. In this respect we are very like England, where enormous fortunes exist side by side with bitter penury, and we are much worse off than France, where colossal private wealth is rarer and where unmitigated poverty is all but unknown. In any large city in America a single block often separates families living under conditions more extremely different than could well be found in all France. And to emphasize these class distinctions, we have imported, mainly into the four million, men from every quarter of the globe, and made up in two-thirds of the states a piebald population unparalleled in any sizable area of the Old World. Most of the so-called mixed races of Europe are fairly pure in comparison, not with the people of New York City, but with those of the Wisconsin plains.

But all these incongruities have never brought a clash? The melting-pot has never boiled over? Well, there have been mutterings. There are some thinkers, and not excitable ones, who have foreseen a race war in store for us or for our children. There are others who fear a new secession as the land fills up if interests grow more contradictory. There are far more who prophesy a conflict of classes amounting to revolution. Possibly we need fear none of these forecasts, though any one of them might have seemed plausible four years ago by the side of a prediction that we should now be at war in Europe.

Whatever may be the danger of the future, the fact that we have had so little friction in the last fifty years has been due mainly to the circumstance that we were all too busy to stop and make trouble. Each tenth of us was too hard pushed to worry overmuch about what the other nine-tenths were doing. Few people want a revolution when they are too rushed to take the time off for it and on the whole too prosperous to feel the need of it. But quiescence may be apathy, not unity. The mere indifference of most of us to the rest of us might be a main reason for our drifting apart. So far there has been more than a man's work for every man, with little time to interfere with other men. But what will happen in the day approaching fast when there is less? How will our sectionalism, our class antagonism, our individualism, measure in that day against our cohesion as one people?

There is no intention here of borrowing trouble from the future. We are not worrying about a clash that may or may not come; we mean solely to mention some of the splendid changes now taking place in regard to our unity as a people. The answer to the questions just propounded no one knows, of course, though everyone has hopes. But the one sure fact is this: that its first crisis having failed to weld it into one, and its second having riven it asunder, our heterogeneous half-continent has had to wait for this its third and most portentous crisis for a great common cause. We have met a problem and a piece of work dwarfing anything that we ever thought would fall to us.

It has come home to every one of us, of whatever region or whatever class. We know that we shall stand or fall together, and all the more because we have now seen the one other country of our size in the world fall before our enemy because divided. A hundred million of us are facing Washington, facing Flanders, facing life and death; and the result in national unity already surpasses all expectation and all precedent among us. Ten million men and women have opened their purses to lend the nation money; not an act of high virtue at a four per cent profit, though the refusal would have been vicious, but a tie of no mean force among those people and between them and the Government. Ten million more will share in the partnership later. Millions more of men and women who little dreamed a year ago of deviating from their daily round at the country's call have gone to camps and hospitals and trenches. There the nephew of Lee has taken the hand of the grandson of Grant, the White Mountain boy is keeping step with the Hoosier, and the young millionaire is swapping anecdotes and "makings" with the plumber—unless the plumber has won his spurs. We have never had a school of equality approaching a draft army facing common work and common peril. It is as democratic as the Subway and as unifying as the college, without the bad air of the one or the manufactured sentiment of the other, and it gives also a fine training in order, precision, rightness that hardly any other American institution affords.

Those who are not yet called to this onerous service are getting at home an appreciable lesson in fraternity. It takes a stringent time like the present to put individual men and classes on their mettle in confederate effort. And classes are approaching each other. A lady throws open her parlors to a congress called by her butler to consider food-saving. In general,—for the exceptions, though noisy, are few,—capitalist and laborer stand shoulder to shoulder straining to do their best. In general, labor gains increasingly for its services, and capital pays the larger bills of the war, a fact that few of the right-minded will deplore. And if the small-salaried man feels the pinch more than either, the tightening of his belt will probably not impede a desirable expansion of his better sentiments. The few who stand aloof and "strut their uneasy hour" are growing lonelier every day. If anyone thinks that they are many, a little reading in the history of the Civil War on either side will soon alter his opinion. He will easily convince himself of the prime fact that never before, not in the war for independence, not in the war for the union, or at any other time or over any other question, has America enjoyed such unanimity.

Based on free consent, a unanimity like this is of incalculable value. It need not interfere with a high degree of diversity in non-essential matters, and human nature may be amply trusted to see that it does not. Small as she is, for instance, that nation whom Michelet loved to call a "person" because in the hour of need she could be of one mind, rejoices in a larger diversity of personal or local habit concerning things not fundamental than we enjoy in this country. If we can preserve the unity we have now gained, and are still to gain, upon non-essentials, or that portion of it that is consonant with freedom of opinion in periods

of smaller strain, if we can make permanent that sense of inter-
dependence between each tract of the country and all the rest,
between each social group and all the others, we shall have won
a great good fortune out of the war.

The measure of all this that we shall preserve doubtless
depends largely on the firmness and wisdom with which we prosecute the war and solve the problems that will arise when we
have won it. At least we have an opportunity that we have
never had before. Is it too much to hope that we may come out
of the war deserving some such phrase as that with which
Michelet crowned his country? Without that single-mindedness
in the face of danger which distinguishes our gallant ally possibly
above all other peoples, the battle of the Marne would never
have been won, our aid might never have been possible, and the
history of centuries might have been reversed. One could hardly
wish a larger gain for his own country than that she, too, prove
worthy of the title so fitly given to happy France.

We may win in cosmopolitanism. For unanimity at home is
no foe to cordiality abroad, but rather, in all ordinary times,
its firm ally. And whether or not we have enjoyed a satisfactory
harmony among ourselves, it is all but universally agreed that we
have been slow to understand and to appreciate our sister nations.
Here again we had too much work at home to worry greatly as
to what was happening elsewhere. We also had a strong tradition of aloofness, wise in its origin among three millions depending on the sailing-ship for their connection with the outer world,
but dubious indeed in its application to a hundred millions furnished with steam and wireless. But whatever the reasons, no
one can well profess that we have been a cosmopolitan nation,
while many would argue that we have been the most isolated of
all great peoples; and this despite the fact that in racial origins
we are about the most international of all and great globe-
trotters to boot.

One of our distinguished ministers to a foreign country was
saying the other day that in general our diplomats are admired
and esteemed abroad as upright gentlemen of fine capacity, but
that for years they have astonished the statesmen of the conti-

nent by their ignorance of what was really going forward in the chancelleries of Europe, or their indifference to it. At home we have produced noble statesmen of whom we are justly proud, but hardly an international figure. In business and finance we have had potentates in plenty, but few whose influence has reached far beyond our own shores—few Rothschilds or Rhodeses. For the protection of South American republics and of our own we have upheld a Monroe Doctrine for a century; and how much do we know about those southern countries under our wing? Pitifully little. The British, French, Spanish, Germans could give us lessons about our nearest neighbors.

If this is true of Ecuador, what, say, of the Balkans? How many of our minds went absolutely void, a few years ago, at the mention of them! Many Parisians of some education could have drawn us a pretty good map of them, sketched their history, named their present rulers, and told us a little about their population and their industries. The stolid indifference of many Americans, especially of those at some distance from centers of discussion, through months and years of the present war, the feeling so humiliating to some of their compatriots that the war was a squabble between powers across the ocean who ought to have had sense enough to keep the peace, and that it was none of our business except as it raised our prices and possibly our incomes,—the feeling which, translated into a thousand placards, read, "No war talk here,"—all this was evidence of an insularity unflattering to America. It is useless to multiply the uncomfortable illustrations. In one word, we were a great people apart.

Well, we are going to get over a great deal of that, and it is high time we were doing so. History does not tell a very reassuring tale of peoples that have striven to live apart, any more than memoirs give a comforting account of recluses. The comparison is not perfect, of course, but it is certain that no nation can cut itself off from the world without stunting its material and spiritual growth. For the nation as for the individual man, "A talent is developed in solitude, a character in the current of the world." Is it permissible to hazard a suspicion that while we had talent in plenty, especially in practical and in inventive efforts, if less in pure science and in the arts, the American character, compared, for instance, with the French or the British, was a little undefined and possibly a bit loose-jointed?

Perhaps, if true, this is no more than the awkwardness of adolescence, and if so, experience is the remedy. And we are now beginning a full experience of those world problems which have been the common heritage of European peoples. Questions once all but academic here have become vital to us as full citizens of the world. We are sharing with the nations that lead in culture and achievement a cause perhaps the greatest that has actuated effort in all time. And our own part in the effort will be large, however slight it may of necessity remain as yet. Our blood and our counsels will mingle with our friends', we shall share in their triumph, and solve with them the problems of settlement that ensue. Our one hope is to do well.

But in the meantime we may gain much that is of great price, and much that is beyond price, out of the association. We may batter down that wall of American misprision and of British disdain that has separated us from the English. We shall surely demolish, if we have not already done so, that notion once so prevalent among us that the Frenchmen of today are only anemic descendants of their lusty forbears, that notion that led a prominent American magazine a few years before the war to conduct a long debate as to whether the French were a decadent race or not. We may put an end to one belief about ourselves, unmerited, if ever reputation was, yet singularly strong in the opinion of most foreigners, that we are a people who live for money. We got the reputation because there were such fortunes to be made here and so many people making them; and no prodigality or philanthropy, though in both we led the world, did much to palliate it. Whole-hearted contribution to a war not for ourselves alone, but for the world, may wipe out the last vestiges of that prejudice. Clearing away a thousand misunderstandings like these, we may conceivably hope to cement in national friendships the foundations of enduring peace.

We may win in modesty. It is a gift which visitors among us

from abroad and observers of our own travelers in foreign countries have not been prone to take as typical of us. To have founded a country on principles so new, borrowed, though they were from thinkers of the Old World, and to have made a wilderness into a world power within a century, give us natural reason for pride in ourselves. But the most reasonably proud Americans —and the present writer would fain be counted among them— have not infrequently smiled or blushed, according to their temperament and the occasion, at irrational exhibitions of boastfulness on the part of their compatriots.

To the thoughtful traveler abroad in other days, perhaps, these words will best commend themselves, for few of us have got as far as Southampton without wondering where the particular boat-load of Americans who shared the voyage could have been collected; and the wonder grew as we kept meeting parties from the boat at strategic points for sight-seeing on the Continent. People like us abroad, of course, especially in France; we are the most generous of their visitors (unless this be a boast!) and we are so happy-go-lucky that we are easy to get along with. But although they give us a warm welcome, they have an honest feeling, more of amusement than of malice, that they must expect a good deal of bragging from us. And we ourselves, when we speak of "spread-eagleism," are usually thinking of our own country. One of our weeklies that has of late been so ferocious on the trail of unwise patriots as to leave too little space to mention the other kind was itself guilty recently of saying that "What distinguishes the statesmanship of President Wilson from that of the other leaders of the Allied cause . . . is nothing but superior rationality." Only that! Even if obviously true, the statement would be exceptionally raw. So far as the present writer knows, America is the first of the Allies to print such a statement. Supposing that an English review had said it of Lloyd-George or a French paper of Clémenceau, how should we feel about it?

Possibly we do not fully deserve the notable reputation for spread-eagleism that we have gained, but in view of the illustrations it is only fair in candor to plead guilty to having lighted a good deal of fire under all the smoke. We could hardly have savored the famous "Yankee in King Arthur's Court" so much if we had not seen ourselves, however caricatured, in him. Many of us have been a little like him, whether in a court abroad or in the bank or grocery at home. We were the people, the brave and the free. We had the red blood, let the blue flow through whose veins it chose. We had the ships and the guns—or we should get them the minute the need came, if it ever did. We thought the French were effete; there is no use denying it, however much we may have had our eyes opened. We thought the English were stupid, more or less *Dundrearys,* and we stopped only too infrequently to ask how *Dundrearys* could manage such an empire so harmoniously. We were the clean-cut race of quick brains. We could lick the world, if the world ever required it.

To be sure, we had a good deal of dirty linen to wash at home. We had political corruption of a scale unknown in the two countries just mentioned. We had poverty undreamed-of in the first mentioned of them. We were coming to hate a captain of industry as much, and as indiscriminately, as we hated a lord. Such things we would debate among ourselves, but let a foreigner approach us upon these topics, and we turned to him our American front and proceeded to show him how, despite any little injustices, our land of promise enjoyed a certain superiority over his own outworn country. Not always did we do this, but too frequently. We may honestly disclaim arrogance; we can hardly prefer a claim to modesty.

But much of that we may now learn. The silence of French heroism may lead us to emulation. The honest confession of British muddling may teach us to acknowledge ours, if we must. The arrogance of Prussia may impress upon us the amiability of its opposite. Congestion on railroads, delays in ship-building, shortages of ammunition, of uniforms, of coal, may set us all so busy mending faults that we shall have time neither for boasting nor for writing articles in deprecation of it.

Far more important, the powerful enemy that confronts us will demand every ounce of strength that is in us and will leave us little breath for words of self-gratulation. A brigand armed with the panoply of wealth and science is holding the world at bay. We shall find him mortal, we shall overpower him, and rid the world of his menace; but we shall know that we did not do it alone, that against him we should have been all but powerless alone, and the lesson will be a good one for our self-esteem. Learning from the British and Gallic veterans, as we must, we shall come to esteem them as we would esteem ourselves. And our foe will so tax our powers before we overcome him, will so rudely shake any over-confidence we may have felt, that in the victory we shall probably feel thanksgiving without vainglory. What veteran victor over Prussia will want to come back and teach his children any form of goosestep? There may have been a little of that when we declared war,—not much, for we had learned a great deal in three years,—but there will probably be less when it is over. There was some of it in and after our clash with Spain, because that was more like an excursion than a war. But the heroes that return from Belgium will be soberer, and despite the acclamations with which we shall receive them, they will find us soberer. Let it be hoped that our modesty and our valor may be equal.

That we may win a great deal more than has been suggested here, or than can be comprehended by one mind considering so large a question, need hardly be intimated. To mention one material benefit, not of the kind, however, that was waived in our first sentences, we may learn enough about economy, personal and national, to add greatly to our well-being. At the least we may hope never again to hear—what some of us used to feel a sort of pride in—that one could feed Paris with the food that New York wastes. At the most we may expect that the education in saving which will come to people of all classes in our spendthrift nation through the Liberty Loans will endure to our benefit long after the war and possibly within a generation offset the huge cost of the struggle.

We may gain in physical manhood, despite heavy losses, by inuring millions of men to work and air. Until one sees a regiment of raw recruits, and remembers that they are chosen men, one scarcely realizes how far physical training has been the affair of the minority in colleges and gymnasiums. For ourselves and from our Allies we may learn a good deal about organization. If we have thought well of ourselves in this respect hitherto, we were usually considering private organizations rather than governmental. Foreigners have often marveled how we could operate a trust so well and a city or state so badly, and many of us have marveled, also. With the Government assuming a large share in the greatest war, in which the control of railroads and of other enterprises is a detail, we shall be more stupid than we should like to believe if we do not reach a higher mark in corporate management.

For many further benefits we may reasonably hope, and doubtless others have occurred to the reader. It may be better for us not to make our prophecies over-specific. Certainly general gain may be predicted a good deal more confidently than this or that particular reform. But if the specific prophecy is the more precarious, it is perhaps also the less important. To say that gain in general, over and above the attainment of our prime and unalterable purpose in the war, may come to us out of all our tribulation and despite all our losses, to state this for our comfort somewhat expressly in reply to a vague opinion still persisting despite of history, that no nation ever goes to war for any reason with results other than damaging, has been the main purpose of this article. And not for our comfort merely, but rather that we may form and foster some idea of what good may come to us, in the belief that its coming and its permanence may be more probable if we receptively anticipate it for the land we love.

DATE

NOV 2 0 70

1 87

GAYLORD